# Who's Who
# in Pacific Navigation

# Who's Who
# in Pacific Navigation

JOHN DUNMORE

University of Hawaii Press
Honolulu

91 92 93 94 95 96   5 4 3 2 1

**Library of Congress Cataloging-in-Publication Data**

Dunmore, John, 1923–
   Who's who in Pacific navigation / John Dunmore.
     p.  cm.
   Includes bibliographical references and index.
   ISBN 0-8248-1350-2
   1. Explorers—Pacific Area—Biography.  2. Pacific Area—Discovery
and exploration.
DU19.D78  1991                   91–19280
910′.91823—dc20                   CIP

*Designed by Paula Newcomb*

# Contents

# Preface

THE CRITERIA FOR INCLUSION in a book such as this are never easy to determine. "Exploration" has been discarded in favor of "navigation" since it could have raised the question of including those who contributed to land exploration, together with those who pioneered research into problems of race, language, religion, mythology, and precolonial history. Even navigation needs to be defined and is deemed to exclude some whose achievements lay solely in coastal surveys, deep-water hydrography, supporting ventures, or sheer survival against great odds. The term as used here is restricted to those who led or played a major role in voyages of exploration and research, with the addition of more secondary figures whose names tend to occur in accounts of voyages, their origin and aftermath, on one condition: that they ventured into the Pacific, that greatest of oceans and the last great unknown on the charts of the world.

Their relative importance cannot be decided by reference to any objective scale of measurement. Early pioneers naturally have the advantages in such a subjective assessment, but an attempt has been made to judge the contenders by their impact on the history of Pacific exploration; that this has to mean its discovery and exploration in historical times cannot be denied, for modern historical approaches require precise evidence that can be assessed and categorized, and many of those who pioneered the earliest exploration and the settlement of the Pacific islands cannot meet those criteria.

The guiding principle, as in any work of reference, has been the likelihood of readers coming upon names of people they would then seek to identify quickly and easily. More thorough enquiries can be made in other works—histories, accounts of voyages, biographies. It is to be hoped that the Bibliography will assist in that second stage.

The limelight naturally and unavoidably falls on the captains and the leaders of expeditions, yet other participants—seconds-in-command, pilots, scientists, artists—deserve mention. They cannot all be given a place here, lest the volume become unwieldy and those names we chiefly seek become lost in the mass. It is assumed that anyone needing to research these secondary, though significant, figures can turn to the accounts of voyages or other more detailed works.

It is in such works too that additional material will be found on these navigators and their achievements. Where these were written by the leader of an expedition or published on his return, they are usually mentioned in the relevant article.

The resources of the National Maritime Museum, Greenwich, and of the Public Road Office, Kew, both in England; of the Service Historique de la Marine, Vincennes, France; of the National Library of Australia, Canberra; of various specialized libraries and museums in Massachusetts, Rhode Island, and New York states have been drawn upon on numerous occasions. Many persons associated with them need to be individually thanked for their assistance, among them Professor Glynn Barratt of Ottawa, Carol Miller and Indulis Kepars of Canberra, Ton Vermeulen of Leiden, Virginia M. Adams of New Bedford, Katherine H. Griffin of Boston, Philip J. Weimerskirch of Providence, Paul Cyr of New Bedford, Gayl Michael of Nantucket, Kay Rieper of Salem, William Asadorian of Queens Borough (New York), Patricia M. Chapman for research in London and Vancouver, and Joyce M. Dunmore for research and other assistance in Wellington. The gathering of information for this work has proceeded over a number of years as a by-product of other research, and during this time assistance has come from a number of people and from institutions in New Zealand, Britain, France, the United States, Australia, and Canada.

All the dictionaries of biography have one thing in common: they are never finalized. The regular appearance of supplements or revised editions enables new information to be added, corrections to be made, new names included. Ongoing scholarly work, sometimes even the chance discovery of old documents, certainly the cooperation of readers with specialist knowledge, all contribute to the accumulation of fresh material. The present work does not pretend to be, alone of all dictionaries of biography, a definitive work. Suggestions and clarification will always be welcome toward a future edition.

# Introduction

FOR COUNTLESS CENTURIES the Pacific Ocean lay devoid of human life, an immensity of water troubled only by repeated volcanic eruptions that cast up hundreds of small islands around which, with endless patience, generations of tiny coral animals then built up reefs in shallow water.

In those distant times there were still land bridges between northern Asia and America and in the south between New Guinea and the Australian continent. Slow migrations of peoples took place from Asia, both along the northern shores and in the south, the migrants stopping, probably for centuries, to develop new techniques so as to adapt to harsh, unfamiliar environments and strange local crops.

Some ventured out to offshore islands, which they took over and settled or used as temporary camping places for fishing or hunting expeditions. The world of the ocean beyond the horizon, however, was a dark place, filled with danger and mystery. Like their European counterparts staring out at the limitless Atlantic, they saw it as the mysterious edge of the world.

Undoubtedly some, driven by curiosity or desperation, overcame their fears and set out westward from the American continent. The prevailing currents make it likely that any who may have succeeded in finding some Pacific island left from the coast of central South America. In the north, drift voyages occurred in a west-to-east direction from Japan or thereabouts.

The Chinese, whose civilization included a knowledge of navigation and direction finding, tended to seek trade routes to the south, eventually as far as the Indian Ocean. The eastern land of Fu-sang was a world of magic, a semimythical place where could be found the herb of eternal youth and sundry enchanters; but those who ventured out in search of it were likely to disappear into the great hole of Wei-lu into which drained all the waters of the world. In more historical times, both China and Japan forbade their subjects to sail from their shores on other than infrequent and strictly controlled trading expeditions. The Pacific remained an unappealing and dangerous place.

The migrations that in time resulted in the peopling of the Pacific Ocean began from the Philippines and southeast Asia. There was no massive population shift comparable to that which occurred in Europe in the years preceding and following the fall of Rome. It was rather a slow movement spanning several thousand years with many stops and starts. The earliest led to the occupation of the Australian continent and the western Solomon Islands as far as Bougainville and thence to the eastern island groups, including New Caledonia to the south and Fiji to the east, with some groups reaching as far as Samoa and Tonga. The Austronesians of Australia and New Guinea did not develop a seafaring culture; the ancestral figures of the Australian people are essentially land-based—snakes, lizards, or other animals.

However, the Melanesians of coastal New Guinea and of the eastern island groups did not lose their association with the sea. Coastal travel was by dugout canoes or outriggers; there was regular contact with offshore and near islands, and the people of the smaller islands developed sophisticated techniques of navigation. Myths often reflect differences between the inland and the island Melanesians, symbolized perhaps by the Vanuatuan story of the seas that flooded in to divide people into bush folk and saltwater folk, a tale that no doubt enshrines some ancient tradition of the breakdown of the land bridges.

Further north, migrations from the Philippines resulted in the settlement of the Marianas and the Carolines, although linguistic differences clearly suggest the arrival of a number of island Melanesians among the southern Carolines and the Gilbert and Marshall islands groups. Attempts to seek more islands farther east were doomed to failure, for the sea currents were unfavorable, and the great expanse of the central Pacific is devoid of habitable island groups. Thus "the people of the small islands," the Micronesians, ended their own odyssey in eastern Kiribati (Gilbert Islands). They evolved a distinctive culture, which included knowledge of star movements and of sea currents. In the Marshalls (Tuvalu), for instance, stick charts served as navigational maps with detailed indications of wind and wave patterns. The outrigger canoe allowed safe crossings between islands over open and often turbulent waters: Micronesian canoe design was in fact quite sophisticated. Having come upon new islands and settled them, the Micronesians could, subject to tribal and other rivalries, maintain some form of contact with their place of departure. A point to bear in mind, however, is that island communities, once they had become self-sufficient, had no real need to maintain such contact, the urge to trade which led Europeans to travel being absent among islanders whose resources varied little from one island to another; barter is warranted only when the items one can obtain differ from those offered in exchange.

The myths, as usual, reflect the culture, and the characters found in the traditional tales have no doubt evolved from real life or ancestral figures. In the Marshall Islands, the brothers Rongelap and Rongerik have given their names to two of the islands. Pälülop, the ancestral canoe captain respected through most of Micronesia, was their grandfather; his son Alulei is honored as the great teacher of the art of navigation and the patron of navigators. The Pälülop-Alulei family is the subject of many stories, which often vary from island to island; it had in Micronesian life a prominence comparable to that of Zeus and his family in ancient Greece.

Both in Micronesia and in Polynesia myths abound about the creation of Pacific islands by gods or half-gods who fished out the island from the depth of the sea. This "fishing out" clearly equates with the discovery of a hitherto unknown island that the ancestral or mythical figure drew out of the empty ocean and thus "created" for his family and their descendants. That this origin of the tale is a real event cannot be challenged, but the actual happening has been so transformed and embroidered upon that the identity of the discoverer has long since been lost. European historians have met with similar problems in endeavoring to reconstruct the events, much closer in time to themselves, of the Trojan War, the founding of the city of Rome, or the court of King Arthur.

The Melanesian-Micronesian areas of settlement do not leave between them convenient corridors along which the migration of a Polynesian race from Southeast Asia could easily have occurred. Their South American origin is also untenable, whatever occasional westerly voyages might have successfully taken place from the American continent. The conclusion seems to be that the Polynesians evolved in the Pacific world itself, probably in eastern Melanesia, where an admixture of Micronesian culture and genetic features was likely. It is a currently accepted view that the eastward migration of western Pacific people ceased some three thousand to three thousand five hundred years ago, the migrants having spread into and settled the larger island groups of Fiji, Tonga, and Samoa. There, in relative isolation, they developed a new culture and evolved new linguistic patterns, those of "the many islands" or Polynesia, with marked differences in each of the island groups, clearly still more Melanesian in the Fiji Islands. Then, social pressures such as an increased population, resulting in greater demands on the food supplies and tribal or interisland warfare, led to renewed migrations. Like most migrations, the drive was along a comparable climatic band, requiring less adaptation to a new environment—that is, toward the east.

Polynesian migrations, with the usual pattern of stops and starts, progressed over the centuries as far as the Marquesas. There is little doubt that attempts were made to continue along the broad easterly band, and there may have been some who made a landfall on the American continent; but, if so, they left no trace. Others went southeast as far as Easter Island, others north to Hawaii, some southwest to the Society Islands and on yet farther to New Zealand.

Such a movement, possibly spread over two thousand years, presupposes a retention or a revival of open sea navigational techniques. The distances were too great to talk of island-hopping, nor can theories of accidental drift voyaging, once a strong challenge to the Polynesian migration story, now be sustained. In 1956 Andrew Sharp had cast doubt on the navigational knowledge and technology of the Polynesians. His role in toning down previously exaggerated but widely accepted beliefs in the sailing abilities of the Polynesian people was significant and important, and he accumulated persuasive evidence that many so-called voyagings in search of a new home were drift voyages successful only where the explorer chanced upon a habitable island. It is now agreed that, although many attempts would have ended in disaster, the ancient navigators possessed the necessary skills to sail back home to report their discovery—the true test of the discoverer—and return to the new island with settlers to set up a new community.

The names of those early discoverers are unfortunately inter-woven with mythological figures and old legends, so that truth and fiction are impossible to disentangle. This phenomenon is not lim-ited to the Pacific world: every culture, indeed every country, has its semimythological heroic figures.

Thus the discoverer of Easter Island, its first king, was Hotu-matua, but nothing precise is known of his voyage, and his lineage is complicated by a claimed affinity with Tangaroa, the first god, and Rongo, another Polynesian god. Maui, who is said to have "fished up" (created or discovered) New Zealand, is a demigod known throughout Polynesia, the central character in many tales and heroic deeds, one of which is the Promethean theft of fire from heaven. Closer to a real human figure is Kupe, who was believed to have been in command of a canoe that sailed from Hawaiki, discov-ered New Zealand, and returned home with news of his find; how-ever, he too is a mythic figure about whom a number of tales embroidered with magic elements are told; even Hawaiki, the ancestral home of the Polynesians, is a shadowy concept, a symbol rather than a locality.

These are but some of the navigator figures of Pacific tradition. They confirm that Micronesians and Polynesians were able to sail into unknown waters in search of new islands, report their discov-eries, and thereby enter their people's oral, magic-filled history; but they do not provide sufficient data for adequate biographies in the historical sense of the term.

This Pacific Ocean lay unknown to the rest of the world for many centuries until the Spanish conquistadors crossed the isthmus of Panama. The first of them to see it, to walk down to it, was Balboa; the first to find a navigable route into it was Magellan. It was Magel-lan who, lulled by what seemed to be a tempting calm ocean of deep blue waters, called it "pacific." He sailed into it, discovered islands and inhabitants, and crossed it from east to west. The wall of dis-tance that had kept the two worlds apart for so long began to crum-ble, and when it did, the age-old cultures of the Pacific Ocean were irretrievably changed.

The Spanish period of Pacific exploration was impressive in its boldness and its extent, yet apart from the Philippines, themselves as much a part of Asia as of the Pacific world, and a few island groups imperfectly positioned on the charts, this period left little that was permanent. Like the Dutch merchants who followed the

Spanish in quick crossings or brief forays, the Spaniards left primarily a fascinating array of names on the maps, some of which have since been erased.

European voyages to the Pacific reflected the ebb and flow of European politics. When the power of Spain began to wane, its role in the Pacific became largely passive, a desperate attempt to preserve the western seaboard of America as an exclusive zone in which not even peaceful foreign traders were allowed.

Spain's alliance with France resulted in the appearance of a number of French ships along the South American coast. They soon began to cross the Pacific to or from China. The attraction was trade with Asia and thence with Europe, but the risks inherent in allowing competitors into their territories alarmed Spanish politicians, and an end was put to this particular threat. More dangerous had been the buccaneers who raided Spanish shipping and settlements. Since these pirates represented a danger not only to Spain but to all the European powers, by concerted action their home bases in the Caribbean and along the Atlantic coast of America were destroyed.

Spain clung to the pretense of exclusiveness until the end of the eighteenth century. Not long after, rebellions in Spanish colonies brought the policy to an end. But already by the middle of the eighteenth century the dominant European powers were Britain and France: Spain had ceased to count. The rivalries between the English and the French were carried into the Pacific; but fortunately, wars between them, although raging in places as far apart as India and North America, never reached the South Seas. Their rivalry was more subtle, kept to the studies of geographers and scientists, the anterooms of politicians, and the parlors of missionaries.

Although their voyages were often born out of this rivalry, or at least affected by it, the navigators of the late eighteenth century owed much of their success to the scientific advances that were being made. The ships were larger, more maneuverable, more dependable. The sciences of navigation and hydrography had made substantial progress. It was now possible to determine latitudes with great precision. Cartographers had a growing fund of geographical knowledge to build on and were ruled by the new scientific spirit, which held imagination and fancy in check. The storage and preservation of food for long voyages improved, as did attitudes toward hygiene. The fight against scurvy, although not completely won, was in its final stages. Above all, the Age of Enlightenment was opening up people's minds, encouraging impartial investigations and systematic study, challenging ancient concepts, and in doing so it spurred on the explorers and made it easier for them to obtain official backing for their voyages.

Missionaries, who had made well-meaning but haphazard efforts to reach the people of the Pacific since the days of the Spaniards, settled in isolated island groups and added their own quota of geographical knowledge. Traders set out, often from the new British colony of New South Wales, and whalers came out from Britain, France, and the young United States. They ventured into areas bypassed by the major navigators, stumbling across unknown islets or into coastal inlets along little-known coastlines.

In the final period, large scientific expeditions set out, from Britain, the United States, France, and Russia, for lengthy voyages that also explored that farthest and final frontier, the Antarctic.

The Pacific Ocean was yielding its secrets. Colonial administrators, writers, artists, anthropologists added their quota to the growing sum of knowledge. In return, the people of the Pacific inspired artists and thinkers from Europe and America. The South Seas attracted tourists in their thousands, many of whom sailed in yachts and schooners into areas where earlier navigators had often only tentatively and fearfully ventured. Some of these were instrumental in improving or correcting the charts; others survived shipwrecks and earned their place in the annals of adventure; yet others, such as Thor Heyerdahl and Eric de Bisschop, set out on raft voyages to test ethnological theories and, if nothing more, earned praise for their determination and their courage. They cannot be included in a book such as this lest the volume become unwieldy and the names readers are most likely to be seeking become lost in the mass. But they illustrate the fact that the history of the Pacific is not a closed chapter in the story of humanity: indeed, it has just begun.

# A Note on Ranks and Titles

A VARIETY OF TITLES have been used by different countries over the centuries. For the sake of readability they have mostly been translated into English. They can only be regarded as an approximation, indicative more of an individual's progression during his career than of a precise placing in some notional international ranking scale. Not only have the structures of rank changed over the centuries, with some titles becoming obsolete, but even where no translation is involved the same term used in two different countries is not synonymous. The term "lieutenant" is a case in point; "captain" can also be confusing, often meaning the master of a ship.

Similarly, titles of nobility, translated into English for the sake of simplicity where they have some relevance, do not indicate an equivalence of rank in different countries.

# Adams

WILLIAM ADAMS was born in September 1564 in Gillingham, Kent, and went to sea from the age of 12. He played a part in fighting the Spanish Armada in 1588 as captain of the supply ship *Richard Duffield*. His next ten years were spent mostly serving in various merchant ships, trading in the Mediterranean.

From 1593 to 1595 he took part in Dutch expeditions in search of a northeast passage around Arctic Russia to the East. This association with Dutch merchants led him to join a fleet of five Dutch ships bound for the Pacific, Adams serving as pilot of the *Hoop*, later transferring to the *Liefde*. The commander was Jacques Mahu *(q.v.)*, who was succeeded by Simon de Cordes *(q.v.)*.

The fleet sailed from the Texel on 24 June 1598, had a slow and difficult Atlantic passage followed by an equally slow struggle through the Strait of Magellan. When the Dutch emerged into the Pacific, on 4 September 1599, they were assailed by a fierce gale. One ship, the *Geloof*, was forced to return to Holland; a second, the *Trouw*, was driven back into the strait and in time made its way alone to the East Indies where it was captured by the Portuguese. The others put in at Spanish settlements along the South American coast, incurring the suspicion and enmity of the Spanish, whose monopoly laws they were breaking.

The *Liefde* and the *Hoop*, now the sole survivors of the fleet (the *Blijde Boodschap* had been confiscated by the Spanish in Valparaiso) sailed from South America on 27 November 1599. The plan was to sail north and west across the Pacific, avoiding the inimical Portuguese and Spanish, and make for Japan and China. The *Hoop*, however, was lost in a storm in late January, probably north of Hawaii, so that only the *Liefde* completed the crossing of the Pacific, reaching Japan on 11 April 1600.

By then only 24 of the original crew of 110 were still alive, and only 6 of those were strong enough to work the ship. Three of the surviving Dutch sailors died within hours of landing, and 3 more died not long after. The *Liefde* was brought to Osaka and later to Edo (Tokyo), and the Dutch, after a period of imprisonment and interrogation, were set free. Their attempts to leave Japan were unsuccessful and led to a bitter falling out and constant quarrels. Adams, however, had impressed Ieyashu, who ruled Japan at that time, and

1

became a trusted adviser, promoting trade between Japan and Holland, building ships, and making several voyages in eastern seas. In 1611 he married a Japanese woman, who bore him two children.

William Adams died in Japan on 16 May 1620. He left his estate in equal shares to his Japanese wife and to Mary Hyn, whom he had married in England in 1589.

## Alcala-Galiano

DIONISIO ALCALA-GALIANO was born in 1762 at Cabra, in southern Spain, entered naval school in 1775, and first saw active service in 1779, gaining wide experience in scientific and hydrographic work. This led him to be appointed to the expedition of Malaspina (q.v.) in July 1789, sailing from Cadiz as lieutenant of the corvette *Atrevida*. The expedition sailed round Cape Horn to Guayaquil, thence to the Galapagos, Panama, and Acapulco.

The Spanish authorities were more interested in discovering the fabled Northwest Passage, which would have rounded off Spanish territories in south and central America as well as provided an alternative route to Europe they might be able to control, than in a circumnavigation; when Malaspina's exploration of the Alaskan coast produced no results, it was decided to mount a special voyage to the northwest coast.

In 1791, accordingly, the viceroy of New Spain appointed Alcala-Galiano to head the proposed expedition. Promoted frigate captain, he took over the schooners *Sutil* and *Mexicana*, the latter commanded by Cayetano Valdes y Flores. Their instructions were to investigate the possibilities offered by Juan de Fuca Strait.

Sailing from Acapulco on 8 March 1792, the two ships dropped anchor in Nootka Sound on 13 May. The Spanish post was now firmly established; and after resting his men, Alcala-Galiano sailed, on 5 June, for the strait, calling at Neah Bay, in present-day Washington state, on the sixth. On the thirteenth, as he rounded Point Roberts, he met the *Chatham* under Broughton (q.v.) and on the twenty-first came upon George Vancouver (q.v.). Relations were friendly, and scientific data were freely exchanged. The British and Spanish ships actually sailed together for some time—until 13 July. Alcala-Galiano completed the circumnavigation of Vancouver Island, emerging into the Pacific from Queen Charlotte Sound on 23

July by Goletas Passage (which he named in full, Canal de la Salida de las Goletas). He then veered south along Vancouver Island to Nootka Sound, which he reached on 1 September, when he once again came upon the English expedition.

Having determined that Juan de Fuca Strait did not lead into a northwest passage, he sailed back to Mexico, arriving at San Blas on 23 November 1792. His reports on the commercial potential of the area he had investigated and his urgings that Spain continue to trade and explore were well received, although not acted upon, being beyond the means of the colonial authorities and rapidly overtaken by the development of war in Europe.

His account of the voyage, *Relación del Viaje hecho por las Goletas "Sutil" y "Mexicana" en el año 1792 para Reconecher el Estracho de Fuca*, was published in 1802 and was widely read.

Alcala-Galiano returned to Spain in 1794 and continued his geographical surveys until the war claimed his services. In 1796 he commanded the *Vencedor* at the battle of Cape St. Vincent, having been promoted to full captain in 1795. He later commanded escort vessels between Cadiz and Mexico and was raised to the rank of brigadier. He was killed in action on 21 October 1805 at the battle of Trafalgar while in command of the *Bahama*.

Galiano Island in the Strait of Georgia, off Vancouver Island, is named after him. Valdes Island, named after the captain of the *Mexicana*, lies just north of it.

## Allen

JOSEPH ALLEN was an American whaler from New England who captained the Nantucket ship *Maro*, built in 1816. He was in the Pacific in 1820, reputedly the first whaler to work on the "Japan grounds," the vast area between the Hawaiian Islands and Japan, and also the first to enter the port of Honolulu.

On 2 June 1820 Allen discovered a barren, rocky island to which he gave the name Gardner's Island. Situated far to the northwest of Hawaii, it is now known as Gardner's Pinnacles. Allen's pioneering expedition proved quite profitable, and he returned to the Pacific in 1821, joined by a growing number of his compatriots. The *Maro* was lost at Rio de Janeiro in 1823, having been run into by a French vessel.

## Anson

GEORGE ANSON was born at Shugborough, Staffordshire, on 23 April 1697 to a well-connected family. Entering the Royal Navy in 1712, he gained rapid promotion. In 1739, with the rank of commodore, he was selected to lead a squadron to the Pacific and particularly to the Philippines to raid Spanish shipping once the expected war broke out. This happened on 19 October, and on 10 January 1740 Anson received his orders.

It was, however, 18 September before he could sail in the *Centurion* from St. Helens, Isle of Wight, with seven other ships. He made for Madeira, Brazil, and Patagonia. In early March 1741 Anson was struggling toward the Strait of Le Maire and Cape Horn in fierce gales and heavy squalls. The ships became separated, the *Centurion* reaching the island of Chiloe alone on 8 May; it went on to Juan Fernandez, arriving on 11 June. Two ships of the squadron eventually joined the *Centurion* there, the sloop *Tryall* and the *Gloucester*, both in a parlous condition, with numerous sick on board as well as a number of dead yet to be disposed of. It took almost three months before Anson could contemplate a raid on the mainland. He sailed in early September and made his first capture of a Spanish vessel on the thirteenth. Then on 13 November came the famous sacking of the town of Paita in Peru, which alerted the Spanish to their vulnerability to foreign raids and to piratical attacks.

By now only the *Centurion* and the *Gloucester* were seaworthy. Anson continued his raids on settlements up the coast as far as Acapulco, looting and destroying Spanish installations. The months went by, the loot increasing, but the strain on the men also growing. In May 1742, Anson left the coast of America for the East. Progress was slow; the *Gloucester* began leaking badly, at a faster rate than the sick crew could pump, and on 16 August, after transferring stores and crew to the *Centurion*, Anson had the ship set on fire. A week later, the English reached the Ladrones Islands (Marianas) and were able to recuperate at Tinian. In mid-October, Anson set sail for Macao, arriving a month later.

George Anson's voyage, appallingly costly in men and ships, did not result in new discoveries, and some of the geographical information gathered from the Spanish was often more confusing than helpful; but it achieved the primary aim the Admiralty had in mind when organizing it, namely, the harrying of Spanish outposts and ships in the Pacific. It was also profitable considering the booty seized, because after refitting in Macao and disentangling himself from arguments with Chinese officials, Anson sailed to the Philippines, in April 1743, in search of the Manila galleon. On 20 June, off Cape Espiritu Santo, he came upon the richly laden *Nuestra Señora de Cobagonda*, and lost no time in transferring all its treasure to the *Centurion*. He then took the *Nuestra* with him to Canton, where he sold it. On 15 December, the *Centurion* sailed for England by way of the Cape of Good Hope, arriving at St. Helens on 15 June 1744.

George Anson joined the Admiralty Board in 1745, although he briefly returned to active service in 1747, and instigated far-reaching and much-needed reforms throughout the Royal Navy. He was given the title of Baron Anson of Soberton in 1747. He died an admiral on 6 June 1762. Several accounts of the circumnavigation were published, starting with Richard Walter's of 1748.

## Arellano

ALONSO DE ARELLANO was captain of the *San Lucas*, a 40-ton patache that formed part of the four-ship squadron of Miguel Lopez de Legazpi *(q.v.)* constructed at Navidad in Mexico. They sailed on 21 November 1564, but on 1 December the *San Lucas* became separated from the other vessels and continued alone on its eastward journey, to complete the crossing of the Pacific to the Philippines.

On the night of 5 January 1565 the Spanish came to an island on which they narrowly escaped being wrecked. Likiep, an uninhabited atoll in a group of thirty-six islets surrounded by a reef, lay in the eastern chain of the Marshall Islands. It had possibly already been sighted by other Spanish navigators. On 7 and 8 January, Arellano came upon other islands, Kwajalein and Lib, the latter being indisputably a new discovery. After this, Arellano maintained a westerly course, making for the heart of the Caroline Islands.

This led to a number of discoveries: Minto Reef on 15 January, Truk on the seventeenth, Pulap on the nineteenth, Sorol on the twenty-second, and Ngulu on the twenty-third. In addition, a number of other islands were seen and some landings were effected, with a bit of trading and several skirmishes. On 29 January, the *San Lucas* reached the Philippines and began a remarkable feat of navigation in the waters around Mindanao, sailing clockwise around the island, going north through the Sulu Sea and, on 22 April 1565 emerging through the San Bernardino Strait into the Pacific to begin the return voyage.

Arellano set a northeasterly course toward the high latitudes, sighting some rocky outliers of southern Japan, probably the lonely island of Sumisu-jima, and after completing a wide arc toward 43° came back upon the coast of Lower California in latitude 27°45' on 16 July, ending his voyage at the port of Navidad on 9 August 1565. He had completed the first west to east crossing of the Pacific.

Arellano endeavored to turn his discoveries to his own advantage, believing at first that the larger expedition had failed. He gained some support in Spain until news arrived of the return of Urdaneta (q.v.) with one of the ships that had set out under Legazpi (q.v.). Arellano was briefly placed under arrest but freed after an enquiry; whether he had deserted or whether he became separated beyond his control remained open. Arellano's attempts to establish himself in the Philippines failed, however, and he died in Mexico in 1579. The account he wrote of his voyage was published in Madrid in 1887 in the Pacheco *Colección*.

## Auribeau

ALEXANDRE D'HESMIVY D'AURIBEAU was born on 25 January 1760 in Digne, southern France, and joined the Navy in 1775. He first served in the *Sultane* in 1777, then in the *Tonnant* as sublieutenant. He transferred to the *Aimable* in 1778, the first of several vessels in which he was to serve during the American War of Independence, including the *Magnanime*, commanded by Vaudreuil, and the *Sceptre*, commanded by Admiral de Grasse, the ship which, in 1782, La Pérouse (q.v.) was to lead on his raid against the British forts in Hudson Bay.

He was promoted to lieutenant in May 1786 and obtained a number of postings in the difficult years prior to the outbreak of the French Revolution. When it happened, in 1789, he was an officer of the *Belette*; a few years later he was given his first command, the *Aurore*.

Although his health was not good, he applied, through relatives, to join the expedition of d'Entrecasteaux (q.v.). He was an experienced officer and very well connected. He was appointed second-in-command to d'Entrecasteaux in the *Recherche*, sailing on 29 September 1791 from Brest with the *Espérance* to search for the lost expedition of La Pérouse. At the same time, d'Auribeau was made a knight of the Order of St. Louis, and in April 1792 promoted to captain.

As the expedition proceeded to Australia, New Zealand, and the numerous island groups of the southwest Pacific, stresses developed on board between conservative royalists like d'Auribeau and supporters of the new revolutionary order. The length of the voyage, the growing shortage of supplies, and psychological strains all took their toll. Kermadec *(q.v.)*, the commander of the *Espérance*, died on 6 May 1793, and d'Auribeau was sent to replace him. Then, on 20 July, d'Entrecasteaux himself died, and d'Auribeau became the effective leader of the expedition, but he was in no fit state to take over, and left Rossel *(q.v.)* to run the ships. By the end of August, d'Auribeau had lapsed into a coma. He recovered during a call at the Dutch settlement of Caieli on Buru Island, but remained bedridden. He began to improve and to take up the reins of command as the ships sailed on to Surabaya. There, in February 1794, he threw his lot in with the émigrés, raised the royalist standard, and had the republican ringleaders arrested. The French authorities, hearing of this, sent out orders revoking his command, but d'Auribeau had already died, on 24 August 1794.

## Balboa

To Vasco Nuñez de Balboa belongs the honor of being the first European to set eyes on what was to become known as the Pacific Ocean or South Seas. He was born, probably in 1475, in Jerez de los Caballeros, Spain; in 1501 he sailed to the Caribbean, where he farmed for a while. His enterprises were not successful, and in 1510 he went with Enciso to the new settlement of San Sebastian, avoiding his creditors, it is said, by having himself conveyed on board concealed in a barrel. The settlement was discovered to be in ruins and Balboa, overcoming the scruples of a wavering Enciso, crossed to Darien on the Central American shore.

As head of the small settlement, Balboa proved to be resourceful, daring, but above all human. He won over the local Indians, who told him of the existence of a great sea beyond the mountain ranges. When news came that the king of Spain was about to have him condemned for overthrowing Enciso, Balboa decided that an important discovery would put him back in the good graces of his sovereign. He set out on 1 September 1513 with 190 Spanish and about 1,000 natives, and after great hardships, struggling through jungle and scrambling over mountains, sighted the Pacific from a hilltop on 25 or 26 September. On the twenty-ninth he formally took possession of the "Great South Sea" on behalf of Spain. He returned to Darien on 18 January 1514 and at once sent news of his discovery to the Spanish court.

King Ferdinand appointed Balboa admiral of the newly discovered ocean and governor of Panama. Balboa repeated the crossing of the isthmus on several occasions, preparing the exploration and eventual conquest of the coast of Peru, but his enemies were intriguing against him, and in 1517 he was sentenced to death on trumped-up charges and executed in the public square of Acla.

## Ball

HENRY LIDGBIRD BALL was born in England in 1757, joined the Royal Navy at an early age, and served in various ships: the *Venus*, *Ramillies*, *Raven*, and *Lark*. He was raised to the rank of lieutenant on 6 May 1779, and in 1787, as commander of the *Supply*, he was selected to join the First Fleet taking convicts and soldiers to New South Wales.

The *Supply*, an armed tender, sailed in May 1787 from Portsmouth and reached Botany Bay in January of the following year. The bay proving unsuitable for a settlement, Ball sailed with the commander, Arthur Phillip, to nearby Port Jackson. Ball surveyed the area and was sent to Norfolk Island on three occasions. On the first of these, on 17 February 1788, he discovered and named Lord Howe Island.

In April 1790 he took the *Supply* to Batavia to buy food for the struggling Australian colony, returning in October. He then took over the chartered vessel *Waaksamheyd* and in January 1791 was asked to bring back John Hunter (*q.v.*) and the shipwrecked crew of the *Sirius*, but he was too ill to carry on. He set off for England in November 1791, reaching Plymouth in April 1792.

He was promoted to commander on his return and once his health was restored took over various ships during the war years of the period 1795–1813. He became a full captain on 9 July 1795, retired on half pay in 1813, and was raised to the rank of rear admiral on 4 June 1814. He died on 23 October 1818. His name is commemorated in Ball's Pyramid, a tall rocky pinnacle close to Lord Howe Island, Mt. Lidgbird on Howe, and Ball Bay in Norfolk Island.

## Banks

JOSEPH BANKS was born on 13 February 1743 in London, the son of a well-to-do family. He was educated at Harrow, then Eton, but attracted as he was by botany he turned from the more traditional academic curriculum of the public schools to the study of natural history. This meant studying alone as best he could, even when he went to Oxford, where he found that the professor of botany did no teaching. Banks therefore engaged a private tutor at his own expense. Largely as the result of his enthusiasm rather than any specific scientific contribution, Banks was elected a Fellow of the Royal Society at the age of 23.

His first experience of overseas travel began in 1766, when he sailed in the *Niger* to Labrador and Newfoundland. He spent 1767 on botanical expeditions in various parts of England; then came the opportunity of joining the expedition James Cook *(q.v.)* was leading to the Pacific. He sailed with a suite appropriate to a man of his wealth—the death of his father in 1761 had brought him a large inheritance—and his growing status as a patron of science. He took with him Daniel Solander, a botanist and naturalist; Herman Sporing, a naturalist; Sydney Parkinson, a botanical artist; Alexander Buchan, a draftsman; four servants; and two dogs.

The *Endeavour* sailed from Plymouth on 26 August 1768. When the ship reached Rio de Janeiro, the suspicious viceroy refused permission to anyone other than the captain to set foot ashore, but Banks managed to go botanizing by setting off in a small boat before daybreak and returning after dark. There was less difficulty when they reached Tierra del Fuego on 11 January 1769, but the cold was so intense that two of Bank's servants, both blacks, lost their lives.

The prolonged stay in Tahiti enabled Banks to make friends with native chiefs who recognized him as a person of rank, although this did not prevent the theft of some of his belongings. On the crossing to New Zealand, there were fish to be caught, birds and algae to be examined. New Zealand provided numerous opportunities for botanizing and for observing the Maoris, though there were a number of unpleasant incidents and several killings. Banks had the pleasure of seeing a major geographical feature named after him—Banks' Island, which turned out to be a peninsula—as well as several varieties of plants.

Australia, which the *Endeavour* reached in April 1770, offered so many botanical treasures that the bay in which he landed, originally called Stingray Harbour, was renamed Botany Bay. The natives here, however, were less easy to approach than the Maoris had been; in addition, as the expedition sailed north from New South Wales, the Great Barrier Reef nearly brought disaster to the *Endeavour* and to Banks' growing collection of natural history treasures. A catastrophe was averted, however, and the expedition continued toward New Guinea and the Dutch East Indies. Malaria and above all dysentery struck the expedition in Batavia, where the *Endeavour* dropped anchor on 10 October. Banks was badly affected, but survived. Parkinson and Sporing, however, did not. Despite the deaths, the ship needed to be repaired and could not leave until late December. There were more deaths on the way home, which was by way of the Cape and St. Helena. The expedition reached England on 13 July 1771.

While Cook went to the Admiralty and to his modest home in Mile End, Banks went to Court and to numerous receptions. Oxford, which had failed to provide him with tuition in botany, gave him an honorary doctorate. When it was decided to send Cook back on a second voyage, with two ships, the *Adventure* and the *Resolution*, Banks took part in the planning, and it was taken for granted that he would accompany Cook. Banks had decided to take not only Dr. Solander with him again and an artist, John Zoffany, to replace the late Sydney Parkinson, but draftsmen, secretaries, servants, even two horn players, making a total retinue of fifteen people. The alterations needed to accommodate all these supernumeraries upset the balance and safety of the vessel, and the entire project was abandoned. Cook sailed without Banks, possibly with some feeling of relief since Banks seemed likely to be the dominant personality on the voyage, while the naturalist set off instead on an expedition to Iceland and the Hebrides.

The cool relations between Banks and Cook did not last long. When Cook was killed on his third voyage, Banks supervised the making of a commemorative medal. He had been elected president of the Royal Society in 1778, a position he was to hold for forty-one years. In 1781 he was created a baronet. His influence grew over the years; he became scientific adviser to the king, was in effective control of the Royal Gardens at Kew, negotiated during wartime to protect the work of foreign scientists, and played a major role in the selection of Botany Bay as a penal settlement—although it proved inadequate compared with nearby Port Jackson.

He died on 19 June 1820. An early romantic attachment to a Miss Harriet Blosset did not survive the separation caused by the voyage of the *Endeavour*, but he eventually married, in 1779, Dorothea Hugessen; they had no descendants.

## Baret

JEANNE BARET (or Baré) was born in La Comelle, near Autun in Burgundy, around 1745. Orphaned and penniless, she fled to Geneva where she worked as a servant, apparently dressed as a male. Later she was engaged as a governess for the young son of the widowed botanist Commerson (q.v.), whom she accompanied on his voyage with Bougainville (q.v.) in the *Boudeuse*, disguised as his valet.

Although the sailors' suspicions had already been aroused by her complexion and her insistence on privacy, it was not until the *Boudeuse* reached Tahiti that her secret was fully revealed. The Tahitians had neither doubts nor qualms, and she had to be rescued from abduction and rape. Baret told Bougainville who she was and he thenceforth extended to her his protection until she disembarked with Commerson in Mauritius.

Described by Bougainville as "neither plain nor pretty," she was hard working and well behaved, helping Commerson with his botanizing work ashore, carrying his notebooks and the varied specimens he collected. She remained on Mauritius with Commerson when the *Boudeuse* sailed on 12 December 1768. Her master died in 1773, and on 17 May 1774 she married Jean Dubernat, a former

NCO in the Royal Comtois regiment. In 1785 she was granted a pension of 200 *livres* by the French government.

Jeanne Baret was not the first woman to cross the Pacific, but she can be credited with being the first to take part in a major circumnavigation.

## Barkley

CHARLES WILLIAM BARKLEY was born in 1761 and worked for the British East India Company until 1786, when he was prevailed upon to transfer his allegiance to the Bengal Fur Company then being managed by John Reid and Daniel Beale. He took over the *Loudoun* (or *Loudon*), which was renamed the *Imperial Eagle* and reflagged in Ostend under Austrian colors to circumvent the East India Company's monopoly.

On 27 September 1786 he married Frances Trevor, the daughter of the Protestant chaplain at Ostend; they sailed on 24 November for Brazil and Cape Horn, arriving at Hawaii in May 1787. After a brief period of recuperation, the expedition sailed, on 25 May, for the northwest coast. Mrs. Barkley thus became the first European woman to set eyes on Vancouver Island and Nootka, where her husband began to buy furs soon after his arrival at the end of June.

Sailing south along the coast, Barkley made a number of discoveries: Clayoquot Sound, Barkley Sound, Frances Island (named after his wife), and Cape Beale. Next came the long-lost Juan de Fuca Strait, whose suspected existence Barkley was now able to confirm, but where he lost six of his men—killed by natives on Destruction Island near the entrance. Shortly after, he sailed for Macao, where he sold his cargo of furs.

Securing another cargo, Barkley set sail for the Île de France (Mauritius) in February 1788, under Portuguese colors, but on arrival in India found himself ill-treated by the company's agents, who were determined to get out of a trade that was becoming unprofitable. Barkley lost most of his charts, journals, and instruments, the bulk of which found their way into the possession of John Meares *(q.v.)*. Barkley on appeal received some compensation, but returned to Europe with his wife.

Barkley sailed again to the Pacific in 1792 in the *Halcyon*, trading again along Vancouver Island and among the Queen Charlotte

Islands, but other traders had benefited from his pioneering efforts, and his role on the coast was negligible. He died in 1832 and his wife in 1845. Frances Barkley wrote her "Reminiscences," a valuable record of the *Imperial Eagle*'s voyage; her husband wrote a "Journal of the Proceedings on Board the *Loudon.*" Neither has been published.

## Barreto

YSABEL DE BARRETO, the wife of Alvaro de Mendaña *(q.v.)*, accompanied her husband across the Pacific on his second voyage. Although haughty and highly conscious of her rank, she was by no means incompetent and fully supported her husband's idealistic approach to exploration and colonization.

The expedition set sail from Paita, Peru, on 16 June 1595, discovered part of the Marquesas, then sailed on to the northern Cooks, the Ellice Islands, and Santa Cruz, making a number of discoveries on the way. During the stay at Ndeni, in the Santa Cruz group, Mendaña died, leaving the effective as well as the nominal command to Ysabel. (Her brother Lorenzo de Barreto, whom Mendaña had appointed captain general, was already sick and survived Mendaña by only one day, leaving Ysabel and two other of her brothers, men of lesser competence, to face Quiros [*q.v.*], the expedition's pilot.) Ysabel planned to sail first to San Cristobal in the hope of finding the *Santa Ysabel*, which had become separated from the other vessels, and also of finding the southern continent that her husband had set out to discover; then by sailing to Manila she could recruit more colonists for a permanent settlement.

Quiros had a more realistic view of the difficulties they all would face and of the condition of their three vessels and their crews. He favored using only one of the ships; in this, as in much else, he was overruled. The enmity that developed between him and Dona Ysabel worsened as time went by.

On 7 November, the expedition sailed for a while on a west-southwest course, but soon altered course toward Manila. The hardships undergone by the crews during this part of the voyage highlighted Ysabel de Barreto's selfishness and sense of superiority. She found it impossible to empathize with the suffering men below deck, and her relationship with Quiros made her even more obdurate. She withdrew into her own small circle, refusing to share any of her store of food and wine with the sick and even using scarce drinking water for washing her clothes. Only Quiros's angry remonstrances persuaded her to give up two jars of oil and allow a calf to be killed. When the Spanish reached Cavite in the Philippines on 11 February 1596, fifty men were dead and many were too ill to work the ship. Dona Ysabel, it must be said, had herself by then given up hope of surviving the voyage, and her withdrawal from shipboard life was due at least in part to a desire to prepare herself for the after-life.

She quickly recovered her spirits, complained bitterly about Quiros and other officers, and then remarried—one Fernando de Castro, a cousin of the retiring governor. The *San Jerónimo* was refitted and revictualed, and in it she sailed to Mexico on 10 August 1596, reaching Acapulco on 11 December.

Don Fernando considered himself Mendaña's heir, claiming through his wife the privileges formerly granted to the navigator, including the governorship of the Solomons. His claim, until swept aside by the Spanish court and in time given up by both himself and Ysabel, delayed Quiros' efforts to mount a new expedition. Ysabel then sank into genteel obscurity, but as nominal head of the Mendaña voyage she could be said to have discovered, on that tragic last leg of the journey, the island of Pakin in the eastern Carolines. Her brother Lorenzo can be credited with the discovery, in a survey around the Santa Cruz Islands in September 1595, of the Swallow Islands, Utupua, and possibly Vanikoro.

## Barrett

GEORGE BARRETT was born in Boston, Massachusetts, in 1773. He worked on whaling ships out of Nantucket, and on 23 July 1819 sailed as captain of the *Independence II* for a voyage to the Pacific and particularly the waters around New Zealand.

On 6 November 1821 he came upon an uninhabited group of islands in the Ellice group, landing on one the following day. He named them the Mitchell's Group. On the eighth he sighted a low island guarded by a coral reef, which he called Independence Island. This was Nurakita, sighted by Mendaña *(q.v.)*. The Mitchells, however, was a new discovery, being the large atoll cluster of Nuku-laelae.

Barrett died on board soon after leaving the Ellice Islands (Tuvalu). The *Independence II* returned to Nantucket on 16 June 1822.

## Bass

GEORGE BASS was born on 30 January 1771 at Aswarby in Lincolnshire, the son of a tenant farmer. He was apprenticed to an apothecary and learned enough of this trade to qualify for service as a naval assistant surgeon at the age of 18. His first ship was the *Flirt*; this was followed by a period in the *Gorgon* and a number of short postings until 1794, when he was appointed to the *Reliance*, which was due to sail to New South Wales.

The *Reliance* arrived in Sydney on 7 September 1795, and Bass soon had an opportunity to develop his interest as a hydrographer and surveyor through exploring nearby coasts and the George River in a small boat. After a voyage to Norfolk Island in the *Reliance*, he carried out more coastal exploration in the *Tom Thumb*. After a further voyage in the *Reliance* to Norfolk Island and Capetown to fetch supplies for the colony, which lasted from September 1796 to June 1797, Bass was given permission to explore the south coast in a whaler.

Leaving Port Jackson on 3 December 1797, Bass sailed toward Tasmania and confirmed its insularity by discovering the strait that now bears his name. In October 1798 he sailed through Bass Strait in the *Norfolk* with his friend Matthew Flinders *(q.v.)*. By now, he was acquiring a reputation in the world of science; he had written a number of papers on natural history and was elected a member of the Linnean Society. But his status as a naval surgeon and the mediocre remuneration it brought him left him dissatisfied. In association with Charles Bishop *(q.v.)*, he turned to trade, sailing with him in the *Nautilus* in May 1799 for Macao, where the *Nautilus* was sold.

Even then, he did not give up his exploring activities. A chart of the voyage he drew up in association with another officer, Roger Simpson, was published in London by the hydrographer Alexander Dalrymple. Bass also carried out some surveying work in the Singapore area while returning to England in the *Rhio*. Arriving there in July 1800, he sailed back to New South Wales in January 1801 in the *Venus*, but trade patterns were changing as the colony became almost self-supporting, and profits were lower than anticipated.

Bass sailed to Dusky Sound in New Zealand and to Tahiti and Hawaii to buy various supplies including pork. Back in Port Jackson in late 1802, he decided to sail to South America in the hope of opening up trade with the Spanish colonies, a dangerous and illegal enterprise. He left Port Jackson in command of the *Venus* on 5 February 1803 and was never heard of again.

In addition to Bass Strait, his name has been given to Bass Island in the Duff group, a part of the Santa Cruz archipelago, and to the Bass Islands, nine small, rocky islets also known as Marotiri in the Austral Islands.

## Baudin

NICOLAS-THOMAS BAUDIN was born on the island of Ré off the Brittany coast on 17 February 1754. After some years in merchant ships, he joined the navy in 1774, his career then making but slow progress owing to his lack of aristocratic connections. Promotion beyond the rank of sublieutenant proved difficult, and Baudin sought service under Joseph II of Austria. He was sent on several scientific expeditions, including a major voyage to the Indian Ocean and the Far East in search of botanical specimens for the gardens of the Schönbrunn Palace.

By this time the French revolutionary wars had broken out, and Baudin made his way back to France. He was selected to lead another scientific expedition, this time to the West Indies, which occupied him from 1796 to 1798. He was regarded as a senior naval officer (a number of his more highly born contemporaries had emigrated or were regarded with suspicion by the republican authorities), with a sound knowledge of navigation and a good practical scientific background. He developed a project for a voyage of exploration to the Pacific which was adopted, but with the emphasis placed on the Australian continent, where much remained to be done. Although there was a minor political aspect to the eventual program, which was finally approved by Napoleon, its main purpose was scientific, and a number of savants were included in the complements of the two ships, the *Géographe* and the *Naturaliste*, which left from Le Havre on 19 October 1800.

After a brief call at Tenerife, the ships sailed for Mauritius. This part of the voyage proved unusually slow—taking five months—and this delay not only depleted the stores but put a strain on shipboard relations that Baudin's authoritarian character, accentuated by already failing health, merely worsened. The expedition sailed on 25 April 1801 for southwest Australia. Cape Leeuwin was sighted on 17 May. Proceeding north, the French vessels sailed toward Rottnest Island, where they became separated in storms. Extensive surveying was done by each ship until they rejoined company at Timor in September.

In mid-November Baudin went south, sailing in a wide arc down the Indian Ocean and east to Tasmania, which was sighted on 13 January 1802. His ambition was to chart the entire east coast, but this proved too vast a task, particularly as the ships were soon again separated. Between them, however, they carried out a great deal of exploration in Bass Strait and along the southwest coast of Australia. Baudin would have been able to claim the credit for surveying a far greater length of hitherto uncharted coast had he not been delayed in his crossing from France to Mauritius, which allowed Matthew Flinders *(q.v.)* to forestall him in much of his work. The two explorers met in what is now known as Encounter Bay on 8 April 1802. The *Géographe* and the *Naturaliste* were reunited in June in Port Jackson. Shortly thereafter, Baudin set out once more for Bass Strait and western Australia, but with a third vessel, the small *Casuarina*, bought in New South Wales as a replacement for the slow and cumbersome *Naturaliste*, which was sent home.

Detailed surveys were made at King George Sound and along the coast to Cape Leeuwin. Further work was done on the west coast and, after a second call at Timor, along the little-known and island-strewn northwest coast as far as Bathurst and Melville islands. On 7 July 1803, his crew exhausted and himself seriously ill, Baudin turned back, setting course for Mauritius, which he reached on 7 August. He died there on 16 September.

In spite of frequent setbacks and endless shipboard dissensions, the expedition achieved a great deal, in both geography and natural history and in the truly astonishing cargo of specimens brought back to Europe.

## Beechey

FREDERICK WILLIAM BEECHEY, son of Sir William Beechey, R.A., a celebrated portraitist, was born on 17 February 1796. He entered the Royal Navy in 1806, attained midshipman's rank in 1807, and saw extensive service during the later stages of the Napoleonic wars. Commissioned lieutenant in March 1815, he was appointed to the *Niger* on the North American station.

In January 1818 he joined the *Trent* under Lt. John Franklin, which sailed with the *Buchan* on an expedition toward the North Pole; its termination near Spitzbergen did not deter Franklin or Beechey from proposing another voyage to the Arctic.

Their suggestions were not accepted, but in 1819 Beechey sailed with William Parry in the *Hecla* to Melville Island. His next appointment, in 1821, was to the warmer climate of the Mediterranean in the sloop *Adventure.* In January 1822 he was promoted to commander, but he needed to recuperate after four years of strenuous exertions; he did not get another appointment until January 1825, when he was given the command of the sloop HMS *Blossom* for a voyage to the Pacific.

The expedition sailed from Spithead on 19 May 1825 for Tenerife, Rio, the Falklands, and Cape Horn, dropping anchor in Valparaiso on 27 October. Within a couple of days, Beechey left for Sala y Gomez, Easter Island, and Pitcairn, of which he wrote a lengthy account. On 29 December he reached Mangareva in the Gambier group, where he remained until 13 January 1826, then beginning a fruitful journey through the Tuamotus. He discovered the islands of Vanavana, which he named Barrow's Island; Fangataufa; and Ahunui, where he found a party of forty shipwrecked Christian Tahitians. He had room for only one man and his family on board, but took them to Tahiti where they could report the wreck and arrange for help.

The *Blossom* reached Tahiti on 18 March. Puritanism was making itself felt over this former South Sea paradise, but the British visitors were still able to be entertained by traditional dances. They weighed anchor on 26 April, sailing north for Honolulu, where they arrived on 20 May. Beechey met the local rulers and later came under the suspicions of the American missionaries, who accused him of attempting to undermine their work. In fact, here as elsewhere, his attitude was fair and impartial. Beechey left Oahu on 31 May for Niihau and then for the northern Pacific.

On 29 June the *Blossom* put in at Petropavlovsk on the Kamchatka Peninsula. Beechey's instructions were to assist captains William Parry and John Franklin in their exploration of the Bering

Strait area. He discovered, however, that Parry had been forced to abandon his ship on Somerset Island and that the crew had made its way back to England. Beechey sailed from the Russian port on 4 July, hoping to rendezvous with Franklin, but there was no sign of him. Beechey nevertheless carried out extensive surveys through and beyond Bering Strait until mid-October.

The *Blossom* sailed to California for supplies, reaching San Francisco Bay on 8 November and Monterey on 1 January 1827. Five days later, the expedition set out to cross the Pacific from east to west, calling at Honolulu on 27 January for a stay of five weeks and reaching Macao on 11 April. Not without difficulty Beechey obtained the supplies, especially medicine, of which he was in need and sailed back to the Arctic at the end of the month, passing through the Bashi Islands, north of the Philippines, and along to the Ryukyu Islands, reaching Petropavlovsk on 3 July 1827.

Beechey's second summer in Arctic waters was as disappointing as the first. Although a few geographical features were discovered, the weather was bad and the cold set in early. And there was no sign of Franklin. On 5 October 1827 the *Blossom* left Bering Strait for Monterey, dropping anchor on the twenty-ninth. During a call for supplies at San Blas, Mexico, Beechey was asked to help transship silver and gold to England. This involved delays that Beechey put to good use to carry out coastal surveys. In Valparaiso, on 29 April 1828, he learned of his promotion to captain. *Blossom* finally reached England in October, being paid off on the twelfth. In December he married Charlotte Stapleton, daughter of a senior army officer.

Beechey's achievements were considerable: not only had he discovered some islands in the Tuamotus and added to our knowledge of Arctic waters, but his reports on the inhabitants of Pitcairn and other Polynesian groups were particularly valuable at a time of transition. Nor were the expedition's contributions to natural history negligible: *Narrative of a Voyage to the Pacific and Beering's Strait . . .* was published in two volumes in 1831. Beechey hoped to return to Arctic waters and drew up a plan for an expedition, which the Admiralty rejected, still hoping that a northwest passage might be found. A proposal to search for the explorer Sir John Ross fared no better. In 1836 Beechey was sent back to the Pacific to carry out hydrographic work along the American seaboard, being given for this expedition *Sulphur* and *Starling*, but ill-health forced him to give up this command. He died on 29 November 1856.

## Belcher

EDWARD BELCHER was born on 27 February 1799 in Halifax, Nova Scotia, of a family of prominent colonial administrators. He joined the Royal Navy in April 1812 and served in the *Abercromby*, then in 1816 in the *Superb*. He was commissioned lieutenant in 1818. His service in the years following included a period in the *Blonde*, commanded by George Anson Byron *(q.v.)*. On his return he was appointed assistant surveyor to the *Blossom*, commanded by F. W. Beechey *(q.v.)*.

The *Blossom* sailed from Spithead on 19 May 1825 for Rio de Janeiro, Cape Horn, and Valparaiso. On 16 November it was at Easter Island, on its way to more lonely islands—Ducie, Henderson, and Pitcairn—to the Gambiers, the Tuamotus, and Tahiti, which it reached in March 1826. The next stage of the voyage took the *Blossom* to Honolulu, Kamchatka, and Bering Strait. The return journey was made by way of San Francisco, the Hawaiian Islands, and Macao, back to the Pacific coast of America, Cape Horn, and Rio. Edward Belcher reached Woolwich on 12 October 1828.

He was promoted commander in 1829, and from 1830 to 1833 commanded the *Aetna* on a long surveying expedition along the African coast. In 1835 he published *A Treatise on Nautical Surveying*. His reputation as a mathematician and hydrographer was now well established, and with his experience of Pacific waters he was an obvious choice to head the expedition of the *Sulphur*, which had sailed from Portsmouth at the end of December 1835 and was now off the South American coast. The expedition's original commander, Beechey, had become too ill to continue and had to be invalided home. Lieutenant Kellett *(q.v.)*, commanding the accompanying schooner *Starling*, had taken over temporarily, but he was too inexperienced and too junior for a major voyage. Belcher received his appointment in November 1836, proceeded to Panama, and crossed the isthmus, where he was met by the *Sulphur*. He continued with the hydrographical work along the coast and sailed for the Hawaiian Islands. He arrived on 7 July 1837 and found himself embroiled in local religious and political squabbles. Dupetit-Thouars *(q.v.)* in the *Vénus* arrived as well, and together the two captains arranged a form of truce. The *Sulphur* then left for Alaska, from Mt. St. Elias to Nootka Sound, down to San Francisco, and on to Central America. Slow, painstaking survey work took up the remainder of 1837 and all of 1838. Only in May 1839 did Belcher get back to Honolulu for a brief respite. On 16 June he made his way back to the northwest coast, finally leaving from Mexico on 25 December 1839 for the Marquesas.

On 20 January 1840, the *Sulphur* dropped anchor in Nuku Hiva, where an observatory was set up. Belcher went on through the Tuamotus to Tahiti, the Cook Islands, Tonga, and Fiji, where he sent Kellett to establish contact with Charles Wilkes *(q.v.)*, whose *Peacock* was also in the archipelago. By June the *Sulphur* was sailing among the New Hebrides (Vanuatu) on its way to the Solomons, New Guinea, and the Moluccas. On 3 September Belcher put in at Amboina and went to Singapore, where instructions were awaiting him to proceed to Canton. The *Sulphur* played a supporting role in the ongoing opium wars and did not leave for England until late 1841. On 19 June 1842 the *Sulphur* dropped anchor at Spithead.

Belcher was made a Commander of the Bath following his return and proceeded to write a *Narrative of a Voyage round the World performed in HMS "Sulphur"*. . . , which appeared in two volumes in 1843. By then he had set out on another surveying expedition, in the *Samarang*, to the East Indies, about which he wrote another *Narrative* in two volumes, published in 1848. He received a knighthood in January 1843 and a pension in 1847. A last voyage awaited him: a search for the lost Franklin expedition. Belcher sailed with the *Assistance* and the *Pioneer* in February 1852. After spending two winters in Wellington Channel among the snow-covered islands of northern Canada, he had to abandon his enterprise and make his way back to England, which he reached in October 1854. He devoted himself to writing an account of the Arctic voyage and various other works, including a long novel on a naval theme.

Sir Edward Belcher became an admiral in October 1872, was granted a Greenwich Hospital pension in 1874, and died in London on 18 March 1877.

## Bellingshausen

FABIAN GOTTLIEB (or, in the Russian form, Faddey Faddeyevich, and in a romanized form, Thaddeus) von Bellingshausen came from a distinguished Baltic family settled on the island of Saaremaa in Estonia, where he was born on 9 September 1778. At the age of 10 he enrolled in the naval corps at Kronstadt, sailed to England as a cadet, and saw active service in the Baltic Fleet from 1797 to 1803.

He sailed with Kruzenshtern *(q. v.)* on his voyage around the globe of 1803–1806. Bellingshausen's growing reputation as an astronomer and a painstaking hydrographer was further enhanced in 1809–1810 when as commander of the *Melpomena* in the Baltic and of the *Flora* in the Black Sea he undertook taxing hydrographic surveys. He was promoted to captain in 1816 and chosen in 1819 to command a major Russian expedition to the Pacific and the Antarctic.

He sailed from Kronstadt on 4 July 1819 with the *Vostok* and the *Mirnyy*, called at Portsmouth to buy scientific instruments, and went on to Rio and South Georgia. The expedition sailed eastward along the Antarctic icefield, remaining south of 60°, and finally made for Australia, anchoring at Sydney on 10 April 1820.

Refreshed and provisioned for the winter, the two ships sailed on 8 May for New Zealand. On 27 May Bellingshausen dropped anchor in Queen Charlotte Sound for a ten-day stop. He visited various settlements and collected a number of artifacts. His reports and those of his officers, together with the material brought back to Russia, are of special anthropological importance, for the people he met were soon to be eliminated, and the local culture destroyed, by Maori raiders from the north.

Bellingshausen continued his voyage, sailing to the Tuamotus, where he discovered a number of small islands: Angatau on 10 July, Nihiru, then Katiu and the Raevski Islands, Fakarava, and Niau. He then sailed toward Tahiti past Makatea, discovering Matahiva, which he named Lazarev Island after the captain of the *Mirnyy*. On 1 August 1820 another island was seen and called Vostok, a name it has kept. Bellingshausen next sailed toward the Fiji group, where three small islands were discovered, including Ono, where valuable artefacts and anthropological information were obtained.

The expedition returned to Sydney on 9 September, preparing for a second swing to the Antarctic on 30 October. Bellingshausen

sighted Macquarie Island but by 29 November found himself surrounded by heavy ice. On 11 January 1821 he discovered an island
which he named Peter I Island, then continued toward the South
Shetlands, where a fortnight later he met a number of British and
American sealing vessels. He veered north for Rio, arriving on 27
March, and ended his voyage in Kronstadt on 25 July 1821.

On his return Bellingshausen looked forward to the official publication of his account of the voyage, but delays occurred, worsened
by the arrest of one of the *Vostok*'s former officers, Konstantin Torson, for his part in the Decembrists' plot of 1825. Bellingshausen
was on active service on the Danube during the war with Turkey in
1828–1829 and unable to supervise or hasten publication when permission was at last given. The two-volume *Dvukratnye Izyskaniia
. . . (Repeated Explorations in the Southern Icy Ocean and a Voyage
round the World)* appeared in 1831, and formed the basis of an
English account in two volumes by Frank Debenham in 1945.

Bellingshausen was appointed governor of Kronstadt in 1839 and
died there on 13 January 1852.

## Bérard

AUGUSTE BÉRARD was born in Montpellier, France, on 24 September 1796, the son of a merchant. He entered the Ecole Navale in
1812 and after the end of the Napoleonic wars had several opportunities to gain experience in the Mediterranean. In 1817 he was
selected to join Freycinet's *Uranie* on a voyage around the world.

Freycinet *(q.v.)* sailed from Toulon on 17 September 1817, making for Gibraltar, Rio, Table Bay, and Mauritius. Exploration proper
began on 12 September 1818 when the *Uranie* reached Shark Bay in
western Australia, although the condition of the vessel did not
allow for a prolonged survey of the coast. Freycinet went up to
Timor, through the Dutch East Indies and north of New Guinea, on
to Guam, and across to Hawaii, where the *Uranie* dropped anchor
on 8 August 1819. After a three-week stay, Freycinet left for New
South Wales, passing between the Cook Islands and the Samoas. He
reached Port Jackson on 18 November and sailed on Christmas Day
to cross the Pacific, passing to the south of New Zealand and turning
Cape Horn on 6 February 1820. The *Uranie* was wrecked at the
Falklands a week later.

Bérard was back in France later in 1820, and after a well-deserved respite was accepted by Duperrey *(q.v.)*, who was about to undertake his own circumnavigation in the *Coquille*. They sailed on 11 August 1822 from Toulon, making for Brazil and the Falklands and turning Cape Horn on 31 December. Three weeks later they anchored in Talcahuano, Chile, and shortly after went on to Peru. Botanizing on an expedition ashore, Bérard was arrested for a time as a suspected spy. There was evidence of considerable administrative dislocation throughout the former Spanish colonies, and the French were not sorry to leave on 22 March for the Tuamotus, Tahiti, the Solomons, and the East Indies. It was now October and Duperey, faced with a great deal of sickness on board, left it to Bérard to oversee the charting of the area while he took the *Coquille* as quickly as possible away from this notoriously unhealthy region into the Indian Ocean and around Australia to Port Jackson, where they anchored on 17 January 1824. The stay lasted until 20 March, when Duperrey sailed for New Zealand and home by way of Rotuma, the Gilbert and Ellice islands, New Guinea, Java, and the Cape. The *Coquille* reached Marseilles on 24 March 1825.

Bérard was promoted to lieutenant on 22 May 1825 and spent the next few years on duty in the Mediterranean. He attained the rank of captain on 22 January 1836. In 1838–1839 he was in the Gulf of Mexico and the West Indies as captain of the *Voltigeur*. Then as commander of the *Rhin* he sailed once more for the Pacific in June 1842. He reached Akaroa, New Zealand, in January 1843 to take over the French naval station; he spent the next three years cruising through the south Pacific, protecting French commercial and colonial interests.

He left Akaroa in April 1846 and gave up his command of the *Rhin* in July. Promoted rear admiral in 1843, Bérard became chief of the naval station at Toulon, where he died on 6 October 1852.

## Bering

VITUS JONASSEN BERING was born at Horsens, Denmark, in 1681. He joined the Danish navy at an early age and in 1703 sailed to the East Indies. However, he then entered the Russian navy and fought in the struggle against Sweden, the "Northern War," which lasted until 1721.

Czar Peter the Great was anxious to discover more about eastern Siberia into which Russian explorers and settlers had advanced throughout the early 1700s. The geodesists Evreinov and Luzhin had been sent to Kamchatka in 1719–1721, but their extensive surveys left in doubt the question of a northern passage between Asia and America. Vitus Bering was despatched from St. Petersburg in February 1725 with another Dane, Martin Spanberg *(q.v.)*, and a Russian, Aleksei Chirikov *(q.v.)*, to explore the waters east and north of Kamchatka. This involved traveling across Siberia to Okhotsk and thence to lower Kamchatka. The country was undeveloped and roadless, and Bering did not reach eastern Siberia until early 1728. A ship had then to be constructed and fitted out. It was named the *St. Gabriel (Sv. Gavrill)* and was ready to sail on 14 July 1728. The first voyage, along the coast of Kamchatka and beyond, took Bering as far as 67° north and seemed to provide adequate confirmation that the two continents were indeed separated. A second voyage was needed, however, and after wintering over in Nizhnekamsk, Bering set out into the northern Pacific toward the Aleutians, but without finding land. He lacked time for a more thorough examination as he was anxious to report back to the authorities. He turned back to Okhotsk and reached St. Petersburg in March 1730.

Bering had passed through the strait that bears his name, but the evidence he brought back from that vast and fogbound region was deemed inconclusive. Of greater importance politically was the closeness of America to Russian Siberia. Bering's proposal for a second expedition from Kamchatka was accepted. The planning was far more thorough, following Bering's previous experience in Siberia, and involved local development with the use of on-site resources.

Bering left St. Petersburg in April 1733 and reached Okhotsk in 1737. The first part of the program was carried out in 1738 by Spanberg, toward Japan. Meanwhile, Bering worked on building two more ships, the *St. Peter* and the *St. Paul*, which were ready by June 1740. He then traveled to the newly founded settlement of Petropavlovsk in southern Kamchatka and sailed with the *St. Peter*, which he commanded, and the *St. Paul*, commanded by Chirikov, on 4 June 1741. Within a fortnight, however, the ships became separated. Chirikov went as far as Sitka, on the Alaskan coast, but found his work hampered by the loss of two boats and fifteen men. He turned west, surveying the Aleutians, and made his way back to Petropavlovsk, where the *St. Paul* dropped anchor on 10 October.

Bering meanwhile sailed south and east in the hope of finding what was referred to as Gamaland. Nothing was sighted until Mt. St. Elias in Alaska appeared on 16 July. He then sailed back west to begin a careful survey of the great Aleutian chain. It was arduous work. Scurvy began to spread through the crew, the ship was often fogbound, there was dissension aboard, and Bering, let it be remembered, was 62 years old. Various islands were discovered and named, and some contact was made with the Aleuts; but food supplies were running low, and storms became frequent from September on. The Russians no longer knew where they were; some thought they had reached the Kurils; Copper Island, discovered on 4 November, was taken for Kamchatka. On 5 November, the *St. Peter* anchored in what is now known as Bering Island, where the expedition decided to winter. On 8 December Bering died. The survivors built a makeshift boat out of the wreckage of the *St. Peter* in which they departed on 13 August 1742, reaching Petropavlovsk on the twenty-seventh.

## Billings

JOSEPH BILLINGS was born at Turnham Green, Middlesex, in 1758. He joined the *Discovery* of James Cook *(q.v.)* on 8 April 1776 as an able-seaman and was discharged into the *Resolution* on 14 September 1779. The expedition left England on 12 July 1776 and returned on 4 October 1780. Billings then served in various merchant ships, one of which brought him in 1783 to St. Petersburg, where he was able to offer his services "as a former companion of Cook," but more practically he drew attention to his experience in the northern Pacific.

He was accepted into the Russian navy as a midshipman, was rapidly promoted to lieutenant, and, two years later, to captain-lieutenant and full captain in charge of exploration in Russia's far eastern waters in association with Gavriil Sarychev *(q.v.)*. He was in Okhotsk in July 1786 and led a voyage to the estuary of the Kolyma River in the East Siberian Sea. His other expedition in 1790 took him to the Aleutian Islands, which were then of considerable commercial interest to Russia. Joseph Billings died in 1806.

## Bishop

CHARLES BISHOP was born in England around 1765 and went to sea in his early teens. The potential offered by the fur trade on the northwest coast attracted numerous merchants and shipowners, and Bishop took the *Ruby* to western Canada in 1794. He explored the Columbia River in May 1795 and also sailed to Hawaii, but his ship was badly damaged in a storm and he decided to cut short his trading activities on the northwest coast and dispose of his furs in Canton. His business negotiations there were complex, as was often the case with independent European traders in China, and Bishop took the *Ruby* to Amboina where he sold it, purchasing the *Nautilus* as a replacement vessel.

He sailed back to Canton and continued his trading activities to Formosa (Taiwan), Kamchatka, Hawaii, and Tahiti. He took on board a group of missionaries whom he conveyed to Sydney, where he arrived on 14 May 1798. He found further opportunities for voyages along the coast and to Norfolk Island. He sailed north from Sydney in May 1799, making for Canton, and passed through the Gilberts and the Marshall Islands, unaware that they had already been discovered. He named the southern Gilberts the Kingsmill Islands, a name that persisted for many years and was found on some charts until quite recently. He discovered the small island of Nonouti and gave the first precise description of Tabiteuea, which he called Bishop's and Drummond's islands. Still used is the name of Nautilus Shoals, which he also identified in the area. He made no discoveries in the Marshalls, although he charted and named several islands in the group.

Bishop went on to Canton, sold his stock of seal skins, and returned to England. He went back to Sydney in August 1801 with George Bass *(q.v.)* with whom he was associated in trading activities. He sailed with Bass to Tahiti to buy pork, but became embroiled in disputes between rival groups of Tahitians. He returned to Sydney, where he suffered a nervous breakdown. Eventually, in 1809, he was sent back to England, where he died in 1810.

## Blackwood

FRANCIS PRICE BLACKWOOD was born on 25 May 1809 of a British naval family and entered the Royal Navy at the age of twelve. He obtained his first command in 1828, and while serving on the East India station took the *Hyacinth* to Australia, contributing valuable hydrographic data on the northeast coastline. He was promoted to captain in 1838 and in 1841 appointed to command the corvette *Fly*.

He sailed from Falmouth on 11 April 1842 accompanied by the cutter *Bramble*. Two scientists, J. B. Jukes (who later wrote the account of the expedition) and John McGillivray, were on board, together with H. S. Melville as artist. The two ships reached the Cape on 19 June, went on to Hobart, and anchored in Sydney on 15 October. Blackwood's main task was to chart the eastern—or outer —edge of the Great Barrier Reef from Breaksea Spit to the shores of New Guinea. This work occupied him from 24 November 1842 to the end of 1843. A second cruise out of Sydney in 1844 took the *Fly* to Cape York and Torres Strait, where Blackwood collected a quantity of valuable artefacts.

After a call at Surabaya, Blackwood returned to the northern Great Barrier Reef and Endeavour Strait. He worked painstakingly in these reef-strewn waters up to the Gulf of Papua and proceeded to survey the coastline. The great Fly River was named after his ship. He went on to Singapore and returned to Sydney by way of the Swan River, thus completing a circumnavigation of Australia. He found awaiting him orders to return home, leaving Lieutenant Yule to continue his survey. The *Fly* sailed from New South Wales on 19 December 1845 and arrived at Spithead on 19 June 1846.

Blackwood then left the navy to enter Jesus College, Cambridge. His scientific achievements had been considerable, and the zoological and ethnological items brought back in the *Fly* exceeded five thousand. He had still more achievements ahead of him. In 1851 he obtained leave to travel to Sweden to observe an eclipse of the sun. He recorded projections of flames from around the disk and wrote an important memoir for the Astronomical Society. He died in Cambridge on 22 March 1854.

### Bligh

WILLIAM BLIGH was born into a family of modest means in September or October 1754 at Plymouth. At the age of 16, he entered the Royal Navy, as James Cook *(q.v.)* had done, as an able-seaman. No ordinary lower-deck sailor, he studied navigation and hydrography, gained experience on coastal patrol duties in the Irish Sea, and in March 1776 was appointed master's mate to Cook, serving on the *Resolution*. He showed himself to be efficient throughout the voyage, displaying little of the irritability for which he later became notorious. Bligh's Cap, off Kerguelen Island, and Bligh Island, in Nootka Sound, Vancouver Island, commemorate his part in the expedition. He was incensed by James King's failure to give him credit for his survey work when King *(q.v.)* wrote up the narrative of the voyage.

After his return to England, Bligh married Elizabeth Betham, of a well-to-do family living on the Isle of Man (she bore him four daughters and died in 1812). Bligh was serving as lieutenant on the *Cambridge* in 1782 when his path first crossed that of Fletcher Christian *(q.v.)*, a young crew member who later served under Bligh on two commercial voyages to the West Indies.

In 1787, through the influence of Sir Joseph Banks *(q.v.)*, the British government bought the merchant ship *Berthia* and refitted it, as the *Bounty*, for a voyage to the Pacific to collect breadfruit plants in the hope of providing an acceptable and cheap diet for slaves in the West Indies. Bligh was placed in command, with Christian as master's mate. The *Bounty* sailed from Spithead on 23 December 1787. An attempt to enter the Pacific by way of the Horn was foiled by wild gales; instead Bligh was forced to sail back to the Cape of Good Hope and Tasmania, where he made his landfall on 19 August 1788. Sailing south of New Zealand and discovering the Bounty Islands en route, he arrived in Tahiti, where the *Bounty* had to remain five months, Bligh purchasing and stowing breadfruit seedlings for the return voyage. On 4 April 1789 he sailed with more than 1,000 plants on board and an unhappy crew whose mood was rapidly worsened as Bligh made increasingly harsh attempts to maintain discipline. On 28 April, all but eighteen mutinied; the mutineers put them and Bligh into the ship's launch. The *Bounty* then sailed away under the command of Christian.

Bligh's 4,500-mile (7,200 km) journey from near the Tonga group to Australia's Great Barrier Reef and then on to Timor is an astonishing feat of determination and navigation. Bligh made for Tofua in the northern Tongas, which he left on 2 May. In the Fiji group, he discovered a number of islands, including Viti Levu and the Yasawa islands. On 14 and 15 May he discovered a number of islands in the

New Hebrides: Mota, Saddle, and the Reef islands. On the twenty-eighth he reached the Great Barrier Reef, landing on one of its islands for what refreshments it could supply, then set off again by way of Torres Strait to Timor. The party in its open boat ended its journey at Koepang on 14 June 1789. Two months later, Bligh sailed for Batavia on the first leg of his journey home. He landed at Plymouth on 14 March 1790.

William Bligh promptly set about writing his account of the disastrous expedition, *A Voyage to the South Sea undertaken by command of His Majesty, . . .* which was published in 1792. Even before it appeared he had sailed with the *Providence* and the *Assistant* on a second, and successful, breadfruit voyage to Tahiti. They left on 3 August 1791 by way of the Cape and Tasmania, continuing as previously south of New Zealand to Tahiti, where he anchored on 9 April 1792. With more than 2,000 plants he left on 19 July, returned to Aitutaki, which he had discovered on his first voyage, and roughly retraced the route he had taken in his launch to Fiji, the New Hebrides, Torres Strait, and Timor. He reached the West Indies in late January 1793, unloaded most of the breadfruit, and made for home, anchoring near Dungeness on 2 August.

War had now broken out. Bligh fought at the Battle of Camperdown in 1797 and at Copenhagen in 1801. Then in 1805, at the suggestion of Sir Joseph Banks, he was appointed governor of New South Wales, a position for which he was temperamentally ill-suited and which ended in 1808 when Bligh was overthrown in the second mutiny of his career. He was able to return to England in 1810, was raised to the rank of rear admiral, and died in London on 7 December 1817.

## Blosseville

JULES-ALPHONSE-RENÉ PORET DE BLOSSEVILLE, the son of Vicomte Bénigne de Blosseville, was born near Rouen in Normandy on 29 July 1802. He joined the Navy in 1818, and as a young officer sailed to the West Indies in the *Railleur.* In 1822 he was selected by Duperrey *(q.v.)* to go with him in the *Coquille.*

The expedition sailed on 11 August 1822, went down to the Falkland Islands, rounded the Horn, and anchored at Talcahuano, Chile, on 20 January 1823. It then crossed the Pacific to the Tuamotus and Tahiti, going on toward New Guinea. At the end of August the *Coquille* was among the Schouten Islands, one of which Duperrey called after Blosseville, an ephemeral name long since forgotten. The expedition sailed around Australia and on to New Zealand, a country that greatly impressed Blosseville. After the *Coquille*'s return to France in March 1825, he wrote a *Mémoire géographique sur la Nouvelle-Zélande*, published as a lengthy report in a periodical in 1826 and reprinted separately in the same year. He wrote a number of other reports on New Zealand, including details of a survey made in the South Island by Captain William Edwardson and several proposals for a penal settlement in this uncolonized part of the world, as well as perceptive comments on other places visited by the *Coquille*.

The last of these reports is dated 1829. By then Blosseville was serving in the Mediterranean. He fought on the *Alacrity* at the Battle of Algiers in 1830. Three years later the French authorities acceded to his request to lead a voyage of exploration to the Arctic in the *Lilloise*. The expedition reached eastern Greenland; it was last seen by fishermen on 15 August 1833.

## Bodega

Juan Francisco de la Bodega y Quadra (sometimes spelled Cuadra) was born in late May or early June 1743 at Lima, Peru. He entered the marine guard at the age of 19, was promoted to ensign in 1767 and lieutenant in 1774. The following year, on 16 March 1775, as captain of the schooner *Sonora* he sailed to the northwest coast in company with the *Santiago*. After the latter turned back, Bodega went on as far as 58°30' north and discovered Bucareli Sound.

Bodega made a second voyage to Alaska in the frigate *Favorita*, sailing from San Blas, Mexico, together with the *Princesa*, on 11 February 1779. The aim was to assess the extent of Russian penetration into northern Alaska and to reassert, by showing the flag, Spanish claims to the northern Pacific seaboard of America, which were being threatened by the Russian advance and by British exploration. This expedition yielded no new discoveries. Bodega was back in San Blas on 21 November 1779. He was made frigate captain in 1780, served for a time in Havana, Cuba, and in Cadiz from 1785, when he was raised to the rank of ship's captain.

He returned to San Blas as local commander in 1789 and was selected to take over the defense of Spanish interests on the northwest coast after the famous Nootka Incident, which almost led to war between Spain and Britain and threatened to trigger a new European war. Bodega, who was known for his tact and geniality, sailed to Nootka in early 1792, took command of the small Spanish base there, and soon displayed his talents. He dealt with English and American traders as well as with local Indians, entertaining visitors with great lavishness. The American navigator Robert Gray *(q.v.)* was so impressed by the Spanish commander that he named his own son after him. Bodega had a second Spanish base built at Neah Bay at the entrance to Juan de Fuca Strait, which he also had surveyed in detail, sending exploration parties into a number of inlets and fiords along the British Columbian and Alaskan coasts, producing detailed maps, and bestowing on geographical features Spanish names that subsist today. His energy was largely instrumental in checking British aspirations along the coast well into the nineteenth century.

Bodega left late in 1792 to spend the winter months in Monterey, California. His health was deteriorating, and he was unable to return to Nootka in 1793. He died in Mexico City on 26 March 1794.

## Boenechea

DOMINGO DE BOENECHEA was born in the Spanish province of Biscay in the 1730s. He joined the navy as a cadet officer in his teens and served with distinction in the Atlantic, the Mediterranean, and off the Spanish American coasts, taking part in a number of engagements. In 1767 he was given command of the small frigate *Santa Maria Magdalena*, in which he sailed to the Pacific.

On 26 September 1772 the viceroy of Peru sent him from Callao in his frigate, now the *Aguila*, with secret instructions to claim any islands he could on behalf of Spain and follow up the investigation of the previous Spanish navigator, Felipe Gonzalez *(q.v.)*. He decided to make for Tahiti, discovering on the way the Tuamotu atoll of Tauere. Other islands seen and named on this voyage had already been discovered by Bougainville *(q.v.)*. On 8 November he reached Tahiti, which he named Amat after the viceroy of Peru. He anchored in Vaiurua Bay, sent his lieutenant, Tomas Gayangos (*q.v.*), to survey the coastline, then sailed for Moorea and home on 20 December, taking four islanders with him. The *Aguila* reached Valparaiso on 21 February 1773.

The following year Boenechea received orders to sail with the *Aguila* and the storeship *Jupiter* back to Tahiti with the three surviving Tahitians and two Franciscan brothers who were to set up a mission station on the island. He left Callao on 20 September 1774, leaving the slower *Jupiter* to follow him as best it could, and again made his way through the Tuamotus. On 29 October he discovered Tatakoto and on 9 November Tahanea. On 13 November he put in at Mehetia, where he took on board several islanders and went on to Tahiti. He reached Tautira in mid-November; there he met up with *Jupiter*. A treaty was signed, providing for a missionary outpost and the sovereignty of Spain over what the Spanish now called the Isla de Amat.

On 7 January 1775 the two ships sailed for Raiatea and Huahine, but Boenechea had fallen gravely ill. The expedition returned to Tahiti, where Boenechea died on 26 January. He was buried ashore on the twenty-eighth, close to a commemorative cross he had had erected. The ships sailed back to Peru on the thirtieth under the command of Tomas Gayangos. According to tradition, Boenechea's burial plot was dug up shortly after the ship's departure to obtain nails from his coffin and other items buried with him.

## Bond

ESSEX HENRY BOND was a captain in the employ of the East India Company who sailed from England to China in 1789 in the *Royal Admiral*, a ship of 914 tons built in 1772. He was involved in supplying the struggling colony of New South Wales and, on his way back to China and India, discovered two islands in the Marshall group. These islands, sighted on 15 December 1792, were the two islets of Namorik atoll on the western fringe of the Marshalls. He named them Baring's Islands.

On the sixteenth, Bond found himself close to a cluster of small islands that he named the Muskillo Islands; they were, however, the islets of Namu atoll, sighted and reported by the Spanish in the sixteenth century.

## Bougainville

HYACINTHE-YVES-PHILIPPE POTENTIEN DE BOUGAINVILLE was born in Brest on 27 December 1781, the son of Louis-Antoine de Bougainville *(q.v.)*. He entered the navy in 1800 after studies at the Ecole Polytechnique, and joined the expedition of Nicolas Baudin *(q.v.)* to Australia and the Timor Sea, sailing in the *Géographe* from France in April 1801 and returning in 1803. He next served in the North Sea and the Channel fleets from 1803 to 1811. He was taken prisoner in 1814, toward the end of the Napoleonic wars.

He was promoted to *enseigne* in 1803, lieutenant in 1808, commander in 1811 and to post-captain in 1821. In 1819–1820 he commanded the *Cybèle* on expeditions to the Far East and the West Indies.

He was destined to lead his own expedition to the Pacific, for in 1822 he was put in charge of the newly built *Thétis*, which, after several voyages to the West Indies and the Mediterranean, sailed for Indochina and Australia. He left, together with the corvette *Espérance*, from Brest, on 2 March 1824 for Santa Cruz, the Cape Verde Islands, Réunion, and Pondicherry, which he reached on 29 June. After a stay of one month, he went on to Malacca, Singapore, and Macao, arriving there on 25 December. His work in Indochina was only partly successful, owing to the emperor's dislike of foreigners, and it was with some feeling of relief that Hyacinthe de Bougainville made for Port Jackson by way of the Anambas, Surabaya, and western Australia.

The *Thétis* and the *Espérance* dropped anchor in Port Jackson on 1 July 1825. Bougainville spent three months there, meeting leaders of society and visiting the district. He sailed on 21 September, making for the south of New Zealand, following mostly the thirty-third parallel, along which some areas of ocean remained imperfectly known, but no new discoveries awaited him on this route. On 22 November he anchored in Valparaiso. There he met another descendant of a Pacific navigator, Captain George Anson Byron *(q.v.)* of the *Blonde*.

The return journey began on 8 January 1826, by way of Cape Horn. Heavy fog prevented Bougainville from calling at the Falkland Islands, where his father had once attempted to establish a French colony. After a stay in Rio, the *Thétis* and the *Espérance* arrived at

Brest on 24 June 1826. They brought back with them an extensive collection of natural history specimens. The account of the voyage was ordered to be printed at government expense, but did not appear until 1837.

Bougainville was promoted to rear admiral in 1838 and served as naval commander at Algiers and as a member of the Admiralty Council. He died in Paris on 10 December 1846.

## Bougainville

LOUIS-ANTOINE DE BOUGAINVILLE was born in Paris on 12 November 1729. His father was a well-born lawyer and local administrator with a wide circle of acquaintances among scientists and geographers. His brother Jean-Pierre was the author of two monographs on voyages of exploration. Louis-Antoine actually started on a military career, joining the Black Musketeers in 1750. In 1754 he was appointed secretary to the French embassy in London and two years later was elected to the Royal Society. By then he had published a treaty on the calculus that had attracted considerable attention.

The outbreak of the Seven Years War resulted in his going to Quebec as aide-de-camp to the French commander Montcalm. Bougainville was wounded on 6 June 1756 and returned to France, where he was promoted to colonel and awarded the Cross of St. Louis. Back in Canada in May 1759, he was present at the battle of the Heights of Abraham, where both Montcalm and the British commander, Wolfe, were killed. Taken prisoner a year later, Bougainville was granted parole to return to France; he fought and was wounded in Germany in 1761.

He conceived a plan to settle displaced French Canadians on the Falkland or Malouine Islands, which were at the time not administered by any European power. For this he was given the rank of captain and sailed with the *Aigle* and the *Sphinx* on 6 September 1763. Protests by Spain, however, led to an agreement between Paris and Madrid to give up the nascent colony. Bougainville sailed in the *Boudeuse* on 15 November 1766 to surrender the Falklands to Spain and to begin a full circumnavigation. His formal duties over, he left for the Pacific by way of the Strait of Magellan, accompanied by the storeship *Étoile*.

The passage through the strait was arduous. After almost two months, on 26 January 1768, the *Boudeuse* and the *Étoile* emerged into the South Seas. After fruitlessly seeking land believed to have been seen by Edward Davis in 1687, Bougainville discovered several islands among the Tuamotus and reached Tahiti on 6 April. He spent nine days there, most of the French being highly impressed by what they imagined to be an unspoilt Eden. With him, he took away a native, Ahu-Toru, whose presence in Paris was to prove a sensation. He then sailed west past the Samoas and the New Hebrides until he came into sight of the outlying reefs of the Australian Great Barrier Reef. Wisely he veered north to New Guinea and the Solomons, through areas almost totally unknown. His passage through the Solomon archipelago is marked by names bestowed on major islands: Choiseul after the minister of the navy and Bougainville after himself.

Their stores badly depleted and their ships in a parlous condition, the French anchored in Port Praslin, New Ireland, from 6 to 24 July 1768. In early September they reached Buru in the Moluccas and later Batavia. They sailed on 16 October for Mauritius, where they anchored on 8 November. The two ships went home separately, the *Boudeuse* leaving on 12 December and arriving in St. Malo on 16 March 1769, the *Étoile* on 1 January 1769, arriving in Rochefort on 24 April.

Bougainville came home to an impressive welcome. He was promoted to brigadier, but his association with the navy was recognized by his being given the rank of captain retroactive to June 1763. His account of the voyage was a European best seller, and he had been paid the homage of having a beautiful flower named after him, the bougainvillea. He began to plan a voyage toward the North Pole, but the American War of Independence broke out, and his next few years were spent on various campaigns in the West Indies and along the Atlantic seaboard of America. There was also time for marriage, to Marie-Josèphe de Longchamps-Montendre.

After the war, he assisted with plans for the expeditions of La Pérouse and d'Entrecasteaux *(q.v.)*. Appointed vice-admiral on 1 January 1792, he felt helpless in the face of constant acts of insubordination by republican sailors; he was imprisoned for two months from 4 July 1794. After the end of the Terror, he became a member of the Bureau of Longitude and the Institute of France. He was appointed senator in 1799 and made an Imperial Count in 1808. He had retired with the rank of rear admiral in February 1802. He died on 20 August 1811 and was buried in the Paris Pantheon.

## Bouman

CORNELIS BOUMAN was born at Oostzaner Overtoom, north Holland, probably around the late 1680s or early 1690s. He had considerable experience as a sailor by the time Jacob Roggeveen *(q.v.)* chose him to accompany him on a voyage to the Pacific as captain of the *Thienhoven*. Bouman sailed from Texel with the two other ships of the expedition on 1 August 1721. There were early difficulties among the various captains, and consideration was given to drop the slower *Thienhoven* from the expedition altogether and to proceed without Bouman. Nevertheless, the voyage proceeded as planned. On 16 December, however, while still in the southern Atlantic, the *Thienhoven* fell behind and lost sight of the other vessels.

Bouman continued south to Staten Eylandt, turned Cape Horn far to the south, sighted the coast of Chile in mid-February, and later in the month reached Juan Fernandez, where the other two Dutch ships found him. He continued with the rest of the expedition to Easter Island, the northern Tuamotus, and the edge of the Society Islands. On 13 June, the Dutch came in sight of the Samoan archipelago. The Manua group, the easternmost, was named Bouman's Islands, and the large island of Tutuila, seen from some distance away, was called Thienhoven.

The expedition sighted nothing more until New Ireland was reached on 17 July 1722. It was sailing into areas controlled by the East India Company, whose monopoly was being infringed. The *Thienhoven* arrived at Japara in northern Java on 10 September to an unfriendly reception. Sailing on to Batavia resulted in arrest and confiscation. Bouman's journal was impounded but later returned to him, so that he took it with him to Holland when he sailed from Batavia in a merchantman on 3 December 1722. The voyage home was slow and circuitous, by way of the Cape, St. Helena, Ascension, Ireland, and the Shetlands, reaching the Dutch coast on 8 July 1723. On the twenty-third Bouman handed his journal to the Committee of Ten of the West India Company, which was preparing a counterclaim against the East India Company. This *Scheepsjournaal gehouden op het Schip "Tienhoven"* was eventually published in Middelburg in 1911. (The spelling *Thienhoven* is more commonly found in English references.)

Little is known of Cornelis Bouman's later life and activities and death.

## Bourayne

JOSEPH-CÉSAR BOURAYNE was born in Brest on 22 February 1768 and joined the navy at the age of 13. He attained the rank of lieutenant in 1793. He was wounded and taken prisoner while serving on the *Atalante*, and spent almost two years in captivity.

He was given command of the *Canonnière* in 1803 and despatched to the Indian Ocean to join the squadron of Rear Admiral Linois. The governor of Mauritius, General Decaen, sent him to Manila by way of Ceylon and Sunda Strait. Bourayne arrived in the Philippines on 30 September 1806. As it was no longer safe for galleons to cross the Pacific, the Spanish asked Bourayne to sail to Acapulco in his warship and bring back supplies.

The *Canonnière* needed refitting. Bourayne left for Mexico on 19 April 1807. Southeasterlies drove him toward Japan, and on 8 May he discovered an island he named Ile de la Canonnière; it was probably Okino-Ogari, one of the Daito group southeast of the Ryukyus. Bourayne proceeded due east, to the north of the Hawaiian group, and finally anchored at Acapulco on 21 July. His was the first French ship to cross the Pacific in sixteen years. He remained in Mexico until 23 October, sailing back to Manila by a route that took him south of Hawaii and through the Marianas. The three million piastres he brought back with him saved the Spanish colony from bankruptcy. The *Canonnière* remained in the Philippines until late March 1808 and reached Mauritius on 13 July with three prizes captured off Sumatra.

Bourayne took part in further naval engagements and was once more taken prisoner. Napoleon I made him a Commander of the Legion of Honor and a Baron of the Empire. Louis XVIII, on his restoration to the throne, made him a Knight of St. Louis. Bourayne died in Brest on 5 November 1817.

## Brind

WILLIAM DARBY BRIND was an English whaling captain born probably in Birmingham in June or July 1794. He went to sea at an early age, soon serving in whaling ships and obtaining his first command in 1819, being employed by London shipowners. He made seven major voyages, his first, in command of the *Cumberland*, taking him to the Bay of Islands, New Zealand, in March 1820. He spent long periods ashore, becoming closely associated with local Maori people and English missionaries. He returned in the *Asp* in 1822–1825 and in the *Toward Castle* on two later occasions, including 1830, when an argument between Maori women, in which he was involved, led to a series of fights ashore known subsequently as the Girls' War.

In 1835 Brind was back in England where, at Gravesend, Kent, he married Eliza Snoswell, who went out with him to New Zealand in 1839. By then, Brind had become increasingly involved with New Zealand, where he had already bought land and built a house. His final command was that of the *Narwhal*, in which he made two voyages before ill health forced his retirement in 1843. He died at the Bay of Islands in 1850, probably on 15 October.

Brind was held in high regard as a seaman. A number of geographical features were once named after him: Brind Rock (now Esperance Rock) in the Kermadec Islands; Brind's Island, a small atoll in the Gilbert Islands; and Brind's Bay (now Matauwhi Bay) in New Zealand.

## Bristow

ABRAHAM (also found as Abram) Bristow was an English whaling captain employed by Samuel Enderby of London. In 1806 he was in command of the whaler *Ocean*, operating in the southern Pacific. On 18 August he discovered an island to the south of New Zealand. He gave it the name Lord Auckland's Island, although it turned out to be a group of six small islands with several rocky islets now known collectively as the Auckland Islands. Returning to the islands in 1807 on the *Sarah*, Bristow formally took possession of the islands and landed a number of pigs; these soon multiplied, providing a source of food for sealing parties left ashore or shipwrecked mariners. Attempts to establish settlements on the islands, including one by Charles Enderby in 1849, all failed.

## Brooke

JOHN MERCER BROOKE was born in 1826 in Florida near what is now Tampa. He joined the navy as a midshipman in 1841 and served on a number of cruises, including one in the sloop *Cyane*, part of the Pacific Squadron, which gave him a chance to sail to Honolulu. He entered the naval academy at Annapolis, graduating in 1847, and served for a time in the Mediterranean.

He carried out hydrographic work with the Coast Survey under Lt. Samuel P. Lee in 1849–1850 and was transferred to the Naval Observatory where, in 1852, he developed a deep-sounding apparatus that was given his name. Brooke's invention gained wide interest and led to his being sent to the Pacific for scientific studies.

The opportunity arose with the despatch of the North Pacific Exploring Expedition under Cadwalader Ringgold (*q.v.*), which sailed from Hampton Roads on 11 June 1853. Brooke was appointed as astronomer and hydrographer and later worked closely with John Rodgers (*q.v.*), who took over when Ringgold's health failed. The expedition of five ships entered the Pacific from the west, by way of the Cape and Hong Kong. Survey work was carried out in the South China Sea, along the China coast, and among the Ryukyu Islands.

When Rodgers began to survey the coast of Japan, from May 1855, he decided not to risk his two ships, the *Vincennes* and the *Hancock*, too far inshore. He accordingly despatched fifteen men in an open boat, the *Vincennes Junior*, under John M. Brooke. In a remarkable feat, Brooke charted and took depths along 450 miles (720 km) of dangerous coastline, reaching Hakodate in June. Further work by the expedition was carried out toward the north, to Sakhalin, Kamchatka, and the Arctic Ocean as far as Herald Island. A shortage of funds forced the expedition to curtail its program. The ships made their way to San Francisco toward the end of 1855, bringing back a large collection of charts and natural history specimens.

Brooke was next given command of his own expedition: a survey of islands, shoals, and other dangers on the route between California and China in the *Fenimore Cooper*, a schooner with a complement of twenty-one men. He made his way from New York to San Francisco in June–July 1858, traveling overland across the isthmus of Panama. The *Cooper* set off on 26 September for Honolulu, arriving on 9 November. Survey work began in earnest when the Americans left on 29 December, making for Necker Island, French Frigate Shoals, and Laysan. This work took up most of January 1859, after which the *Cooper* returned to Honolulu.

Clearing Honolulu on 9 March, Brooke headed southwest for Johnston Island, then for Guam; he arrived on 12 April for a three-week stay after which, continually sounding at great depths, he sailed to Hong Kong, where the *Fenimore Cooper* dropped anchor on 19 May. From China, Brooke sailed, on 23 June, for the Ryukyu Islands and Japan. He dropped anchor in Edo Bay, Yokohama, on 13 August. The *Fenimore Cooper* was to travel no further: a few days later the ship grounded during a storm and it soon became evident that it could not be repaired. The Americans spent six months ashore. On 10 February 1860, Brooke and a number of his men sailed home in the *Kanrin Maru*, the first Japanese warship to make the crossing to California; he reached San Francisco on 17 March and proceeded to Washington, D.C., again by way of Panama, to supervise the preparation of his reports and charts. The full report was not completed: the Civil War broke out, and Brooke resigned from the navy in April 1861 to offer his services to the State of Virginia. He served Virginia with the rank of commander as Chief of the Bureau of Ordnance and Hydrographer, then until his retirement in 1899 was on the staff of the Virginia Military Institute as Professor of Physics and Astronomy. He died on 14 December 1906 at Lexington, Virginia.

## Broughton

WILLIAM ROBERT BROUGHTON was born probably in England in 1762, but there is little on record of his early life, except that he joined the Royal Navy as a youth, old enough to be taken prisoner by rebellious colonists in Boston in 1776. He subsequently rose to the rank of lieutenant aboard the *Burford* and in 1790 was appointed to command the *Chatham* for an expedition to the North American coast with the *Discovery* under Vancouver (*q.v.*).

The *Chatham* was not ready until 6 January 1791, and further delays meant that the two ships did not sail from Falmouth until 1 April. They went down to the Cape of Good Hope and set off across the Indian Ocean, going to southwestern Australia and, passing to the south of Tasmania, on to New Zealand. Vancouver anchored in Dusky Sound on 2 November 1791. Three weeks later the expedition left, refreshed after the hardships of a difficult voyage, only to be separated in a wild gale. Broughton decided to make for Tahiti and, while sailing to the east of New Zealand, discovered a new island group, which he named the Chatham Islands. It was 29 November 1791. Broughton landed and took formal possession of the islands, which now form part of New Zealand.

The *Chatham* reached Tahiti on 26 December and was joined by Vancouver's *Discovery* four days later. On 24 January 1792, the expedition sailed for Hawaii, arriving on 1 March. After a brief stay, Vancouver left for North America to begin a survey of the coast, with the *Chatham* sailing on ahead to Nootka Sound, where the *Discovery* joined it on 28 August. Broughton had carried out valuable survey work in the Columbia River and along the deeply indented coastline, and when the *Chatham* set out from Nootka on 12 October 1792 he felt he could look forward to more useful hydrographic work; negotiations with the Spanish authorities bogged down, however, and Vancouver decided to send Broughton to Europe. The *Chatham* was taken over by Peter Puget *(q.v.)* while Broughton traveled across Mexico from San Blas to Vera Cruz and on to England. He was then sent to Madrid as a specialist adviser during the seemingly endless negotiations.

William Broughton returned to active service to continue the survey work of Vancouver. Given command of the *Providence*, he sailed on 15 February 1795 for the Canaries and Rio, then to the Cape of Good Hope and Australia, dropping anchor at Sydney on 27 August. After refitting, he went on to Tahiti and Hawaii, where he learned that Vancouver had returned to England. The *Providence* sailed to the northwest coast, dropping anchor in Nootka Sound on 27 February 1796. There he found a message from Vancouver, whose work was finished, sending him to Monterey. Broughton's instructions were broad, so that he was able to decide with his officers which surveys he should turn to next. A decision was made to sail to the northwest Pacific, and Broughton crossed the ocean once more, calling at the Hawaiian Islands and reaching Hokkaido, Japan, on 12

September 1796. The Japanese made it clear that he was not welcome, but Broughton nonetheless made a running survey along the coast of Hokkaido to the Kurils and back to Honshu and the Ryukyus before sailing to Macao.

Broughton purchased a small schooner, the *Resolution*, since hydrographic work in little-known and unfriendly waters was too dangerous for a single vessel. It proved to be a wise decision. He left Macao on 28 April 1797, sailing north along the coast of Taiwan, but on 17 May he struck a coral reef. The *Providence* sank, little being saved from the wreck. Broughton sailed to Whampoa in the *Resolution*, discharged his surplus men, and turned back to continue his survey in the *Resolution*. It was 26 June. He sailed round Japan and along the west coast of Hokkaido up the Gulf of Tartary between Sakhalin and the mainland—although like other Europeans before him, he did not realize that Sakhalin was an island. He then turned south toward the eastern coast of Korea and on to Macao, where he dropped anchor on 27 November 1797. After resting his crew and repairing his ship, he set sail for England, arriving in February 1799.

In 1804 he published *A Voyage of Discovery to the North Pacific Ocean*, but he could not rest on his laurels; when war broke out again, Broughton was called back to active service. In 1809, commanding the *Illustrious*, he went to the West Indies and in 1810 to the Indian Ocean, where he took part in the capture of Mauritius, and to the Dutch East Indies for the expedition against Java. He was back in England in 1812; his health was failing, and when peace came he retired to Italy. He died at Florence on 12 March 1821.

## Burney

JAMES BURNEY was born in London in 1750, the son of a notable music historian. He went to sea at the age of ten, in the *Princess Amelia* and later in the *Magnanime* patrolling the coast of Brittany, then aboard the frigates *Niger* and *Aquilon*, and finally in 1770–1771 in the Indiaman *Greenwich* bound for Bombay. He joined the *Resolution* under James Cook (*q.v.*) on 17 December 1771 as an able seaman; in January 1772 he was promoted to lieutenant upon being transferred to the expedition's other vessel, the *Adventure*. On his return, he served in the *Cerberus*, spending most of 1775 on the North American station.

Burney had a further opportunity to sail with Cook when he was appointed on 10 February 1776 to the *Discovery* as first lieutenant. After the death of Charles Clerke *(q.v.)*, Burney was transferred to the *Resolution*, but when a further reorganization was called for, he returned to the *Discovery*, in September 1780. After his return to England, Burney commanded the frigate *Latona* for a cruise to the North Sea and in May 1782 took the *Bristol* to India. He was invalided out in 1784.

Burney is the author of *A Chronological History of the Discoveries in the South Sea or Pacific Ocean*, published in five volumes in 1803–1817, and *A Chronological History of North-Eastern Voyages of Discovery*, published in 1819. He was raised to the rank of rear admiral in 1821 and died on 17 November of the same year.

## Butler

CAPTAIN BUTLER was master of the merchant ship *Walpole*, which took supplies to New South Wales in 1794. On the return voyage, sailing north on 17 November 1794, he came upon a small island in the Loyalty Islands that he named Walpole Island.

The uninhabited island was a rich source of guano for many years. It has retained the name of Walpole Island.

## Buyers

JOHN BUYERS sailed to China in 1799 as first officer of the merchant vessel *Barwell*. He learned of the lucrative fur trade along the northwest coast of America and on his return to England persuaded a group of merchants to finance an expedition in a brand-new ship, the *Margaret*. With his friend John Turnbull *(q.v.)* as supercargo, Buyers sailed from England on 2 July 1800 for the Cape of Good Hope, Bass Strait, and Port Jackson, New South Wales, where the *Margaret* dropped anchor in January 1801. Turnbull remained in Australia while Buyers sailed to North America. His speculations on the coast were a failure, and Buyers returned to Australia.

Meantime, Turnbull had gone to Norfolk Island on a whaling ship. Buyers sailed there to pick him up and together they sailed, on 9 August 1802, for Tahiti, arriving on 24 September. After a stay of a month, buying pigs and selling spirits, the two partners left for

Huahine and Raiatea, finally reaching Oahu, in the Hawaiian Islands, on 17 December. The *Margaret* left Hawaii on 21 January 1803 for Tahiti.

On 10 March, Buyers discovered an uninhabited atoll, which he named Phillips Island, and shortly after a smaller atoll, which he called Holt's Island. On the thirteenth, he made another new discovery but apparently did not name these islands, now known as Makemo, Taenga, and Faaite, all part of the Tuamotu archipelago. The *Margaret* reached Mehetia on the sixteenth and Tahiti shortly after. Turnbull disembarked while Buyers sailed along the coast and among the Society Islands in search of pigs and pearls. The ship was wrecked on a reef in the western Tuamotus. Buyers and seventeen of his men eventually struggled back to Tahiti on a makeshift raft.

In September 1803, Turnbull and Buyers obtained a passage back to Port Jackson, calling at Tonga on the way and finally reaching New South Wales at the end of the year. They sailed to England on 16 March 1804 in the *Calcutta*, their long odyssey coming to an end there in June.

## Byron

GEORGE ANSON BYRON, the only son of George Anson Byron, the grandson of John Byron *(q.v.)*, and a cousin of the English poet, was born at Bath, Somerset, on 8 March 1789. He joined the Royal Navy as a volunteer in December 1800, gradually working his way up to midshipman and lieutenant, seeing service during the Napoleonic wars. He attained the rank of captain in June 1814.

On 19 April 1824, his cousin died in Greece, and George Anson became the seventh Lord Byron. A few weeks later, King Kamehameha II (Liholiho) landed in England from the whaler *Aigle*, captained by Valentine Starbuck *(q.v.)*, with a party that included Queen Kamamalu. Within six weeks both sovereigns had died of measles. An embarrassed British government decided to send back the royal remains to the islands with full honors. Captain Lord Byron was chosen for this task. He sailed in HMS *Blonde* from Spithead on 29 September 1824. Several senior naturalists were also selected to join the expedition. Among the *Blonde's* officers was Lieutenant Edward Belcher *(q.v.)*.

The *Blonde* went by way of Madeira, Brazil, and Valparaiso, where Byron dropped anchor on 4 February 1825. He sighted Hilo on 3 May, stopped at Maui two days later, and arrived off Honolulu on the sixth; the bodies were taken ashore for a ceremonial funeral. Byron stayed a month at Honolulu, leaving for Hilo with Queen Ka'ahumanu and a party of chiefs on 7 June.

During his lengthy stay in the Hawaiian Islands, Byron went to Kealakekua, where James Cook (q.v.) had been killed, and erected an inscribed cross to his memory. He finally sailed on 18 July 1825, intending to make for Tahiti. On the twenty-ninth, he discovered Malden Island, which he named after his surveying officer; it forms part of the Line Islands. Byron next sailed to Starbuck Island, which he named, and on to Mauke in the Cook Islands. But his attempts to reach Tahiti were foiled by contrary winds and currents, and on 10 August he veered east for Valparaiso. Three weeks later he reached the Chilean port and began to refit his ship for the return voyage to England by way of Cape Horn. The *Blonde* dropped anchor at Spithead on 15 March 1826.

The *Blonde* expedition produced results of interest to naturalists and ethnographers, and gave rise to useful reports, some of which, by the naturalists Andrew Bloxam and James Macrae, have since been published.

Captain Lord Byron retired as an admiral on 20 May 1862 and died in London on 2 March 1868.

## Byron

JOHN BYRON was born on 8 November 1723, the second son of the fourth Lord Byron. His naval career began around 1737. In 1740 he joined the *Wager*, one of the squadron in which Anson (q.v.) was due to sail to the Pacific, as a midshipman. The *Wager* struck rocks north of the Strait of Magellan, and Byron did not get back to England until 1746, having suffered great privations meanwhile, but also having shown leadership and initiative during these troubled years.

He was compensated for his sufferings by being given various commands: the frigate *Syren* in December 1746; the *Augusta*, 50 guns, in 1753; the *America*, 60 guns (which took part in an expedition against Rochefort) in 1757; and the *Fame*, 74 guns, in which he went to Canada. By this time, he had earned the nickname "Foul-weather Jack."

When the Seven Years War ended, he went on half-pay until selected to command the *Dolphin* to survey and take possession of the Falkland Islands, then to pass through the Strait of Magellan and search for a northwest passage along the northern American coastline. The *Dolphin* sailed on 21 June 1764 in consort with the sloop *Tamar.* The two ships finally emerged into the Pacific on 9 April 1765, but Byron, claiming that his ships were in no condition to sail to California and northwestern America, struck out on a westerly course across the southern Pacific.

His decision to ignore his instructions has been the subject of arguments ever since. In hindsight, his decision was not unwise, for the hoped-for northern passage from the Pacific to Hudson Bay does not exist, and his ships would not have had an easy or a fruitful time in the labyrinth of inlets and islands of the British Columbian coast. But to achieve renown, he needed to make a major discovery along his self-chosen route, either Davis Land—which did not exist—or the lost "Islands of Solomon"—which he failed to find. He did not even have the consolation of discovering Tahiti; he sailed past 500 miles (800 km) or so to the north and left it to Wallis *(q.v.)* to discover a year later.

Byron's track across the Pacific took him north from the Strait of Magellan to Masafuera, well off the coast of Chile, then to the Tropic of Capricorn and roughly west-northwest. On 7 June 1766 he discovered two small islands, part of the northern Tuamotus, which he named the Islands of Disappointment, an appropriate name in view of what awaited him. He continued, sighting occasional small islands until he reached the Tokelau group. Had he continued on his westward course he would have stumbled upon the Solomons, but a few days later he veered north.

On 2 July he discovered an island in the Gilbert group, to which his own name was given, but his longitudes are not precise enough for it to be identified; it was probably Nukunau. On 31 July the *Dolphin* and the *Tamar* anchored in Tinian, where a stay of nine weeks helped to restore the crews, by now ridden with scurvy.

Byron then went to Batavia by way of the northern Philippines and on 9 May 1766 finally reached England. The voyage had produced few tangible results—the discovery of four or five small islands and some valuable descriptions of native peoples and arte-facts. It did lead to a desire on the part of the Admiralty to find out more about the southern and central Pacific—the *Dolphin* was promptly sent back under the command of Samuel Wallis.

John Byron was not condemned for neglecting his original in-structions. His voyage spurred further English expeditions; in fact, he probably helped to plan Wallis'. Besides, he was too well con-nected to be punished or even reprimanded. He spent the years 1769–1772 as governor of Newfoundland, was promoted to rear admiral in 1775, and to vice-admiral in 1778. He died on 10 April 1786, two years before the birth of his grandson, George Gordon, Lord Byron, who was destined to bring the family name greater fame in the world of literature. Another grandson, George Anson Byron *(q.v.)* commanded the *Blonde* on a later expedition to the Pacific.

## Careri

GIOVANNI FRANCESCO GEMELLI CARERI, a native of Naples, com-pleted a voyage around the world and, in June 1696, sailed from Manila to Acapulco in the famous Manila galleon, going by way of Guam along an easterly route to the north of the Hawaiian Islands. He sighted the American coast in the neighborhood of present-day San Diego, California. The crossing had taken more than two hun-dred days, ending in early 1697. Careri then traveled overland to the Atlantic coast to find passage to Spain and home again.

His fame rests on the colorful and informative account of his voy-age, *Giro del Mondo*, published shortly after his return, which con-tains excellent descriptions of daily life on the great, slow galleons making their lonely way across the Pacific. An edited translation by A. Churchill appeared in 1963 as *A Voyage to the Philippines*.

## Carteret

PHILIP CARTERET was born in Jersey, Channel Islands, on 22 Janu-ary 1733. His naval career began in 1747 when he went to Ply-mouth, serving first as a captain's servant, then in January 1748 as a volunteer in the *Monmouth*. In November 1751 he was transferred to the *St. Albans*, in which he sailed to the coast of Guinea, then to the *Augusta* and the *Vanguard*, sailing mostly in Mediterranean waters. He qualified as a midshipman in 1755, and in 1757–1762 during the Seven Years War, served on the *Guernsey*. He was promoted to third lieutenant in June 1757 and to second lieutenant in August 1758.

In 1764 he was approached by John Byron *(q.v.)*, under whom he had served on several occasions. Byron, who was to sail to the Pacific in the *Dolphin*, appointed Carteret first lieutenant of the *Tamar*, the *Dolphin*'s consort. They sailed on 21 June and emerged into the Pacific on 9 April 1765. Three weeks later, at the island of Masafuera, Byron transferred Carteret to the *Dolphin*. The original plan had been to sail north along the American coast in search of a northwest passage, but Byron decided to strike across the Pacific, reaching Tinian in the Marianas at the end of July and making a few, very minor discoveries on the way.

Carteret was back in England in May 1766 and was almost immediately selected to take part in another voyage to the Pacific.

Carteret was to command the *Swallow*, a sloop of 14 guns, which would accompany the *Dolphin*, now placed in the charge of Samuel Wallis *(q.v.)*. They sailed from Plymouth on 21 August, making for Madeira and reaching the Strait of Magellan on 17 December. The passage to the Pacific was one of the longest on record, and the *Swallow* was once given up for lost. The ship had already shown during the voyage from England that it was a wretched sailer, difficult to work and to steer. For a time, Carteret considered turning back and not delaying the *Dolphin* any further, but Wallis wanted to draw on Carteret's previous experience of the Pacific. Wallis also rejected Carteret's suggestion that he join him in the *Dolphin* as adviser and allow someone else to return with the *Swallow*.

The ships emerged into the Pacific on 11 April 1767, after a four-month struggle through the strait, but in fog and bad weather the two ships became separated and, this time, never rejoined.

Carteret struggled alone toward Juan Fernandez which he found, on 8 May, to have been fortified by the Spanish. He nevertheless refilled his water casks at Masafuera, sailed north to seek the islands of San Ambrosio and San Felix, without success, and with no better luck spent some time looking for the southern continent. On 2 July, however, he discovered a small island that he named Pitcairn. Further islands came into view in mid-July, on one of which, part of what he called the Duke of Gloucester's Islands, a landing was effected. These were part of the Tuamotu archipelago. Progress was slow, while scurvy made rapid advances. Then, on 12 August, more land was seen; Carteret named it Queen Charlotte's Islands.

He had come to the northern sector of the Santa Cruz group and discovered Vanikoro, where La Pérouse *(q.v.)* was to be wrecked some twenty years later. He then went on to the Solomons, without recognizing them for what they were, and discovered the island of Ndai. On 24 August he discovered the Kilinailau Islands, also known as Carteret Islands, and the next day the large island of Buka. Soon after, he reached New Britain and put into a small bay called English Cove, where the ship was repaired and food and water taken on board. On 9 September he found a strong current was bearing the *Swallow* toward an inlet. It was a strait, St. George's Channel, which separated New Britain from what he now named New Ireland. Soon after, he discovered that another substantial island lay off the northwest of New Ireland; he called the passage between the two Byron Strait, and the land, New Hanover.

There were more islands still. He named the group the Admiralty Islands, but the area was not unexplored. He did, however, give the first precise description of Aua and Wuvulu to the southwest of the Ninigo group. He made his way to Mindanao, in the Philippines, then south between Borneo and the Celebes, where the Dutch were suspicious of his motive in sailing among their colonial possessions. He spent from 21 December 1767 to 22 May 1768 in the small port of Bonthain in the southern Celebes and another three months in Batavia. The Dutch carpenters doubted, when he sailed in mid-September, that the *Swallow* would ever reach Europe; but he made it to South Africa, spending from 28 November 1768 to 6 January 1769 at Table Bay, and on 20 May 1769 finally dropped anchor at Spithead —"to our great joy."

Carteret was raised to post rank in 1771. He commanded the *Druid* in 1777 for an expedition to the West Indies and in 1779 took the *Endymion* across the Atlantic to join Admiral Rodney but he was invalided back in 1781. He retired formally in 1794 as a rear admiral and died at Southampton on 21 July 1796.

## Cary

JAMES CARY was born in New England in the 1770s and went to sea on various whaling vessels, eventually serving as first mate to Uriah Swain in the *Mars* in 1799–1801. In 1803 he sailed from Nantucket in command of the whaler *Rose*.

While on his way to Canton, Cary discovered an island to the southwest of the Gilbert group, which he named Rose Island. It was Tamana. Cary reached Canton in May 1804, stayed a month to take on an extra cargo, and sailed by way of Dampier Strait, between New Guinea and New Britain, to Port Jackson in New South Wales. He went on south of Tasmania toward the Indian Ocean, encountering fierce storms that forced him to put into Capetown in October. He finally reached Nantucket on 28 December 1804. James Cary left on a further voyage in 1805 but died at Canton before completing it.

## Cary

NATHANIEL C. CARY was born in Nantucket in 1797. His mother was a member of a well-known naval family, the Coffins. The Carys, allied to other Nantucket seafarers, were among the first Nantucketers to sail to China. Nathaniel commanded a number of trading and whaling ships—from Nantucket, New Bedford, and Boston, but also from Dunkirk.

On 16 August 1832 he sailed from New England in command of the whaler *Gideon Barstow* bound for the Pacific. Sailing north from the Society Islands, he came upon a low-lying island that did not appear on any chart, to which he gave the name Barstow's Island; this was Morane, in the Gambier archipelago (it may have been previously sighted by Moerenhout [*q.v.*]).

Nathaniel Cary returned home on 29 December 1835; he took out the *Gideon Barstow* again in June 1838; it was wrecked, however, at Cocos Island in the Indian Ocean. He returned to the Pacific Ocean four times, in the *Charles Drew*—July 1842 to March 1844, August 1844 to May 1846, and in November 1849; on this last occasion the whaler was lost at Honolulu on 22 October 1850—and in the *Nimrod*, which sailed from New Bedford on 13 September 1851 and returned on 26 March 1854. Cary's health began to fail during this voyage, and he came home sick in 1852. He recovered, however, dying at Nantucket in his ninetieth year in 1887.

## Castro

KNOWLEDGE OF FRANCISCO DE CASTRO'S voyage and person is shadowy and indirect. He sailed in 1538 from the Moluccas, probably from Ternate, for Mindanao, at the behest of the governor, Antonio Galvano. With him went two priests to convert natives of islands they encountered on the way.

They sailed north and, like a number of Portuguese navigators, were blown east to the edge of the Caroline Islands. It appears likely that he landed on the islands of Yap, Ulithi, and Fais. Castro's destination, however, was the Philippines, and having restored his crew he went on toward Mindanao. The islands may have been discovered before Castro's visit. The only source for this voyage is Galvano's own account of exploration in this region, his *Tratado dos descubrimientos.*

## Cavendish

THOMAS CAVENDISH (the contraction Candish is sometimes found) was born, probably in 1555, near Harwich in Suffolk and educated at Cambridge. In April 1585 he sailed from Plymouth with Sir Richard Grenville to the West Indies and Virginia, returning on 18 September. He was eager, however, to emulate the voyage of Sir Francis Drake *(q.v.)* and sailed from London on 10 June 1586 with three ships, the *Desire,* the *Content,* and the *Gallant,* and 123 men, going to Plymouth and finally sailing on 21 July for the Canaries, Sierra Leone, the Cape Verde Islands, and Cape Frio in Brazil.

On 23 November Cavendish left Brazil for the Strait of Magellan, discovering on the coast of Patagonia a harbor that he named after his own vessel. It is today known by its Spanish equivalent, Puerto Deseado. He left there on 28 December, entered the strait on 6 January 1587, and emerged into the Pacific on 24 February. He sailed north along the coast of Chile, looking for settlements to raid. He lost several men when a small party attempted a landing on 1 April but was more successful near Africa, capturing a number of small ships and attacking Spanish settlements ashore.

On 25 May he reached Guayaquil, where he refitted; on 7 June he sailed for Guatemala and Acapulco. After carrying out more raids, he went up to Cabó San Lucas, the southern extremity of California, to await the Manila galleon. On 14 November 1587 the great *Santa Ana* hove into sight and was captured. Cavendish transferred its rich cargo to his ship and burned the galleon. Then, leaving the *Content* behind, he sailed on 19 November across the Pacific to the Ladrones, which he reached on 3 January 1588, then on to Samar and Capul islands south of Luzon, passing between Panay and Negros to the Sulu Sea, the Strait of Lombok, along the south coast of Java to the Cape of Good Hope (where he arrived on 19 March), thence to St. Helena (8 June) and finally, Plymouth, where his *Desire*, the only ship to complete the voyage, received a tumultuous welcome on 10 September 1588.

Cavendish set out on 26 August 1951 for an even more ambitious voyage to the Pacific and the East, with the *Leicester, Roebuck, Desire*, and two other vessels. He again went to Brazil, Port Desire, and the Strait of Magellan, but he encountered much greater difficulties and part way through the strait, on 15 May, he turned back to Port Desire, intending to try the Cape of Good Hope route. He died at sea on his way to St. Helena in June 1592.

## Cécille

JEAN-BAPTISTE THOMAS MÉDÉE CÉCILLE was born in Rouen, Normandy, on 16 October 1787. He first went to sea in merchant ships, then joined the navy in 1808, taking part in the defense of Marseilles in 1810. A lieutenant from 1816, he obtained his first command in 1820, when he took the *Expéditive* to the West Indies. He was a frigate captain by 1829 and in 1835 was given command of the *Héroïne.* He was then ordered to the Pacific to protect whalers and other interests.

He sailed from Brest on 1 July 1837, spent a short time in Rio, and went on by way of the Cape to King George Sound, Hobart, and Port Jackson. He reached the Bay of Islands, New Zealand, on 20 May 1838, sailed down to Akaroa in the South Island, and on to the Chatham Islands, where the crew of the whaler *Jean Bart* had recently been massacred. On 27 November he was in Tahiti, where French settlers and missionaries were being harassed by the local ruler. On

4 December he sailed for Valparaiso and home, reaching Brest on 17 July 1839.

He had been promoted to full captain in 1838. It was proposed to send him back to the Pacific in 1841 in the *Érigone,* but this plan was canceled when he was appointed to head the China naval station. He was made a rear admiral in 1844 and vice-admiral in 1847. Two years later he was appointed the French ambassador to London. He became a senator in 1853 and, in 1859, was made a Count of the Roman Empire in recognition of the help he had given to missionaries in the Pacific and in the East. He died in St. Servan, Brittany, on 9 October 1873.

## Cermeño

SEBASTIÁN RODRIGUEZ CERMEÑO was born in Portugal in 1550. As a young man he joined the naval service, making his way to South America. He was probably the pilot of the *Santa Ana,* captured by Thomas Cavendish *(q.v.)* off California on 14 November 1587.

Cermeño returned to the South American coast and sailed to the Philippines where, in 1595, he was given command of the *San Agustin* with instructions to make for California as far north as the winds and currents would permit and then to search south along the coast for natural harbors where the galleons coming from Manila might find refuge in case of necessity.

On 4 November 1595 Cermeño made a landfall in the neighborhood of 41°45′ north, in the vicinity of Point Saint George, near the present Oregon-California state line. He proceeded southward as instructed, but the *San Agustin* was wrecked in December and the voyage to Mexico had to be completed in the ship's boat. He reached Jalisco, near San Blas, on 7 January 1796.

Cermeño reported on a number of bays and inlets, but he did not enter them and so could not provide any precise details. He named one of these bays Bahia de San Francisco, and so was regarded by some as the discoverer of San Francisco Bay. The problem was further confused by an English cartographer changing the name to Bay of Francis Drake.

Details of Cermeño's later career and date of death are not known.

## Chamisso

LOUIS-CHARLES-ADELAIDE (ADELBERT) DE CHAMISSO was born at Boncourt in the province of Champagne in 1781 but was forced by the Revolution of 1789 to leave France at an early age with his family. The Chamissos eventually made their home in Berlin, and the youth became a lieutenant in the Prussian army in 1801. He was taken prisoner by Napoleon's army and was allowed to return to France as a civilian, devoting himself to botanical and other studies.

He offered his services as a botanist and writer to the *Riurik* expedition under Kotzebue *(q.v.)* and was accepted, joining the ship in Copenhagen in August 1815. His relations with Kotzebue became tense as the circumnavigation progressed, the two men's temperaments and backgrounds being very different. Chamisso's account of the voyage, however, once allowance is made for his dislike of Kotzebue, is a valuable document, lively and filled with useful information about the islands visited, in particular the Hawaiian group. It was written as a diary *(tagebuch)*, and the scientific notes were included in Kotzebue's published account. Chamisso's *Reise um die Welt* was published in Leipzig in 1836.

Soon after his return to Europe, in July 1818, Chamisso was appointed custodian of the Berlin Botanical Gardens; he also continued to devote himself to literature. He died on 21 August 1838 in Berlin.

## Cheyne

ANDREW CHEYNE was born in the Shetland Islands in 1817 of a land-owning and fishing family. He worked on one of the family fishing vessels, but by 1840 was in Sydney, where he is recorded as sailing to the Bay of Islands, New Zealand, as master of the brig *Bee*. On 7 August 1841 he sailed as supercargo of the *Diana*, ostensibly for New Guinea but in fact to the Isle of Pines, New Caledonia, buying sandalwood, and eventually to China by way of the eastern Carolines, Guam, and Manila, reaching Macao on 28 March 1842.

In June 1842 he was back in Sydney preparing to sail once more to Melanesia for sandalwood, this time as captain of the brig *Bull*. He left on 26 July for New Caledonia, the Loyalty Islands, and north to

Ponape in the Carolines, where he remained while the *Bull* continued on its way to China. He organized a third expedition to trade between Melanesia and the East: the *Naïad* left from Macao in June 1843 through the Philippines to the Palaus and the Carolines and around the Solomons. The *Naïad* sailed through the islands until November 1845, when the ship had to be abandoned at the island of Aneytum, north of New Caledonia. Cheyne then sailed in 1846 in the *Starling*, going from China to the New Hebrides (Vanuatu) and the Solomons; he returned to Scotland in 1848.

He obtained his first-class mariner's certificate in 1849 and his master's ticket in 1851. In between he had sailed to Australia and back. He married in the Shetlands in 1852 and took his bride on the *Lady Montague*, of which he had been given command for a circumnavigation. He sailed from Plymouth on 9 August 1852 for the Cape, Tasmania, the Isle of Pines, Ponape, Hong Kong, and Manila, then crossed the Pacific to San Francisco and Callao, where the *Lady Montague* had to be sold. The couple finally reached England in November 1854. Cheyne returned to the East and Australia, engaging in various trading ventures in New Guinea and the Palau Islands. He was killed on the island of Koror in the Palaus in February 1866.

Cheyne published in 1852 *A Description of Islands in the Western Pacific Ocean* and in 1855 *Sailing Directions from New South Wales to China and Japan; including the Whole Islands and Dangers in the Western Pacific Ocean*. The journals of his 1841–1844 voyages, edited by Dorothy Shineberg, were published in 1971. His writings are full of valuable ethnographic and historical information.

## Chirikov

ALEKSEI ILICH CHIRIKOV (or Tchirikov) was born in 1703 and graduated from the Russian Naval Academy in 1721. In 1725 he was appointed as one of the two lieutenants of Vitus Bering *(q.v.)* and set out toward eastern Siberia. The expedition had to struggle with the problems of overland travel and of obtaining supplies for an arduous voyage. It was not until the spring of 1728 that the participants could start building a ship, the *St. Gabriel (Sv. Gavrill)*, in Kamchatka, in which they sailed on 14 July. The voyage involved sailing north into what is now the Bering Sea and through the strait into the

Arctic Ocean as far as 67°18′, charting the Siberian coast as they went. The fog was too thick to see the nearby American coast. On 2 September the *St. Gabriel* was back in Kamchatka.

Chirikov went home in 1730 but was soon to return to Siberia for another expedition with Bering. This began officially in 1733, but Bering wanted to ensure that the ships and the supplies were adequate for the major undertaking being planned and he did not reach Okhotsk until 1737. Two ships were then built, the command of the *St. Paul (Sv. Pavel)* going to Chirikov. The expedition sailed from Kamchatka on 4 June 1741, sailing southeast and east until 20 June, when the two ships lost sight of each other.

Chirikov sailed east and northeast until 15 July 1741, when he sighted a mountainous and forested coast; it was the northwest coast of America, and he was the first European to reach it. From this point, Cape Addington, he sailed north toward what are now Baranof Island and Chichagof Island; on the eighteenth, he entered a strait—Lisianski Inlet—at the northern end of the latter island and sent two boats ashore, neither of which returned. He veered west until, on 1 August, he reached the Kenai Peninsula in the Gulf of Alaska; he then sailed off the Aleutian chain, anchoring off Adak on 9 September and later sighting the islands of Agattu and Attu. Scurvy was affecting the crew, and Chirikov was endeavoring to return to Kamchatka as quickly as he could. Even so, a number died, including his lieutenants Chichagov and Plautin and a French naturalist, Delisle de la Croyère, before the *St. Paul* could drop anchor in Petropavlovsk harbor on 10 October.

In May 1742 Chirikov set out again to seek Bering's vessel, which had still not returned. He went back to the Aleutians and took the opportunity to determine as precisely as he could the position of Attu. But there was no sign of Bering's *St. Peter*; it was in fact at the time being broken up to build a smaller but seaworthy craft, and Bering himself was already dead. Chirikov returned to Kamchatka, having gathered little new information during this voyage and holding the belief, shared by Bering's officers, that the Aleutians were offshore islands of the American coast. The achievements, however, of what is known as the Great Northern Expedition were considerable and provided valuable data for cartographers of the northern Pacific, in whose work Chirikov participated after his return to Russia.

He was promoted to commodore admiral. He died in Moscow in November 1748. His name has been given to capes on Kyushu Island, Taui Guba, Attu, and in the Anadyr Gulf; Vancouver *(q.v.)* named Chirikof Island, south of the Alaska Peninsula, in his honor.

## Christian

FLETCHER CHRISTIAN was born near Whitehaven, Cumberland, in September 1764, the son of a lawyer. He had a good education, but had a wish to go to sea. At the age of 18, he served in the *Cambridge*, whose complement included Lt. William Bligh *(q.v.)*. He later sailed to the East Indies in the *Eurydice*, but transferred to the *Britannia*, a merchant vessel trading in the West Indies, under Bligh's command. On their second voyage, Bligh ordered him to be treated as an officer.

On 7 September 1787 Christian joined the *Bounty* as master's mate for a voyage to Tahiti, where it was proposed to collect breadfruit plants and take them to the West Indies. The *Bounty* sailed from Spithead on 23 December 1787, making for Cape Horn, but when gales proved too wild, veering back toward the Cape of Good Hope and Tasmania. On 2 March 1788 Bligh gave Christian "a written order to act as lieutenant." The *Bounty* arrived in Matavai Bay, Tahiti, on 26 October. The stay was a long one—more than five months—during which Bligh found it increasingly difficult to maintain discipline and to hold his temper under control. The attractions of the island and Bligh's increasing and excessive harshness combined to create a dissatisfied and rebellious crew. Things worsened after the *Bounty* weighed anchor on 4 April 1789, and on the twenty-eighth, while the *Bounty* was sailing south of Tofua, a number of the crew, Christian among them, mutinied. They set Bligh and eighteen loyalists adrift in the ship's launch to make their way as best they could to the Dutch East Indies.

Fletcher Christian was now in charge of the *Bounty*. The breadfruit plants were thrown overboard and the ship's course changed back to the Society Islands. It was obvious that any stay at Tahiti would need to be brief, as a search for the men of the *Bounty* would start there. Some other island refuge was needed, preferably off the beaten track.

On 29 May Christian put in at Tubuai, but thefts and an attack by the natives made it clear that it would not provide the required safe asylum. The *Bounty* went to Tahiti for supplies, leaving sixteen of the mutineers behind and, with a number of Tahitian women to provide wives, set out in search of another island. Eventually, after a reconnaissance in the Tonga group, Christian selected Pitcairn, where he arrived on 15 January 1790. The stores were ferried ashore and the *Bounty* set on fire to remove any clue that might attract the attention of a passing ship.

Pitcairn did not prove to be an island paradise. Arguments and fights soon broke out, followed by several killings. Fletcher Christian was murdered toward the end of 1793. Reports that he was seen in England were unsubstantiated and highly improbable. No ship called at Pitcairn until 1808, when Mayhew Folger *(q.v.)*, from the Boston ship *Topaz*, met descendants of the mutineers and revealed the story of the Pitcairners to a world that took some time to accept his report as credible.

## Clerke

CHARLES CLERKE was born in Weathersfield, Essex, in 1741, the son of a well-to-do farmer. He entered the Royal Navy at the age of 12. He served in the *Bellona* and almost lost his life in 1761 in an engagement with a French warship. He sailed as a midshipman in the *Dolphin* under John Byron *(q.v.)* during Byron's voyage to the Pacific of June 1764 to May 1766. However, he did not stay with the *Dolphin* when it set out in August 1766 for a second circumnavigation under Samuel Wallis *(q.v.)*. Instead, he served in the West Indies and in 1768 was accepted for the *Endeavour*, which was to sail to Tahiti under James Cook *(q.v.)*.

When the *Endeavour* left Plymouth on 26 August 1768, Clerke held the rank of master's mate. However, upon the death of Zachary Hicks in May 1771, he was formally promoted to third lieutenant. The *Endeavour* was back in England in July 1771, and Cook began to prepare his second circumnavigation. Clerke joined him, this time as second lieutenant of the *Resolution*, the vessel commanded by Cook himself. Clerke, who had a low opinion of this ship, until it was refitted, kept on friendly terms with Sir Joseph Banks *(q.v.)*, who had refused to sail on it. The *Resolution*, with the *Adventure*, sailed on 13 July 1772, making for the Cape and the southern Indian Ocean. A call was made in New Zealand in March to June 1773 and again in November after a sweep through islands of the central Pacific. The *Adventure* had become separated from its consort, so the *Resolution* set off alone for an exploration of Antarctic waters and a second sweep through the islands. On the homeward journey, a group of rocks off South Georgia were surveyed and named Clerke Rocks. On 30 July 1775 the *Resolution* was back in England.

Clerke did not have much time to rest after his more than three years at sea (he was involved in rescuing his brother from financial disaster, and the problems this caused him affected his health). Yet another voyage was planned, and he was given the command of the *Discovery*, the other ship, the *Resolution*, being again under the command of James Cook. The *Discovery* sailed on 1 August 1776, more than a fortnight after the *Resolution*. The two ships soon rejoined; they entered the Pacific via the Cape of Good Hope and sailed for New Zealand and the islands of the central Pacific. In August 1777 the ships were sailing among the Society Islands when it became evident that Clerke was suffering from tuberculosis. Since the expedition was bound for Alaska and the Arctic, he seriously considered the suggestion of William Anderson, the ship's surgeon, who was similarly affected, that they stay behind, but eventually proceeded along the northwest coast and back to Hawaii, where Cook was killed on 14 February 1779.

Clerke then took command of the expedition. His health had continued to deteriorate, but he was determined to complete Cook's work. He sailed from the Hawaiian Islands on 15 March, sailing west and north in increasingly cold weather for Kamchatka. He was often too ill to leave his cabin. In June he sailed north through Bering Strait until the end of July, when the ice proved an insuperable barrier to further exploration. Clerke died just before reaching the port of Petropavlovsk in Kamchatka on 22 July 1779. He was buried at Petropavlovsk at the foot of a tree on the twenty-ninth. He left all his collections to Sir Joseph Banks.

## Clipperton

JOHN CLIPPERTON first appears in the Pacific as the chief mate and carpenter of the *St. George*, who with twenty-one others mutinied against Dampier *(q.v.)* in Nicoya Gulf in present-day Costa Rica in July 1704. They sailed in a 40-ton Spanish vessel that Dampier's buccaneering crew had recently captured.

Clipperton went to the Mexican coast, when he captured two Spanish ships; one of them was so old that he sank it; the other he ransomed for 4,000 Spanish dollars. Anxious to avoid meeting the *St. George*, Clipperton proceeded to cross the Pacific, but he sheltered first in a lonely island lying almost 1,800 miles from the American continent in roughly the same latitude as Nicoya Gulf. The uninhabited island, which now bears Clipperton's name, is a French possession. It is a deserved tribute, for Clipperton, in crossing the Pacific to the Philippines, a voyage of more than 7,000 miles, in such a small vessel showed himself to be a skillful navigator. From the Philippines, Clipperton sailed to China, where he obtained a passage in a Dutch ship to Europe.

Clipperton returned to the Pacific in 1719 as second-in-command to Shelvocke (q.v.), whom he then nominally replaced as the expedition's leader. Rivalry between the two men began almost as soon as they set sail from England on 13 February 1719, and the *Success* and the *Speedwell* soon separated. Clipperton waited for Shelvocke at the Canary Islands in March 1719, but the latter's *Speedwell* did not materialize, nor was there any meeting of the two ships at any of the other prearranged rendezvous, the Cape Verde Islands and Juan Fernandez, where the *Success* arrived on 7 September 1719. Although Clipperton's crew was weakened by sickness and desertions, he nevertheless succeeded in capturing three Spanish vessels.

But manning these prizes strained his resources of manpower. His later attempts at capturing further Spanish vessels resulted in a set of failures that led his crew to various mutiny attempts. By chance, and two years after leaving Plymouth, the *Success* came across the *Speedwell* off the Mexican coast. The meeting ended in recriminations, and on 7 March 1721 Clipperton set off across the Pacific. The *Success* reached Guam on 13 May with a crew greatly weakened by scurvy. Although they were at first given some provisions, the Spanish governor considered Clipperton—who was drunk most of the time and incapable of running the ship—to be nothing but a pirate and ordered him fired upon. However, the *Success*, although damaged by the guns of the Spanish battery, got away to Amoy and eventually to Canton.

Clipperton took the *Success* to Batavia, whence he shipped out for Europe aboard a Dutch merchantman. He reached his home in Galway in June 1722, where he died a week later.

## Colnett

JAMES COLNETT (records also show him as Collnett) was born probably in 1753 at Plymouth and entered the Royal Navy in 1771, serving on the *Hazard* and *Scorpion*; at this point he was accepted as a midshipman with the *Resolution* under James Cook *(q.v.)*, which he joined in December 1771. He was the first to sight New Caledonia, on 4 September 1774, an event commemorated in the name Cape Colnett on the northwest coast of the island. The expedition was back in England on 29 July 1775, and Colnett subsequently served with the crew of the *Juno*.

Colnett was next appointed master of the *Adventure* and, in February 1779, was promoted to lieutenant, serving in the *Bienfaisant* and *Pégase*. In 1786 he was placed on half pay and took command of the *Prince of Wales*, fitted out by Richard Cadman Etches and his associates to trade on the northwest coast. In company with the *Princess Royal*, Colnett sailed from England in September, turned Cape Horn, and reached Nootka Sound on 7 July 1787. He met George Dixon *(q.v.)*, proceeded up the coast, discovering Klaskish Inlet on the way, and after several weeks of reasonably successful trading sailed for Hawaii. The two ships returned to the coast in the spring, Colnett then cruising in Prince William Sound and along the Alaskan coast. On 18 August 1788 they returned to Hawaii, where they obtained supplies before sailing for China; they reached Macao on 12 November 1788.

There, Colnett teamed up with John Meares *(q.v.)* and the Etches group to set up the "Associated Merchants trading to the North West Coast of America." John Etches sailed back to England in the *Prince of Wales* while Colnett took over a snow, the *Argonaut*, and returned to Nootka. There, on 3 July 1789, Colnett was arrested by the Spanish authorities, who claimed the whole area on grounds of prior discovery. This "Nootka Incident" almost led to war between the major powers. Colnett was not released until 9 July 1790. He was able to trade for furs (sea otter skins) once the international dispute was resolved in October 1790. He sailed for Hawaii on 3 March 1791 and reached Macao on 30 May only to find the Chinese had banned the importation of furs.

Colnett succeeded in selling part of his cargo on the northern coast of China while on an unsuccessful trading voyage to Japan, which remained a closed world. He gave up and returned to England in 1792, where he disposed of the balance of his stock. He returned to the Pacific in the *Rattler*, provided by the Admiralty for survey work; interest was centered on facilities for the growing whaling industry. Colnett sailed on 7 January 1793 for Rio, Cape Horn, and the Galapagos Islands, which he reached on 25 June 1793. He pressed on to Cocos Island, where he anchored on 25 July, the island of Socorro off the Mexican coast, and various harbors along the American coast. He returned to the Galapagos in March 1794, went down to the coast of Chile, turned Cape Horn, and was back in England on 2 November.

James Colnett was promoted to commander soon after his return, on 19 December 1794, and to captain on 5 October 1796. The conflict that had developed following the French Revolution brought back to active service officers who, like him, had been placed on half-pay. But Colnett did make one more voyage toward the Pacific in 1802–1803 when he commanded the *Glatton*, taking convicts to New South Wales.

Colnett also worked on writing *A Voyage to the South Atlantic and round Cape Horn into the Pacific Ocean*, which was published in 1798. He died in September 1806.

## Commerson

PHILIBERT COMMERSON was born on 18 November 1727 in Châtillon-sur-Chalaronne, France. He studied botany at Montpellier and traveled extensively through France. In 1764 he settled in Paris, writing and taking part in research, acts that brought him in contact with a number of French scientists. He was selected to join the Bougainville *(q.v.)* expedition of 1766 as botanist and surgeon aboard the *Étoile*.

He was tireless in collecting natural history specimens whenever he could go ashore, helped by his "valet," Jeanne Baret *(q.v.)*. His exuberant support for the ideas of Jean-Jacques Rousseau and for the theory of the "noble savage" led him to write laudatory letters and articles on the subject of Tahiti that played an important part in giving rise to the myth of the South Sea island paradise.

Suffering from seasickness and finding it difficult to get on with the *Étoile's* officers, he left the ship in Mauritius. He continued his botanical work in Mauritius, and on his death on 13 March 1773 he left a large collection of scientific papers, most of which were never published.

One week later in Paris, the Académie des Sciences, unaware that he had died, elected him an associate member.

## Cook

JAMES COOK, the son of a day laborer, was born on 27 October 1728 in the Yorkshire village of Marton-in-Cleveland. There was no seafaring tradition in his essentially agricultural background. His education was mere elementary tuition given by a farmer's wife, as was that of most boys of his lowly class, with the added advantage of further study at a small local school.

At the age of 17, he was apprenticed to a grocer in the nearby fishing port of Staithes, but eighteen months later he transferred to Whitby to work for a shipowner and coal merchant. This gave James the chance to work as an apprentice and soon as a seaman on colliers plying between Whitby and other ports on the east coast. He gained wider experience and rose to the position of mate, until in June 1755 he volunteered to join the Royal Navy as an able-seaman. He was soon promoted to master's mate.

The Seven Years War (1756–1763) provided opportunities for young men of talent to learn, to display their ability, and to rise through the ranks. James Cook took part in a number of bloody engagements and earned promotion to master's rank; this was in 1757 when navy regulations barred anyone with so little length of service from receiving a commission, even in wartime. He served first in the frigate *Solebay*, then in the *Pembroke*, in which he went to Canada. Here Cook carried out the meticulous survey work for which he became famous, his first published chart appearing in London in 1759 following his survey of Gaspé Bay. After the fall of Quebec, Cook was transferred to the *Northumberland*, the flagship of Admiral Colville.

The work Cook performed from both ships was recognized after the war when he was sent to Newfoundland for further hydrographic surveys. His precise observations of an eclipse of the sun in 1766, invaluable to determine the longitude of Newfoundland, brought him to the attention of the Royal Society. His recognized ability as a navigator in imperfectly charted waters, his precise hydrographic reports, and his work on the eclipse made him an obvious preference to command a ship the Admiralty was planning to send to the Pacific to observe the transit of Venus and to carry out exploration in southern latitudes in the hope of discovering the rumored southern continent. For this, Cook was commissioned first lieutenant.

The *Endeavour*, in which he sailed from Plymouth on 26 August 1768, was a sturdy bark built in Whitby. Cook took the ship south to Madeira and Rio, turned Cape Horn, and sailed through the Tuamotus to Tahiti, where he anchored on 13 April 1769. The transit of Venus was duly observed, and on 9 August Cook set out in search of the southern continent. On 7 October he came upon the east coast of northern New Zealand and began a detailed survey of both its islands that lasted until 1 April 1770. He sailed almost due west toward the Australian continent, discovering and naming New South Wales and almost losing the *Endeavour* on the Great Barrier Reef. He went on, south of New Guinea, to Timor and Batavia, where he anchored on 11 October. The ship was in need of extensive repairs and did not leave until 26 December, sailing south into the Indian Ocean for the Cape of Good Hope and home. It was back in England on 12 July 1771. This first voyage earned international acclaim, but the narrative was left to Dr. John Hawkesworth, who produced a more literary account than Cook could have done (and took a great many liberties with the text).

Cook was soon asked to lead a second expedition to the Pacific. He sailed with two vessels, the *Resolution* and the *Adventure*, the latter being commanded by Tobias Furneaux *(q.v.)*, on 13 July 1772, once again from Plymouth. Cook now held the rank of commander; he would be promoted to post-captain on his return.

This voyage to the high southern latitudes would finally determine that the southern continent did not exist. The expedition sailed south to the Cape of Good Hope, then to the Antarctic until, at the end of December, the ice shelf barred further progress. Cook sailed northeast to the Crozet Islands, then south and east again along latitude 60° south. Then it was time for sailing to New Zealand. Cook entered Dusky Sound on 26 March 1773 and on 11 May anchored in Queen Charlotte Sound; there he found the *Adventure*, from which the *Resolution* had been separated since 8 February.

On 7 June the ships set out for the Society Islands and Tonga. On 3 November the *Resolution* was back in New Zealand, but the *Adventure* had again disappeared. This time the separation was final. Cook sailed three weeks later to continue his exploration of the southern Pacific, reaching on 30 January 1774 the latitude of 71°10', farther south than anyone had yet sailed. The *Resolution* then veered north, toward the Marquesas and Tahiti, where Cook dropped anchor on 22 April. After more exploration, in Tonga, Fiji, the New Hebrides, and New Caledonia, Cook again made for New Zealand, discovering Norfolk Island on the way, and reached Queen Charlotte Sound on 18 October.

The voyage home began on 10 November 1774, more or less due east toward Cape Horn, with further exploration in the high latitudes of the southern Atlantic, to South Georgia and the Sandwich group, then north to the Cape and to Plymouth, reaching England on 29 July 1775. Cook took steps to ensure the account of his second voyage would follow his own narrative and not be rearranged into an inaccurate literary production. This task took up a great deal of his time while pressure mounted to send him on a third expedition.

The *Resolution* was to sail in July 1776 together with the *Discovery*, commanded by Charles Clerke *(q.v.)*, but they left separately, Cook on 12 July and Clerke in early August. They joined up at Capetown on 10 November. The expedition made for Australia by way of the Crozet and Kerguelen islands, put in for a brief stay in Tasmania, and went on to New Zealand, where Cook anchored on 12 February 1777. After a fortnight, the two ships sailed away to the north, to the Cook Islands and Tonga, for this third voyage was directed at the northern Pacific, the first having covered the central area and the second the south.

After a call at Tahiti in August, Cook sailed to Christmas Island and the Hawaiian group, which he called the Sandwich Islands, and on to the northwest coast of America, which he sighted near latitude 45° north on 7 March 1778. He followed it to Alaska as far as the beginning of the Aleutian chain and in early November turned south for Hawaii. He reached Maui on 26 November and was able both to get supplies and continue his survey of the newly discovered group. On 17 January 1779 he dropped anchor in Kealakekua Bay. He could now rest his men and enjoy the welcome the islanders gave him. There were minor incidents during the fortnight's stay, but when the expedition sailed out on 4 February, there was no reason to feel alarm. A gale, however, damaged the ships and forced them back. On the eleventh they were at anchor in the bay. Two days later Cook and four marines were killed in a sudden attack by islanders. The expedition continued without him to Kamchatka, Bering Strait, and China, reaching England on 4 October 1780.

Elizabeth Batts, whom Cook had married on 21 December 1762, died on 13 May 1835. None of their six children survived her.

## Cooke

EDWARD COOKE (sometimes referred to as Edmund Cooke), born on the island of St. Christopher around 1675, accompanied Woodes Rogers *(q.v.)* on his circumnavigation. Cooke had already sailed with a number of trading and privateering voyages in the period 1690–1700 with mixed success, having been twice taken prisoner by the French.

When the Rogers expedition was being planned, Edward Cooke was given command of the *Duchess*, Rogers commanding the larger *Duke*. They sailed on 1 August 1708 by way of the Canaries and Cape Horn, which they turned in early January 1709, and put in at Juan Fernandez Islands. The rest of the year was spent on raid and plunder along the coast of South America, including the capture of three prizes, which, renamed the *Beginning*, the *Increase* and the *Marquis*, they added to their own *Duke* and *Duchess*.

For a time, Cooke commanded the *Beginning*, later taking over the larger *Marquis*. A Spanish frigate was then taken and renamed the *Batchelor*. Cooke, in charge of the *Marquis* sailed across the Pacific, leaving Puerto Seguro in Lower California on 10 January 1710 and reaching Guam on 11 March. When the *Marquis* was sold in Batavia, Cooke transferred back to the *Duchess* as second captain. The last stage of the circumnavigation was completed by way of the Cape and Holland.

Cooke's account of the voyage, which he succeeded in getting published just ahead of Woodes Rogers' own narrative, was a great success. *A Voyage to the South Sea and round the World* appeared in two volumes in 1712; it is less well written and somewhat less reliable than Rogers' book, but nevertheless is filled with colorful details and observations that appealed to contemporary readers; it has not lost its attraction even today.

Edward Cooke drowned in 1732, the year of Woodes Rogers' death.

## Cordes

SIMON DE CORDES, who took over command of an expedition of five Dutch ships following the death of Jacques Mahu *(q.v.)* in September 1598, was born in Antwerp or, according to other reports, in Amsterdam, around the year 1559. A Catholic, he had close family associations with traders in Lisbon. A trader of some repute himself in Holland, he joined with others in the expedition of five ships, which sailed from Rotterdam in June 1598.

Progress was slow, the ships not reaching the Strait of Magellan until April 1599. Opposing winds further delayed the fleet, which suffered great hardships and did not emerge into the Pacific until 4 September. Once this painful navigation was completed, violent gales scattered the ships: the *Geloof*, commanded by Sebald de Weert, made its way back through the strait, sighted some outliers of the Falkland Islands, and reached Holland in June 1600. The *Trouw*, with Simon's nephew Balthasar on board, eventually made its way to the island of Chiloe where, in March 1600, an attempt was made, as had originally been planned by the Dutch, to support rebellious Indians against their Spanish overlords; when this scheme failed, the survivors sailed to the Spice Islands, Balthasar and all but six of those remaining being killed at Tidore on 5 January 1601. The small *Blijde Boodschap*, captained by Dirck Gerritszoon, was captured by the Spanish at Valparaiso. Cordes in the *Hoop* effected several landings on the coast, in one of which, on the island of Mocha, in November 1599, he was killed. The *Hoop* eventually sailed north and set off across the Pacific but was lost somewhere to the north of Hawaii. The fifth ship, the *Liefde*, with William Adams *(q.v.)* on board, reached Japan in April 1600.

## Cowley

WILLIAM AMBROSE COWLEY, born in the late 1650s, was an English adventurer who joined the buccaneering expedition of John

Cook in Virginia in April 1683. He is reputed to have taken a Master's degree at Cambridge. His contribution to historical knowledge rests on his having kept a record of the voyage of the *Batchelor's Delight*, which turned Cape Horn in mid-February 1684 and dropped anchor at Juan Fernandez Islands on 23 March, falling in with another buccaneer, John Eaton *(q.v.)*. Cook died in July, being succeeded by Edward Davis *(q.v.)*.

After some months of fairly unprofitable raiding and cruising along the South American coast, Cowley transferred to Eaton's *Nicholas* as master. Further cruising proved to be again unprofitable, there being little Spanish shipping about. Eaton and Cowley set out on 22 December 1684 for Guam, where they arrived on 15 March, having suffered greatly from scurvy. In April the *Nicholas* sailed for Canton and after a refit cruised among the Dutch East Indies until January 1685 when Cowley left the ship and made his way to Batavia and then to the Cape of Good Hope and England, where he arrived in October 1686.

Cowley's journal is lively and filled with observations on the people he met and navigational details. It is, like many documents of its type, not entirely reliable. It was published in 1699. Nothing is known of his later life.

## Cox

JOHN HENRY COX was a British merchant trading in Canton who saw great possibilities in the fur trade. He became associated with expeditions to the northwest coast as early as 1785, assisting in organizing voyages by Hanna and Meares *(q.v.)*. He was living in England in 1788 and had built a brig, the *Mercury*, in which he sailed from Gravesend on 26 February 1789, depending for navigational guidance on the knowledge of Lt. George Mortimer *(q.v.)*.

He sailed by way of Tenerife and the Cape of Good Hope, reaching Amsterdam Island on 29 May; he remained on the island, gathering seal skins, until 9 June. At the beginning of July, Cox landed on the Australian continent, then sailed south of it until 5 July, when he landed in Tasmania—at Oyster Bay, which he named. He stayed almost a week, establishing contact with the shy Tasmanian aborigines, and continued toward the Austral Islands and Tahiti, where he dropped anchor on 12 August 1789. The stay lasted until 2 September, when Cox sailed for Kealakekua Bay, Hawaii, where he arrived on the twenty-third.

The *Mercury* left a couple of days later for Unalaska, where it dropped anchor in late October. Little trade followed in this area, which was regularly visited by Russian dealers, and the season was too advanced to tarry in these latitudes. Cox sailed for Canton on 6 November, calling at Tinian on 12 December and reaching Macao Roads on 27 December. He arrived back in Canton a few days later.

The period was a troubled one for fur traders. The Spanish had halted trade at Nootka Sound, while the Chinese authorities were starting to restrict the importation of furs. Cox had other interests in Canton than the fur trade, but he died on 5 October 1791.

Several geographical features on the northwest coast bear his name: Cox Point and Port Cox, in Clayoquot Sound, which Meares named after him, and Cox Island, one of the Scott group, named by Hanna.

## Crignon

PIERRE CRIGNON was born in Dieppe, Normandy, toward the end of the fifteenth century. A poet as well as a geographer and astronomer, he won prizes in poetry in Rouen before sailing from Dieppe on 28 March 1529 with the two Parmentier brothers, Jean and Raoul, on the expedition of the *Sacre* and the *Pensée*. Both Parmentiers died in Sumatra, leaving Crignon to bring the ships back to France. This he had achieved by the end of 1530, as his poem on the death of the brothers was published in Dieppe in 1531. He also wrote an account of the voyage and a treatise, *The Pearl of Cosmography*, now lost. His writings display a knowledge of the western Pacific that has led some historians to suggest that he sailed eastward from Sumatra and brought the ships home by way of Cape Horn or the Strait of Magellan. The evidence supporting his claim to be listed among the earliest Pacific navigators remains, however, very slight and is mainly based on the interpretation of imprecise charts and treatises.

## Crocker

STEPHEN R. CROCKER was born in October 1807 at Barnstable, Massachusetts. He worked on various ships and on 31 July 1836 sailed from Bristol, Rhode Island, as master of the *General Jackson*, owned by members of the local Wolf family. The campaign lasted for more than three years, Crocker returning to Bristol on 6 December 1839, during which time he had sailed throughout the northern and southern Pacific Ocean.

On 28 January 1839 he came upon a low-lying, inhabited island, part of the Tokelau group, which was known as Duke of Clarence Island and is Nukunonu. Then on 14 February he discovered an uncharted island farther south that he called D'Wolf Island after the *General Jackson*'s owners, William H. D. Wolf and James D. Wolf; it is the island of Fakaofo.

Stephen Crocker left the sea during the 1840s and turned to farming. He died at Barnstable on 12 November 1888.

## Crozer

THE AMERICAN WHALING CAPTAIN ''CROZER'' from Boston is credited with the discovery of Kusaie (Kosrae), also known as Ualan, in the Ponape group of the Caroline Islands. Crozer was in command of the whaler *Nancy* when, on 24 December 1804, he sighted a high island, which he named Strong Island. The high peak of this island is now known as Mt. Crozer. The report of this discovery comes from the French navigator Duperrey. However, no information is available on Crozer, which may be a misreading of Crocker, a patronymic of a New England whaling family.

## Crozet

JULIEN-MARIE CROZET was born on 26 November 1728 in Port-Louis, Brittany. He first served as a pilot's boy in September 1739 with a merchant vessel bound for India and China. He transferred to the navy during wartime from August 1745 to November 1748, then returned to ships of the French India Company. He was recalled for wartime naval service in March 1758, serving as a lieutenant in the *Volant*, and fought and was taken prisoner off the coast of Senegal.

Once freed, he was promoted to fireship captain and saw active service until January 1761, when he resumed his position with the India Company. In 1770 he was lieutenant in the *Duc de Praslin*. In Mauritius he met Marion du Fresne *(q.v.)* under whom he had served in the *Robuste* and later in the *Duc d'Argenson* during the Seven Year War. The collapse of the India Company left few openings for men like Crozet, who gladly accepted Marion du Fresne's offer to sail as his second-in-command in the *Mascarin*.

The expedition, consisting of two ships, sailed on 18 October 1771, first for the Cape and then on 28 December southeast across the Indian Ocean. A number of islands were discovered in January 1772 including, on the twenty-fourth, the Crozet Islands.

On 3 March the ships sighted Tasmania and three days later anchored in Blackman's Bay. Soon after, the French sailed for New Zealand, which they reached on 25 March, and spent from 4 May to 12 July in the Bay of Islands. The stay was marred by tragedy, Marion du Fresne and a number of his officers and men being killed in a sudden ambush by Maoris on 12 June. This made Crozet the effective leader of the expedition, the commander of the second ship, the *Marquis de Castries*, being young and inexperienced.

Crozet readied the ships for an earlier departure than had been expected, carried out reprisals against the natives, and sailed northward toward Tonga and the Marianas. On 26 September 1772 the ships anchored at Guam, their crews badly afflicted with scurvy. After recuperating, the French sailed for the Philippines, reaching Manila on 7 December. The *Mascarin* needed extensive repairs and did not leave until 9 March 1773. On 7 April Crozet was back in Mauritius. He made his way to France in November and obtained a new command, that of the *Ajax*, in which he sailed to the Indian Ocean. On his way home, in March 1775, he met James Cook *(q.v.)* at the Cape. The two had long discussions; on his next voyage Cook, using Crozet's charts, surveyed the islands the French had discovered in the southern Indian Ocean. Crozet was back in France in 1776 and captained the *Elizabeth* during the war against England. He died in Paris on 24 September 1782.

## Crozier

FRANCIS RAWDON MOIRA CROZIER was born in England, probably in 1796. He joined the Royal Navy in 1810, first served in the *Hamadryad*, and was then appointed to the *Briton* under Sir Thomas Staines *(q.v.)* who was about to sail to the Pacific.

*Briton* left Spithead on 30 December 1813 for Rio and the Cape.

Orders were countermanded, and Staines sailed instead for Cape Horn and the Pacific. He reached Valparaiso on 21 May 1814, went on to Callao and the Galapagos, spent a fortnight in the Marquesas, and in September came upon the English mutineer settlers of Pitcairn. The *Briton* then returned to Valparaiso and home, arriving at Plymouth on 7 July 1815.

Crozier next traveled to the Cape as mate of the sloop *Doterel* and on his return to England was appointed to the *Fury*, beginning a long period of Arctic exploration with William Edward Parry. Promoted to lieutenant in 1826, Crozier next served in the *Stag* and later in the *Cove*. A commander, in 1837, he was appointed to command the *Terror* under the orders of James Clark Ross *(q.v.)* with the *Erebus*, for a voyage to the Pacific and Antarctic, which lasted from 1839 to 1843. He was then selected for another voyage to the Arctic under Sir John Franklin with the *Terror* and the *Erebus*. Crozier sailed on this last voyage in May 1845. Details of his fate were not known for many years: Crozier took over command on 11 June 1847 when Sir John Franklin died, the ships having been trapped in ice since September 1846, and is estimated to have finally succumbed in late April or May 1848.

## Dampier

WILLIAM DAMPIER was born at East Cocker, Somerset, in May 1652, the son of a tenant farmer, but he was orphaned at an early age and placed with the master of a ship in Weymouth who took him on a voyage to Newfoundland. He subsequently sailed to Bantam in the Dutch East Indies and served in the Dutch War of 1673–1674, but was invalided and put ashore. He served as an under-manager on a plantation in Jamaica, but after six months returned to sea, working mostly in ships engaged in the coastal trade in the Caribbean.

In 1679 he joined a party of buccaneers, crossed the Isthmus of Panama, and went raiding along the coast of Peru. He is recorded as visiting the islands of Juan Fernandez in 1681. He then returned to the Atlantic; in 1683 he fell in with another group of buccaneers in Virginia and sailed with them to the Pacific by way of Cape Horn. The purpose once more was buccaneering along the American coast, but the Spanish were on their guard, and the raiders made for the Galapagos Islands. Further raids on Spanish settlements met with little success, and Dampier joined Captain Swan *(q.v.)* of the aptly named *Cygnet*, whom he persuaded to sail across the Pacific.

With a smaller vessel commanded by the *Cygnet*'s mate, Teat, they sailed from Cape Corrientes, in present-day Colombia, on 31 March 1686, and reached Guam on 20 May. The *Cygnet* went on to Mindanao, where Swan was eventually left behind, Dampier sailing to China, the Spice Islands, and Timor. On 4 January 1688, he reached Australia, the first Englishman to visit the continent. Cygnet Bay in King Sound and Dampier Land in the north of western Australia commemorate his visit. A few weeks were spent along this bleak shore, and then Dampier began to make his way back toward Sumatra and India. He eked out a living by showing a tatooed native whom he took to England with him, arriving there in September 1691.

Resting from his travels, Dampier sold the "Painted Prince" whom he had brought to England and turned to farming, but his main activity was the writing of an account of his adventures, which appeared in 1697 under the title *A New Voyage Round the World*; this was an instant success and made him known to English society and the world of learning.

He used his newly gained influence to obtain command of a voyage of exploration to Australia and the southwestern Pacific. He sailed in the *Roebuck* on 14 January 1699. It was an ill-equipped and poorly crewed ship that took him, nevertheless, by way of the Canaries and Bahia, to western Australia, where he arrived in late July.

They sailed northward to Shark Bay and the group of islands now known as Dampier Archipelago. He put in at Timor for much-needed supplies; on 1 January 1700 he sighted New Guinea. Sailing off its northern coast, he discovered the islands that lie to the northeast; not identifying them as consisting of several large islands, he named them all New Britain. Forced to turn back to Timor by the state of his ship, he passed through Dampier Strait, arriving at Timor in May and going on to Batavia. On the way home the rotten *Roebuck* foundered at Ascension Island in February 1701. Dampier was taken back to England by visiting merchantmen to face a court-martial. Although his reputation as a navigator was unimpaired, he was, probably rightly, judged unfit to command a ship of the Royal Navy.

The success of another book, *A Voyage to New Holland*, and the outbreak of war gave Dampier an opportunity to take up a new command, this time a privateer, the *St. George,* in which he sailed on 30 April 1703 for Kinsale in Ireland, where the *Cinque Ports* joined him, then on to Rio and into the Pacific by way of Cape Horn. On 7 February 1704, Dampier anchored at Juan Fernandez Islands with Captain Stradling of the *Cinque Ports.* French vessels drove them off, and raids on the Spanish-controlled mainland proved abortive. The crews became increasingly dissatisfied, one—Alexander Selkirk *(q.v.)*, who has acquired immortality as the sailor on whom Daniel Defoe modeled his Robinson Crusoe—being left at his request on Juan Fernandez. By the end of the year, the *St. George* was so unseaworthy that Dampier abandoned it and crossed the Pacific in a Spanish ship he had captured. The *Cinque Ports* soon after foundered off the American coast.

When he reached the Dutch East Indies, he was imprisoned as a pirate, having lost the commission that showed him to be a privateer. In time, however, he made his way back to England, where in 1707 he published a *Vindication of his Voyage.*

Dampier sailed to the Pacific once more, not as a captain, but as a pilot to Woodes Rogers *(q.v.)*, who sailed from Bristol on 2 August 1708 and reached Juan Fernandez on 1 February 1709. Alexander Selkirk was still there, but he refused to be taken off until he became convinced that Dampier was not in command. As a privateering cruise, the voyage was more successful than that of the *St. George*, Rogers sailing from the American coast with rich loot in January 1710 and arriving at Guam on 11 March. Dampier was back in England on 14 October 1711.

William Dampier had taken part in four major voyages and had three times circumnavigated the globe. His last years were spent endeavoring to obtain his share of the prize money he felt was due to him, but he died in March 1715 in London in relative poverty.

## Darwin

CHARLES ROBERT DARWIN was born at Shrewsbury, Shropshire, England, on 12 February 1809. He at first studied medicine and theology, but was more attracted by the natural sciences. In 1831 he was appointed naturalist to the *Beagle* expedition under the command of Capt. Robert Fitzroy *(q.v.)*.

They sailed from Portsmouth in December for Cape Verde Islands and entered the Pacific through the Strait of Magellan, surveying the coast of South America and going on to the Galapagos Islands, where young Darwin was greatly impressed by the fauna and was led to speculate on what he later referred to as "the transmutation of species." His interest was also aroused by fossils during his geological observations.

The *Beagle* subsequently crossed the Pacific to Tahiti, New Zealand (where the expedition put in at the Bay of Islands), Australia, Tasmania, Mauritius, Brazil, and the Azores. The voyage ended in October 1836, Charles Darwin then assisting Fitzroy with compiling the *Narrative of the Surveying Voyages of His Majesty's Ships "Adventure" and "Beagle"*, being responsible for the third volume. Darwin became secretary of the Geological Society and worked on his theory of evolution by natural selection and on other natural history projects. Finally, in 1859, having learned that another naturalist was independently arriving at the same conclusions as he, he published his epoch-making work *On the Origin of Species.* He spent the rest of his life expanding on different aspects of his theories. He died at Down, Kent, on 19 April 1882.

## Davis

LITTLE IS KNOWN of Edward Davis' early years. Some believed he was of Flemish birth, but his name is clearly English—unless one prefers the name David, by which many French and Spanish navigators called him, in which case a Low Countries origin is not too improbable.

In 1683 Davis was sailing in the *Batchelor's Delight* in company with a motley group of buccaneers. He was second-in-command to Capt. John Cook, whom he succeeded in July 1684 when Cook suddenly died. From all accounts, including that of William Dampier *(q.v.)*, Davis was an able leader and surprisingly sober and humane for one of his calling, but he was illiterate, and most of what is known about him is second hand.

His claim to fame rests on a report that in 1687, after almost three years spent cruising in Pacific waters and raiding Spanish settlements, Davis sighted a low sandy island at latitude 27°20′ south, with behind it a range of higher land. At the time the *Batchelor's*

*Delight* was on its way from the Galapagos to Juan Fernandez. The longitude remained vague, and Davis Land, as it became known, was sought in vain by a succession of navigators well into the nineteenth century. The land may have been a sighting of the islands of San Felix and San Ambrosio, but the mystery may never be resolved. Indeed Beechey *(q.v.)*, of HMS *Blossom*, speculated that Davis' island might have disappeared in some later cataclysm.

Davis sailed back into the Atlantic by Cape Horn at the end of December 1687 and made for the Caribbean, where the leading buccaneers were imprisoned. He returned to England around 1690, to receive a couple of years later his share of the prize money restored by royal order. He may be the Edward Davis who deserted in Madagascar in 1697 to join Captain Kidd and eventually give evidence against him at the famous pirate's trial.

## Delano

AMASA DELANO was born in Duxbury, Massachusetts, on 21 February 1763. When the American War of Independence broke out he served first in the army, then in 1777 joined the crew of a privateer. He rose rapidly through the ranks, made voyages to the West Indies and Europe, and in March 1790 sailed from Boston as second officer of the *Massachusetts*, a large armed merchantman of 800 tons, 36 guns, on a voyage to the East Indies and China. The *Massachusetts* reached Macao on 30 September, but the enterprise was a commercial disaster, and the ship was sold in Canton.

Delano was left stranded with his fellow officers; he found work repairing a ship damaged in a typhoon and also had an opporunity of sailing to the northwest coast. In April 1791 he was taken on as an officer in the *Panther*, which was accompanied by the smaller *Endeavour*, for a voyage from China to the Palau Islands, which he reached on 9 June, later going on to islands off the western tip of New Guinea and to Amboina. The expedition returned to western New Guinea in the hope of discovering a strait that some believed divided the island. Unsuccessful in this, the expedition crossed over to the north coast of Australia and west to Timor. After a second visit to the Palaus, Delano made for Macao, where the expedition dropped anchor in March 1793.

On 10 November 1799 Delano sailed once more from Boston, in

command of the sealing ship *Perseverance*. Most of his time was spent along the South American coast, among the Galapagos and at Juan Fernandez and Easter islands. He completed a circumnavigation by way of Canton, Mauritius, and the Cape of Good Hope. He was back in Boston on 1 November 1802.

On 25 September 1803 he again took the *Perseverance* into the Pacific, accompanied by his brother Samuel in charge of the schooner *Pilgrim*. Most of 1804 was spent around Tasmania; in October 1804 the two ships sailed for Peru, then went north to the Galapagos and Hawaii before crossing to Macao. They began their return journey in January 1807, reaching Boston on 26 July 1807.

Amasa Delano's fame rests largely on his lively and informative account of his travels, which includes keen observations on the peoples and islands visited: *Narrative of Voyages and Travels in the Northern and Southern Hemispheres, comprising three voyages round the world together with a voyage of survey and discovery in the Pacific Ocean and Oriental Islands* was published in Boston in 1817. Delano died in Boston in 1823.

## Dennett

THOMAS DENNETT was the captain of the transport ship *Britannia*, which sailed from England in late 1796 with a cargo of convicts for the penal colony at Port Jackson, New South Wales. His brutality toward the convicts, which resulted in six deaths, led to his being tried on arrival in Australia and to instructions by the British government for stricter controls on board convict transports, including the appointment of an official representative of the Crown on each ship. Dennett had apparently hoped to settle in New South Wales; he had bought some eighty acres of land, which he named "Woodmancote," in Vaucluse Bay. This purchase is dated 6 July 1797, but soon after, he left for England by way of Canton.

On the way, the *Britannia* came upon four islands in the Marshall group, to which Dennett gave European names. Only one of these, Hunter Island, was a true discovery, the small island of Kili. However, although they had been seen by Spanish navigators in the sixteenth century, Dennett gave the first precise reports on Namu, Lib, and Ailinglapalap.

Thomas Dennett died in London in 1798. He was apparently a

man of substance, of Irish birth, as his will made a number of important bequests of his wife in County Cork and also to his mother and sister. He left the Vaucluse Bay property, which proved to be prime real estate, to the unborn child of Elizabeth Rafferty "left by me pregnant at Sydney."

## Dillon

PETER DILLON was born in Martinique, in the French Caribbean, on 15 June 1788, but was taken to Ireland as a youth. He joined the British Royal Navy and served at the Battle of Trafalgar. In 1806 he sailed to the East, probably in a merchantman, and worked in various ships trading among the Polynesian islands and with Fiji. In 1813 while third officer on the snow *Hunter* he was involved in an affray with some Fijians on a sandalwood-buying expedition. He barely escaped with his life, earning fame for resourcefulness and courage. The height from which he repelled his attackers is still known as Dillon's Rock.

Shortly after his marriage to Mary Moore, the daughter of a Sydney trader, in 1814, he moved to Calcutta, concentrating on trade between Bengal and Australia. In 1822 he bought the brig *Calder*, 200 tons, in which he sailed to Australia, New Zealand, and South America. He seems also to have gone on to the Falkland Islands and possibly Buenos Aires. He sailed back by way of Tahiti, Tonga, Fiji, and the New Hebrides, where he bought sandalwood, reaching Sydney on 25 February 1825. He soon set out once more for Valparaiso, but the *Calder* was lost in a gale off the Chilean coast.

Dillon then turned to the *St. Patrick*, a ship of 430 tons, in which he owned a share. He bought out his partner and took the *St. Patrick* to the Tuamotus, Tahiti, and New Zealand. On his way to Calcutta he put in at Tikopia in the Santa Cruz group, where in 1813 after the Fiji affair he had set ashore two men from the *Hunter* and a Fijian woman. All three were well. One of them offered for sale the silver guard of a sword of European manufacture, obtained from the nearby island of Vanikoro. Dillon rightly assumed that these articles must have come from the wreck of La Pérouse's two ships, which had vanished in 1788. He hurried to Calcutta and showed his evidence to the British authorities, who provided him with a better vessel, the *Research*, for a return voyage to Vanikoro.

Dillon reached the island on 8 September 1827 and collected enough relics to prove beyond all doubt that his assumption had been correct. He took the relics to France, where he was received by King Charles X, who awarded him the Legion of Honor, together with an annuity of 4,000 francs. After publishing an account of his voyage he returned for a time to Sydney, basking deservedly in his fame. Neither Britain nor France, however, gave him an official position—such as a consulship—which he craved and which would have ensured his financial security. He died in relative poverty in Paris on 9 February 1847.

Dillon was an able navigator with a thorough knowledge of the islands and peoples of the Pacific. He was also a larger-than-life character and a great storyteller with the endearing habit of bestowing titles of nobility on the islanders who served under him. His own *Narrative* and the memoirs of men who served under him contain valuable information about Pacific navigation and ethnology.

## Dixon

LITTLE IS KNOWN of George Dixon's early life. He first appears in records in April 1776, when by warrant he joined the *Discovery*, commanded by James Cook *(q.v.)*.

Dixon was back in London in October 1780. He had recognized the potential for trade on America's northwest coast and in August 1784 wrote to Sir Joseph Banks *(q.v.)* suggesting an overland expedition by way of Quebec and the Great Lakes, putting himself forward as guide and astronomer. Nothing came of this proposal, but in the following year he became associated with a group of merchants and Nathaniel Portlock (a shipmate from the *Discovery*) in a trading venture. Richard Etches and Company (known as "The King George Sound Company") obtained a license from the South Sea Company to trade on the northwest coast. Two ships were fitted out: the *King George*, commanded by Portlock, and the *Queen Charlotte*, commanded by Dixon.

The expedition sailed from London on 29 August 1785 and reached Cook Inlet, Alaska, on 19 July 1786. After several weeks of slow trading, Portlock and Dixon went to Hawaii for the winter; in the spring of 1787 they sailed to Prince William Sound, Alaska, where they met John Meares *(q.v.)*, who had spent the winter months there and was in dire need of assistance. They helped him in exchange for his promise not to trade on the northwest coast.

On 14 May Dixon separated from Portlock. In July he identified and named the Queen Charlotte Islands, and soon after this came upon another English trader, James Colnett *(q.v.)*. He then sailed to Hawaii for supplies, arriving among the islands on 5 September. He was eager to leave for China to sell his substantial cargo of furs and left on 18 September from Waimea Bay. He passed through the southern Marianas, past Tinian and Saipan. The *Queen Charlotte* dropped anchor in Macao Roads on 9 November. When Portlock joined him a couple of weeks later, they disposed of their cargo and bought a stock of tea to take back to England. They sailed for home on 9 February 1788, making for the Indian Ocean, but separated for a while in April. Dixon reached England a few weeks after Portlock, dropping anchor off Dover on 17 September 1788.

George Dixon's account of his travels, *A Voyage round the World*, appeared in London in 1789, but it is largely the work of William Beresford, his supercargo. This publication was followed by an exchange of pamphlets with Meares, whose account of his own voyage took credit for the work of others and cast aspersions on Dixon.

George Dixon kept up his interest in the northwest coast and pressed for further explorations and a search for the Northwest Passage, holding discussions with the hydrographer Alexander Dalrymple and endeavoring to enlist the support of Sir Joseph Banks. He was on the point of taking part in a voyage of exploration to Hudson Bay for the Hudson Bay Company, but this came to nothing. He seems instead to have settled in Gosport as a teacher of navigation and was probably the author of *The Navigator's Assistant*, published in London in 1791. His date of death is not known.

## Douglas

WILLIAM DOUGLAS was a merchant captain who became associated with John Meares *(q.v.)* in 1787. In January 1788 in Canton, Meares arranged for the purchase of two ships, the *Felice Adventurer*, to be commanded by himself, and the *Iphigenia* (or *Efigenia*) *Nubiana*, to be commanded by Douglas, both ships sailing under Portuguese colors on 22 January. They reached the Philippines in early February, but as Douglas' vessel was slow and heavy, Meares decided to go on ahead, leaving on 10 February.

Douglas sailed on the twenty-second, and on 9 March discovered, so he believed, a new island, which he named Johnstone's Island, and on 4 April another, which he called Moore's Island. These were not discoveries, but small islands of the large Caroline archipelago. On 5 June Douglas arrived off Cape Trinity in Alaska and shortly after entered Cook Inlet. In July he started down the coast, trading for furs, and joined Meares in Friendly Cove on 27 August, remaining there until 27 October, when he sailed for Hawaii without Meares but in company with Captain Funter's *North-West America.*

Reaching Maui on 7 December, Douglas began a stay of four months, landing his Hawaiian passenger, the chief Kaiana (whom he had brought with him from Canton), and replenishing his stores for a return voyage to the northwest coast.

The *Iphigenia* sailed for the coast of America on 18 March 1789, but by now the Spanish authorities had sent forces to Nootka to put an end to what they considered an infringement of their monopoly rights. When Douglas arrived at Nootka, his ship was seized and part of its cargo confiscated. Douglas protested that he was sailing under the protection of the Portuguese flag and succeeded in obtaining his release. The *Iphigenia* sailed for Macao, arriving on 5 October 1789.

William Douglas died in the latter part of 1791. He had made one true discovery on what was essentially a trading voyage: on 19 March 1789, the day after he left the Hawaiian Islands, he had come upon the uncharted rocky island of Nihoa, northwest of Niihau.

## Downes

JOHN DOWNES was born at Canton, Massachusetts, on 23 December 1784, of a seagoing family. He first went to sea as an assistant to his father, who was serving in the *Constitution.* He was appointed acting midshipman in 1800 and midshipman in 1802. Promoted lieutenant in 1807, he joined David Porter *(q.v.)* in 1809 as first lieutenant of the *Essex* and was involved in a number of campaigns during the 1812 war, capturing and refitting as a privateer the British vessel *Georgina.*

In 1818 Downes was ordered to the *Macedonian,* in which he spent several years cruising in the Pacific. In 1828 he was given the command of the *Potomac* and then with the rank of commodore headed the United States Pacific station. The Pacific cruise of the *Potomac,* which lasted from 1831 to 1834, was recorded by Downes' secretary, Jeremiah N. Reynolds, and published in New York in 1835 under the title *Voyage of the United States Frigate "Potomac" during the circumnavigation of the globe.* An account by Francis Warriner appeared in Boston in the same year.

John Downes ended his sea service with this major voyage, turning to shore duties and becoming commander of the Boston naval yard. He died at Charlestown, Massachusetts, on 11 August 1854.

## Drake

FRANCIS DRAKE was born near Tavistock, in Devonshire, in the 1540s (possibly as early as 1540 or as late as 1545), the son of a tenant farmer who may have seen some service as a sailor. Apprenticed to a mariner at an early age, by 1567 Francis Drake was master of his own ship, the *Judith,* in which he sailed with John Hawkins to the Gulf of Mexico on a slave-trading voyage that ended in disastrous failure. Drake was more fortunate with two voyages to the Caribbean in 1570 and 1571. On the third occasion, sailing in May 1572, he traveled across the Isthmus of Panama far enough to catch a glimpse of the Pacific Ocean.

Having built up a reputation as an able commander and an efficient privateer, Drake was secretly commissioned by Queen Elizabeth I to lead an expedition against the Spanish colonies on the Pacific seaboard of America. He sailed from Plymouth on 13 December 1577 with five ships and 166 men. Two ships were abandoned in the Plate River estuary; the other three struggled through the Strait of Magellan from 20 August to 6 September 1578, emerging into a wild Pacific gale. One ship disappeared, another returned to England. Only Drake's *Golden Hind,* blown far to the south, was left to carry on. Drake sighted a southern land but whether the "Elizabethides" were isolated islands or a first sighting of Cape Horn no one can say for certain.

The lonely ship sailed northward, raiding Valparaiso and other settlements along the coast and collecting a rich booty, until there were no more Spanish outposts to be seen. After April 1579 the Spanish were free of the *Golden Hind:* it was sailing beyond California toward Oregon and possibly got as far north as Vancouver Island, in the hope of finding a northwest passage that might lead back to the Atlantic and England. There was none, and Drake put in to what may have been San Francisco Bay to careen his ship in preparation for the voyage home which, with the entire coast of Central and South America on the lookout for his loot-laden ship, could now only be by way of the East. Drake, well received by the local Indians, claimed northern California for England, naming it New Albion.

On 23 July 1579 he set sail, heading westward across the Pacific. There was no landfall until 30 September, when he fell in with islands at 8° to 9° north latitude. Although Drake, from the thievish disposition of the natives, believed that he had come to Magellan's Ladrones, they were probably some of the Palau Islands. A fortnight later, the *Golden Hind* reached Mindanao, sailed on to the Celebes (where it narrowly escaped being wrecked on a reef), continued to southern Java, and began the long haul home by way of the Cape of Good Hope and Sierra Leone. Drake entered Plymouth harbor on 26 September 1580 to a triumphant welcome. The booty he had brought with him enabled Queen Elizabeth to pay off England's foreign debt. Not surprisingly, she knighted him on board the *Golden Hind.*

Late in 1585 Drake sailed again with a large fleet to the West Indies and later earned greater fame when he masterminded the defeat of the Spanish Armada. Further ventures were less successful, however. He died of dysentery on his last voyage to the Caribbean, on 23 January 1596, and was buried at sea.

He had married Mary Newman in 1569. She died in 1583. His second wife was Elizabeth, daughter of Sir George Sydenham. Neither wife bore him any children.

## Du Bouzet

JOSEPH-FIDÈLE-EUGÈNE DU BOUZET was born of a noble family in Paris on 19 December 1805. After studying at the École Navale, he joined the expedition of Hyacinthe de Bougainville *(q.v.),* sailing from Brest in the *Thétis* on 2 March 1824 for Manila, Macao, Indochina, and Australia, returning to France on 24 June 1826 by way of Cape Horn. He served in the Mediterranean and along the coast of Algeria. On 7 September 1837 he sailed for a second voyage to the Pacific in the *Zélée* under Dumont d'Urville *(q.v.)*; he was now a lieutenant. The expedition ended in Toulon on 6 November 1840.

On 23 March 1841 he took over the *Allier*, in which he sailed to New Zealand, arriving on 7 November. At the request of the Catholic bishop Pompallier, Charles Lavaud *(q.v.)*, the French representative in New Zealand, sent du Bouzet to the island of Futuna to bring back the remains of the missionary Peter Chanel. Du Bouzet, escorting Pompallier in the *Sancta Maria*, reached Futuna on 18 January 1842 and left two days later, going back to Akaroa, New Zealand, where he arrived on 13 February 1842. He then transferred to the *Aube*, Lavaud intending to return to France in the *Allier*. Du Bouzet himself set off for France on the *Aube* in March 1842.

On 26 October 1845 du Bouzet sailed from Brest in command of the *Brillante*. He sailed for Valparaiso by way of Tenerife and Rio, then began a slow voyage along the American seaboard of Callao, Monterey, and Acapulco, and back to Valparaiso. He sailed from there on 23 February 1847 and called briefly at Callao before setting out for Tahiti, Samoa, Tonga, Wallis, and Rotuma, then going to Honolulu. In August he was in New Caledonia, where he rescued a group of French missionaries who were under attack by the islanders; he took them to Sydney, where he spent the period 11 September to 4 October. His return journey took him to New Zealand and back to Valparaiso; he carried out further missions along the coast, to Coquimbo, Paita, and Guayaquil, before setting off for Rio, which he left to sail to France on 27 April 1849.

In 1851–1853 he commanded the Levant naval station, with the *Pandore* and the *Gomez*. Then in March 1854 he was appointed governor of French Oceania. He sailed in the *Aventure*, called at Tahiti, and went on to New Caledonia, where his ship was wrecked on the Isle of Pines during the night of 28–29 April 1855. He was forced to return to France for a court-martial, was acquitted, and sailed back to Tahiti in October 1856. After completing his term in 1858, he was promoted to rear admiral and transferred to command the naval forces in Algeria and subsequently, in 1860–1863, the French naval station in Brazil. He died on 22 September 1867.

## Duclos-Guyot

SECOND-IN-COMMAND of Louis de Bougainville *(q.v.)* both during his expedition to the Falkland Islands in 1763 and on his voyage around the world in 1766–1769, Nicolas Pierre Duclos-Guyot was born in St. Malo, Brittany, on 12 December 1722 and entered the service of the French India Company at the age of 12. He displayed outstanding qualities and by 1743 was promoted to lieutenant.

When the war of the Austrian Succession broke out he served in a number of privateers, after which, in 1749–1755, he went on a lengthy commercial voyage to the Pacific coast of South America. The Seven Years War saw him returning to the command of privateers and soon obtaining a commission in the navy. In 1759 he sailed to Canada, where he met Bougainville, distinguishing himself in various engagements and in a bold action in the St. Lawrence River, for which he was promoted to fireship captain.

After his two voyages with Bougainville, he commanded a number of merchant ships on voyages to China and India. Finally, in 1776, opportunities opened up for him in the navy. He became the port captain of Mauritius in 1778, received the Order of St. Louis, and in 1781 commanded the *Osterlay* on a voyage to Buenos Aires. He retired on a pension as full lieutenant in 1784 but was recalled to active service in 1792 for an expedition to Santo Domingo. He died near St. Malo on 10 March 1794.

## Du Fresne

MARC-JOSEPH MARION DU FRESNE (or Dufresne) was born in May 1724 in St. Malo, Brittany, into a family of local merchants who had associations with the seaborne trade. He entered the French India Company's service at the age of 11 and during the War of the Austrian Succession commanded various privateers operating from St. Malo.

After Culloden he was sent to Scotland to bring back the defeated Young Pretender, Charles Edward. This mission completed, he served in the French navy; he was taken prisoner in 1747. After the war he returned to the India Company, sailing to the Indian Ocean and China. When war broke out again he served in Brittany, much of the time outwitting the British who were blockading the coast; he was also called in as adviser on a proposal to effect a landing of French troops in Scotland. He attained the rank of fireship captain in 1759 and was made a Knight of the Order of St. Louis in 1761.

He then returned to trading in eastern waters, carried out hydrographic surveys in French Mauritius, and acted for a time as harbormaster in Port Louis, where he settled, trading with the Seychelles and India and speculating in land. The liquidation of the French India Company caused him some financial difficulties, and he welcomed the opportunity in 1771 of setting off for the Pacific with two naval vessels on a voyage that was to combine trade with exploration.

The primary purpose of the expedition was to return the Tahitian, Ahu-toru, to his homeland. Ahu-toru had been taken to France by Bougainville (q.v.) in 1768 and after being lionized in Paris had been sent to Mauritius in the hope of finding a passage on some Pacific-bound vessel. Marion du Fresne was provided with the *Mascarin* and the *Marquis de Castries.* He sailed from Port Louis on 18 October 1771, going to the nearby islands of Bourbon (Réunion) and Madagascar to take on supplies and also to get away from an epidemic of smallpox ravaging Mauritius. Nevertheless, smallpox killed Ahu-toru and removed the need to sail for Tahiti. Du Fresne endeavored to recoup some of the costs of the expedition by sailing to Capetown and then started a search for the southern continent in high latitudes. He discovered various islands in the southern Indian Ocean—Marion Island, Prince Edward Island, the Crozets—spent several days in Tasmania, and went on to New Zealand.

He sighted Mt. Taranaki on 25 March 1772, naming it Pic Mascarin, and sailed north as far as Spirits Bay, where a gale later caused severe damage to the vessels and the loss of several anchors. On 4 May the expedition anchored in the Bay of Islands. The next five weeks were spent exploring the bay and repairing the ships. This leisurely stay enabled the French to explore the coast, to trade, and to set up camps ashore.

Communication with the Maoris was made possible by the use of an extensive Tahitian vocabulary prepared by Bougainville and Ahu-toru. There were occasional incidents related to thefts, but nothing occurred to mar friendly relations until 12 June, when du Fresne went ashore with a fishing party. All were suddenly attacked and killed. A second party was similarly attacked the following day. In all, twenty-five officers and men lost their lives. Du Fresne's second-in-command, Crozet *(q.v.)*, and the captain of the *Marquis de Castries*, set about immediately to secure the ships, abandoning the camps and fighting off minor raids.

The French ships were unable to depart promptly, as repairs were incomplete and timber at an inland camp could not be retrieved. They sailed on 13 July for the central Pacific and the Philippines.

The reasons for the killing of Marion du Fresne may never be known. The local Maoris were overrun by a rival tribe a few years later, and no reliable traditions survived. It is likely that the French transgressed in some way, until it became imperative to get rid of them: a stay of five weeks with no clear signs of an early departure created serious economic and cultural strains. And if the local Maoris feared a permanent French settlement, intertribal politics would have exacerbated the situation.

The stay, remarkable for its length and the closeness of the contacts established between the visitors and the indigenous people, produced many pages of records of early Maori life. Marion du Fresne's own journals have not so far been found, but there are extensive notes in the logs and records of his officers, as well as charts and drawings.

The events of July 1772 strengthened the view held in France that New Zealand was a country inhabited by dangerous natives and so was unsuitable for colonization.

## Duhaut-Cilly

AUGUSTE BERNARD DUHAUT-CILLY was born on 26 March 1790 at St. Malo, Brittany. After a brilliant and lively career during the Napoleonic wars, starting in 1807, he sailed for a time in the Indian Ocean under the famous privateer Robert Surcouf. He then transferred to the merchant navy. He was given command of the *Héros*, a small merchantman, which left Le Havre on 10 April 1826.

He reached Rio in May, turned Cape Horn in July, and dropped anchor at Valparaiso on 3 August. He spent many months trading along the California coast with limited success. Competition was severe and duties prohibitive. In October 1827 Duhaut-Cilly was back in Peru; he then went back to Monterey, to the Russian settlement of Bodega near San Francisco, to Santa Barbara, and to San

Diego. He decided to make for Hawaii, which he reached in September 1828. He sailed on 15 November for Canton, where he arrived on 26 December; after a stay of three months he sailed home by way of Sunda Strait, Reunion, and St. Helena; he was back in Le Havre on 19 July 1829.

Duhaut-Cilly was an educated man with a rare gift for literary descriptions, and his work *Voyage autour du Monde, principalement à la Californie et aux îles Sandwich*, which he wrote on his return and which was published in two volumes in 1834, enjoyed a well-deserved success.

He died at St. Servan, near his native town, on 26 October 1849.

## Dumont d'Urville

JULES-SÉBASTIEN-CÉSAR DUMONT D'URVILLE was born at Condé-sur-Noireau, Normandy, on 25 May 1790, the son of a district judge. After his father's death, he was brought up by his mother and her brother, the Abbé de Croisilles. He joined the navy in 1807, but saw little service, as the British navy was blockading French ports. He married in 1816 Adèle Pépin, daughter of a Toulon watchmaker, whom his mother considered so beneath him that she refused ever to meet her daughter-in-law.

In 1819 he had the opportunity to join the *Chevrette*, which was about to carry out hydrographic work in the Mediterranean. He was instrumental in arranging the purchase by France of the Venus de Milo, which a peasant on the Greek island of Melos had just unearthed. For this he received the Légion d'Honneur and promotion to the rank of lieutenant; his scientific work earned him membership of the Linnean Society and the Société de Géographie. He was also selected to take part in the voyage of the *Coquille*, commanded by L. I. Duperrey *(q.v.)*.

On his return in 1825 Dumont d'Urville was promoted to commander and given the *Coquille*, renamed for the occasion *Astrolabe*, for a return voyage of exploration in Pacific waters. His energy and his daring transformed the expedition into a major undertaking, far superior in importance to Duperrey's. He sailed from Toulon on 25 April 1826, making for Tenerife, the Cape Verde Islands, Trinidade, the Cape of Good Hope, and King George Sound in southwestern Australia, which he reached on 7 October. Arriving in Port Jackson,

New South Wales, on 2 December, he discovered that his survey of uninhabited bays had aroused suspicion about possible French colonization plans. He stayed only nineteen days, then made for New Zealand to explore parts of the coast that James Cook *(q.v.)* had not surveyed in detail. He spent from 11 January to 22 March 1827 on this work, discovering French Pass and d'Urville Island and sailing into what was to become Auckland Harbour. His route next took him to Tonga, Fiji, New Ireland, and New Britain, and by way of northern New Guinea back to the Australian continent. This time he gave Port Jackson a miss, preferring to anchor in Hobart.

The final part of his voyage took him to Vanikoro, where La Pérouse had been wrecked. After erecting a monument to La Pérouse's memory, he began his journey home by way of Guam, the Carolines, Batavia, Mauritius, and Capetown. The *Astrolabe* finally dropped anchor in Marseilles on 25 February 1829.

The hydrographic and scientific results of the expedition were impressive. Thousands of natural history specimens and drawings were handed over to the authorities, but d'Urville felt that official recognition was slow and inadequate. His proud and abrupt manner did not help his case. In 1830 he was asked to command the ships that conveyed the deposed Charles X to exile in England. He then applied himself to overseeing the publication of accounts of the *Astrolabe* expedition, but by 1835 he was practically in retirement. Finally, he was placed in charge of a new expedition, this time with two ships, the *Astrolabe* once again and the *Zélée*. He sailed from Toulon on 7 September 1837.

The expedition was to concentrate on the Antarctic regions, which were now attracting attention. The two ships sailed south to Port Famine in the Strait of Magellan, then to the South Shetlands and the South Orkneys. The tip of the Antarctic peninsula was named Louis Philippe Land, after the King of France, other names—Adélaïde, Joinville—also honored the royal family. After more than three months of arduous exploration d'Urville left this inhospitable area for Talcahuano, in Chile, where the expedition anchored on 6 April. D'Urville next went on to the Marquesas, Tahiti, Fiji, Vanikoro once more, and Guam, arriving on 1 January 1839. The following months were spent among the Dutch islands. After a call in Hobart, the two ships sailed back to the Antarctic, where Adélie Land was discovered and named after d'Urville's wife. The homeward journey took him back to Hobart and on to New Zealand, then through Torres Strait to the Indian Ocean and St. Helena. The expedition reached Toulon on 6 November 1840, again bringing back thousands of natural history specimens and artists' drawings.

D'Urville, his wife, and their only surviving son were killed in a railway accident near Paris on 8 May 1842.

## Duperrey

LOUIS-ISIDOR (ISIDORE) DUPERREY was born in Paris on 21 October 1786; he joined the navy at the age of 17, sailing as a novice in the *Vulcain*, then in the *Républicain*, mostly operating off the coast of Brittany. In 1809 as a sublieutenant he served in various ships in the Mediterranean and was appointed to the expedition of Freycinet *(q.v.)*, during which he carried out useful survey work. On his return in 1820 he was promoted to full lieutenant and awarded the Cross of St. Louis.

With the help of Dumont d'Urville *(q.v.)* he planned a voyage of exploration to the Pacific, which received government approval in November 1821. He was allocated the *Coquille*, a corvette of 380 tons, and sailed from Toulon on 11 August 1822.

The route took the expedition to Tenerife, Trinidade, and Brazil, which, having just proclaimed its independence from Portugal, was naturally suspicious of the arrival of a European warship. The *Coquille* obtained some stores and left on 30 October for the Falklands, where the remains of Freycinet's ship, *Uranie*, which had struck a submerged rock close to the shore, were still visible. Cape Horn was turned on 31 December; on 20 January 1823 the *Coquille* dropped anchor in Talcahuano, Chile. Duperrey then sailed to Peru, carrying out hydrographic surveys off the coast.

The crossing of the Pacific from east to west took the French to the Tuamotus, where they discovered the island of Reao, then to Tahiti, where they anchored on 2 May, finding to their astonishment that this renowned South Seas paradise was turning into a strict, puritanical society ruled by fundamentalist English missionaries. Duperrey sailed from Matavai Bay on the twenty-second, going on to Bora Bora. On 9 July he finally left the island group, making for the southwest toward Tonga, intending to go to Port Jackson, but this was not to be. Storms and mountainous seas forced him northward toward the Santa Cruz Islands and the Solomons.

On 9 August the *Coquille* was in sight of Bougainville Island, and a couple of days later it was possible to anchor in Port Praslin in New Ireland. It was a much-needed pause in the strenuous voyage, as a number of men were sick and exhausted. On 21 August the *Coquille* sailed away, continuing on a westerly course toward Waigeo, Caieli, and Amboina. Cholera was ravaging the Dutch colony, and Duperrey sailed as soon as he could to Timor and into the Indian Ocean, rounding the Australian continent to make once more for Port Jackson, which he reached on 17 January 1824. He stayed in New South Wales until 24 March, leaving for New Zealand with five passengers, including the missionary George Clarke.

The stay in the Bay of Islands lasted from the fourth to the seventeenth of April and produced valuable data on early New Zealand. The *Coquille* then sailed toward the Fijis, but only Rotuma was sighted on the thirtieth. Of greater interest was the ship's passage through the little-known Gilbert and Ellice islands in May and through the Carolines in June. A group of islands was seen that did not appear on the charts; they were named the Îles Duperrey, another island receiving the name of d'Urville: they were Mokil and Losap-nama, possibly new sightings but more probably sighted by Spanish navigators in the sixteenth century.

In July, Duperrey sailed south again, toward New Guinea and the Dutch East Indies. Passing through Sunda Strait on 17 September 1824, he made for Mauritius and home, reaching Marseilles on 24 March 1825 after thirty-one months of navigation. He was promoted to frigate captain, received the Legion of Honor in 1836, and was elected to the Academy of Science in 1842. He wrote numerous papers on hydrography and physical geography. Duperrey's contributions to science during and after his voyage of exploration justify as much as did the voyage of the *Coquille* the reputation he enjoyed for the remainder of his life. He died on 10 September 1865.

## Dupetit-Thouars

ABEL AUBERT DUPETIT-THOUARS was born in August 1793 at Turquant, near Saumur, France, of a well-to-do family with naval links. He joined the navy in 1804 and served in the North Sea and in the Mediterranean during the Napoleonic wars, by the end of which he became an *enseigne*. Four years later he was promoted to lieutenant and to frigate captain in 1826. He took part in the Algerian campaign and remained as naval adviser on coastal defenses until he was sent to the Pacific in the *Griffon* to join the French naval station protecting the American seaboard. He was made a full captain in 1835.

In 1836 he was appointed to command an expedition to the Pacific to look after French commercial and political interests. He sailed in the *Vénus* from Brest on 29 December 1836 for Rio and Cape Horn. He sailed south to well below Staten Land and emerged into the Pacific in early April 1837, dropping anchor in Valparaiso on the twenty-sixth. Storms kept him there until mid-May, when he sailed for Callao. On 14 June he left for Hawaii, carrying out hydrographic work on the way, and put in at Honolulu on 8 July.

A bitter and complex struggle was going on between French missionaries and traders and the Hawaiian rulers, backed by American missionaries. Dupetit-Thouars found himself cooperating with Captain Belcher *(q.v.)* of the *Sulphur* in upholding the claims of French and English nationals. The dispute was settled at least temporarily but with some acrimony, and on the twenty-fourth both captains sailed away, Dupetit-Thouars making for Kamchatka. He arrived at Petropavlovsk on 31 August 1837 and left on 16 September for the Aleutians searching for islands that appeared on a number of charts but did not in fact exist. This work completed, he made for California, anchoring in Monterey Bay on 18 October. Supplies were scarce and even water was difficult to obtain after a long summer drought. Dupetit-Thouars sailed on 14 November to carry out survey work along the coast down to Acapulco, which he reached in early January.

A fortnight later, the *Vénus* left for Easter Island, where the French spent several days before turning back to Valparaiso by way of Juan Fernandez. They remained there from 18 March to 28 April 1838, then sailed to Callao, Paita, the Galapagos, and the Marquesas, where Dupetit-Thouars, arriving on 2 August, carried out a detailed survey. The next stop was Tahiti, where the situation was even more tense than at Hawaii. He anchored on 28 August and on 9 September was joined by Dumont d'Urville *(q.v.)* with the *Zélée* and the *Astrolabe*. When they left, in mid-September, the problems appeared to be resolved. Dupetit-Thouars went on to the Cook Islands, Rarotonga, and New Zealand, putting in at the Bay of Islands on 13 October.

Their stay lasted until 11 November, when the *Vénus* sailed for

New South Wales. After three weeks in Sydney, Dupetit-Thouars sailed for home, by way of Cape Leeuwin, Mauritius, and the Cape. The *Vénus* ended its voyage at Brest on 24 June 1839.

Dupetit-Thouars, a rear admiral after 1841, sailed back to the Pacific to take charge of the French Pacific naval station. In 1842 the Tahiti problem came to a head. Dupetit-Thouars arrived in September in the *Reine Blanche* to bring Tahiti under French protection. This move was only a temporary solution, and Dupetit-Thouars returned the following year to proclaim French sovereignty.

His term in Oceania ended in 1844. He returned to France, was raised to the rank of vice-admiral in 1846, and became a member of the Admiralty Council in 1849, the same year in which he entered the French parliament. He died in Paris on 16 March 1864.

## Eaton

JOHN EATON, about whose early life little is known, was captain of the *St. Nicholas*, which he had fitted out in London in 1683 for the purpose of raiding Spanish settlements in the Pacific. He first raided the Atlantic coast of South America, then turned Cape Horn in March 1684. He put in at Juan Fernandez in April with John Cook and Edward Davis *(qq.v.)* of the *Batchelor's Delight*. After six months of limited success along the South American coast, Eaton and Davis parted.

Taking four hundred sacks of flour as his share of the prize and the buccaneer William Ambrose Cowley *(q.v.)* as his master, Eaton sailed away on 2 September 1684. Further attempts at piracy off the coast having failed, he sailed on 22 December for Guam. Scurvy ravaged the crew, but eventually, on 15 March, the *St. Nicholas* reached Guam. After spending five weeks recuperating and reprovisioning the ship, Eaton and Cowley sailed for the Ladrones group (Marianas) and Canton, where they arrived in May. The rest of the year was spent in the East Indies until the *St. Nicholas* reached Timor, where the buccaneers split up and went their separate ways.

Eaton is recorded as having been in Batavia in March 1686 and eventually making his way back to England.

## Ebrill

THOMAS EBRILL was an English trader active in the central Pacific from the 1820s. He married Eleanor Henry, sister of Samuel Pinder Henry *(q.v.)*, with whom he developed a sugar cane plantation in Tahiti. In April 1826 he brought the first cargo of sandalwood to Sydney in the *Minerva*. A second shipment of twenty-eight tons, probably from the New Hebrides area, was taken to Sydney in 1827. Thereafter Ebrill went pearl fishing in the Tuamotus. As trade developed in the Pacific, he engaged in various enterprises until his death on 2 November 1842 at the Isle of Pines, New Caledonia, when he was attacked by Melanesians, his crew killed, and his brig, the *Star*, burned.

Thomas Ebrill was credited with discoveries made in the Tuamotus in 1833, especially in the Actaeon Islands, but the records are very imprecise and most, if not all, of the Actaeon group had been sighted by Quiros *(q.v.)*.

## Edwards

EDWARD EDWARDS was born in England in 1741 and joined the Royal Navy in the mid-1750s. He was involved in a number of campaigns, gaining wide experience and rising to post-captain in 1781. He earned a reputation as a strict disciplinarian, if lacking in imagination and initiative, and was chosen as particularly suitable to command the *Pandora*, a 24-gun frigate, for a voyage to the Pacific to seek and to bring home the mutineers of the *Bounty*.

Edwards sailed from Portsmouth on 7 November 1790 for Cape Horn and the southeastern Pacific. His route took him toward Easter Island and the Tuamotu archipelago, passing well to the north of Pitcairn Island, where a number of the mutineers had sought refuge. On 16 March 1791 he reached Ducie Island and shortly after discovered a low island, which he named Carysfort; it is Tureia in the Tuamotus. Edwards pressed on to Tahiti and was successful in capturing a number of mutineers whom he incarcerated in an iron cage built on deck, the infamous "*Pandora's* box."

Leaving Tahiti on 9 May for Aitutaki and Palmerston in the northern Cook Islands, he sailed on to the Tokelau group, landing on 12

June on an island he called Duke of Clarence's Island; this was Nukunonu, a discovery. He then pressed on to the Samoas, where he became separated from the accompanying schooner *Resolution*, commanded by Oliver *(q.v.)*. On 8 August he came upon a lonely island, which he named Grenville Island; this was another discovery, Rotuma. Four days later, two small islands were added to the list, Mitre and Cherry, which are Fataka and Anuta, lying to the west of the Santa Cruz group. On the previous day, he had sailed past the danger known as Pandora Reef.

He then sighted Vanikoro, part of the Santa Cruz Islands. It was known, having been reported on by early Spanish voyagers and by Carteret *(q.v.)*, but unfortunately Edwards failed to land there or even sail close to it; had he done so he would in all probability have solved the problem of the lost expedition of La Pérouse *(q.v.)* and rescued survivors of the wreck that had occurred a mere three years earlier. All Edwards did was to name it Pitt's Island.

He sailed on into Torres Strait to be wrecked in his turn: the *Pandora* struck a reef on 28 August and sank within hours, Edwards making no attempt to save the mutineers imprisoned in their cage. Those who survived owed their lives to officers of the stricken ship.

The expedition took to the boats and made its way to the Dutch East Indies, where it found Oliver and the *Resolution*. The journey home was completed through the assistance of the Dutch and eventually in the British vessel *Gorgon*, which dropped anchor in England on 20 June 1792.

Captain Edwards was acquitted at the court-martial that followed the loss of the *Pandora* and resumed active service, although a substantial part of British public opinion cast a severe judgment on his harshness and his inhumanity toward the mutineers, some of whom were acquitted. He was promoted to rear admiral in 1799 and died in 1815.

## Egui

BERNADO DE EGUI (sometimes referred to as de Guia) was a Spanish captain, commanding the *Santo Domingo de Guzman*, who sailed from Guam in early 1712. On 6 February he came upon an uncharted island, which he named Los Garbanzos. It was Ulithi in the Carolines.

Little else is known about Egui, whose voyage is first referred to in the writings of the Spanish missionary Juan Antonio Cantova, who visited the Carolines in 1722.

## Elcano

JUAN SEBASTIÁN ELCANO (or del Cano) was born in 1476 in the Basque town of Guetaria, Spain. He sailed with Magellan *(q.v.)* and after his leader's death brought the *Victoria* back to Seville, thus completing the first circumnavigation of the globe.

Elcano had had a brush with death during the early part of Magellan's voyage, on the occasion of an abortive mutiny at Port San Julian, southern Argentina, when the mutineers placed him in reluctant command of the *San Antonio.* He was sentenced to death along with a number of others, but not executed. When Magellan was killed in the Moluccas, Elcano took charge of the *Victoria*, sailing to Tidore, Timor, and Europe. He proved himself an able commander, struggling against a severe shortage of provisions and inimical Portuguese, and finally dropped anchor in Seville on 8 September 1522.

He set out for the Pacific a second time in July 1525 as chief pilot on the expedition of Loaysia *(q.v.)*. Unhappily, the *Sancti Spiritus*, in which he sailed, was wrecked at the Cape of the Eleven Thousand Virgins at the entrance to the Strait of Magellan in early 1526. He survived and was able to transfer to the flagship *Santa Maria de la Victoria*, taking over when Loaysia died on 30 July 1526. However, he too died, on 4 August 1526, somewhere in the mid-Pacific.

## Entrecasteaux

JOSEPH-ANTOINE BRUNY D'ENTRECASTEAUX was born in Aix-en-Provence in November 1737. The family belonged to the higher level of the French public service, and when he joined the navy in 1734 he was breaking with tradition. Well-connected, he was soon promoted to *enseigne* (sublieutenant) and in 1770 to lieutenant. He served in the Mediterranean, especially in the Levant, and in the Atlantic, taking part in the American War of Independence.

He had obtained his own command in 1777 and attained the rank of post-captain in 1779. He was appointed assistant director of ports and arsenals four years later, but a ghoulish murder committed by his nephew forced him to seek a post abroad. He went to the Indian Ocean as commander of the French naval station and later governor of the French Indian Ocean colonies.

It was during this period that he sailed to Canton in the *Résolution* and the *Subtile* against the prevailing monsoon winds, a near-impossible task he carried out without loss. In 1791 he was promoted to rear admiral and selected to lead an expedition in search of the overdue ships of La Pérouse *(q.v.)*. He was given command of two vessels, the *Recherche* and the *Espérance*, with instructions to carry out extensive hydrographic and scientific work in addition to looking for the lost expedition among the myriad islands of the southwest Pacific. The task was daunting enough, but it was further complicated by the revolutionary mood of a number of scientists and officers aboard.

D'Entrecasteaux sailed from Brest on 29 September 1791, making for Tenerife, Capetown, and Tasmania. Extensive surveys were made along the south coast of Tasmania, where he spent almost six weeks before going on to New Caledonia, the Solomons, and the Dutch West Indies. The confused situation back in Europe resulted in a cool reception by the authorities, who reluctantly supplied him with water and food. After a week, d'Entrecasteaux went on to Timor, sighted on 19 October 1792, and south toward Cape Leeuwin at the southwest tip of Australia. He sailed along the south coast of the continent, discovering the Recherche Archipelago and Espérance Bay in December. By early January 1793 supplies were so low that he was forced to give up this highly productive exploration and make once again for Tasmania. Thus he was robbed of the opportunity of discovering Bass Strait, the existence of which he had deduced.

The two ships arrived in Recherche Bay, Tasmania, on 21 January 1793, thus completing a full circle around Australia. The channel named after d'Entrecasteaux during their first visit was further explored, the charts were revised and improved, and friendly relations were established with the natives. As no Tasmanian aborigines survive, reports brought back by the French are now invaluable anthropological documents. The ships sailed out on 27 February making for New Zealand, north of which a new archipelago, the Kermadec group, was discovered, and Tonga. They continued to

New Caledonia, the Loyalty Islands, and the Santa Cruz Islands. It was here that the French sighted Vanikoro, where La Pérouse had in fact been wrecked and where a few survivors might still have been living, but they did not stop or land. By this time, the expedition was severely affected by sickness and exhaustion. D'Entrecasteaux went on to explore part of the Solomons and the islands east of New Guinea, but on 20 July he died as the expedition was wending its way back to the Dutch East Indies. Kermadec, who commanded the *Espérance*, had died earlier.

The expedition limped into the port of Caieli, on Buru, on 3 September 1793 and eventually made its way to Surabaya, where political friction among the French and the uncooperative attitude of the Dutch brought about its final disintegration. Many of the documents and specimens brought back by the expedition, although sent on to France, were intercepted by the English and not released for some years.

Although the collapse of the expedition overshadowed its achievements, these were considerable and eventually gained international recognition.

## Erskine

JOHN ELPHINSTONE ERSKINE was born at Cardross, Perthshire, on 13 July 1806 of a distinguished Scottish family. He entered the navy on 6 May 1819 and served from 1826 in various ships until he obtained his first command, that of the *Arachne* in 1829. The following year he transferred to the *Grasshopper* and in 1836 the *Harlequin* on a tour of duty in the Mediterranean. He was promoted to captain in June 1838 and on 6 August 1841 became flag captain of the *Illustrious* on the North America and West Indies station. He was back in England in 1845.

He was appointed captain of the *Havannah* on 24 February 1848 and sailed to the East Indies. In 1849 the governor of New Zealand, Sir George Grey, asked him to undertake a survey of the southwest Pacific. Erskine sailed from the Bay of Islands on 25 June 1849 and made for Niue, Samoa, Tonga, Fiji, and the New Hebrides (Vanuatu). The *Havannah* continued on to the Loyalty Islands, to New Caledonia and its offshore Isle of Pines, and then to New South Wales for rest and repairs, reaching Sydney on 7 October. Erskine returned to New Zealand the following year, completing his mission by way of New Caledonia, the Solomons, and Vanuatu. He wrote an account of this voyage, supplying valuable ethnographic information, under the title *Journal of a Cruise among the Islands of the Western Pacific*, published in 1853.

The *Havannah* spent 1851 as part of the Australia station. Erskine then returned to England and after a period of active service took command of the *Monarch* for a cruise to the Baltic; in 1855–1856 he commanded the *Orion* in North America and the West Indies. He became a rear admiral in 1857 and a vice-admiral in 1864. In the following year he entered the House of Commons as Member for Stirlingshire, a constituency he represented until 1874. He retired from the navy in 1873 and died in London on 23 June 1887.

## Espinosa

GONZALO GOMEZ DE ESPINOSA (or Espinoza) sailed with Magellan *(q.v.)* as *alguacil mayor* (senior constable) of the fleet. After the death of Magellan on 27 April 1521, Espinosa took over command of the *Trinidad* and soon overall command of the expedition. With the *Victoria*, the *Trinidad* proceeded through the Sulu archipelago to the south of Mindanao and reached Tidore in the Moluccas on 8 November 1521. The *Victoria* was able in time to continue the journey; but the *Trinidad*, an unseaworthy vessel, was unable to set sail until April 1522. Attempts to get to America failed, and Espinosa was forced to return to the Moluccas, which by now were under the full control of the rival Portuguese. The ship and the cargo were seized, the men arrested and put to work building a fort at Ternate. The impounded *Trinidad* foundered not long after.

Eventually, Espinosa and three others were released and made their way back to Spain to face litigation and poverty.

Espinosa discovered a number of islands: the Sonsorol Islands on the western fringe of the Carolines on 6 May 1522, the island of Agrigan (less probably, Asuncion) in the northern Marianas on 11 June, and later, the Maug Islands in the same area, where he was able to effect a landing. On this latter occasion, one of his men deserted and some four years later managed to make his way to Guam.

## Fanning

EDMUND FANNING was born in Stonington, Connecticut, on 16 July 1769. He was well connected, one of his uncles being a British general. He was at one time offered a commission in the Royal Navy, which he declined, preferring to throw in his lot with the American colonists.

He went to sea at the age of 14, working on a coaster. By the age of 22 he was first mate aboard a sealing vessel, the *Betsey*, bound for the South Shetlands. In 1793 he obtained his first command, a West Indian brig. Then, in 1797 he sailed from New York in the *Betsey*, this time in command, bound for the Pacific. He turned Cape Horn toward the end of the year, obtained a cargo of seal furs in January, February, and March on Masafuera Island, and made for the Marquesas, where he rescued an unsuccessful missionary, William Crooke. But Crooke, having barely escaped with his life on Tahuata, was made welcome by the people of Nuku Hiva, and Fanning left him there when he sailed on 29 May 1798 for China.

In the lonely mid-Pacific he came upon an uncharted island on 11 June, a second one on the twelfth, and a coral reef on the fourteenth. These were new discoveries: Fanning Island, Washington Island, and Kingman Reef. Fanning continued toward Tinian, which he reached in mid-July and where he rescued some shipwrecked Europeans, and to Canton, which he left in late October to complete his circumnavigation by way of the Cape of Good Hope. He was back in New York on 26 April 1799.

In January 1800 he took command of the corvette *Aspasia* bound for South Georgia. He collected 57,000 fur skins, which he subsequently sold in Canton, arriving back in New York on 4 March 1802.

He continued to press for American exploration of the Pacific and the Antarctic and was instrumental in despatching the brigs *Seraph* and *Annawan* to the Antarctic in 1829. His memoirs, *Voyages around the World*, published in 1833, were deservedly popular, and he played a significant role in sending out the expedition of Charles Wilkes *(q.v.)*. Edward Fanning died in New York on 23 April 1841.

## Fearn

JOHN FEARN was captain of the British trading vessel *Hunter*, which sailed from New South Wales to the Hawaiian Islands in 1798. While in latitude 22°40′ and approximately at longitude 171°50′ east, he came upon an uncharted island, which he named Hunter Island. It is situated to the east of New Caledonia, a peak in the Hunter Island undersea ridge, and is administered by New Caledonia. Proceeding north, Fearn sighted an inhabited island to the west of the Gilbert group, which he called Pleasant Island; it retained its name until 1888, when it was annexed by Germany and reverted to its native name, Nauru. On his return Fearn gave details of Eniwetok, which had been discovered in early days by the Spanish, but was imperfectly known. John Fearn is sometimes confused with another John Fearn (1768–1837), a captain in the Royal Navy, who retired from the service to devote himself to philosophy; the discoverer of Nauru, however, was not in command of a navy ship, but of a modest snow.

## Fernández

JUAN FERNÁNDEZ was born in Spain in the early 1530s and came to Chile in 1550 or 1551 where he acquired considerable experience as a pilot, boatswain, and eventually master, operating largely out of Santiago. In February 1574 he was in command of the *Nuestra Señora dos Remedios* sailing from Valparaiso to Callao in Peru. He began his return journey on 27 October, sailing away from the coast to catch the southern currents and southeast trade winds. On 6 November he sighted two islands, which he named San Félix and San Ambor (San Ambrosio), and on the twenty-second he came upon a further two he named Santa Cecilia; these became known as the Juan Fernandez Islands.

He can be credited with the discovery of San Felix and San Ambrosio, but the islands that bear his name had probably been sighted by earlier Spanish navigators. Fernández was back in Chile in November, his reputation greatly enhanced. He was sent, probably in 1575 but certainly in 1576, to make further discoveries, or at least to obtain more precise information about what he had seen. He sailed from about 40°5′ on a west-southwest course and after a month at sea apparently came to a land about which increasingly romantic reports began to spread—that it was a vast country with fine rivers and well-dressed inhabitants. It could have been Easter Island, possibly even Tahiti, less plausibly New Zealand or even Australia. The reports gained a great deal from the general belief in the existence of a vast southern continent.

Juan Fernández settled in Santiago and died there in 1599.

## Fitzroy

ROBERT FITZROY was born on 5 July 1805 in Suffolk. He was the grandson of the Duke of Grafton and the son of General Lord Charles Fitzroy. After studies at Rottingdean, Harrow, and Portsmouth Naval College, he sailed in the *Owen Glendower* to South America; he also served in the Mediterranean and the Channel. He was promoted to lieutenant in 1824 and was flag lieutenant to Admiral Ottway in 1828.

Following the suicide of the captain of the *Beagle*, Fitzroy was given the opportunity to take over command and bring the ship back from Tierra del Fuego to Britain to 1830. His command was confirmed for a major voyage of exploration. The *Beagle* sailed on 27 December 1831. On board was the young scientist Charles Darwin *(q.v.)*, who later achieved fame for his *Origin of Species*, which drew on many of the observations he had made during the voyage, which lasted almost five years.

Fitzroy sailed to Santa Cruz and Rio, to Tierra del Fuego and the Falklands. By early 1834 the Atlantic part of the voyage was complete, and the *Beagle* made for Valparaiso. Surveys of the Chilean and Peruvian coasts took up much of 1835. Part of September and most of October were spent on a detailed survey of the Galapagos. In November, Fitzroy was among the Tuamotus, making for Tahiti. On 19 December 1835 he sighted New Zealand, anchoring two days later in the Bay of Islands.

The stay in New Zealand lasted until the thirty-first; the *Beagle* then sailed for Sydney, arriving on 12 January 1836. The expedition went on to Tasmania and King George Sound in western Australia. In March, Fitzroy crossed the Indian Ocean to the Cocos Islands and eventually made for home by way of Mauritius, the Cape, St. Helena, and the Azores. He dropped anchor in Falmouth on 17 November 1836. The following month he married Mary Henrietta O'Brien, daughter of a general.

On his return Fitzroy began editing the charts and sailing directions that resulted from the voyage and working on his stolid *Narrative of the Surveying Voyages*, which appeared in 1839. Darwin's much briefer and more readable account, which made up the third volume, came out as a separate book in 1845 as *The Voyage of the "Beagle"*.

Following the publication of the *Narrative*, Fitzroy worked as one of the Elder Brethren of Trinity House and, in 1841, was elected Member of Parliament for Durham. Two years later he went to New Zealand as colonial governor, a post he held until the beginning of 1846. He became acting superintendent of Woolwich Dockyard, commanded the *Arrogant* for a time, but retired from active service in 1850. His wife died in 1852. In 1854 he was appointed to head the new meterological office. He then remarried, to Maria Isabella Smyth, the daughter of a landowner. He was promoted to rear admiral in 1857 and vice-admiral in 1863, but he suffered a breakdown and committed suicide on 30 April 1865. Maria survived him.

## Flinders

MATTHEW FLINDERS was born at Donington, Lincolnshire, on 16 March 1774. He joined the Royal Navy in 1789 and had an early opportunity to sail into the Pacific when he was chosen as a midshipman in the *Providence* under Captain Bligh *(q.v.)*.

They left England on 3 August 1791 and reached Tasmania on 8 February 1792, going on to Tahiti to collect breadfruit plants. The stay lasted from 9 April to 19 July, Bligh then transporting the plants to the West Indies and returning to England on 2 August 1793. Flinders subsequently served in the *Bellerophon* and departed for Australia as an officer with the *Reliance* in early 1795. A fellow officer was George Bass *(q.v.)*, with whom in 1797 he sailed in a whaleboat and showed that Tasmania was an island. In September 1798 Flinders went with Bass in the schooner *Norfolk* to confirm the existence of Bass Strait. This they did by circumnavigating Tasmania.

Flinders, now a lieutenant, was back in England in August 1800, publishing an account of his surveys, which he dedicated to Sir Joseph Banks *(q.v.)*. This move led to his receiving official support for a comprehensive survey of the Australian coast. He took command of the *Investigator* and sailed from Spithead on 18 July 1801. He reached Cape Leeuwin on 6 November and went on to King George Sound, where he spent most of December and the first few days of January 1802. Once he had reached the eastern side of the Great Australia Bight, he entered unknown waters and made a number of new discoveries.

Still charting the coast, he met on 8 April 1802 in Encounter Bay the Frenchman Baudin *(q.v.)*, who was doing the same thing from the opposite direction. Each continued on his way, and Flinders dropped anchor in Port Jackson on 9 May.

On 22 July the *Investigator*, accompanied by the brig *Lady Nelson*, set out for the next stage of the voyage. Flinders sailed north along the coast of New South Wales, but he soon found the *Lady Nelson* so slow and unreliable that he sent it back to Port Jackson while he went through the Great Barrier Reef by what is now called Flinders Passage. He turned Cape York, discovered and named the Wellesley Islands, and continued his coastal survey to Cape Arnhem, but was forced by the condition of his ship to abandon his hydrographic work and to make as speedily as possible for western Australia, the south coast, and Port Jackson by way of Bass Strait. He dropped anchor in Sydney Cove on 9 June 1803, having completed the first circumnavigation of Australia.

Flinders sailed for England on 10 August 1803 in the *Porpoise*, accompanied by the *Cato* and the *Bridgewater*. On the seventeenth the *Porpoise* and the *Cato* were both wrecked on a reef while the *Bridgewater* sailed on. Flinders managed to struggle back to Port Jackson, where he was given the schooner *Cumberland* as a replacement vessel. When he arrived at Mauritius, a French colony, on 15 December, he discovered that war had again broken out; lacking a passport for the *Cumberland*, he was detained until June 1810. He reached England on October 1810 and worked on the narrative of his expedition, *A Voyage to Terra Australis*, which was published in two volumes on 19 July 1814, the very day on which he died, aged 40.

## Folger

MAYHEW FOLGER was born in Nantucket, Massachusetts, around the year 1775. Related to other New England sailing families, he went to sea at an early age. On 5 April 1807 he sailed from Boston in command of the *Topaz*, owned by Boardman and Pope, on a sealing voyage.

Going by way of the Cape of Good Hope and Kerguelen Island, the *Topaz* put in at Hobart, Tasmania, in October, and then sailed for the Chatham Islands and the Antipodes Islands, near New Zealand. In need of supplies and with so far only a mediocre catch of seals, Folger then sailed for the central Pacific, and on 6 February 1808 reached Pitcairn Island, where he discovered descendants of the mutineers of the *Bounty* and Alexander Smith (John Adams), the last survivor of the men who had mutinied against Captain Bligh *(q.v.)*.

His brief stay was sufficient for Folger to provide a report to the British naval authorities at Valparaiso at the end of September 1808. Extracts from the log of the *Topaz* were sent in 1809 to the British Admiralty by the commander-in-chief of the naval station in Brazil, Folger being by then on his way home to Boston. However, the Admiralty was too preoccupied with the war with France to concern itself with Pitcairn.

Mayhew Folger returned to sea in 1810, but in 1813 he wrote direct to the Admiralty with additional information on the mutineers. No action was taken, and Folger's role in the discovery, even Folger himself, were forgotten until British naval ships, starting with the frigate *Briton* on 17 September 1814, began to call at the isolated island.

## Forster

JOHANN GEORGE ADAM FORSTER (usually referred to as George Forster, and in modern German reference works and biographies as Georg) was born near Danzig, in eastern Prussia, on 26 November 1754. With his father, Johann Reinhold Forster *(q.v.)*, he went to Russia and, in 1766, to England.

While his father wrote and taught, George engaged in translation work. In 1773 he accompanied his father on the second voyage of James Cook *(q.v.)*, with the functions of natural history assistant and artist. Even more important, perhaps, was his role in keeping the peace between his cantankerous father and the rest of the *Resolution's* complement.

George Forster carried out his father's ambition to produce an account of the voyage, as the elder Forster had been effectively blocked by James Cook from writing his own, and George's English was better than his father's. In what was almost a race between Cook and the Forsters, George's version won, being published in March 1777, six weeks before Cook's. The elder Forster's more scientific account came out a year later.

George Forster returned to Germany to take up a post as professor of natural history at Cassell University, where he remained from 1778 until 1784. A German translation of his narrative of the Cook expedition appeared between 1778 and 1780. In 1784, George Forster transferred to the university at Vilna, where he held a professorship until 1788, when he became librarian to the Elector of Mainz.

He was an early supporter of the French Revolution, and he favored the incorporation of the territories on the left bank of the Rhine into the new French Republic. He went to Paris in 1793 to carry on negotiations, and died there on 10 January 1794.

## Forster

JOHANN REINHOLD FORSTER was born in Dirschau (present-day Tczew), near Danzig, on 22 October 1729. He was educated locally and in Berlin. In 1748 he enrolled at Halle University to study theology; he was ordained in 1751, although his real interests lay in science. Following the death of his father in 1753 he became a man of some means. In February 1754 he married Justina Nicolai; on 26 November 1754 his eldest son, Johann George Adam (q.v.) was born.

The Seven Years War created great difficulties for the region, which was occupied by Russian troops. Later, in 1765, Forster was invited by the Russians to make a report on the Volga region. By now his interest in natural history was well established. He took his son George with him to assist with the botanical part of his work. Inadequately recompensed for his work, Forster left Russia for London, where he arrived in late October 1766. There followed a period of severe financial difficulties but of considerable scientific writing and lecturing that made the two Forsters known to an ever-widening circle of influential people. The elder Forster's cantankerous character magnified setbacks and slights, but his energy and ambition more than made up for his frequent tactless actions. In June 1772,

Sir Joseph Banks *(q.v.)* having decided that the quarters provided for him in the *Resolution* were inadequate, Forster was appointed as naturalist to accompany James Cook *(q.v.)* on his second expedition.

The voyage, which began on 13 July 1773 when the *Resolution* and the *Adventure* sailed from Plymouth, was an epic circumnavigation that was not completed until 30 July 1775, when the *Resolution* anchored at Spithead, the *Adventure* having reached England a year earlier. It took the *Resolution* down to the Antarctic, farther than any vessel had ventured before, twice to New Zealand, and through many of the islands of the central Pacific from Easter Island to Tahiti, Fiji, and the New Hebrides. The return home was by way of Cape Horn and across to the Cape of Good Hope. There was much to occupy the Forsters during those long months, and they responded to the challenge with characteristic energy.

It had become Johann Reinhold Forster's impression that he would write the official narrative of the voyage. This became an obsession, but English was not his native tongue, and Cook was, like many others, unhappy about what the writer Hawkesworth had done with the account of his first voyage. Rejected for this task, the elder Forster prevailed on his son, who was a quicker and better writer of English, to produce a narrative before Cook did. George Forster's *A Voyage round the World* appeared in March 1777, beating James Cook's *A Voyage towards the South Pole and round the World* by a few weeks. Johann Reinhold's own *Observations made during a Voyage round the World*, devoted mainly to scientific and philosophical comments, came out in 1778. He spent the next two years on further writings and attempts to promote various schemes, but he increasingly alienated his supporters. In 1780 he took up a professorship at Halle University in Germany, rising to pro-rector in 1790, but he was otherwise frustrated in his ambitions. He died at Halle on 9 December 1798.

## Freycinet

THE FREYCINET FAMILY was one of ancient lineage, whose ancestors had settled in Saulce-sur-Rhône, Dauphiné, France, in quite early times. Louis de Saulces de Freycinet's two eldest sons, Henri and Louis, sailed to the Pacific, and a grandson, Charles, was four times prime minister of France.

Henri was born in 1777 and Louis in 1779. Both joined the navy in January 1794, serving first in the *Heureux* and escaping from the dangers that faced young aristocrats in the darker days of the Revolution. The British blockade of French ports gave them few opportunities for acquiring experience at sea, but in 1800 they were both selected for the Baudin expedition, one to each ship, with the rank of *enseigne*. Baudin *(q.v.)* was a hard taskmaster and criticized Henri as "too young" (at 23) for the duties entrusted to him; but Henri was an able officer and carried out valuable survey work in Australia and in fact took over command of the *Géographe* when Baudin fell ill.

After the expedition's return to France in 1804, Henri went back to active service, was wounded and taken prisoner in the West Indies, and, after his release, was appointed to a shore position at Rochefort. He subsequently became governor of the island of Bourbon (now Réunion), of French Guiana, of Martinique, and the Maritime Prefect of Rochefort. He died, a rear admiral, in 1840.

Louis de Freycinet was requested to assist the naturalist François Péron with compiling the official account of Baudin's voyage and, when Péron died, to complete it. Publication was completed between 1807 and 1816, by which time Freycinet had begun planning his own voyage of exploration. His proposal was approved, and he sailed in the *Uranie* on 14 September 1817 from Toulon, bound for Gibraltar, Tenerife, Rio de Janeiro, and Australia by way of Capetown and Mauritius.

Smuggled on board and at first dressed as a man was Louis' wife, Rose Marie, who accompanied him for the entire voyage, a breach of naval regulations that the authorities eventually agreed to overlook.

The expedition reached Shark Bay, in western Australia, on 12 September 1818. It discovered a commemorative pewter plate left by the Dutch navigator Vlamingh in 1697 to commemorate his and an earlier voyage. (The plate was taken to Paris but eventually—in 1947—returned to Australia.) The *Uranie* then sailed to the East Indies, the Marianas, Guam, and Hawaii, anchoring in Kealakekua Bay on 8 August 1819. The stay in this island group lasted until 30 August and provided valuable information on early island life.

The expedition then made its way back to Australia, sailing almost due south toward the Samoas and the Cook Islands. East of the Samoan group the French came across an apparently undiscovered island; they named it Rose Island, not realizing that Roggeveen *(q.v.)* had seen it and named it Vuyle Eylandt in 1722. They sailed on toward the Tongan group and sighted Australia on 13 November, anchoring in Neutral Bay, Sydney, five days later. The growth of the colony since Freycinet's previous visit, seventeen years earlier, greatly impressed the visitors.

Leaving on 25 December, the *Uranie* made for high latitudes, passing to the south of New Zealand and turning Cape Horn on 6 February 1820. Then, on the fourteenth, it struck a rock while putting in at the Falkland Islands and was lost. Finally rescued, the French made their way back to France aboard a three-master that Freycinet purchased and renamed the *Physicienne*. On 13 November 1820 they were back in France. A court-martial exonerated Freycinet for the loss of the *Uranie* while the scientific community hailed the impressive collection of natural history specimens his expedition had gathered and managed to save from the wreck.

Louis de Freycinet devoted most of his remaining years to writing and supervising the publication of the official accounts of his voyage, which appeared between 1827 and 1839. He died in 1842. His wife had predeceased him, dying of cholera in 1832 at the age of 37.

## Funnell

WILLIAM FUNNELL was a mate serving with Dampier *(q.v.)* in the *St. George*, which sailed from England on 30 April 1703 for the Canary Islands, Brazil, and the South Seas on a buccaneering voyage. The *St. George* entered the Pacific by way of Cape Horn in late January 1704, went to Juan Fernandez Islands, and spent most of the year raiding along the coast of South America with mixed success. One large Spanish vessel, the *Asunción*, was taken almost by chance, and Funnell was sent to it by Dampier as prize master. However, Dampier was anxious only for the ship's stores of food, of which the buccaneers were in great need, and refused to let Funnell spend time searching for gold coins he believed were hidden in the hold. An attempt to capture the Manila galleon failed, and the condition of the creaky *St. George* kept worsening; in January 1705 Funnell and a number of others parted from Dampier, accepting his offer of the small *Dragon*, an early capture from the Spanish, in which on 1 February he set sail for the Dutch East Indies.

When the *Dragon* made its way into Amboina, the Dutch arrested

Funnell and his companions and auctioned off the ship and its contents. Released after nearly four months, Funnell sailed home in a Dutch vessel, reaching England on 20 August 1706. He then found a publisher for his journal, which appeared as *A Voyage round the World* in 1707. It contained enough criticism of Dampier for the latter to respond on his return to England with *Vindication of his Voyage to the South Seas*, published in the same year. Funnell's date of death is not recorded.

## Furneaux

TOBIAS FURNEAUX was born on 21 August 1735 at Swilly, Devon. He joined the navy in his teens and by 1755 was serving as midshipman. During the Seven Years War, he sailed in the *Marlborough* to the West Indies. He took part in various raids and engagements, rising to the rank of lieutenant. In December 1760 he was appointed second lieutenant of the *Melampe*, a frigate operating mostly in the Channel and off the coast of Brittany. In July 1762 the ship sailed to West Africa and in March 1763, Furneaux now being first lieutenant, to Barbados, where he transferred to the *Ferret*. The war being over, he returned to England and was placed on half-pay until July 1766, when he was appointed second lieutenant of the *Dolphin*, which was about to sail out to the Pacific under Samuel Wallis *(q.v.)*.

The *Dolphin* left Plymouth on 21 August 1766, passed through the Strait of Magellan, and emerged into the Pacific on 11 April 1767 after almost four months of hard struggle, only to become separated from its consort, the *Swallow*, never again seen on the voyage. The *Dolphin* sailed on westward, making a number of discoveries, the most important of which was Tahiti. Wallis went on to Tinian, which he reached on 19 September, and sailed home by way of Batavia and the Cape, dropping anchor in the Downs on 19 May 1768.

In December 1770 Furneaux was appointed to the *Trident* and shortly after to the *Torbay*, the captain of which was Samuel Wallis. However, late in 1771 Furneaux, with the rank of commander, was chosen to command the *Adventure*, sister ship to the *Resolution*, commanded by James Cook *(q.v.)*. The expedition sailed from Plymouth on 13 July 1772. They made for Madeira and Table Bay, then set off to explore the Antarctic. The cold and ice created great difficulties requiring all of Cook's skills as a navigator to overcome. On 17 January 1773 the Antarctic Circle was crossed for the first time in history, but the icefield forced a retreat. On 8 February in a gale compounded by fog the two ships lost sight of each other.

Furneaux sailed for New Zealand, the agreed rendezvous in case of separation. On the way he put in for five days at Adventure Bay, Tasmania, and surveyed some of the east coast, narrowly missing the discovery of the strait that separates Tasmania from the rest of Australia. On 7 April the *Adventure* dropped anchor in Ship Cove, New Zealand, where on the eighteenth the *Resolution* joined it. On 7 June the two ships set off for further explorations, this time toward Tahiti. On 12 August an island was discovered; named Furneaux Island, it has reverted to its native name of Marutea. A few days later the expedition reached Tahiti where the *Adventure*'s sick, fairly numerous, had a chance to recover and Furneaux had the opportunity to assess the changes that had occured over the previous six years.

On 8 September at nearby Raiatea, Cook allowed Furneaux to take aboard the *Adventure* a young Tahitian, Omai (more correctly, Mai), who traveled with him to England, where he became a celebrity before, in time, returning to his native island. The ships were on their way to Tonga and New Zealand, but on 29 October a gale once more separated them, and this time they did not rejoin. The *Adventure* was held up by further bad weather, and when it finally reached Ship's Cove, in early December, the *Resolution* had already left.

Furneaux's stay was marked by tragedy. On 17 December 1773 an entire boat's crew—ten men and a midshipman—were massacred by Maoris while ashore collecting wood and water. He decided to sail for home by way of Cape Horn, setting out to cross the Pacific on 18 December, across a vast empty ocean. Rather than turning along the Argentinian coast, however, he thought it wiser to continue eastward toward the Cape of Good Hope, where provisions would be available. He reached Table Bay on 19 March 1774, left again on 10 April, and anchored at Spithead on 12 July.

After a period of rest, Furneaux took over command of the *Syren*, a new frigate. He was commissioned captain on 10 August 1775 and in January 1776 joined Admiral Parker's squadron off the coast of North America. On 6 November 1777 the *Syren* was lost and Furneaux taken prisoner. He was released early in 1778, exonerated by a court-martial, and served for a while in the *Isis*, but he was to be soon invalided back to England. There he died on 28 September 1781.

## Gaetan

JUAN GAETAN (also found as Gaytano and Gaetano, since he was of Italian origins) sailed with Ruy López de Villalobos from Mexico to the Philippines on 1 November 1542. In August 1543 Villalobos sent the *San Juan* back to America, but the attempt was unsuccessful. The *San Juan* set out again by way of New Guinea in 1545.

Gaetan's claim to fame rests on his account of Villalobos' voyages, which the Italian historian Ramusio printed in his famous compilation *Delle Navigationi e Viaggi* (Venice, 1550). But he was also believed to have reported the discovery of the Hawaiian Islands in 1542 on the outward journey. Less plausible is the theory that Gaetan sailed on another expedition in 1555 during which he discovered an island group he called Islas de la Mesa and which were part of the Hawaiian archipelago. Useful though his account of the 1542 expedition has proved, the claims relating to the discovery of Hawaii are highly circumstantial and dependent on charts of doubtful accuracy.

## Gallego

HERNÁN GALLEGO was born at Coruna, Spain, sometime in 1514 or 1515. Little is known of his early years, but he was no doubt an experienced seaman by 1557, when he was appointed pilot of a ship sent from Valdivia, Chile, to explore the coast down to the entrance of the Strait of Magellan. The expedition was disastrous, costing the lives of some seventy men. Gallego's next ten years were spent as pilot on ships sailing along the Spanish Pacific seaboard.

In 1567 he was appointed pilot-major of the *Los Reyes*, one of the two ships selected for the voyage of exploration of Alvaro de Mendaña (*q.v.*); Gallego had overall responsibility for the expedition's journey, being the most experienced man on board either ship. His longitudes and latitudes, however, were subject to a fairly wide range of errors which, although not unusual in those days of unsophisticated instruments, made the identification of some of the islands discovered and their correct positioning on successive charts a particularly difficult task.

After leaving Callao on 19 November 1567, the two ships sighted a number of small islands and reefs and on 7 February came upon a large island that the Spanish named Santa Ysabel, part of what became known as the Solomon Islands. There a brigantine was constructed, the *Santiago*, to carry out detailed exploration among the numerous islands, Hernan Gallego being put in charge as pilot, with Pedro de Ortega *(q.v.)* as commander. They set out on 7 April, discovering Malaita, the Florida group, Guadalcanal, Savo, the Georgia group, and Choiseul. After completing the circuit of Santa Ysabel (a difficult and at times dangerous navigation), the *Santiago* rejoined the two ships on 5 May. The *Santiago* went out again on 19 May, still with Gallego as pilot but commanded by Hernando Henriquez *(q.v.)*. On this occasion, San Cristobal, Ulawa, Olu Malau, and Ugi were discovered. On a third local voyage, starting on 4 July, this time under Francisco Muñoz Rico, still with Gallego as pilot, the small islands of Santa Catalina and Santa Ana were discovered.

The expedition set off for home on 17 August 1568, Gallego persuading Mendaña that the best route was across the Pacific to Mexico. To some extent he was correct, as a direct route to Peru would have presented serious difficulties, but an alternative would have been the Philippines. As it was, the expedition struggled to Lower California, which Gallego sighted on 19 December. His knowledge of the coast and his acquaintance with Spanish officials in Mexico facilitated the repairing of the ships and the final voyage home, which ended at Callao on 11 September 1569.

The later life of Hernán Gallego is obscure. He probably died in a wreck in 1570. But a man of that name bequeathed an estate to the Augustinian Friars of Chile in 1606, by which date he would have been in his eighties. A more important legacy is his "Relación" of the Mendaña expedition, which exists in manuscript in a long and a shorter version and is the most important single source of information on the voyage.

## Gardner

GEORGE WASHINGTON GARDNER was born in 1778 in Massachusetts and was related by marriage to the naval Nantucket family the

Coffins. He went to sea at an early age and in 1809 was given command of the whaling ship *Sukey*, sailing from Nantucket for the Pacific on 11 July and returning on 6 June 1811.

He returned to the Pacific the same year, sailing as captain of the *William Penn* on 9 November, but the ship was captured on 4 December 1813 and taken to the Cape of Good Hope. Gardner was later given the *Globe*, in which he made three whaling voyages from Nantucket to the Pacific: from 21 October 1815 to 1 January 1818, 3 March 1818 to 29 May 1821, and 9 August 1820 to 3 May 1822.

His next ship was the Nantucket whaler *Maria*, in which he made two voyages to the Pacific—from 17 November 1822 to 27 April 1825 and from 17 July 1825 to 2 June 1828. It was on the first of these that he discovered an island in the Austral group to which he gave the name Maria Island; it is still uninhabited and has received various names over the years such as Hull Island and Sands Island; its native name is Nororutu.

George Gardner died in 1838.

## Gardner

JOSHUA GARDNER was a whaling captain from Nantucket, Massachusetts, who sailed in command of the *Ganges* in the mid-1820s. Late in 1825 he came upon an island at 4°20′ south and 174°22′ west, which he named Gardner's Island. Known as Kemins or Kimins Island in the Phoenix group, it is now generally referred to by its native name, Nikumaroro. The discovery, reported in the *Nantucket Enquirer* of December 1827, is sometimes credited to Gardner's fellow captain, Joshua Coffin.

## Gayangos

TOMAS GAYANGOS was born at Logrono, northern Spain, probably in the late 1730s. He was a midshipman based at Cadiz in 1755, a junior lieutenant in 1760, and a full lieutenant in 1772, by which time he was serving on the Pacific coast of Spanish America.

He was appointed to the *Aguila* under Domingo de Boenechea (*q.v.*) sailing to Tahiti. A gentle person, he was popular with the Tahitians and made a friend of the chief of Hitiaa, who had welcomed Bougainville (*q.v.*) a few years earlier.

Following the death of Boenechea during the *Aguila*'s second voyage to Tahiti, Tomas Gayangos, as senior lieutenant, took over command in January 1775 and brought the *Aguila* and its consort, the *San Miguel*, back to Callao. He was clear of Tahiti by 30 January, sailing southeast; on 5 February he came upon an island that he named Santa Rosa; it was a new sighting, the island of Raivavae in the Austral group. The *Aguila* dropped anchor at Callao on 8 April 1776, being joined by the *San Miguel* five days later.

Tomas Gayangos returned to Europe the following year, serving on the *Poderoso* under Juan de Langara. He saw active service on a number of occasions during the hostilities with Britain, under Langara and under Casa-Tilly. He was promoted to commander in 1779, captain in 1782, commodore in 1789, and rear admiral in 1794. He died at Cadiz in 1796.

## Gilbert

THOMAS GILBERT was a merchant navy captain who worked for the East India Company and private shipowners; he was given command of the *Charlotte*, which sailed from England on 13 May 1787 for Botany Bay with convicts and soldiers for the new penal settlement, as part of the First Fleet. The fleet reached New South Wales in January but soon moved to a better anchorage at Port Jackson.

Following the landing of convicts and soldiers, together with supplies for the colony, Gilbert prepared to sail back to England by way of Canton to collect a cargo for the voyage home. He left on 6 May 1788 in company with the *Scarborough*, commanded by John Marshall *(q.v.)*. He got ahead of Marshall for a while, but the two ships kept together for most of the voyage.

On 27 May, Gilbert, ahead of the *Scarborough*, discovered an island south of the New Hebrides (Vanuatu), to which he gave the name of Matthew Island, and on 18 June came upon the first three of a succession of islands through which both ships passed. They were Abemama, Aranuka, and Kuria, all discoveries in the large group that became known as the Gilbert Islands (Kiribati). Some of the islands and atolls sighted during the following ten days had already been seen by early Spanish voyagers, but a number were true discoveries that can be credited to both Gilbert and Marshall. Their charts and sketches provided the first overall picture of this part of the Pacific and its scattered archipelagos.

In addition, Gilbert had some contacts with the islanders, who came out to their ships in canoes, although the information gathered about the Gilbertese is fairly general.

Arriving in China on 9 September, Gilbert took on a cargo of tea for the East India Company and continued on his way to England, where the *Charlotte* was sold. Little is known of his life after 1789, the year in which his account of the journey—*Voyage from New South Wales to Canton*—was published in London. The *Charlotte* worked on the London to Jamaica run and subsequently in Canadian waters, being lost off Newfoundland in 1818.

## Golovnin

VASILII MIKHAILOVICH GOLOVNIN was born on 8 April 1776 at Gulynki, Ryazan, and graduated from the Naval Cadet School in 1792. Like a number of his contemporaries, he served with the British Royal Navy, from 1801 to 1805. On his return, the valuable code of signals he compiled brought him to the attention of his superiors.

His first expedition, when he was given command of the naval sloop *Diana*, began in 1807 and, through a series of misfortunes, kept him in the Pacific area until 1813. The *Diana* sailed to Kamchatka, arriving on 5 October 1809, having been held by the British for thirteen months at Capetown.

In 1810 he sailed to the Russian settlements on the northwest coast of America and returned to Kamchatka to prepare for a full survey of the Kurils in 1811. He had with him the skilled navigators Khlebnikov and Novitzsky, and together they drew up meticulous charts of the Kuril chain; these charts made a major contribution to European knowledge of the area. Unfortunately, he landed on Kunashir off Hokkaido and was taken prisoner when he came upon a strong Japanese garrison. The *Diana*, under Petr Rikord, escaped and hastened to Okhotsk to report the incident. Golovnin was not released until October 1813.

He returned to Russia during the final stages of the Napoleonic wars; when peace was declared he was sent on a second voyage to the Pacific. He sailed in 1817 in the sloop *Kamchatka*, by way of Cape Horn and South America. He crossed the Pacific to Kamchatka, which he reached in May 1818, thence across to the Russian outpost of Novo Arkhangelsk (Sitka) in Alaska, down to Fort Ross, back across the Pacific to the Hawaiian Islands, the Marianas, Manila, the China Sea, Sunda Strait, and home by way of the Indian Ocean and the Cape of Good Hope; he dropped anchor at St. Petersburg in September 1819. Although he achieved little in the way of new discoveries. Golovnin's expedition brought back a vast store of scientific and astronomical information.

After his return Golovnin was appointed assistant director of the Naval Cadet School and, in 1823, quartermaster general of the navy. He was then promoted to the rank of vice-admiral. He died at St. Petersburg of cholera on 29 June 1831.

He published a number of books on his voyages. The *Diana* expedition resulted in *Notes of Naval Captain Golovnin on his Adventures as a Prisoner of the Japanese* (St. Petersburg, 1816), followed by *Abbreviated Notes of Golovnin on his Cruise* (St. Petersburg, 1819) and *Recollections of Japan* (London, 1819); the second expedition produced *The Journey of the sloop "Kamchatka" from Kronstadt to Kamchatka* in 1819 and *A Journey round the World* in 1822, both published in St. Petersburg. The southernmost settlement of the island of Kunashir, formerly known as Tomari, has been renamed Golovnino by the Russians to commemorate the locality where he was arrested by the Japanese.

## Gonzalez

FELIPE GONZALEZ Y HAEDO was born in Santona, northern Spain, in 1703. After some years as an apprentice, he was accepted with the rank of pilot in the Spanish navy, serving in the *San Bernardo*, engaged on troop transport, and in the *Santiago* before sailing to the Indies in the *Aranzusu* in 1730. He spent the next twenty years in various naval vessels, taking part in a number of campaigns and sailing between Cadiz, Mexico, and the West Indies. In 1741 he was formally incorporated into the Spanish Royal Navy with the rank of ensign.

Promoted frigate lieutenant in September 1751 and full lieutenant in May 1754, he joined the *Poderoso* in 1758 and in the following year sailed with the Victoria squadron escorting Charles III and the royal family from Naples to Barcelona. He spent the next few years on active service in the Atlantic and the Mediterranean until 15 January 1766, when he was raised to the rank of frigate captain and sailed to Vera Cruz as second-in-command of the *Firme*. In 1769 he went to Callao in the *San Lorenzo*, 74 guns, with troop reinforcements for Peru and Chile and was ordered to sail in search of the island of David or Davis, which Surville *(q.v.)* had hoped to discover.

Surville's *Saint Jean-Baptiste* had put in at Callao with its crew in a parlous state, seeking assistance, while technically in breach of Spain's monopoly rights over the Pacific seaboard of South America. Anxious to forestall any French claim to islands in the southeast Pacific, the Spanish viceroy, Manuel de Amat, despatched Felipe Gonzalez, his senior and most experienced naval commander, in the *San Lorenzo*, with the *Santa Rosalia*, 36 guns, under Antonio Domonte. Gonzalez sailed, as instructed and in line with Surville's original plans, along the twenty-seventh parallel, leaving from Callao on 10 October 1770.

On 15 November Gonzalez came to an island he named San Carlos; he took formal possession of it in the king's name and after six days sailed on westward. Sighting no further land, for indeed there was nothing ahead of him for many hundreds of miles, he turned back toward Peru, arriving at Callao on 28 March 1771, after a call at the island of Chiloe in December.

Although the viceroy was convinced that Gonzalez had found the legendary island of David, it soon became apparent that he had merely rediscovered Roggeveen's Easter Island.

Gonzalez remained in Peru for a time, but further campaigns called him back to Spain. He had been promoted to full captain in October 1770; he rose to the rank of brigadier in December 1782 and sailed in the *San Eugenio* to Montevideo, Valparaiso, Talcahuano, and Callao, his main function being the protection of Spanish shipping along the Pacific coast. He returned to Cadiz in 1787. Promoted to commodore in 1789, he served as honorary adviser to the navy; he died in Madrid on 27 October 1792.

## Gore

JOHN GORE was born in the American colonies, probably in Virginia in 1730—his antecedents are unclear—and went to sea in 1755. He served as a midshipman in various ships in the Mediterranean, the Atlantic, and the West Indies. In early 1764 he was appointed master's mate to serve in the *Dolphin*, commanded by John Byron *(q.v.)*. The *Dolphin* left, accompanied by the *Tamar*, on 21 June 1764, reached the Falklands in January 1765, and entered the Pacific in April. The expedition passed through the Tuamotus, the Tokelaus, and the southern Gilberts, anchoring at Tinian in the Ladrones on 31 July. Returning by way of Batavia and the Cape, Byron reached England on 9 May 1766.

The *Dolphin* was promptly sent back to the Pacific under Samuel Wallis *(q.v.)*, and John Gore again sailed on it. Leaving Plymouth on 22 August 1766, Wallis entered the Straits of Magellan on 17 December, emerging into the Pacific on 11 April 1767. He discovered a number of islands as he made his way across the ocean, including Tahiti. Continuing to Tinian, Batavia, and the Cape, the expedition was back in England on 20 May 1768.

Gore was to have very little respite. He was appointed third lieutenant to the *Endeavour*, commanded by James Cook *(q.v.)*, which sailed from Plymouth on 26 August 1768. The *Endeavour* followed the usual route from Cape Horn to the Tuamotus and Tahiti, where Cook observed the transit of Venus, then sailed to New Zealand (which Cook circumnavigated and charted), crossed the Tasman Sea to Botany Bay and up the coast of New South Wales, sailed through Torres Strait to southwest New Guinea, and on to Batavia, the Cape, and home. The *Endeavour* dropped anchor in the Downs on 12 July 1771.

After more than seven years of arduous service, broken only by two brief periods of leave, Gore was entitled to a rest. He signed off and went on half-pay. James Cook soon began preparations for a second circumnavigation and became involved in a dispute with Sir Joseph Banks *(q.v.)*, who decided not to join him. Instead, Banks planned a voyage to Iceland and took with him Gore, who "out of mere friendship chose to take the trip." They sailed in the *Sir Lawrence* on 12 July 1772, called at the Hebrides, and reached Iceland on 25 August. The stay lasted almost two months, the *Sir Lawrence* arriving back in Scotland in November.

A period ashore gave Gore time to marry—or at least to indulge in some domesticity—and to start a family, but Cook was to call on him once more. Cook had returned from his second voyage on 30 July 1775 and was invited to undertake a third one. Gore was appointed first lieutenant to the *Resolution* in February 1776. The ship sailed from Plymouth ahead of its consort, the *Discovery*, on 12 July 1776, for the Cape, Tasmania, New Zealand, and the islands of the central Pacific. The major work of exploration, however, was carried out in the north, where the Hawaiian group was discovered and the northwest coast of America explored.

Cook was killed in Hawaii on 14 February 1779. In the subsequent reorganization, Gore took command of the *Discovery*. Then, on 22 August, Cook's successor, Charles Clerke *(q.v.)*, died, and Gore became captain of the *Resolution* and overall commander of the expedition. He brought the two ships back to England, by way of Macao and the Cape, and because of storms rounded the north of Scotland, anchoring off the Nore on 4 October 1780.

John Gore was promoted to post-captain on his return and given a pension by being appointed by Greenwich Hospital, taking the position on the establishment left vacant by Cook's death. Gore died on 10 August 1790 at Greenwich.

## Gray

ROBERT GRAY was born on 10 May 1755 at Tiverton, Rhode Island. He is believed to have served in the navy on the colonists' side during the American War of Independence. By 1787 he was in command of a trading vessel belonging to two merchants planning to send an expedition to the northwest coast and was selected to captain the sloop *Lady Washington*, which sailed from Boston on 30 September 1787 with the *Columbia* under John Kendrick *(q.v.)*.

Progress down the Atlantic was slow. Upon rounding Cape Horn, the two vessels became separated on 1 April 1788. Gray then made his way north, making his landfall on 4 August near Cape Mendocino, California, and on 16 September reaching Nootka Sound, where he met John Meares *(q.v.)*. Kendrick arrived a week later. The two ships wintered in Nootka. On 16 March 1789 Gray sailed south as far as Juan de Fuca Strait, then back north to Graham Island. On 23 May he returned to Nootka to repair his ship. There Kendrick took over the *Lady Washington*, giving Gray the *Columbia*. Gray sailed for China on 31 July with a cargo of furs, going by way of the Hawaiian Islands, where he spent three weeks laying in stores, and reaching Canton on 17 November 1789.

On 12 February 1790 the *Columbia* sailed for home with a call at

Ascension Island on 16 June. Completing what was the first American circumnavigation, Gray arrived in Boston on 9 August 1790. This pioneer voyage was not a financial success—especially as the *Lady Washington* kept on accumulating losses. Nevertheless, Gray left almost immediately for a second expedition. The *Columbia* sailed from Boston on 28 September 1790 and reached the northwest coast on 3 June 1791. Gray began trading for furs along the coast from Juan de Fuca Strait up to Clarence Strait in Alaska and on 18 September put into Clayoquot Sound for the winter. There he had built a sloop, the *Adventure*, which he placed under the command of Robert Haswell, his first officer.

The two vessels sailed out on 2 April 1792, the *Adventure* going north. Gray sailed in the opposite direction, met Vancouver *(q.v.)* off the mouth of the Quillayute River, and on 7 May discovered what is now Gray Harbour. On the eleventh he entered the estuary of the great Columbia River, the major discovery of his voyage. He sailed back north to rejoin the *Adventure*, put into Nootka Sound, sold *Adventure* to the Spanish, and on 3 October set off for the Hawaiian Islands and Canton. Having sold his cargo of furs and taken on a stock of oriental goods, Gray sailed for Boston, where the *Columbia* dropped anchor on 29 July 1793.

Robert Gray later served as master on various Boston coastal vessels and commanded the privateer *Lucy* during the troubles with Britain and France at the end of the century. He is believed to have died of yellow fever on a voyage to South Carolina in mid-1806, leaving a widow and four daughters but very little else.

## Grijalva

HERNÁNDO GRIJALVA was one of the Cortes' most able sea captains. He carried out a series of voyages of exploration along the Pacific coast of America from 1532 to 1536, first in the *San Lazaro*. In 1533 he discovered the island of Socorro, which he called San Tomas, and shortly thereafter the islands of San Benedictino, which he named Los Inocentes. Returning to the continent to latitude 20°20′ south, he went on to Acapulco and then surveyed the coast along the Gulf of Tehuantepec.

From 1534 to 1536 he helped Cortes on his various and largely unsuccessful attempts to search for pearls and establish a colony in Lower California. In the following year, Cortes sent him with two ships to the assistance of Pizarro, who was being hard pressed by Mango Ynca in Cuzco, Peru. Once this was achieved, Grijalva was authorized to sail across the Pacific to the Moluccas, searching on the way for islands reported to abound in gold.

Grijalva sailed from Paita with the *Santiago* in April 1537, roughly along the equator, and discovered an island he named Acea in latitude 2° north; this may well be Marakei in the northern Gilberts. Later, the Spanish came upon another island which, for the natives' occupation, they called the island of fishermen, Dos Pescadores, which is probably Abaiang in the same Gilbert group.

Not long after this, Grijalva's crew mutinied, complaining that he had neither discovered any islands of value nor succeeded in finding a wind that would bring them home. So they killed him and struggled on to western New Guinea, where the *Santiago* foundered. Seven survivors were ransomed by the Portuguese governor of the Moluccas in 1539 and thus survived to give an account of the voyage, the first crossing of the Pacific made along and south of the equator.

## Guevara

SANTIAGO DE GUEVARA was a brother-in-law of Juan Elcano *(q.v.)* and sailed with him in the expedition of Loaysia. He was in charge of the 50-ton patache *Santiago*, which left from Coruna on 24 July 1525 and entered the Pacific by the Straits of Magellan on 26 May 1526, shortly after which a gale scattered the fleet.

Finding himself alone, Guevara headed north toward Mexico. On 11 July land was sighted, which was part of the coast of Central America, and on the twenty-fifth the Spanish landed at Mazatlan near Tehuantepec, thus making the first direct voyage from the tip of South America to Mexico.

What happened to Guevara after that is not clear, but one of his crew is recorded as having joined the *Florida* under Saavedra *(q.v.)* in October 1527, dying on the voyage to the Ladrones (Marianas).

## Hagemeister

KNOWN IN RUSSIA AS LEONTII ADRIANOVICH GAGEMEISTER, Hagemeister was of German origin, his German name being Karl August Ludwig von Hagemeister. He was born in 1780, studied at the Naval Cadet School, and like many of his contemporaries, served with the British navy, notably in the Caribbean, returning to Russia in 1805.

With the rank of lieutenant, he sailed in the *Neva* from Kronstadt across the Atlantic and Indian oceans and eventually to the Russian settlements in North America. In 1808 and 1809 he explored the coast of Alaska and sailed to Kodiak Island and to Honolulu, where he spent three months. He then sailed to St. Petersburg (traveling overland across Siberia), arriving in 1810.

In 1816 he was given the command of the Russian American Company vessel *Kutuzov*, in which he sailed to the northwest coast, completing a circumnavigation that brought him back to St. Petersburg in 1820; during this time he served as governor of Russian North America. His major achievements came in 1828–1830 when in the *Krotkii* he completed his second circumnavigation. He was accompanied by Professor Ermann, from Berlin, who carried out magnetic observations, but the more important work of the expedition consisted of hydrographic surveys, especially in the Marshall Islands, which were still imperfectly charted.

Hagemeister was credited with the discovery of an island that he named Prince Menshikov Island; it has been identified with Apataki atoll, which had been seen by both Roggeveen and Cook *(qq.v.)*. He died in 1834. A small island and a strait off Alaska still bear his name.

## Hall

THERE IS LITTLE direct information about this John Hall—the name is not uncommon. He is reported as being the captain of a trading vessel, the *Lady Blackwood*, on a voyage from Calcutta to Mexico in 1824. On 2 April, Hall was sailing through the Caroline Islands when he discovered a small group of islands, whose position he determined. Three years later, the French navigator Duperrey *(q.v.)* noted a report in the *Annales Maritimes* detailing Hall's discoveries. Duperrey correctly deduced that the island group was north of Truk Island and credited the discovery to John Hall; Duperrey bestowed on them the name of Hall Islands, which they still retain in addition to their native names, Nomwin and Murilo.

## Hamelin

FERDINAND-ALPHONSE HAMELIN, the nephew of Jacques-Félix Emmanuel Hamelin *(q.v.)*, was born in 1796 at Pont-Lévêque, Normandy. He joined the navy in 1807 and took part in numerous campaigns. Promoted to rear admiral in 1842, he was appointed commandant of the French Pacific naval station in 1844. He sailed from Rochefort in July 1844 for Valparaiso, Callao, the Marquesas, and Tahiti, where he arrived on 21 December 1844. France had just established a protectorate over the Society Islands, and Hamelin found himself faced with a difficult political situation. He sailed in the *Virginie*, accompanied by the *Héroïne* and the *Triomphante*, reaching Callao on 21 March 1845. He returned to Tahiti in July to continue negotiations with the British representatives. After his return to France he was raised to the rank of vice-admiral. He commanded the Black Sea squadron in 1853, was made a full admiral in 1854, and served as minister of marine from 1856 to 1860. He died in 1864.

## Hamelin

JACQUES-FÉLIX EMMANUEL HAMELIN was born at Honfleur, Normandy, in 1768, the son of an apothecary. His early career was spent in merchant ships trading to Africa and the West Indies. His middle-class background would have allowed him little opportunity for advancement in the navy, but the Revolution, which resulted in the emigration of many officers and changed the structure of the navy, created a demand for experienced mariners. Hamelin had seized every opportunity to learn the art of navigation and the theory of hydrography.

In 1795 he served as a sublieutenant in a hard campaign in the Mediterranean, and in the following year took part in the abortive attempt to land French troops in Ireland. The British blockade of the French coast restricted further naval actions to occasional cruises, in which Hamelin several times took part. By 1799 his organizational ability had earned him a shore position—the command of St. Malo harbor—but he was eager to return to sea. Now with the rank of frigate captain, or commander, he was appointed to command the *Naturaliste*, one of the two ships allocated to Baudin *(q.v.)* for a voyage of exploration in Australian waters.

The *Naturaliste* was a slower vessel than Baudin's own *Géographe*, but Hamelin's skill and daring took him closer inshore than his superior and produced valuable surveys of the Australian coast and some significant discoveries. The expedition sailed from Le Havre on 19 October 1800, to Mauritius, western Australia, Timor, Tasmania, and Port Jackson. In November 1802 Baudin decided to rid himself of the slow and cumbersome *Naturaliste*. Hamelin sailed with Baudin on 18 November as far as King Island, in Bass Strait, and three days later set out for France. He reached Mauritius on 2 February 1803, but was subsequently captured in the Channel and taken to Portsmouth, being later released through the intervention of Sir Joseph Banks *(q.v.)*, finally arriving at Le Havre on 7 June 1803.

Hamelin was promoted to captain, given the cross of the Legion of Honor, and made a baron. His career continued to prosper; he was posted to the "Grande Expédition" planned against England, and although this undertaking was canceled, he had one moment of glory against the English when commanding the frigate *Vénus*. He eventually became director of the Dépot des Cartes et Plans and a rear admiral. He died in 1839.

Cape Hamelin, near Cape Leeuwin, and Hamelin Pool, both in western Australia, are named after him.

## Hanna

NOTHING IS KNOWN of James Hanna until 15 April 1785, when he sailed from Macao in the 60-ton brig *Harmon* on the first commercial voyage made to the northwest coast of America. It is even unclear which flag he sailed under, but his financial backer was John Henry Cox, an English merchant living in China.

Hanna reached Nootka Sound in August and, in spite of an early affray with local Indians, he purchased 560 otter pelts with which he returned to Macao, where he arrived in December. The skins sold for an excellent price, and a second expedition was organized with a larger ship, *Sea Otter*.

James Hanna sailed in May 1786, again making for Nootka and arriving once more in August, but he discovered that he had been forestalled by another trader, James Strange *(q.v.)*, and could buy only some 50 pelts. Hanna was thus forced to sail up the coast in search of more skins and explore a number of sounds and inlets. He gave the name of Cox Island to the north of Vancouver Island and that of Nova Hibernia to the Queen Charlotte Islands. On 1 October he sailed back to Macao, where he dropped anchor on 8 February 1787.

In spite of rapidly growing competition in the fur trade, the voyage of the *Sea Otter* was profitable, and a third expedition was planned. However, James Hanna died at Macao a few months after his return.

## Hasselborough

FREDERICK HASSELBOROUGH was the captain of the sealing vessel *Perseverance* owned by Campbell & Co. of Sydney. The spelling Hasselburg is also to be found. He left New South Wales in 1810, making for New Zealand. In October–November 1810 he came upon two detached islands well to the south of New Zealand that he named Campbell and Macquarie. Although he was the discoverer of Campbell Island, the presence of wreckage on Macquarie suggests that someone had preceded him there but evidently had not survived to report the discovery.

Hasselborough was himself drowned in a boating accident at Campbell Island with two of his men on 4 November 1810, his fate and his discovery being reported to his employers when the *Perseverance* returned to Port Jackson on 8 January 1811.

## Hawkins

RICHARD HAWKINS, born in 1562, the only son of the privateer and associate of Francis Drake, Sir John Hawkins, made England's final attempt at raiding the Spanish possessions along the Pacific coast of America. He had sailed on a raiding voyage to the West Indies in 1582 under his uncle William, captained a galliot in Drake's expedition to the same area in 1584–1585, and served under Drake against the Spanish Armada in 1588. Two years later he went out with his father to Portugal in a failed attempt to capture the Spanish treasure fleet.

On 12 June 1593 he set out with the *Dainty* and the *Fancy* from Plymouth, supposedly on a voyage of discovery. Scurvy soon affected the crew, and on 10 December, when he ran into a storm off the River Plate, the *Fancy* deserted. Land was discovered farther south, which he named Hawkins' Maidenland in honor of Queen Elizabeth. It was in all probability a sighting of the Falkland Islands. On 15 February 1594 he entered the Strait of Magellan, emerging into the Pacific on 29 March.

Any pretense at exploration was promptly abandoned. Hawkins plundered Valparaiso. This gave the Spanish authorities time to organize their defenses. Hawkins was first attacked off Pisco; in mid-June, while sailing to Ecuador and Panama, he was outmatched by two Spanish ships and forced to surrender. He was sent to Spain in 1597 and repatriated to England in 1602. He was later knighted, became Member of Parliament for Plymouth, and a vice-admiral. He died in London on 17 April 1622.

His *Observations in his Voyage into the South Sea* was published in that same year.

## Hayes

WILLIAM HENRY (BULLY) HAYES was born sometime between 1828 and 1832 in Cleveland, Ohio, went to sea at an early age, and is believed to have been dismissed from the U.S. Navy in 1846, having seen service in the China seas. He then worked on merchant ships, obtaining his master's ticket in 1854 or therabouts, engaging in trade in California, Australia, East Asia, and various Pacific islands.

Having lost his ship, the *Ellenita*, off Samoa in October 1859, he went to Australia, where he was briefly imprisoned for debt. He then joined a vaudeville troupe as manager, going with it to New Zealand in September 1862. In 1864 he went to Australia, and obtained a ship, which he lost on arrival in New Zealand to creditors.

With his next ships, the *Shamrock* and the *Rona*, he traded extensively between New Zealand and various Pacific islands. From 1867 to 1875 he traded among the islands, using Samoa as his base and showing great navigational ability and an unparalleled knowledge of island groups, passes, and reefs. This knowledge enabled him on several occasions to avoid capture by British and American authorities—for by then he had acquired a reputation for sharp dealings, gun and alcohol running, and other nefarious activities. His nickname was actually *bulli*, a Samoan term meaning "evasive" or "slippery" bestowed on him by a local missionary.

His luck came to a temporary end in Guam in 1875 when the Spanish authorities arrested him, sending him to prison in Manila. He was freed after nine months and resumed trading, but he was killed on board his own ship in April 1877 during a voyage from the Marshall Islands to Kusaie (Kosrae) in the Carolines.

## Henriquez

HERNÁNDO HENRIQUEZ was lieutenant *(alférez general* or *alférez real)* on the expedition led by Mendaña *(q.v.)* in 1567. On 3 May 1568 he was sent with Hernán Gallego *(q.v.)* in the brigantine the Spaniards had constructed for coastal explorations in the newly discovered Solomon Islands. Although Gallego was the pilot, Henriquez was the senior officer and in better health than Gallego, who was affected by fever, possibly malaria. Henriquez can therefore be credited with important discoveries made by the brigantine during late May and June, namely the islands of San Cristobal, Ulawa, Olu Malau, and Ugi.

## Henry

SAMUEL PINDER HENRY was born in Tahiti on 8 February 1800, the eldest son of the missionary William Henry. After studying in Sydney, he returned in 1814 and settled with his father in Moorea. The Tahitian king, Pomare II, supported the English missionaries, including the Williams family. Samuel became a sailor and trader, making a first voyage in the islands in command of Pomare's *Haweis*. In 1821 the king appointed him sole agent for disposing of his cargos in Sydney. During the 1820s he sailed on a number of occasions on trading voyages among the islands and to New South Wales, dealing in mother-of-pearl and sandalwood and, on at least one occasion in 1822, in muskets.

Henry was associated with the missionary John Williams and the French trader J. A. Moerenhout *(q.v.)*. He was a partner with his brother-in-law Thomas Ebrill in a sugar cane enterprise, which, however, did not prosper, owing to a shortage of local labor. In 1831 he sailed with Captain Sandilands of the *Comet* from New South

Wales to Pitcairn Island to assist in the removal of the islanders to Tahiti. He was later appointed port pilot of Papeete, where he died on 9 June 1852.

Moerenhout reported in his *Voyages*, published in 1837, that it was Samuel Henry who discovered Rimatara, one of the Austral Islands. This discovery was probably made during Henry's 1821 voyage.

## Hergest

RICHARD HERGEST was born in London in 1754. He served first in the *Augusta*, then in the *Marlborough*. On 16 December 1771 he transferred to the *Adventure* as an able-seaman and sailed with James Cook *(q.v.)* on his second voyage to the Pacific, leaving on 13 July 1772 from Plymouth and returning three years later, on 29 July 1775. After serving in the *Ramillies* and the *Dublin*, Hergest was recalled to sail with Cook on his third voyage. Hergest had held the rank of midshipman from January 1773, but he transferred to Cook's *Resolution* on 10 February 1776 as an able-seaman, later rejoining the midshipmen. He took an active part in the events surrounding the death of Captain Cook; above all he developed further the friendship he had established with Vancouver *(q.v.)* during the previous voyage: Vancouver was to refer to him as "for many years my most intimate friend."

Hergest was commissioned lieutenant on 19 October 1780, shortly after the conclusion of the voyage. He was due for leave, since he had been at sea almost without a break for ten years. He saw service again but did not reenter the Pacific until 1792: Vancouver's expedition to the northwest coast needed approvisioning, so in 1791 he was sent in command of the *Daedalus* to take supplies to him in North America. In view of their long association, it was a logical choice, and in fact Hergest had almost sailed in Vancouver's ship. The passage as far as the Marquesas Islands was arduous, and when Hergest reached the archipelago on 22 March 1792 things went no better. The *Daedalus* broke its cable in a gale and, worse still, caught fire. The cargo, already damaged through faulty stowage, was further affected by this disaster.

The fire was put out, and the *Daedalus* struggled along to the Hawaiian Islands. Hergest anchored in Oahu, where, on 11 May, he was set upon by a party of islanders and killed together with his astronomer, Gooch. The *Daedalus* sailed on to Nootka, assisting Vancouver for a while, and then crossed the Pacific to Port Jackson, arriving in April 1794.

Vancouver avenged his friend's murder when he went to Oahu in 1793 by prevailing on a chief to identify and execute the alleged culprits. He also included an account of Hergest's voyage in his own *A Voyage of Discovery to the North Pacific Ocean*, published in 1798, while Aaron Arrowsmith, in his 1794 "Planisphere," used names bestowed by Hergest on several Marquesas islands; as a consequence Hergest was credited for some years with having made new discoveries in the Marquesas.

## Hsü Fu

HSÜ FU is a semimythical Chinese navigator who is believed to have sailed in 219 B.C. for the three islands of Fu-sang, a mysterious country to the east of Asia. Having obtained the permission of the emperor Shih Huang Ti, he left from the ancient city of Lang Yu in Shantung Province. He returned some time later and reported success, having met various magicians or officials, including the "Magician of the Sea" at Chih Cheng Palace on P'eng-lai Island who asked for a tribute of young men and maidens.

The emperor was persuaded and allowed Hsü Fu to leave on a second expedition, possibly in 215 B.C., with his colonists. Hsü Fu was never heard of again. It is likely that he had reached Japan. Whether he successfully carved himself a small kingdom in Japan, which, apart from the early Ainus, was still underpopulated, can only be speculation.

## Hudson

WILLIAM LEVERRETH HUDSON was born in New York in 1794 and was serving in the U.S. Navy as a midshipman in 1816. He became a close friend of Charles Wilkes (*q.v.*), who in 1838 selected him as second-in-command of the United States Exploring Expedition and captain of the 650-ton sloop *Peacock*.

The fleet sailed from Norfolk, Virginia, on 18 August 1838 for Cape Verdes and Rio, *Peacock* proving the fastest sailer. The ships left Rio on 6 January 1839, making for Tierra del Fuego, Hudson sailing southwest to penetrate beyond James Cook's most southerly reaches before going on to Valparaiso, where the remainder of the fleet joined him in May. Wilkes then organized a thorough survey of the Tuamotu archipelago. The islet of Ahii was given the name of Peacock Island, just as Nanomanga would be called, equally ephemerally, Hudson Island.

In September 1839 *Peacock* rejoined the other ships in Matavai Bay, Tahiti, where she remained until mid-October for repairs. The next survey was that of the Samoan islands, *Peacock* being assigned the island of Upolu. The ship then made for Sydney, arriving on 26 November. The expedition sailed on 26 December for the Antarctic and New Zealand, but during this arduous part of the voyage Hudson's ship was badly damaged by ice and forced to return to Sydney. Hudson rejoined Wilkes at the Fijis in June. After a survey of this multi-island group Wilkes sailed for Honolulu, where Hudson joined him on 30 September 1840, the vessels having once again separated to cover as wide an area of ocean as possible. After a refit, *Peacock* was sent back to Samoa for further surveys, Wilkes meanwhile carrying out exploration work among the Hawaiian Islands before leaving in April 1841 for the northwest coast.

After completing his work in Upolu, Hudson sailed to the Ellice Islands (Tuvalu), arriving at Funafuti on 14 March 1841. The area was little known, although Hudson's Island (Nanomanga) had been discovered earlier, as had Fakaofo in the Phoenix group, which Hudson has often been credited with discovering. His next survey was in the Gilberts, which, Hudson complained, were inaccurately placed on the charts. This work meant that the *Peacok* returned later to Honolulu, missing Wilkes, who had already left for North America. After a brief respite, Hudson sailed on 21 June for the Columbia River, where he arrived, accompanied as usual by the small schooner *Flying Fish*, on 17 July. In attempting to get over the bar, the *Peacock* grounded and was lost.

Determined to pursue the survey of the coast, Wilkes purchased a brig, the *Thomas H. Perkins*, which he renamed *Oregon*. Work continued as far down as San Francisco Bay until 2 November 1841, when the fleet sailed for Honolulu, the Philippines, and Singapore, where the *Flying Fish* was sold. The *Oregon* arrived in New York a few weeks after Wilkes, at the beginning of July 1842.

Hudson had sailed with Wilkes as a lieutenant. He was promoted to captain in 1855, and in 1857–1858 commanded the steamer *Niagara*, which laid the first cable across the Atlantic. He died at Brooklyn, New York, on 15 October 1862.

## Hunter

JOHN HUNTER was born on 29 August 1737 at Leith, the port of Edinburgh. He went to sea at an early age and was shipwrecked while with his father off the coast of Norway. He enrolled as an able-seaman in the *Centaur* in 1755 and took part in a number of war-time engagements, serving among others in the *Royal Ann*, the *Princess Amelia*, and the *Royal George* under Admiral Durrell. By 1780 he was a lieutenant of the *Berwick* under Rodney; he later served in various ships under Admiral Howe, who became First Lord of the Admiralty in 1783.

In 1788 Hunter was appointed to the First Fleet preparing to sail to Botany Bay under Capt. Arthur Phillip. He was given command of the *Sirius* in which, on 2 October 1788, he also sailed to the Cape to fetch supplies for the new settlement. He returned in May 1789 but later lost the *Sirius* on Norfolk Island. He sailed instead in the Dutch snow *Waaksamheyd*, making for England. Passing east of the main Solomons chain he discovered a group of five low islands, which he named Stewart Islands. The *Waaksamheyd* reached Plymouth in April 1792.

Hunter returned to New South Wales in 1795 in the *Reliance* to take over as the colony's governor. He became a rear admiral in October 1807 and a vice-admiral in July 1810. He died in London on 13 March 1821. His *Historical Journal*, published in London in 1793, is a valuable record of his voyages and of early colonial Australia.

## Ibargoitia

JUAN DE IBARGOITIA, a frigate lieutenant in the Spanish navy, sailed from Manila on 15 July 1800 as commander of the *Filipino* for San Blas in Mexico. In March and April 1801 he sailed back and surveyed a number of the Caroline Islands, drawing plans and writing reports.

He is credited with the discovery of Pulusuk, Onon (Onoune), and probably Puluwat, which may have been sighted by Mortlock *(q.v.)* but of which Ibargoitia gave the first precise description and longitude.

## Ingraham

JOSEPH INGRAHAM was born in Boston and baptized there on 4 April 1762. He probably served in the navy during the Revolutionary War and subsequently sailed to the East. In October 1787 he sailed under John Kendrick *(q.v.)* in the *Columbia* to the northwest coast. Upon the return of the *Columbia* to Boston in August 1790, Thomas H. Perkins, a merchant, outfitted the *Hope* for Pacific trade and placed Ingraham in command.

Ingraham wasted no time and sailed by way of Cape Horn, entering the Pacific in early 1791 and making in the first instance for the Marquesas and Hawaii. On 19 April he sighted two islands, which he named Washington and Adams, followed by two more, which received the names Federal and Lincoln. More islands were encountered on the twentieth and twenty-first. The group became known as the Washingtons; they formed part of the Marquesas and included several discoveries for which Ingraham eventually received the credit: Ua Pou (Adams), Ua Huku (Washington), Nuku Hiva (Federal), Eiao, and Hatutu. He provides some useful ethnological information about the islanders in his *Journal*, a four-volume work. In May he was in the Hawaiian Islands, but he hastened to the northwest coast, aware of the fierce competition developing among traders. He arrived off the coast in June and after some initial difficulties obtained 1,400 skins.

He then sailed back in October to Hawaii and across the Pacific to Macao, where he found the Chinese had placed restrictions on the sale of furs. His worries were not helped by his falling seriously ill; by an irony of fate he was attended to by the surgeon of the *Solide*, the ship of Etienne Marchand *(q.v.)*, who had recently been to the Marquesas and now discovered to his chagrin that Ingraham has preceded him there and robbed him of several new discoveries.

In 1792 Ingraham returned to the northwest coast, going to Nootka in July where he found his fears realized: excessive competition from traders of various nations had unbalanced the market and reduced profitability. His second visit to the coast resulted in a substantial loss, and he made his way back to Boston, arriving early in 1793. Joseph Ingraham was commissioned a lieutenant in the U.S. Navy in June 1799 and was appointed to the brig *Pickering*, which sailed from Newcastle, Delaware, on 20 August 1800 and was never heard of again.

## Jacquinot

CHARLES-HECTOR JACQUINOT was born on 4 March 1796 at Nevers, France. Joining the navy at the age of 16, he rose successively to the rank of *enseigne* in 1820, lieutenant in 1825, and frigate captain in 1836.

In 1826 he was appointed first officer of the *Astrolabe*, in which Dumont d'Urville *(q.v.)* carried out a lengthy circumnavigation, returning to France in February 1829. He was not appointed captain upon the conclusion of the expedition as d'Urville requested because he lacked the appropriate seniority. D'Urville kept in touch with him, however, and looked forward to having him along as a second-in-command on the next voyage to the Pacific he was planning.

From 1837 to 1840 Jacquinot commanded the *Zélée* during d'Urville's second expedition. Promoted full captain on his return, he was given the task of supervising the publication of *Voyage au Pôle Sud et dans l'Océanie*, the official account of the expedition, following d'Urville's death, a task that did not really suit his nature.

He was appointed rear admiral in February 1852. He served in the Crimean War and was raised to vice-admiral in December 1855. He served as a naval administrator from 1857 but was put on the semiactive list in 1861 and died in 1879.

## Johnston

CHARLES JAMES JOHNSTON was born in England in 1765; he joined the Royal Navy in 1787, serving at first aboard the sloop *Savage* and later in various ships during the wars with France. He rose steadily through the ranks and was appointed governor of the naval hospital at Madras in 1802.

Promoted to captain in September 1806, he was given command

of the *Cornwallis*, in which he sailed to the Pacific. On 14 December 1807 he came upon two small islands enclosed by a reef, some seven hundred miles west-southwest of Honolulu. He named them at first Cornwallis Island, but they soon became known as Johnston Island, a name they have retained. Strictly, Johnston is the larger island, the other, half a mile to the northwest, being Sand Island, sometimes referred to as Agnes Island.

After his return to England, Captain Johnston continued in the service. He was a vice-admiral in the 1840s, retiring on half-pay as a rear admiral in 1850 and being finally pensioned off in April 1854. He died at Cowhill, near Dumfries, Scotland, on 16 October 1856.

## Jones

THOMAS AP CATESBY JONES was born at Hickory Hill, Virginia, on 24 April 1790. A midshipman from 22 November 1805, he began his career at Norfolk, then transferred to New Orleans under Captain Porter, spending seven years on operations directed against slave traders. He was promoted to lieutenant in May 1812 and to master commandant in 1820.

In 1825 he was appointed for the first time to command the U.S. Pacific Squadron, his flagship being the *Peacock*. He sailed to the Hawaiian Islands, enforcing the payment of certain debts, looking for deserters from American merchantmen, and supporting American missionaries against claims made by the British consul.

In 1836 Jones was appointed to head the South Seas Surveying and Exploring Expedition, a post he resigned in December 1837 after a dispute with the secretary of the navy. He returned to the Pacific in 1842 to command the Pacific Squadron. While at Callao he received information that led him to believe war had broken out with Mexico, and he sailed north, taking possession of Monterey on 19 October. He was relieved of his command to appease the Mexican government, but not otherwise censured. Two years later he returned to the Pacific to head the Pacific Squadron, and after the Mexican War helped to transport refugees out of Southern California. However, an argument over funds caused him to be once more relieved of his command.

Jones retired in 1855 and died at Sharon, Virginia, on 30 May 1858.

# Joy

GEORGE FOLGER JOY was born in 1796 in Massachusetts and served on a number of ships, including whaling vessels. His first recorded voyage to the Pacific was on the *Boston*, a whaler that sailed from Nantucket on 18 December 1822. He returned to New England on 9 May 1825.

On 30 May 1824 he had met the French captain L. I. Duperrey *(q.v.)* near the Marshall Islands. He reported to Duperrey his discovery on the twenty-fifth of an atoll of eight islets at latitude 4°45'. This was the island of Ebon, a detached atoll in the southwestern sector of the Marshalls.

This was to be Joy's only discovery in the Pacific, to which he returned on at least seven occasions between 1825 and 1849, mostly on whaling expeditions, the whalers he commanded being, in addition to the *Boston*, the *Golden Farmer*, *Zenas Coffin*, *Charles and Henry*, and *Columbia*. He died in Massachusetts in 1876.

# Kellett

HENRY KELLETT was born at Clonacody, Ireland, on 2 November 1806 and entered the navy in 1822. After five years serving in the West Indies he was appointed to the *Eden*, Capt. William Owen, for operations in Africa. He was promoted to lieutenant in 1828 and three years later was posted to the survey ship *Aetna* under Edward Belcher *(q.v.)*.

In 1835 Kellett left the *Aetna* to take over command of the *Starling*, which accompanied Beechey's *Sulphur* on a major surveying expedition to the Pacific. They sailed from Portsmouth on 24 December 1835, making for Madeira, Tenerife, Rio, and Montevideo, but when they reached Valparaiso on 6 June, Beechey became too ill to continue and was invalided home. Kellett took over command of the expedition for the rest of 1836 and carried on with surveying work. He then handed over command to Edward Belcher, who had been sent out from England to take charge of the expedition, and sailed with him to the Hawaiian Islands, Alaska, and California. The year 1838 was spent on survey work along the Central American coast; there was another call at Honolulu in 1839, but work along the American littoral took up most of that year; then the

expedition set off across the Pacific to the Marquesas, the Tuamotus, Tahiti, and on to Fiji, where in June 1840 Kellett was sent off to
make contact with the expedition of Charles Wilkes *(q.v.)*, who was
also in the archipelago. The final stage included the New Hebrides
(Vanuatu) and New Guinea, Kellett sailing on ahead to Amboina,
where Belcher joined him on 3 September 1840. The expedition
went home by way of Singapore and Canton, reaching Spithead on
19 June 1842. Kellett, however, stayed with the *Starling* in the East
and did not return to England until mid-1843.

Kellett had been raised to the rank of commander on 6 May 1841
and to post rank on 23 December 1842. In February 1845 he was
given command of the survey ship *Herald* in which he sailed to the
Pacific, carrying out hydrographic work along the coast between
Panama and Guayaquil. This work, however, was interrupted during the summer months of 1848, 1849, and 1850 when Kellett sailed
to Bering Strait and Arctic waters to assist in the search for the expedition of Sir John Franklin. It was not until late 1850 that the *Herald*
began its voyage home across the Pacific to Hong Kong, Singapore,
and the Cape, reaching England in mid-1851.

The continuing search for Franklin took up Kellett's next four
years. He sailed in the *Resolute* in February 1852 under the orders of
his old captain, Sir Edward Belcher, for Baffin Bay and Lancaster
Sound, wintering at Melville Island. The next year brought severe
hardships, and in May 1854 Belcher ordered the *Resolute* abandoned, overriding Kellett's objections. The ship's company returned
to England in another vessel, arriving in September 1854. The *Resolute* had meanwhile drifted through Lancaster Sound and been taken
over by an American whaler; after refitting, it was formally handed
back to Britain in December 1856.

Henry Kellett, who had been appointed commodore at Jamaica in
1855, was promoted to rear admiral in June 1862, vice-admiral in
April 1868, and then knighted a year later. He served as commander-
in-chief in China from 1869 to 1871 and died at Clonacody on
1 March 1875.

## Kendrick

JOHN KENDRICK was born about 1740 in Harwich, Massachusetts.
He went to sea at an early age, working on a whaler in the Gulf of St.

Lawrence and later serving as a soldier in the Seven Years War. He married in 1767 and acted as master of various ships sailing between Boston and southern ports. During the American War of Independence, he commanded ships under letters of marque, preying on British merchantmen. He lived at Edgartown, Martha's Vineyard, until 1778, when he settled in Wareham.

He had built up a solid reputation as a navigator when he was offered the command of the *Columbia*, which with the *Lady Washington* was being outfitted by a group of Boston merchants led by Joseph Barrell to sail to the northwest coast. The two ships left Boston on 30 September 1787 but became separated during a gale off Cape Horn on 1 April 1788. The *Lady Washington*, commanded by Robert Gray *(q.v.)*, reached the northern coast first, but the two ships rejoined in Nootka Sound on 23 September 1788. Kendrick's ability as a leader is open to argument. He had sailed to Juan Fernandez, where he spent late May and early June, and had been delayed when his ship had suffered in various storms. The voyage had already lasted a year. Kendrick and Gray wintered on the northwest coast, obtaining furs to take to China.

Kendrick decided to transfer to the *Lady Washington*, and on 30 July 1789 he sent Gray with the *Columbia* to Canton while he continued to trade off the coast. After a couple of months, Kendrick sailed for China by way of Hawaii, arriving in Macao on 26 January 1790. His transactions there were prolonged and obscure. He seems at times to have behaved as though the *Lady Washington* belonged to him. He altered the sloop to a brigantine and sailed north to Japan, later returning to the northwest coast. He found the presence of Spanish vessels there a potential danger and traded slowly and cautiously until September 1791, when he returned to China.

He reputedly bought some land in Alaska, but like his other transactions, the purchase was not profitable. He sailed again for the northwest coast in 1792, but the *Lady Washington* was dismasted in a gale, and months of inaction followed. In 1793 and 1794 Kendrick was back sailing on the coast. In December 1794 he was at Oahu in the Hawaiian Islands, en route to China, when on the twelfth he was killed in a freak accident: another American vessel, in saluting, inadvertently fired a loaded cannon, hitting the *Lady Washington* amidships.

Kendrick was an able-seaman and a kind-hearted leader, but he was no businessman: his hopes of recouping his mounting losses by one more voyage ended at each attempt in failure.

## Kent

JOHN RODOLPHUS KENT was born in England, but neither the place nor the date of his birth is known. He joined the Royal Navy and was in New South Wales in 1820. As captain of the schooner *Prince Regent* he sailed to New Zealand from Port Jackson on 15 February 1820 and carried out coastal surveys along the northern coasts. He returned twice to Australia, the second time in October 1820, and in 1821 sailed to Hawaii with the *Prince Regent*, which was to be given to Kamehameha II on behalf of King George IV, and the cutter *Mermaid*.

Kent was back in Port Jackson on 24 January 1823. On 7 May 1823 he sailed again for New Zealand to investigate the likelihood of a flax trade being successfully established around Foveaux Strait in the far south. Until his return to Australia in August, he also carried out a number of coastal surveys in the South Island. On 5 November he went back to southern New Zealand in command of the brig *Elizabeth Henrietta*.

Back in Australia in March 1825 he decided to leave government service and took command of the sealing vessel *Elizabeth*, sailing from Port Jackson on 14 March 1826 for southern New Zealand, the Seal Islands, and eventually Hokianga on the western coast of northern New Zealand. It was here that he decided to settle in April 1827, working as a trader and sailing to Australia and back on a number of occasions in command of small trading vessels.

He died at Kahawai, not far from present-day Auckland, on 1 January 1837.

## Kermadec

JEAN-MICHEL HUON DE KERMADEC was born in Brest, France, on 12 September 1748 into a family long associated with the sea. He joined the navy in 1766, becoming a sublieutenant within a few years and a full lieutenant in 1779. He took part in a number of campaigns, distinguishing himself particularly during the American War of Independence, which earned him the Cross of St. Louis. In 1785 he went on to Mauritius, where he became a close friend of d'Entre-casteaux *(q.v.)*, with whom he sailed in the *Résolution* on the famous expedition to China against the prevailing monsoon winds.

D'Entrecasteaux selected him to command the *Espérance* for the expedition in search of La Pérouse *(q.v.)*. Since he was a member of the Academy of Marine, Kermadec was closely associated with the planning of the expedition and supervised the fitting out of the two vessels selected for it at Brest.

Kermadec's health was not really up to the strains of an arduous voyage, and when the *Recherche* and the *Espérance* sailed from Brest on 29 September 1791, it must have been with some misgiv-ings on his part. He seconded d'Entrecasteaux with skill and devo-tion, and there were few difficulties in his ship as it followed the *Recherche* around Australia and through the numerous archipelagos to the north. His promotion to captain from 1 January 1792 was well deserved. But during the second stay in Tasmania, in February 1793, Kermadec developed a fever from which he never recovered. North of New Zealand the pilot of the *Recherche*, Joseph Raoul, discovered the island that now bears his name; the island group of which it formed part was named the Kermadecs.

Kermadec died on 6 May 1793 while the expedition was charting the coast of northern New Caledonia. To prevent his body being dis-interred by the natives, he was secretly buried on the offshore islet of Poudioué. A number of geographical features in addition to the Kermadecs bear his name: the Huon River in Tasmania, where Huonville has since been built; Huon Islet in New Caledonia; Huon Gulf and Huon Peninsula in northeast New Guinea; and the great Kermadec Trench and Kermadec Ridge.

## Khromchenko

VASILII S(ERGEIVICH) KHROMCHENKO (also found under Krom-chenko and Khramchenko) was born in 1792 and first sailed to the Pacific as mate of the *Riurik* under Kotzebue *(q.v.)*. Kotzebue highly commended him for his willingness and ability, and in 1821 Khrom-chenko gained further experience when he surveyed Bristol Bay in Alaska. He obtained his own command, the *Elena*, in 1828, sailing to Port Jackson, through the Marshall Islands, where he carried out hydrographic operations, and to Sitka on the northwest coast. In

1831 he set off once more to the Pacific as captain of the transport ship *Amerika*, again going to Port Jackson, and spending part of 1832 in the Marshall Islands. He died in 1842.

## King

JAMES KING was born in 1750 in Clitheroe, Lancashire, the son of a clergyman. He entered the Royal Navy at the age of 12 and served on the Newfoundland station and in the Mediterranean. He became a lieutenant in 1771 but in 1774 decided to study science in Paris and later at Oxford. He was recommended by Dr. Hornsley, professor of astronomy, for the third voyage of James Cook *(q.v.)* and joined the *Resolution* in February 1776.

The *Resolution* sailed from Plymouth on 12 July 1776, making for the Cape of Good Hope, Tasmania, and New Zealand. In March 1777 the expedition was on its way to the Society Islands, discovering Mangaia and Atiu in the southern Cooks, and Tubuai in the Austral Islands. Following their departure from the Society Islands, the English discovered the Hawaiian group and went on to explore the northwest coast of America. On his return to the Hawaiian Islands, Cook was killed on 14 February 1779.

The death of the commander led to a reorganization of Cook's two ships and their crews. James King became the *Resolution*'s first lieutenant, replacing John Gore *(q.v.)*, who took over the *Discovery*. The expedition sailed to Kamchatka to begin an arduous exploration of Arctic seas. It lasted from June to August 1779. On 22 August, as the two vessels neared the coast of Kamchatka, Charles Clerke *(q.v.)*, who had taken over after Cook's death, died of tuberculosis and exhaustion. Another reorganization was necessary. King took over command of the *Discovery*, in which he sailed on 10 October for Macao and home. Almost a year later, on 4 October 1780, the two ships arrived in the Thames.

Promotion soon came: James King became a post-captain. In 1781 he was appointed to the *Crocodile* on Channel service and toward the end of the year to the *Resistance* for escort duties to the West Indies. His main task, however, was the completion of the narrative of Cook's third voyage, for which he was eminently qualified. He authored the third volume of *A Voyage to the Pacific Ocean in the Years 1778 . . . 1780*, which appeared in 1784. King's tuberculosis forced him to give up his naval career and to seek rest in a warmer climate. He moved to Nice, southern France, in 1783 and died there toward the end of October 1784.

## Koster

JAN KOSTER (or Coster) was captain of the *Arend*, which under Jacob Roggeveen *(q.v.)* sailed to the Pacific with the *Thienhoven* and the *Afrikaansche Galey*, leaving from Texel on 1 August 1721.

Koster was the most experienced of the three captains (Roggeveen, who was not a sailor, but a lawyer, took passage on the *Arend*, which with 32 guns and a complement of 110 men was the largest of the three vessels). He had been in the service of the Dutch East India Company and had sailed to the East at least three times prior to 1718. In September 1718 he was discharged from the company's service because, while captain of the *Noordbeck*, a merchantman returning to Holland, part of the cargo turned up missing. At the time of his departure from Texel with Roggeveen, he was probably in his forties and can therefore be assumed to have been born in Holland in the mid-1670s.

The instructions issued to him survived and provide a valuable insight into the proposed expedition. The intention was to enter the Pacific by way of Cape Horn, explore the southeast Pacific (seeking in particular David Land and Terra Australis), and return by the same route, thereby respecting the monopoly of the Dutch East India Company over the Spice Islands (now Indonesia). The first part of the plan was followed, but at a shipboard meeting in June 1722 it was decided to press on toward the west across the Pacific. One possibility was to make for New Zealand, which was not under the East India Company's control, but Koster argued strongly against this option. The expedition accordingly sailed for the Dutch East Indies, reaching Japara in northern Java on 10 September 1722 and Batavia on 4 October.

The ships were impounded and the navigators placed under arrest. The *Arend* was used by company officials for a trading voyage to Persia. Koster's journal was sent to Holland, where it was tabled at the inevitable litigation that arose out of the dispute between the Dutch West and East India companies, but it has unfortunately been lost. Jan Koster sailed on 3 December 1722 for Holland in a Dutch merchantman, arriving at Texel in July 1723. Within a few days of his return, he was giving evidence before the Committee of Ten of the West India Company. The legal arguments dragged on for several years, while Koster waited for his arrears of pay to be settled. The date of his death is unknown.

## Kotzebue

OTTO EUSTAFEVICH VON KOTZEBUE (or Kotsebu) was born in Tallinn (then called Reval), Estonia, on 30 December 1788. He was the son of the German dramatist August von Kotzebue, who wrote a play on La Pérouse *(q.v.)* in 1798. He entered the Naval Cadet School and was selected to join the expedition of Kruzenshtern (1803–1806) as a cadet in the *Nadezhda*. Kruzenshtern *(q.v.)* developed great respect for Kotzebue's ability and determination during the voyage and took the young man under his protection. When Count Romanzov, the grand chancellor, proposed that a Russian expedition should seek the much-yearned-for Northwest Passage through Bering Strait, Kruzenshtern recommended that, whatever the purpose, the expedition should be led by Kotzebue. Together they went to Abo, in Finland, in 1814 to arrange for the construction of a ship. Kruzenshtern then went to London to buy scientific instruments.

In January 1815 Kotzebue went to fetch the new ship, the *Riurik*, which was launched in May. All was ready by July, and on the thirtieth the expedition sailed from Kronstadt for Copenhagen and Plymouth. On 5 October 1815 the *Riurik* left Plymouth for Cape Horn and the Pacific. In mid-February 1816 it put in at Concepción, Chile. A call at Easter Island in March met with a hostile reception, and Kotzebue sailed on to the Tuamotus, where on 25 April he discovered Tikahau, which he named Kruzenshtern Island. Sighting Penrhyn (Tongareva) at the end of the month, he went on to the Marshall Islands, part of which he mapped in detail, and to Kamchatka. He was in time to explore the Bering Strait area in July and to explore part of northern Alaska and the northwest coast, leaving his name to the vast Kotzebue Sound off the Seward Peninsula. By early October he had reached San Francisco Bay, where he rested his crew for a month before going on to Hawaii.

Kotzebue spent from 24 November to 14 December 1816 in the

Hawaiian Islands and sailed again to the Marshalls, where he made various small discoveries in the Radak and Ralik chains, bestowing Russian names on these atolls (which, however, have reverted to their native names). He left in March 1817 for Unalaska, carried out more surveys along the Alaskan coast, and returned to Hawaii in September. On 14 October 1817 he left Oahu for home, reaching the Cape of Good Hope on 29 March 1818 where he met Freycinet *(q.v.)* of the *Uranie*. Kotzebue arrived back at Reval on 23 July 1818.

His achievements were considerable. He published a detailed account of his voyage with a valuable *Atlas* in 1821–1823 by which time he was already preparing a second expedition in the frigate *Predpriatie*. He sailed on 28 July 1823, called as before in Denmark and England for supplies and equipment, and left Portsmouth on 15 September for Tenerife, Rio, and Cape Horn, which he turned on 25 December. After a brief stay in Chile, the *Predpriatie* sailed for the Tuamotus. Kotzebue discovered an island he called Predpriatie, which is Fangahina, as well as Aratika, before dropping anchor in Tahiti on 14 March 1824. He then went on to survey the Samoan group and continued to the Marshalls, furthering his survey of the Radaks, and sailing to Petropavlovsk in June. The summer months were spent on hydrographic work along the Aleutian chain, going to the Russian trading post at Sitka and down the American coast to San Francisco.

The return voyage took the *Predpriatie* across the Pacific to Hawaii and back to the Marshalls—where on 9 October Kotzebue discovered Bikini Atoll (which he named Escholtz after a scientist who sailed with him on both voyages)—Guam, the Philippines, and the Cape of Good Hope. After a brief call at Portsmouth, Kotzebue dropped anchor at Kronstadt on 10 July 1826. The account of this second circumnavigation was published in 1828 and translated into English in 1830.

Kotzebue eventually retired to Reval, where he died on 15 February 1846.

## Krenitsyn

LITTLE IS KNOWN of the early life of Peter Kuzmich Krenitsyn (or Krenitzin). In association with M. D. Levashov, he led the first government-sponsored expedition to the Aleutian Islands, setting out in 1764 from St. Petersburg. In 1768 he set out from the mouth of the Kamchatka River to survey the islands of Umnak, Unalaska—whose latitude he determined with precision—Unimak, and the western shores of the Alaska Peninsula.

He returned to Kamchatka in 1769 and drowned in the Kamchatka River before he could set out again. The journals and charts of the expedition were sent back to St. Petersburg and were used to compile a notable map of the Aleutian Islands, which appeared in 1777. This information was also drawn upon by the Englishman William Coxe for his 1780 work, *Account of the Russian Discoveries between Asia and America.*

His name is commemorated in the Krenitzin Islands in the central Aleutians.

## Kruzenshtern

IVAN FEDOROVICH KRUZENSHTERN (or Krusenstern, also known as Adam Ivan) was born at Hagudi, Estonia, on 19 November 1770. He graduated from the Naval Cadet Corps in 1788 and took part in the battle of Gotland in the Gulf of Finland. Like a number of young cadets of the time he was sent to England as a volunteer in 1793 to gain experience with the British navy. This enabled him to travel to America, India, and China. On his return to Russia in 1799 he wrote a memoir on the relative advantages for Russia of sailing to China by way of the Cape of Good Hope and Cape Horn. He obtained the support of the czar for a circumnavigation that was to put his ideas to the test.

Lisyansky *(q.v.)* went to England, where he obtained two ships, renamed the *Nadezhda* and the *Neva*. Kruzenshtern was to captain the *Nadezhda* and command the expedition, while Lisyansky was put in charge of the *Neva*. The ships sailed from Kronstadt on 7 August 1803, making first for Copenhagen, then to Falmouth for further supplies, finally leaving on 5 October for Cape Horn, which was rounded on 3 March 1804. The ships became separated three weeks later. Kruzenshtern went to the Marquesas, putting in at Nuku Hiva on 5 May. A week later the *Neva* rejoined its consort. A great deal of ethnologic information on the Marquesas was obtained during this stay, which lasted almost two weeks. The Russians were helped by two European residents of the island, one of whom, Cabri, a heavily tattooed Frenchman, was taken back to Europe.

The ships next made for Hawaii, where, by arrangement, they separated, the *Nadezhda* setting course for Kamchatka. On July 13 the ship arrived at Petropavlovsk, where much-needed repairs could be carried out. On 6 September it left for Nagasaki, where Kruzenshtern hoped to establish contact with the Japanese. He arrived at the harbor entrance on 8 October but was not allowed into the inner harbor until 22 December. Earlier negotiations with Japan had given rise to the hope that a Russian ambassador would be accepted, and one was actually on board; but the attempt to establish relations was a failure, and Kruzenshtern sailed out on 17 April. He returned to Petropavlovsk along the coast of Honshu and Hokkaido and went on to Sakhalin and the Kurils, so that his time was not totally wasted.

Leaving Kamchatka on 5 July 1805, he continued his survey of Sakhalin; he concluded that it was not an island, but a peninsula attached to Asia. He returned briefly to Petropavlovsk before sailing for Macao on 9 October. He arrived there on 20 November 1805 and was joined by the *Neva* a fortnight later. The Chinese authorities were not sure whether the two Russians were warships or merchant vessels that could be allowed to trade, as Lisyansky had on board a rich cargo of furs for sale. The English head of the East India Company helped to smoothe the problems; the furs were sold, passports were issued, and the *Nadezhda* and the *Neva* weighed anchor on 9 February 1806. They proceeded south through the China Sea to Sunda Strait and the Indian Ocean and arrived back in the Baltic on 19 August 1806.

The expedition was successful in every respect bar the Japanese enterprise. The scientific, hydrographic, and ethnographic work was considerable. Kruzenshtern's *Voyage around the World in the Years 1803–1806*, published in three volumes in 1809 to 1812, was complemented by Lisyansky's own account and by the narrative of the expedition's scientist G. H. von Langsdorff, but most influential was Kruzenshtern's great *Atlas of the Southern Sea*, published in St. Petersburg in 1827.

Kruzenshtern became inspector in 1811 and director in 1827 of the Naval Cadet Corps, a post he held until 1842. The publication of his papers took up much of his time; he assisted in the planning of Kotzebue's voyage *(q.v.)*, was a founding member of the Russian Geographical Society, and was elected a member of the Royal Society of London. He became an admiral in 1842 and died at Reval on 24 August 1846.

## La Giraudais

FRANÇOIS CHESNARD DE LA GIRAUDAIS was born in St. Malo, Brittany, in 1727 and first went to sea at the age of five with his father, under whom he served aboard the *Saint Laurent* in 1744 during the War of the Spanish Succession. He was wounded while a lieutenant on the *Lys* and taken prisoner. During the Seven Years War he commanded a privateer and was once more taken prisoner. When he was freed he took over the *Machault* and served with particular dash and bravery in Canada and Newfoundland. It was then that he met Bougainville *(q.v.)*, who asked him to assist with the establishment of a French settlement on the Falkland Islands.

For this he was put in charge of the *Sphinx* in 1763. When the settlement had to surrender to the Spanish, he returned (in 1767) in command of the *Étoile* and with the rank of fireship captain. He then accompanied Bougainville during his circumnavigation, sailing by way of the Strait of Magellan and the Tuamotus to Tahiti, the Samoas, and the New Hebrides, then to New Guinea, the Solomons, and the Moluccas. His ship was slower and more cumbersome than Bougainville's *Boudeuse* and required extensive careening in Mauritius. The *Étoile* finally anchored in Rochefort on 24 April 1769 after an absence of twenty-seven months.

La Giraudais returned to Mauritius, where he engaged in commercial operations with only moderate success. He died in Zanzibar on 30 November 1775.

## Langara

CAYETANO DE LANGARA Y HUARTE was a relative and probably a younger brother of Juan de Langara y Huarte (1730–1806), captain general of the Spanish fleet. Little is known of his early career, but in 1770 he sailed under Felipe Gonzalez *(q.v.)* on the *San Lorenzo* to Easter Island. During the period of Spanish activity in the southeastern Pacific and particularly in the Society Islands, he served in Peru and Chile, being entrusted in 1772 with negotiations on behalf of the viceroy during a spate of rebellious activities involving the *Astuto* and the *Septentrion*. He was an obvious choice to command the *Aguila* following the death of Boenechea *(q.v.)*, when the viceroy decided to get a report on the Spanish mission recently established at Tahiti.

Langara sailed from Callao on 27 September 1775 with stores for the missionaries but found the two men dispirited after less than a year among the islanders. He took them on board and brought them back to Callao, where he arrived on 17 February 1776.

Langara returned to Europe and served in several ships, being given command of the *Paula Primera*, a 1,400-ton floating battery of 21 guns, based in the Spanish port of Algeciras during the long siege of Gibraltar. The *Paula Primera* was set on fire during the battle of September 1782, and Langara is believed to have lost his life during this engagement.

## Langerie

JEAN-BAPTISTE FORGEAIS DE LANGERIE was captain of the *Comtesse de Pontchartrain*, a merchant vessel that circumnavigated the globe from west to east, the first ship to do so. The *Pontchartrain* sailed in February 1714 from St. Malo, Brittany, passed through Sunda Strait on 25 August, and dropped anchor in Canton at the end of September.

After almost a year in the East, on 7 September 1715, the *Pontchartrain* sailed with a cargo of Chinese goods for South America, accompanied by the *Brillant*, commanded by Jacques Louvel. They went north of Taiwan toward Okinawa and reached Tres Marias Islands, off the coast of Mexico, on 26 October 1715. After a brief stay, they continued their trading voyage as far as Arica in northern Chile. There were further opportunities for trade along the South American seaboard, but Langerie sailed home to St. Malo in 1716, thus completing his circumnavigation. Louvel, on the other hand, stayed on the coast, taking advantage of the relaxation of the Spanish monopoly rights, which favored French merchants; this situation was coming to an end, however, and the *Brillant* was captured by a Spanish punitive expedition in 1717.

## Langle

PAUL-ANTOINE FLEURIOT DE LANGLE was born at the chateau of Kerlouet, Brittany, on 1 August 1744. He joined the navy in 1758, took part in a campaign to the West Indies, and was wounded on his return, off Ushant, in 1760.

He rapidly recovered and served in various ships, sailing to the West Indies once more, to Guiana, and to the Mediterranean. He began to earn a reputation in scientific circles for his work on longitudes, was appointed to the Académie de Marine, and made a Knight of the Order of St. Louis in 1778. He held various commands during the American War of Independence, when he met La Pérouse *(q.v.)*, under whom in 1782 he took part in the daring raid on British settlements in Hudson Bay, northern Canada.

Back in France in 1783 he was promoted to the rank of post-captain and married Georgette de Kérouatz, niece of a senior naval administrator. His scientific background combined with his naval experience and his friendship with La Pérouse made him an ideal choice for the command of the *Astrolabe*, the second ship of the La Pérouse expedition. Indeed, for a time, rumors circulated in Paris that he was to lead the expedition.

The *Astrolabe* and the *Boussole*, which La Pérouse commanded, sailed from Brest on 1 August 1785, making for the South Atlantic and, by way of the Strait of Le Maire, for the Pacific. The ships called at Chile, Easter Island, and Maui in the Hawaiian Islands before going on to Alaska, down to California, and across to China. The strain of navigating in the relatively unknown waters around Japan, Korea, and Siberia, coupled with his painstaking scientific work, began to take its toll on de Langle, who was compelled to appoint a young officer, Law de Lauriston, to take over his hydrographic and scientific tasks. It may have impaired his judgment or shortened his temper for, on 10 December 1787, in spite of La Pérouse's strong entreaties—which fell just short of a direct order—he decided to go ashore in a bay on Tutuila, in the Samoan group, to refill the ship's water casks. The tide was low, and he was forced to leave his boats and some of his men some distance from the shore.

He was killed along with eleven others when the islanders attacked in force.

## Langlois

JEAN-FRANÇOIS LANGLOIS was born at La Lucerne, in the department of Manche, France, on 26 June 1808. He first sailed in merchant ships out of Cherbourg and from 1826 in whaling ships from Le Havre. He obtained his first command of a whaling vessel in 1833.

In 1837 as captain of the *Cachalot* he set out for the Pacific. From May to August 1838 he was whaling off the coast of New Zealand and became attracted to the commercial possibilities of Banks Peninsula and Akaroa Harbour. He persuaded local Maori to sell him an ill-defined area of land for a thousand francs and sailed back to France, where he spent most of 1839 obtaining support for a colonizing company, the Compagnie Nanto-Bordelaise, which despatched on 20 March 1840 the ship *Comte de Paris* under Langlois, who then planned to go whaling in her; the French government had already sent out the corvette the *Aube* under Capt. C. F. Lavaud *(q.v.)*.

The *Comte de Paris* reached Banks Peninsula on 17 August 1840. From December 1840 until April 1841 Langlois went on a whaling expedition in this vessel, returning to Akaroa to rest his crew and setting out again in May on a voyage that took him as far as Tonga. He was back at Akaroa in February 1842 and after a more lengthy stay returned to France, where he arrived in October 1842. He spent much time attempting to pursue his claims and to persuade the French government to proclaim French sovereignty over the small colonial enclave. In 1847 he endeavored to set up a French whaling company and in 1851 became manager of a large fishing concern, but he did not return to the Pacific and retired in 1857 in Paris. Nothing is known of his later years.

## La Pérouse

JEAN-FRANÇOIS DE GALAUP was born in Albi, southwest France, on 23 August 1741. When he joined the French navy as a "garde de la Marine" in November 1756 he added the name of one of the family's country properties, the farm of La Pérouse, to his own and in later years when he frequented the court became known as Comte de la Pérouse.

He served in a number of ships during and between the long wars that opposed France and England during the second half of the eighteenth century, taking part in numerous campaigns in Canada, Newfoundland, the West Indies, the Indian Ocean, and America. In 1782, as the American War of Independence was in its closing stages, he carried out a daring and dangerous raid deep into Hudson Bay, northern Canada, destroying the British posts there, but he also helped to repatriate prisoners and took care to ensure that supplies were left for those who stayed behind to face the harsh winter. This humane behavior won him praise in France and earned him the goodwill of the British authorities, who readily cooperated when he began to plan his voyage of exploration.

By 1783 he was a post-captain, a Knight of the Order of St. Louis, and influential in French naval circles. He became a close adviser to Count Claret de Fleurieu, a senior naval administrator, with whom he began to plan an expedition to the Pacific to survey in particular areas that James Cook (q.v.) had not been able to reconnoiter. It was at this time that he married Eléonore Broudou, daughter of a minor official from French Mauritius, whom he had been courting since 1777 but had been unable to marry in the face of the vehement opposition of his father, who considered the Broudous of an altogether inappropriate social class for a Galaup.

The expedition was meticulously planned, advice being obtained from a number of scientific societies. King Louis XVI took a personal interest in the preparations and amended some of the original instructions. Two ships were allocated, solid storeships, the *Boussole* and the *Astrolabe*, the latter being placed under the command of de Langle (q.v.).

The expedition sailed from Brest on 1 August 1785, called briefly at Tenerife, Trinidade, and Brazil, and passed through the Strait of Le Maire, reaching the port of Talcahuano in Chile on 24 February 1786. On 17 March the voyage of exploration proper began when the ships sailed for Easter Island, Maui in the Hawaiian group, and northern Alaska. The northwest coast of America was surveyed in detail, an achievement marred by the loss of twenty-one men drowned in a boating accident during a stay in Lituya Bay. The French continued on to Monterey, the major Spanish settlement in California, where they remained from 15 to 24 September. They then sailed westward across the Pacific, discovering Necker Island and French Frigate Shoals, and arrived in Macao on 3 January 1787.

In February they set out for the Philippines to begin the most dangerous and the most productive part of the voyage. Formosa (Taiwan), Korea, and Japan were closed worlds that Europeans were forbidden to approach. Their coastlines and surrounding seas were largely unknown, the charts quite unreliable. The *Boussole* and the *Astrolabe* sailed north along the coasts of Tartary and Sakhalin until shallow waters near the northern tip of Sakhalin forced them to turn back. In August they passed through the strait that separates Sakhalin from Hokkaido and that still bears today the name of La Pérouse. They continued along and through the chain of the Kuril Islands, anchoring in the Russian settlement of Petropavlovsk in southern Kamchatka on 7 September.

There, La Pérouse received news from France of his promotion to commodore and fresh instructions from Paris. Instead of sailing to New Zealand or home by way of the Moluccas, options still open to him, La Pérouse was ordered to sail to Botany Bay, where, reports had it, the English were planning to establish a colony. The new route still allowed La Pérouse to carry out further exploration in the northwest and central Pacific. But when the expedition was exploring the Samoas it suffered its second major reverse: on 11 December 1787 de Langle and eleven officers and men were killed in Tutuila in a sudden and still unexplained attack by a large crowd of Samoans. La Pérouse continued his survey of the Samoan and Tongan groups, attempted unsuccessfully to land on Norfolk Island, and on 26 January 1788 dropped anchor in Botany Bay, where the First Fleet under Captain Phillip had arrived a few days earlier.

The *Boussole* and the *Astrolabe* set out from New South Wales on 10 March to return to the Tongas and to explore New Caledonia and the adjacent archipelago. The plan was to return to France by way of Torres Strait, western Australia, and the Indian Ocean, thereby completing a voyage of exploration that would have lasted more than four years. Sometime in June 1788, however, a cyclone struck the vessels by night and drove them against reefs surrounding the small island of Vanikoro in the Santa Cruz group. Details of the wreck did not come to light for forty years (see under *Dillon*); as far as Europe was concerned the expedition had vanished. Fortunately, the journal of La Pérouse as well as other reports had been despatched to France with letters and other documents from various ports of call, so that the expedition's achievements could be recorded.

Many valuable drawings, however, and most of the natural history collection went down with the two ships.

## Laplace

CYRILLE-PIERRE-THÉODORE LAPLACE was born at sea on 7 November 1793, joined the navy during the Empire, and fought in various campaigns in the Indian and Atlantic oceans and in the West Indies. Promotion came quickly even though the postwar period offered few opportunities for young officers to display their talents: he became a lieutenant in 1823, received the Cross of St. Louis in 1825, and was promoted to frigate captain in 1828. He was well connected—he was the brother-in-law of Baron Tupinier, the director of ports and arsenals—but the reports of his commanding officers all bear witness to his ability and his resourcefulness.

He was chosen to command the *Favorite* on a voyage to the Far East and the Dutch East Indies, with the option of returning home by way of the Pacific and Cape Horn. Laplace did not hesitate to choose the longer way home rather than go back along the now well-worn Indian Ocean track.

The *Favorite*, a corvette of 680 tons, 24 guns, sailed from Toulon on 30 December 1830. After a brief call at the French West African outpost of Gorée, Laplace sailed around the Cape of Good Hope and reached the island of Bourbon (Réunion) on 1 April 1831. Buffeted and endangered by a series of hurricanes, the *Favorite* sought a safer anchorage in Port Louis, Mauritius. Eventually, at the beginning of May, the French set out for a survey of various small islands in the Indian Ocean and for French settlements in India. Narrowly avoiding being wrecked near Madras, they left on 2 August for Malacca and Singapore—which they found a dreary colony—then on to Manila, which was more enjoyable despite an epidemic of cholera, and Macao, where they dropped anchor on 21 November. Late December to early March 1832 was spent on surveys and negotiations along the coast of Indochina, an important but frustrating part of the voyage.

The *Favorite* sailed to the Natunas group north of Borneo and to the little-known Anambas. On 9 April Laplace reached Surabaya, where the Dutch authorities, disturbed by news of the overthrow of King Charles X, were polite but distant. Dysentery contracted in the unhealthy port did not make things any easier for the French, who left as soon as they obtained sufficient supplies for the next stage of the voyage, which took them through Madura Strait to Australia. On 11 July Laplace reached Hobart, grateful for a healthy climate and a chance to send his sick to a hospital. Leaving Hobart on 7 August, he made for Sydney, where he was made welcome but where rumors spread after his departure on 21 September 1832 that he was on his way to claim New Zealand on behalf of France.

He was indeed on his way to New Zealand, first sighted at the end of September, and he spent ten days in the Bay of Islands. The presence of a large French corvette in New Zealand waters led a number of Maori chiefs to write, after some prompting, to King William IV asking for his protection. Unaware of the concern he had caused, Laplace was on his way to Easter Island; but dysentery reappeared, and he sailed direct to Valparaiso where he arrived on 14 November.

The *Favorite* reached France on 21 April 1833 after an absence of twenty-eight months. Laplace handed over his charts and a large collection of natural history specimens. The first volume of the official account of his voyage appeared in 1833.

Laplace was soon to return to the Pacific. He sailed in the *Artémise* from Toulon on 20 January 1837. He again called at Gorée, but bad weather forced him to put into Capetown for repairs and supplies. Things were no easier on the way to Bourbon, where the *Artémise* dropped anchor on 26 May. After a call at Mauritius, the expedition went on to the Seychelles and to Trincomalee, where supplies were cheaper and more plentiful than in Mauritius. The French called at Pondicherry on 4 August, but on the way from Madras to Calcutta cholera broke out among the crew, causing a number of deaths.

In October, Laplace sailed to Sumatra, then back to India, putting in at Goa and Bombay. On 4 February 1838 he began a voyage of exploration to Muscat, Socotra, and Bander Abbas at the entrance to the Persian Gulf in "truly frightful heat." He was back in Trincomalee at the end of May and in Pondicherry in early June; he then began the Pacific stage of his voyage, going to Pulau Penang and Malacca, his men now affected by an outbreak of dysentery; nineteen died before he reached Indochina, but the others had recovered by the time he dropped anchor in Manila on 30 August. The *Artémise* needed repairs: the ship did not sail again until 16 October, to make for Tasmania by way of Macao, Batavia, and Sunda Strait.

The French spent from 25 January to 18 March 1839 in Hobart and Sydney, then sailed across the Tasman Sea to the northern tip of New Zealand and the Society Islands. The *Artémise* struck a reef and was almost lost off Tahiti; it limped, with all pumps hard at work, into Papeete on 23 April. Repairs took two months, Laplace sailing on 22 June for Honolulu, where he anchored on 9 July. In both places, his task had been to ensure equality of treatment for French missionaries and French traders.

Earlier plans to go to Kamchatka had to be abandoned because the season was too advanced. Laplace sailed instead to the Russian settlement of Bodega on the California coast where he had discussions with the governor; he then continued south to San Francisco and Monterey, getting supplies, and on to Callao, Valparaiso, and Concepción. He turned Cape Horn on 12 January 1840, his crew now suffering from an epidemic of smallpox. He reached Rio on 4 February and anchored finally in Lorient on 14 April. The *Artémise*, too old and too badly deteriorated to be repaired, was turned into a naval hulk.

Laplace supervised the writing and publication of an account of the voyage. The first volume appeared in 1841, but later volumes followed more slowly: Laplace was a good if prolix writer with a literary and philosophic bent. He also had his naval career to pursue: he became a vice-admiral in 1853. The Revolution of 1848 also caused delays, so that the sixth and final volume did not appear until 1854. Laplace died at Brest in 1875.

## Laughlan

DAVID LAUGHLAN was a British merchant captain who traded in the East and in Australia. In August 1812 he was sailing in charge of the vessel *Mary*, north of the Louisiade Archipelago when, on the sixteenth, he sighted a group of islands surrounded by reefs that did not appear on any charts. These five islands and several islets due east of Woodlark Island are now known as Laughlan's Islands, or Nada by their native name.

## Lavaud

CHARLES-FRANÇOIS LAVAUD was born at Lorient, France, on 25 March 1798, the son of a naval officer. He first sailed from Lorient in December 1810 in the *Nymphe* for the Indian Ocean and the Dutch East Indies, returning to France in December 1811. He went to sea again in 1815–1818, sailing to Newfoundland, the West Indies, and Africa. Appointed ensign in 1819, he served in a succession of ships, including the *Moselle*, in which he first sailed to the Pacific.

Promoted lieutenant in May 1826, he served in the Mediterranean and in 1829 received his first command, that of the *Philomène*, bound for the Newfoundland station, where he gave evidence of his administrative and diplomatic skills. A corvette captain in September 1832, he carried out a number of missions in American waters and in the West Indies. In August 1839 he was given command of the *Aube* and despatched to New Zealand to give support to a planned French settlement on the South Island.

Lavaud sailed from Brest on 19 February 1840, arriving at the Bay of Islands by way of Africa, the southern Indian Ocean, and the south of Tasmania on 11 July. He discovered that Britain had already taken over New Zealand and claimed sovereignty over the area where the French colonists were about to settle. He handled the difficult situation in which he found himself with a great deal of tact and eventually left New Zealand in the *Allier* in January 1843, sailing back to Brest by way of Tahiti, Valparaiso, Cape Horn, and Rio, reaching Brest in October.

Now a full captain, he took command of the *Psyché*. In September 1846 he was named governor of the French establishments in Oceania. He arrived at Papeete, Tahiti, on 21 May 1847 in the *Sirène*, and soon found himself embroiled in a difficult situation. He dealt ably with a wide range of problems, but left with few regrets on 3 April 1850. He was back in France in August, and in 1852 was appointed naval prefect of the port of Lorient.

Promoted to rear admiral in June 1853, Lavaud was chosen to serve on the Admiralty Council in 1860. He retired in March 1861. He died at Brest on 14 March 1878. He left a number of valuable comments and reports on the Pacific, in addition to his administrative papers on the problems he found in New Zealand and Tahiti.

## Lazarev

ALEKSEI PETROVICH LAZAREV, the younger brother of Mikhail
Petrovich Lazarev (the eldest, Andrei, was also a naval officer) was
born in 1791. He served in the Adriatic in 1807 and was given land-
based appointments in Italy in 1810. Popular with members of the
nobility, he was appointed to the imperial yachts *Tserera* and *Neva*;
nevertheless, at the end of 1818 he sought a change from high society and, hoping to further his naval career, obtained a transfer to the
*Blagonamerennyi*, which was to sail as part of the expedition of
Vasilev *(q.v.)*. He sailed from Kronstadt in July 1819 and returned in
August 1822, having entered the Pacific by the Cape of Good Hope
route and completed the circumnavigation by way of Cape Horn.
Aleksei Lazarev wrote a valuable and detailed account of the voyage
which, however, edited by A. I. Solovev, was not published until
1950.

On his return he secured an appointment to the Baltic Fleet, but
he soon went back to courtly duties. However, political upheavals,
which probably had a part in the nonpublication of his "Notes on
the Voyage," affected his career. In spite of some later promotion, he
died in obscurity on the family estates in 1862.

## Lazarev

MIKHAIL PETROVICH LAZAREV was born in Vladimir, near Moscow, in November 1788 of a well-to-do family. He entered the Naval
Cadet Corps in 1800, and in 1803 was sent to England to gain experience with the British navy. After a full four years, he returned to
Russia in 1808 and for the next five years served in the Baltic Fleet.

In 1813, when barely twenty-five years of age, he was given command of the French-built supply ship *Suvorov*. His mission was to
sail to the Russian America Company's outposts of Petropavlovsk in
Kamchatka, Kodiak Island, and Novo Arkhangelsk on Sitka Island.
While sailing through the northern Cook group he discovered on 17
September 1814 an uninhabited island he named Suvorov (the name
remains, more usually spelled Suwarrow). It is an atoll consisting of
twenty-five small islets. Lazarev returned to the Baltic in 1816, having successfully completed his task without provoking any political
unease among the other European nations with interests on the
northwest coast.

Russia was by now planning major expeditions to the Pacific. Lazarev's obvious organizational ability and his recent expedition to the Pacific led him to be appointed captain of the sloop *Mirnyy*, which was to accompany Bellingshausen *(q.v.)* commanding the *Vostok*. The two ships sailed from the Baltic on 4 July 1819, going to Copenhagen, Plymouth, and then south to the Antarctic. The South Georgia and South Shetland islands were reached late in the year, but on 18 January 1820 the *Mirnyy* almost came to grief on a heavy ice floe. Then, with supplies low, the *Vostok* made for Port Jackson, leaving Lazarev to follow in his slower vessel. *Mirnyy* rejoined the *Vostok* in early April, and on 8 May the two set off again, for Queen Charlotte Sound, New Zealand. The stay was of considerable ethnographic value; the Russians then went to Rapa, the Tuamotus, and Tahiti. Late in July, Bellingshausen discovered the small island of Matahiva, which he named Lazarev Island. In August the ships set course for Port Jackson, where they anchored on 9 September. After a further swing toward the Antarctic and the South Shetlands, the expedition sailed for Rio and home, arriving back in Kronstadt on 25 July 1821.

Lazarev's next command was the *Kreiser*, in which he carried out a major cruise from 1822 to 1825. He then took over the *Azov*, in which he fought at the Battle of Navarino (1827). He was promoted to rear admiral and in 1828–1829 organized the blockade of the Dardanelles as part of the ongoing struggle against Turkey. He then transferred to the Baltic Fleet, but in 1833 became commander-in-chief of the Black Sea Fleet and military governor of Sebastopol. He died in Vienna in April 1851.

## Legazpi

MIGUEL LOPEZ DE LEGAZPI (found also as Legaspi) was born in Spain around 1510; he first studied law but joined the army, serving in Mexico and rising to the rank of alcade and head clerk of the local administration. He was a friend of the Augustinian monk Andres de Urdaneta *(q.v.)*, who was regarded as highly knowledgeable in matters relating to the Pacific. The presence of Urdaneta on an expedition to the western Pacific, in effect toward the spices of the orient, provided a missionary pretext for an undertaking that challenged Portuguese claims to exclusivity.

Four ships sailed from Acapulco under Legazpi's command, with

Urdaneta on board, on 21 November 1564. One of these, the *San Lucas*, disappeared on the thirtieth. On 9 January 1565, the island of Mejit, the easternmost of the Marshall group, was discovered and, because of the appearance of the islanders, named Los Barbudos. The next day, more islands were discovered—Ailuk and Jemo—and, on the twelfth, Wotho. The expedition then sailed on to Guam and reached Samar in the Philippines on 14 February. On 27 February the fleet anchored off Cebu, where some resistance was encountered. On 8 May Legazpi laid the foundations for the fort and city of San Miguel and began to establish and strengthen Spanish dominion over the Philippines.

The *San Pedro* was sent back to America in June 1565, but Legazpi remained in the Philippines. The large island of Mindanao proved much more difficult to pacify than Luzon, and the Portuguese sent a small fleet in 1568 to endeavor by threats and arguments to force Legazpi to leave, but he was a skilled negotiator and had learned to use tribal rivalries to his advantage. He was also being reinforced by troops and settlers from Mexico. In 1569 he was formally promoted to governor and captain general. On 19 May 1571 he took possession of Manila. He died there on 20 August 1572. His name is commemorated in Legazpi, a city of southeast Luzon.

## Le Maire

JACOB LE MAIRE was born in 1585, the son of an Amsterdam merchant, Isaac Le Maire, who had tried for many years to break through the monopoly of the Vereenigde Oost-Indische Compagnie (East India Company). Earlier attempts had been stillborn because of the company's control of the Cape and the Strait of Magellan route. By 1614, however, Isaac Le Maire and associated merchants from the town of Hoorn obtained permission to trade in the East and in the Pacific on condition a new passage into the South Seas was discovered.

Isaac was too old to sail himself, so he had recourse to an experienced seaman, Willem Schouten *(q.v.)*, and appointed his son Jacob as supercargo and general supervisor of an expedition of two ships, the *Eendracht*, captained by Schouten, and the smaller *Hoorn*, commanded by Jan Schouten, Willem's brother.

The ships sailed from Texel on 14 June 1615, making for Africa and South America. They reached Port Desire on the coast of Patagonia and proceeded to refit the ships before beginning the search for a new pass south of the strait, but in an attempt to burn off the weeds that had attached themselves to the *Hoorn* the ship caught fire and had to be abandoned. The *Eendracht* left on 13 January 1616, sailed south, and discovered a new island, which the Dutch named Staten Landt, and a wide channel they called the Strait of Le Maire; it led to open water and to the tip of South America, which they called Cape Hoorn, first sighted on 29 January. From there, the way was open, without breaching the East India Company monopoly, to the Pacific Ocean.

The *Eendracht* next made for Juan Fernandez Islands and soon after veered west. On 9 March, Jan Schouten died. Then, on 10 April, the Dutch were in sight of the Tuamotus and began an impressive series of discoveries: Pukapuka was the first, followed by Takaroa, Takapoto, Manihi, and Rangiroa. Several landings were made, resulting in clashes with the islanders, who stole whatever they could, and shots were fired. In May discoveries were made in the Tonga group: Tafahi (called Cocos), Niuatobutabu (Traitors), Niuafou (Good Hope). On 19 May the Hoorn Islands of Futuna and Alofi were added to the map. The Dutch stayed there for a fortnight, believing themselves very near the Solomons if not among them. After discoveries in the Bismarck Archipelago, on 25 June 1616 Le Maire came upon the large island of New Ireland, which he took to be New Guinea; smaller discoveries included the Tanga, the Lihir and the Tabar islands until, on 2 July, the Dutch added, without identifying it as a separate island, New Hanover.

The *Eendracht* was now leaving the area of the Pacific unfrequented by Europeans and nearing the East India Company's sphere of influence. On 3 and 4 July, Le Maire discovered a number of small islands in the Admiralty group and not long after could name Biak and Supiori the "Schouten Eilanden" off western New Guinea. On 17 September the expedition reached the Dutch post of Ternate on Gilolo (Halmahera), where they were well received. After a rest the ship continued to Jacatra, where it dropped anchor on 28 October. The situation now changed for the worse, the Dutch governor-general flatly rejecting Le Maire and Schouten's claim that they had entered the South Seas by way of some new and totally unknown passage. He impounded the *Eendracht*, took over most of its crew, arrested the two leaders, and sent them to Holland by the next homebound ship, which happened to be under the command of another Pacific navigator, Van Spilbergen *(q. v.)*.

Jacob Le Maire died at sea not long after his departure, on 22 December 1616. His father set in motion a successful process of litigation against the East India Company and eventually obtained compensation for the losses sustained.

## L'Hermite

JACQUES L'HERMITE the younger was born at Antwerp in January 1582 of a family of merchants. When the Spanish conquest of the city in 1585 drove Protestants to safer Dutch territories, the family moved to Amsterdam and later to Rotterdam, where they became associated with the Dutch East Indies Company. In 1605 Jacques L'Hermite went out to the East Indies with the fleet of Cornelis Matelief and served in various capacities for a number of years, taking part in a number of military operations in eastern waters.

By 1612 L'Hermite had returned to Holland and was established as a merchant in Amsterdam, married and well connected. The long struggle between Spanish and Dutch had ended, temporarily, in the truce of 1609. Then, in 1618, Prince Maurice of Nassau, whose party L'Hermite supported, established himself in power by a coup d'état. The truce petered to an end in 1621, and the Dutch States-General—with the active cooperation of Prince Maurice—planned an expedition to the Pacific seaboard of South America, where they hoped that a Dutch military and trading base could be set up.

The fleet, which became known as the Nassau Fleet, was ready by the beginning of 1623. It consisted of eleven ships carrying sixteen hundred men of whom more than a thousand could be used for military actions against the Spanish and later provide garrisons. It sailed on 24 April 1623, making for the Cape Verde Islands, Sierra Leone, and Annabon, not reaching Le Maire's Strait until February 1624. The ships sailed close to Tierra del Fuego, along Nassau Bay, discovering a small island to which the Dutch gave the name L'Hermite. The main discovery, however, was determining that Cape Horn was not part of the mainland but a promontory at the south of a smaller island.

Once they reached Pacific waters, the ships were scattered in a gale; they reunited at Juan Fernandez in April. Preparations were then made for attacks on Spanish settlements in Peru. On 5 May they arrived off Mala, south of Callao, just a few days after the despatch of a rich convoy of silver to Panama. This despatch had depleted the Spanish naval forces, such as they were, but the viceroy succeeded in putting together a sizable force of soldiers and volunteers to prevent any effective landing by the Dutch intruders.

On 2 June 1624 Jacques L'Hermite, who had been in ill health for some time, died off Callao, his place being taken by Geen Huygen Schapenham (q.v.), who eventually took the fleet across the Pacific and on to the Dutch East Indies.

## Lisyansky

YURII FEDOROVICH LISYANSKY (or Lisiansky) was born at Nezhin, near Kiev, in August 1773 and enrolled at the Naval Cadet Corps in 1786 after which, like a number of promising graduates of the period, he went to England to serve in the British navy as a volunteer. His long association with Kruzenshtern (q.v.) began there: he traveled with him to the Cape of Good Hope in the warship *Raisonable* (but did not continue with him to India and Canton).

When Kruzenshstern obtained permission in 1802 to organize a voyage around the world, Lisyansky was sent back to England to purchase suitable ships for the expedition. In February 1803 Lisyansky bought and equipped two ships, which were renamed *Nadezhda* and *Neva*. He was then appointed captain of the *Neva* and second-in-command of the expedition. He had brought both ships to Kronstadt on 5 June; they were ready to sail in August, first for Copenhagen, then for Falmouth to lay in additional supplies and equipment. Leaving on 5 October, the ships made for the island of St. Catherine, Brazil, where the *Neva*'s masts had to be repaired. This repair led to a stay of some six weeks, the ships leaving on 4 February 1804 and rounding Cape Horn on 3 March. Three weeks later the ships became separated. Lisyansky went to Easter Island, which he sighted on 16 April, but weather prevented a landing. There was no sign of the *Nadezhda*, so he sailed on to the Marquesas, where the two ships rejoined on 11 May. A week later they sailed for Hawaii where, by arrangement, they separated, Kruzenshtern going to Kamchatka while Lisyansky anchored in Kealakekua Bay, where he obtained supplies, and later in Waimea Bay, Kauai, where the local ruler came on board.

Lisyansky sailed for the northwest coast on 20 June 1804, going to Kodiak Island, which he reached on 10 July. He learned that the Russian settlement at Sitka had been taken by the Indians; he went to its aid and returned to Kodiak in November, remaining until 14 June 1805. He then spent the summer months along the northwest coast, surveying and buying furs. His hydrographic contributions were particularly important, and he gave their present name to a number of islands.

The *Neva* left for Canton in September, almost coming to grief on the way on an uncharted reef on the night of 15 October 1805. In the morning it was seen that the reef was one of a number surrounding a small island. It was named—and remains—Lisyansky Island. The uninhabited island forms part of the northern Hawaiian Islands.

On 3 December the *Neva* reached Macao and was reunited with the *Nadezhda*. Lisyansky was anxious to dispose of his cargo of furs, as only the *Nadezhda*'s costs were being met in full by the czar, and the proceeds of the *Neva*'s trade were urgently needed. After some protracted negotiations the furs were sold and Chinese goods taken aboard for the return voyage. The ships weighed anchor on 9 February 1806 and made for the South China Sea and Sunda Strait. They subsequently became separated in dense fog, and Lisyansky continued alone from 15 April, although he had a brief sighting of the *Nadezhda* in the South Atlantic on 26 April. The two ships made their own way back to Kronstadt, the *Neva* dropping anchor there on 19 August 1806. The expedition was rightfully hailed for its achievements: it was the first circumnavigation by a Russian expedition.

Lisyansky returned to active service in the Baltic Fleet, but he retired from the navy in 1809. He worked on the narrative of his voyage, which was published in St. Petersburg in two volumes in 1812 and in London in 1814. It was accompanied by a valuable collection of maps and drawings. He died in St. Petersburg in February 1837.

## Loaysia

GARCIA JOFRE DE LOAYSIA (or Loyasia) sailed with seven ships in July 1525 from Coruna, Spain, to follow the route to the Moluccas blazed by Magellan *(q.v.)*. He proceeded to the Strait of Magellan, but at the entrance, one ship was wrecked and two others turned back. The remaining four vessels made their way through the winding waterways, emerging into the Pacific on 15 May 1526. Four days later a wild northeasterly gale struck the little fleet.

As a result of this storm one caravel, the *San Lesmes*, disappeared. Whether it made its way to Amanu, in the Tuamotus, as some believe, or was wrecked somewhere farther south, whether east or west, no one can state with certainty. The pinnace *Santiago* struggled on to Spanish outposts on the coast of America. The caravel *Santa Maria del Parral* reached Mindanao, where it was wrecked so that almost nothing is known of its crossing.

Loaysia's own flagship, the *Santa Maria de la Victoria*, sailed on, but its captain died en route on 30 July 1526. He was succeeded by Juan Sebastian del Cano and Alonso de Salazar *(qq.v.)*, who brought the caravel to Guam on 4 September 1526.

## Lütke

FEDOR PETROVICH LÜTKE (or Litke) was born at St. Petersburg on 17 September 1797 and joined the navy in 1813. He sailed around the world with V. M. Golovnin *(q.v.)* in the sloop *Kamchatka* in 1817–1819. In 1821 he was appointed to lead a voyage of exploration to Novaja Zemla, the eastern Barents Sea, and the White Sea, returning in 1824.

Then came the opportunity of leading his own expedition to the Pacific. Lütke sailed in the sloop *Senyavin* with the *Moller* as consort, having a number of noted naturalists on board. Leaving Kronstadt on 16 August 1826, he entered the Pacific by Cape Horn, calling at Valparaiso and going up the northwest coast to Sitka, where he dropped anchor in June. Summer months were spent on survey work in the Bering Sea, but Lütke's main work was carried out in the Caroline Islands, beginning in November 1827 and taking up most of 1828.

Lütke's report on the Carolines was detailed and precise. The inadequate information previously available led him to believe that a number of small islands and atolls he came upon were discoveries, but only one can be truly credited to him: the island of Eauripik in the western Carolines, discovered on 12 April 1828. However, his charts of the archipelago, published in his *Voyage autour du Monde* at St. Petersburg in 1835–1836, earned him a well-deserved reputation, further enhanced by an excellent monograph on his work in the Bering Sea. Lütke completed his circumnavigation by way of the Cape, returning to Kronstadt in 1829. His accounts of the voyage occupied him for the next few years and were published between 1834 and 1836 with a French edition in the latter year.

He continued his career in the Russian navy, making valuable contributions to the sciences and in particular to the study of tidal movements. He served as military governor in Tallinn and Kronstadt between 1850 and 1857, became an admiral in 1855, and president of the St. Petersburg Academy of Sciences in 1864. He was also elected a member of the Paris Académie des Sciences, while in 1873 the Russian Geographical Society created the Lütke Gold Medal in his honor.

Fedor Lütke died at St. Petersburg on 8 August 1882.

## McClure

JOHN MCCLURE was the English captain of the snow *Panther*, 200 tons, which was fitted out by the East India Company for an expedition of discovery and survey (but also trade) to the Carolines, New Guinea, and Australia. On board as officer was Amasa Delano *(q.v.)*. The *Panther* left with the smaller *Endeavour* from Macao Roads on 27 April 1791.

The first call was at the Palaus, where they arrived on 9 June, remaining until the twenty-seventh. McClure continued on his way to western New Guinea, sailing among its offshore islands from 19 July. A call was made in September at Amboina, and in mid-October McClure was back on the New Guinea coast, seeking the strait that rumor claimed divided the great island. Exploring along the southwest coast, he entered a wide bay; the bay, however, ended in a river mouth, the Muturi, and a small group of islands; it was known for many years as McCluer [sic] Gulf but is now generally referred to by its Indonesian name, Teluk Berau. During this survey, the English were attacked by the natives, who killed the *Panther*'s surgeon.

Satisfied that no strait existed, McClure withdrew and eventually made his way to the northern Australian coast and from there to Timor, where he stayed for almost two months, from late January to

24 March 1792, before going on to Benkoelen (Bengkulu), Sumatra, for a refit. Sickness killed many of the crew, and the *Endeavour* was so infested with vermin that it had to be scuttled in shallow water to clear it of insects, later being refloated.

McClure sailed for Batavia on 17 August 1792 and later returned to the Palau Islands by way of the Sulu Sea. He remained there from 20 January 1793 to mid-March, then made his way back to Macao, where the two vessels were sold off. Knowledge of this voyage comes primarily from Delano's book, *Narrative of Voyages and Travels*, published in Boston in 1817.

## Magellan

FERNÃO DE MAGALHÃES (Ferdinand Magellan) was born in Sabrosa or nearby Oporto, in Portugal, probably in 1480. After some time as a page in the household of Queen Leonora, he went to the East with Francisco de Almeida in 1505, took part in the battle of Diu in 1509, and fought in Malacca in 1509 and 1511. He was back in Portugal in 1513 and was wounded in Morocco. For reasons that remain open to argument, he fell out with the Court of Portugal and offered his services to Spain. His proposal to seek a route to the Moluccas by way of the South Seas was eventually accepted. It would provide Spain with access to the Spice Islands by routes Portugal did not control.

On 20 September 1519 Magellan sailed from Sanlúcar de Barrameda with five ships, including his own *Trinidad*. Petty rivalries and the sailors' fear of the unknown caused a series of mutinies and near-mutinies that began to plague the expedition by the time the ships reached the Cape Verde Islands. In January 1520 they arrived at the estuary of the River Plate and at the end of March put into Port San Julian in southern Argentina. During Magellan's stay there, one mutiny occurred and one of the ships was wrecked. With the coming of the southern spring, the expedition set out again, and on 21 October sighted the entrance to what is now known as the Strait of Magellan.

The journey through the tortuous unknown strait, during which one ship was lost by desertion, took thirty-eight days. On 28 November 1520 the *Trinidad*, the *Concepción*, and the *Victoria* emerged into the ocean. Magellan was fortunate in meeting no storms and accordingly bestowed on it the name of Pacific Ocean.

Because he encountered very few islands, it is impossible to determine with any accuracy his track to Guam, which he sighted on 6 March 1521. It is generally accepted that, sailing north off the coast of Chile, Magellan veered west-northwest before reaching latitude 30°5′ and made a first landfall on Pukapuka (which he named San Pablo) or one of the nearby islands that form part of the Tuamotu archipelago, before continuing on to either Caroline Island (Los Tiburones) or, less probably, nearby Vostok, part of the Line Islands.

Guam and Rota, discovered in March, provided food for the starving and scurvy-ridden crews, but there were irritating thefts by the islanders, earning them the name Islands of Robbers (Ladrones), now replaced by the broader and more pleasant title Marianas. Ten days later the three ships finally reached the Philippines, completing the first crossing of the Pacific, the first islands spotted being Samar and Cebu. Magellan made an alliance with the latter island's ruler, an alliance he was soon forced to honor by supporting the Cebu ruler against nearby Mactan. On 27 April 1521 Magellan, underestimating the resources of the enemy, was killed.

Following his death, the rajah of Cebu turned against the Europeans, who then sailed for the Moluccas, burning the *Concepción* because they had not enough crew to sail it. On 26 November they reached Tidore, where the *Trinidad* was eventually broken up. The *Victoria* sailed for home on 21 December 1521 with a cargo of spices, limping into Seville on 8 September 1522. Eighteen men out of the original number completed this first circumnavigation of the globe.

## Mahu

JACQUES MAHU (or Mahieu: the family apparently originated from France) was born in 1564, according to some reports, in Cologne, where, it can be assumed, his parents had fled from the war-torn Low Countries. He worked for a time in Bergen-op-Zoom but moved to Rotterdam, where he became a merchant of some standing.

With a number of other merchants, including Simon de Cordes (*q.v.*), he organized an expedition of five ships to the Pacific: the *Hoop, Geloof, Liefde, Trouw,* and *Blijde Boodschap.* They were well armed and well equipped because the Dutch had in mind the arming of natives against their Spanish conquerors, but food supplies were less adequate.

The expedition sailed from Rotterdam in June 1598. The crossing of the Atlantic proved slow and painful. Scurvy broke out and Mahu died before even reaching the Strait of Magellan, on 24 September 1598.

The expedition was almost a total failure. The *Hoop* sailed as far north as the latitude of the Hawaiian Islands, where it vanished; the *Geloof* turned back to Holland from the Strait of Magellan; the *Liefde* reached Japan, the *Trouw* reached Tidore, and the *Blijde Boodschap* was captured by the Spanish in Chile.

## Makarov

STEPAN OSIPOVICH MAKAROV was born on 27 December 1848 at Nicolaev, Ukraine, and graduated from the naval school in 1865. He was promoted to ensign in 1869 and served first with the Pacific Ocean Squadron, then from 1871 with the Baltic Fleet and from 1876 with the Black Sea Fleet.

In 1886 he led a major Russian scientific expedition to the Pacific in the corvette *Vitiaz*. He sailed through the Strait of Magellan to the Marquesas and the Hawaiian Islands, on to Yokohama, the Sea of Japan, the Sea of Okhotsk, and Kamchatka, completing his circumnavigation by the Philippine Islands, the Indian Ocean, and the Suez Canal before returning to Kronstadt in 1889. Research centered on hydrology and meteorology, with detailed analyses of water temperatures at various depths and the velocity of sea currents. In addition to scientific papers and reports, Makarov published *"Vitiaz" and the Pacific Ocean* in two volumes (St. Petersburg, 1894).

Stepan Makarov returned to service with the Baltic Fleet in 1890. He completed a second circumnavigation in 1894–1896, reversing the route he had followed earlier, sailing from St. Petersburg to the Mediterranean and the Suez Canal, to the Far East, and thence across the Pacific to North America and Cape Horn. In 1899 he was appointed governor of the port of Kronstadt until the outbreak of the Russo-Japanese War in 1904. Admiral Makarov was appointed commander of the Pacific Ocean Squadron on 1 February and organized the defense of Port Arthur with energy and efficiency. Unhappily, his flagship, *Petropavlovsk*, struck a mine off the port on 13 April 1904, and he went down with his ship and his six hundred men.

## Malaspina

ALESSANDRO (ALEJANDRO) MALASPINA was born at Mulazzo, Italy, on 5 November 1754. After studying at Palermo, he joined the Spanish navy in 1774, making a number of voyages to the Atlantic and to China. In 1784 he was given command of the frigate *Astrea*, sailing from Cadiz on a voyage around the world that took him to South America, the Philippines, and the Cape of Good Hope.

In 1789 Malaspina was put in charge of a major scientific expedition with the 306-ton *Descubierta* and *Atrevida* commanded by José Bustamente y Guerra. The complement included the noted botanists Luis Nee and Thaddeus Haenke as well as six artists. Malaspina sailed from Cadiz on 30 July 1789, making for Montevideo, the Falkland Islands, and Cape Horn, then working his way up the South American coast to Valparaiso, Callao and Guayaquil, thence to Panama, Realajo (Nicaragua), and Acapulco.

The Spanish authorities were anxious to defend their claims to the northwest claim, which were being endangered by the British and the Russians in search of furs. Malaspina had orders to carry out detailed exploration along the northern coast and to find if he could the rumored Strait of Anian. He sailed from Acapulco on 2 May 1791, going up to Cape Engano and Yakutat Sound, in the Gulf of Alaska. The great Malaspina Glacier, to the north of Yukutat, commemorates his work; another tribute to him is Malaspina Strait between Texada Island and the mainland in the Strait of Georgia, in present-day Canada. The Strait of Anian, however, did not exist, and Malaspina sailed slowly down the coast to the Spanish outpost of Nootka. On 28 August 1791 he left Nootka for Monterey, in Spanish California, where he arrived on 10 September.

The expedition, having rested and taken on supplies, then crossed the Pacific to Guam, Sonsorgon in the Philippines, Macao, and Manila. Planning to return to the Pacific, Malaspina left Manila for Zamboanga in Mindanao, passed through the Celebes Sea, and eventually entered the Tasman Sea. On 25 February 1793 he reached Doubtful Sound in the southwest of New Zealand. His visit left a number of Spanish names to New Zealand topography: Bauza Island, after one of his cartographers, Felipe Bauza; Malaspina Reach in Doubtful Sound; and Mt. Malaspina in the southern New Zealand mountains, among others.

Malaspina then crossed the Tasman to New South Wales, sighting the Australian coast on 12 March 1793 and anchoring in Sydney Cove the next day. During the month they spent at Port Jackson, the Spanish set up an observatory ashore and made a number of botanical excursions inland. On 12 April they started on their homeward voyage, sailing east back across the Pacific, calling at Vavau, Tonga, in May. Malaspina was well received, and on the thirtieth he formally proclaimed the annexation of the islands on behalf of the king of Spain. He then sailed to Callao and after his call there went south to turn Cape Horn, making once more for the Falklands and Montevideo. He was back in Cadiz in July 1794.

He was at first honored for his achievements and promoted to brigadier general. He returned for a time to Italy and started work on an account of the voyage. However, his critical comments on Spanish colonial administration and on the likely disaffection of the colonists if reforms were not undertaken led to his arrest on 23 November 1795. His papers were taken from him, and the projected publication was stopped, although information from Bauza's charts was able to be used by English and other cartographers. The drawings, however, were scattered, and many were lost; his advice on developing the American colonies was of course disregarded by the Spanish authorities and unrest and eventually uprisings became inevitable.

Alessandro Malaspina spent seven years in jail, being freed in 1802 through the intervention of Italian friends of Napoleon. He was banished from Spanish soil and returned to Italy, where he died on 9 April 1809 at the age of fifty-four. A journal written by an ensign on the *Descubierta*, Francisco Xavier de Viana, was printed in Montevideo in 1849, but no account of this major Spanish expedition was published until 1885, almost a century after its departure from Cadiz: *Viaje Político-científico alrededor del Mundo por las Corbetas "Descubierta" y "Atrevida" al mando de los Capitánes de navío D. Alejandro Malaspina . . . desde 1789 a 1794*, edited by Novo y Colson (Madrid, 1885).

## Marchand

ETIENNE MARCHAND was born in Grenada, West Indies, in 1755. The island was at the time still a French colony. Marchand served in the merchant navy, rising to captain and gaining wide experience in navigation. He was on his way home from Bengal in 1788 when he met Nathaniel Portlock *(q.v.)* at St. Helena. The information he obtained from the Englishman led him to draw up a plan for a voyage to the Pacific to buy furs.

Back in Marseilles in August 1789, he persuaded the firm of J. and D. Baux to finance an expedition. He sailed in the *Solide*, 300 tons, on 14 December 1790, passed through the Strait of Gibraltar a fortnight later, and made for Tenerife and Cape Verde. He made no further call until he reached the Marquesas, by way of Cape Horn, on 12 June 1791. He anchored in Tahuata two days later and on the twentieth sailed west-northwest for another island barely glimpsed against the setting sun: it was Ua Pu. He named it Marchand, then went on to make further sightings; but he had been preceded by Ingraham *(q.v.)*, and only Motu Iti, northwest of Nuku Hiva, was a true discovery. Marchand called the group Îles de la Révolution and claimed them on behalf of France.

On 24 June Marchand sailed for the northwest coast and spent a month trading for furs from Cape de Engano to the Queen Charlotte Islands. He then went to Hawaii for supplies and on to Macao by way of the northern Marianas. He was in Macao by 27 November; but finding that trading in furs was now banned by the authorities, he sailed within a fortnight for Mauritius and home. On 14 August 1792 he dropped anchor in Toulon, having completed one of the speediest circumnavigations of the eighteenth century.

The voyage, through no fault of his own, was a financial disaster, although his own account, published in 1792, and a later major narrative by a senior naval administrator, the Comte de Fleurieu, had a considerable influence. Marchand died on the island of Réunion on 15 May 1793.

## Marshall

NOT A GREAT DEAL is known about John Marshall, whose first name sometimes appears as William. He was a merchant captain, mostly in the services of the East India Company, who was given command of the transport *Scarborough*, part of the First Fleet, which sailed to Botany Bay, New South Wales, from England on 13 May 1787. The voyage was slow and strenuous, but the fleet reached Botany Bay in January 1788, the *Scarborough* discharging its cargo of convicts, soldiers, and supplies and undergoing repairs.

On 6 May 1788 Marshall sailed from New South Wales together with Thomas Gilbert *(q.v.)*, who commanded the *Charlotte*. Their route took them northwest and north toward Norfolk Island and the New Hebrides (Vanuatu) and into an area of the southwest Pacific where a number of new islands were discovered. As Marshall was sailing in company with Gilbert, it is not easy to decide which discoveries were made by which ship; but the two big groups of scattered islands were named the Gilbert Islands and the Marshall Islands, the latter being the more northerly.

The discoveries were made from 18 to 30 June 1788, and, although a number of the islands reported and charted had probably been sighted by early Spanish voyagers, many were unknown and can be credited to Gilbert and Marshall. These include Maiana, Tarawa, Makin, Arno, Majuro, Maloelap, Erikub, and Wotje. Most of the islands were given English names by Gilbert, who may be regarded as the leading figure, although his prominence may be due to his account of the voyage published in 1789, information about Marshall's role being more indirect. Marshall, however, gave the name of Lord Mulgrave to Milli, discovered on 25 June, and Gilbert named the northern group the Marshall Islands because at the time the *Scarborough* was a little ahead of the *Charlotte*. (Gilbert, however, was highly displeased with Marshall's firing at some approaching proas or canoes, thus making it difficult to talk or trade with the islanders, although Marshall did so in the belief that they were intent on attacking his ship.) The islands have all reverted to their native names.

Leaving the Marshalls, the two ships made for Tinian for supplies and reached China on 9 September; after loading tea and other goods they made their way back to England.

Little is known of John Marshall's later life, except that he is recorded as having made one further voyage to New South Wales.

## Martin

LOPE MARTIN first came to prominence as pilot of the *San Lucas*, which sailed from Mexico in 1564 under the command of Arellano *(q.v.)*, became separated from the other ships of the expedition, reached the Philippines in January 1565, and eventually made its way back to America.

On 1 May 1566 Martin set out from Acapulco as pilot of the *San Gerónimo* to go to the aid of Legazpi *(q.v.)*. On the way, a mutiny broke out, the captain, one Pedricon, being killed. The causes of this mutiny are obscure, but it is clear that Lope Martin was the ringleader, and it is suspected that he was also responsible for Arellano's defection of 1564. Whatever the true reasons, Martin later fell out with a number of the mutineers on board the *San Gerónimo* or became the victim of a countermutiny by some of the officers and men who had remained loyal, and he was marooned with several followers on the atoll of Ujelang in the Marshall Islands on 21 July 1566, the *San Gerónimo* continuing to the Marianas and the Philippines.

During the time when he was de facto commander of the *San Gerónimo*, Lope Martin may have discovered several islands in the Marshall group; but details are too uncertain to identify them, and he cannot even be credited with discovering Ujelang, where he probably ended his days, as Legazpi had sailed by it in 1565.

Lope Martin is referred to as a Portuguese; he was a native of Ayamonte near the present Portuguese-Spanish border.

## Martinez

ESTEBAN JOSÉ MARTINEZ FERNÁNDEZ was born on 9 December 1742 at Seville, entered naval college at 13, and went to sea within three years. By 1773 he was serving as second pilot at San Blas, on the Pacific coast of Mexico.

Martinez sailed with Juan Perez *(q.v.)* as second officer of the *Santiago*, which left from San Blas in January 1774. The expedition sailed as far as the coast of Alaska, discovering Nootka Sound and probably Juan de Fuca Strait. From 1775 to 1788 Martinez was engaged in supplying Spanish posts in the Mexican province of

Sonora and in California. In 1786 he piloted the two ships of La Pérouse *(q.v.)* into Monterey harbor.

La Pérouse's comments to the Spanish authorities were interpreted as more evidence of Russian penetration into Alaska. The viceroy despatched Martinez on a reconnaissance of the north. He sailed from San Blas in *La Princesa* on 8 March 1788 accompanied by the *San Carlos*, commanded by Gonzalez Lopez de Haro. They went as far as Kodiak Island and Unalaska in the Aleutians, where Martinez obtained information about a proposed Russian outpost in Nootka. On his return to San Blas on 5 December, he accordingly proposed that Spain should preempt the Russians by setting up a post in Nootka before they could do so. The viceroy accepted his proposal and sent Martinez to Nootka; he arrived on 5 May 1789 to find several foreign vessels and their commanders already there, including the American John Kendrick *(q.v.)*. Martinez, however, was more concerned about English challenges to the Spanish monopoly. He eventually captured four English vessels associated with the enterprises of Meares and Colnett *(qq.v.)*, although he released two of these that were flying the Portuguese colors. This action, the so-called Nootka Incident, almost led to war between England and Spain.

Martinez had surveyed Juan de Fuca Strait in June and July and became convinced that it would eventually lead through inland waterways to the Mississippi River. He formulated plans for a permanent Spanish settlement at Nootka from which trade could develop through an envisaged Spanish base in the Hawaiian Islands and thence to the Philippines and Asia; but his orders were still only to show the flag on the northwest coast, so, unable to winter in Nootka, he sailed back to San Blas at the end of October 1789. He returned to Nootka in 1790, sailing under Francisco Eliza of the *Princesa*.

The Nootka Incident caused Martinez to be overtaken by events and outranked by newly appointed officers; he sailed back to Spain in September 1791, but returned to San Blas in 1795. He continued to press for Spanish settlements along the northwest and California coasts as further voyages to California strengthened his belief in the potential of this vast area. He died at Loreto, Baja California, on one such voyage on 28 October 1798.

## Maurelle

FRANCISCO ANTONIO MAURELLE (sometime found as Mourelle) was born at San Adrian de Corme, on the coast of Galicia, north-western Spain, in 1754. He began his naval career as an apprentice pilot in November 1768, sailed on a number of expeditions from 1770, and was appointed ensign in 1776, rising steadily in rank to frigate lieutenant in 1787. Reports refer to him as "outstanding as a pilot, in manoeuvres, tactical operations and discipline, of proven bravery, talented and zealous."

In 1775 Maurelle was serving on the west coast of Mexico when he was appointed pilot of the schooner *Sonora* commanded by Bodega y Quadra *(q.v.)*. They sailed from San Blas on 16 March 1775, making for Spain by way of the island of Socorro and sailing north as far as the Alexander archipelago; they arrived home on 3 November.

In 1780 Maurelle went to Manila with a contigent of marines and was then placed in charge of the *Princesa*, formerly known as the *Nuestra Señora del Rosario*. He first sailed to the east coast of Luzon, putting in at Sisiran, where his final orders reached him, requiring him to proceed to America. He weighed anchor on 21 November 1780, intending to sail by the central and south Pacific instead of the more usual northern route, because it was an unfavorable time of year for such a route. It resulted in his making a number of discoveries.

On 8 January 1781, while making for New Ireland, he came upon the Hermit Islands; on the thirteenth he encountered Tench Island in the Bismarck group; then on 26 February he discovered Fonualei in the Tongan archipelago. Further discoveries or firm sightings were made in the Vavau group, where the Spanish landed. On 21 April he discovered the island of Toku in the Tongas, and on 3 and 6 May, Nanumanga and Nanumea, respectively, in the Ellice Islands (Tuvalu). Maurelle's reports were later praised by Captain Bligh *(q.v.)* for the accuracy of his latitudes, "though he seems to have been a poor unhappy wanderer about this sea."

Unhappy Maurelle certainly was when he was unable to proceed eastward along this route. He veered north and northwest to Guam to refresh his crew and complete the crossing by the northern route. He put in finally at San Blas on 21 September 1781. He wrote a record of his voyage under the title *Noticia de la navegacion de la fragata "Princesa" al mando del alférez de fragata D. F. Maurelle.*

Maurelle went on to a successful career in the Spanish navy, taking part in a number of engagements against English forces and during the Napoleonic wars. He was raised to the rank of admiral in 1818 and given the Grand Cross of the Order of San Hermenegildo in 1819. He died at Cadiz on 24 May 1820.

## Meares

JOHN MEARES was born in England probably in 1756 and joined the Royal Navy in 1771 as captain's servant in the *Cruiser*. He served in various ships until 1778, when he was promoted to lieutenant. The American War of Independence was by then being fought, and Meares saw action on a number of occasions. When peace came, however, in 1783, he saw few prospects for himself in the naval service and transferred to the merchant navy.

He obtained command of an India-bound vessel and once in Calcutta set up a trading partnership. He then turned his attention to the northwest coast of America, where a lucrative fur trade was opening up. On 12 March 1786 he set out in the 200-ton snow *Nootka*. This should have enabled him to reach the coast in time for the summer season, but Meares was first required to sail for India, so the *Nootka* did not make Alaska until August. In spite of competition from other traders, he began to buy furs; he also, unwisely, decided to winter in Prince William Sound, northern Alaska. He and his crew suffered great hardship, their ship icebound, and scurvy rampant. In May, Portlock and Dixon *(qq.v.)* discovered Meares and came to his rescue. He was able to resume trading down the coast and then make for Canton by way of Hawaii, where he anchored in August 1787 and gave a passage to China to Kaiana, brother of Kauai's ruler.

Meares reached Canton in October, ahead of Portlock, and was able to dispose of his stock of furs without too much difficulty. He found support from several English merchants for a return voyage to the northwest coast, which would also enable him to take Kaiana back to Hawaii. On 22 January 1788 he sailed from Canton in the *Felice*, accompanied by the *Iphigenia*, commanded by William Douglas *(q.v)* both flying the Portuguese flag. However, Meares soon left the slower *Iphigenia* behind, transferring Kaiana to it, and sailed on alone. On 9 April he discovered the lonely pinnacle rock of Lot's Wife (Sofu Gan), north of the Marianas, and on 11 May reached King George's Sound (Nootka Sound), where he built a trading hut. He spent several weeks cruising down the coast of Vancouver Island to Juan de Fuca Strait, which he formally claimed on behalf of England, and south to Oregon.

The *Iphigenia* joined him, although Meares was determined he would not sail back across the Pacific with it as consort. In September Meares launched a 40-ton schooner he had had built, the *North-West America*, the first vessel to be constructed on the coast. Its purpose was to keep with the *Iphigenia* as tender. On 24 September he sailed away in the *Felice*, making for Hawaii, where he arrived on 17 October, going on to Waimea Bay in Kauai a week later. Meares finally dropped anchor in Macao Roads on 5 December.

John Meares then teamed up with James Colnett *(q.v.)* and his own backers to set up the Associated Merchants Trading to the North-West Coast of America. Colnett sailed in April 1789 in the *Argonaut*, followed by Charles Duncan in the *Princess Royal*. These teamed up with the *Iphigenia* and the *North-West America* at Nootka, but all four were captured by the Spanish authorities, who were endeavoring to put an end to British encroachment on what they considered to be their territory.

Meares' two ships, which still flew the Portuguese flag, were soon released; but when he heard of the Spanish intervention, Meares sailed for England to raise the issue at the highest levels. Thus developed the Nootka Incident, which almost led to war between Spain and England. Part of the eventual agreement between the two nations, signed in October 1790, provided for compensation to Meares for losses incurred as a result of the incident. In the same year, Meares published the narrative of his travels, *Voyages made in the years 1788 and 1789 from China to the North-West Coast of America*, which included *An Introductory Narrative of a Voyage performed in 1786 from Bengal in the ship "Nootka"*. It was a handsome and timely production, but it contained exaggerated claims and disparaged the work of other navigators, especially George Dixon, who brought out *Remarks on the Voyages of John Meares*. This in turn sparked further pamphlets in defense of each man; the argument went on until 1792. Posterity has ruled in favour of Dixon.

On 26 February 1795 Meares was promoted to commander; but although war had again broken out, he does not appear to have seen active service. He died in 1809.

## Mendaña

ALVARO MENDAÑA DE NEYRA (Negra) was born at Coruna, Spain, in 1541 or 1542. Little is known of his early years, but, like many other young Spaniards with few prospects at home but some useful relations, he went to Peru to seek his fortune. His uncle, Pedro de Castro, who had been appointed governor-general at Lima, was persuaded to send an expedition to the Pacific in search of the gold-rich Terra Australis, reputed to lie somewhere to the west of Peru. Mendaña was placed in overall command in spite of his relative youth: he was only 25 at that time. Two ships were provided, the *Los Reyes* and the *Los Todos Santos*, respectively commanded by Hernan Gallego and Pedro Sarmiento *(qq.v.)*.

The ships sailed from Callao on 19 November 1567, steering west-southwest. No land was seen, even after the route was altered to northwest, until 15 January 1568. They had passed between the Marquesas and the Tuamotus and reached the northern end of the Ellice Islands chain. The island was inhabited, but as the currents were too strong Mendaña was not able to land and obtain supplies; he named it Isla de Jesus. Later, a dangerous reef was discovered, which he called Baxos de la Candelaria; it was probably Ontong Java or possibly Roncador Reef—the uncertain longitudes and a recurrent error in Gallego's latitudes plagued the expedition.

On 7 February, having altered their course to southwest, the Spaniards came upon a large mountainous island to which they gave the name Santa Ysabel. It was their first sighting of the island group that became known as the Solomon Islands and the expedition's greatest discovery. Mendaña landed, established a camp ashore, and had constructed a small brig, the *Santiago*, in order to carry out a detailed survey of the archipelago.

Mendaña spent six months among the islands, hoping to christianize the natives and eventually colonize the archipelago; but although he was a gentle man with a degree of humanity and sympathy toward the natives rare in his day, there were inevitably clashes and deaths. On 17 August 1568 the two ships, in need of repair and fresh supplies, set off for home. A number of discoveries were made on the way: Namu, an atoll in the Marshall group on 17 September, and Wake Island on 3 October. On the sixteenth the two ships became separated in a storm, both crews by then greatly suffering from sickness and lack of food.

The *Los Reyes* reached Lower California on 19 December, finally dropping anchor on 22 January 1569 in the bay of Santiago de Colima, where the *Los Todos Santos* joined it three days later. By March the crews had sufficiently recovered to sail back to Peru, reaching Callao on 11 September.

Mendaña at once proposed a return expedition to found a colony in the Solomons, but his uncle had been recalled to Spain, where Mendaña, finding no support in Peru, joined him. Although he eventually returned to South America with the king's support for his project, local officials were less than helpful, and the incursion of Francis Drake *(q.v.)* in the Pacific, followed by other English raiders, added to delays. It was not until 16 June 1595 that he was finally able to sail from Paita with a fleet of four ships. With him went his wife and her three brothers, people as different from his own idealistic self as anyone could be.

On 21 July Mendaña came upon an inhabited island, which he named Magdalena, and soon others came into view: Mendaña had discovered Fatu Hiva, Motane, Hiva Oa, and Tahuata, part of what are known as the Marquesas, a name he gave them in honor of the viceroy of Peru who had supported his undertaking, the Marqués Hurtado de Mendoza. Continuing his westerly route, Mendaña left the islands on 5 August, discovering the Danger Islands, or Pukapuka, in the northern Cook group a fortnight later and Nurakita in the Ellice Islands on the twenty-ninth.

Then on 7 September the ships reached a new land—which, however, was not part of the Solomons, for Mendaña had not sailed far enough, but Santa Cruz, or Ndeni. One of the ships, the *Santa Ysabel*, then disappeared. Mendaña landed and proceeded to establish a camp and lay out a city; but dissension broke out among the soldiers and the crews, and there were skirmishes and murders, Mendaña being seemingly unable to maintain discipline. His health was deteriorating rapidly under the weight of privations and disappointments, and on 18 August 1595 he died, having unwisely named his wife, Ysabel de Barreto *(q.v.)*, as his successor.

The expedition disintegrated, effective navigational direction being taken over by Quiros *(q.v.)*.

## Millett

CHARLES MILLET was born at Salem, Massachusetts, in 1793. He went to sea at an early age and in 1825 sailed to Sumatra in the *Ann* for the firm of Henry Prince and Company. In the following year he took the ship *Ann* to Mocha and in 1827 opened up trade between Zanzibar and Salem. He made other voyages—to Madagascar, Canton, and Manila—for various Salem merchants, and on 27 April 1832 sailed in the *Tybee*, owned by N. L. Rogers and Brother, for Australia, where he arrived in October 1832, laying claim to being the first American merchant captain to drop anchor in the harbor and thereby opening up trade between the United States and Australia. The *Tybee* returned to Salem by way of Cape Horn, reaching home in 1833. Millett made several other voyages to the Pacific, being recorded as sailing to New Zealand in 1837. He died at Salem on 6 June 1878.

## Moerenhout

JACQUES ANTOINE MOERENHOUT was born on 17 January 1796 at Ekenren near Antwerp, which was at the time annexed to France. He joined the French army in 1812 and fought in Germany until May 1814. After working in commercial enterprises in Antwerp, he went to Chile around 1826 as Dutch consul and with the intention of setting up in business. He went to Tahiti and Pitcairn in 1828–1829 and made up his mind to settle in Tahiti.

It was during his first voyage, from Chile to Tahiti in the *Volador*, that he made what were believed to be discoveries. On 1 March 1829 he came to an island he named Bertero, after his friend the Italian botanist Carlo Bertero. It was probably Minerva Reef. He next came upon an uncharted island in the Tuamotus, which he called Moerenhout; it was Maria Atoll. Other islands reportedly seen at the time cannot be reliably identified.

After traveling to Europe and the United States in 1836, Moerenhout returned to Tahiti as American consul, in which capacity he became embroiled in local politics and particularly in the disputes between French missionaries, whom he assisted, and the English missionary Pritchard. In 1838 he was appointed French consul and became highly influential as French influence over the territory increased. In the face of continuing English hostility, however, he was transferred to Monterey in 1845 and to the Los Angeles consulate in 1859.

He died in Los Angeles on 11 July 1879. Moerenhout's major contribution to our knowledge of the Pacific is his *Voyage aux îles du Grand Océan*, published in two volumes in 1837.

## Monteverde

JUAN BAUTISTA MONTEVERDE sailed from Manila in January 1806 in command of the Spanish ship *Palas*, bound for Peru. On 18 February he was passing through the Carolines archipelago when he sighted an island that did not appear on any chart. He named it Dunkin, but it has since been identified as Nukuoro. It is an atoll consisting of some forty islands and is noteworthy for being populated by Polynesians, the farthest west these people have been found. Monteverde also came upon the island of Oroluk nearby, but although he gave some complementary information about it, the atoll was not unknown. Monteverde can be credited only with the discovery of Nukuoro.

## Morales

LUIS MORALES was born at Tordesillas, Castile, on 29 September 1641 and entered the Jesuit order in 1658. After studying at Salamanca, he went to Mexico, whence he sailed for the Marianas. He traveled tirelessly among the islands from the late 1680s, greatly contributing to establishing the geography of this complex archipelago and working on vocabularies of the local language.

He was eventually transferred to the Philippines and after a voyage back to Europe sailed to Mexico, where he served for some years. He sailed for the last time across the Pacific, from Acapulco to Manila, and died on 16 June 1716.

## Morrell

BENJAMIN MORRELL, JR., was born on 5 July 1795 at Stonington, Connecticut, the son of a shipbuilder. He gained some experience as a youth working on local ships; but in 1812, having joined an expedition against English shipping that ended in disaster, he spent eight months as a prisoner in Newfoundland. A second voyage, in a privateer, again resulted in his being captured. After his release in May 1815, he served in several vessels until June 1822, when he obtained the command of a sealer, the *Wasp*, in which he went to the Falklands, the Antarctic, and the Pacific coast of South America, returning on 18 May 1824.

In July 1824 he sailed from New York with the schooner *Tartar*, going to the Hawaiian Islands. On 6 July 1825 he landed on Lisianski Island and later on Pearl and Hermes Reef. He next went to the Galapagos and made his way home by way of the Falklands, reaching New York on 8 May 1826. He then took over the *Antarctic*, in which he went to Africa. On 2 September 1829, accompanied by his wife, Abby Jane, he sailed for Tristan da Cunha and the Indian Ocean, thence to the Auckland Islands south of New Zealand. On 20 January 1830 he put in at the Bay of Islands, New Zealand, where he spent just under a week before sailing for the Philippines by way of the Carolines. A number of islands he claimed to have discovered on the way were already known, although in fairness to him it must be said that some he believed to be unknown were quite recent discoveries.

From Manila, Morrell went to the Fiji group and west to the Solomons, where he was attacked by natives in "Massacre Islands" or Tauu, losing fourteen of his men. This incident forced him to return to Manila, after which in September he sailed back to Tauu, rescued one survivor from the attack, and exacted revenge on the islanders. After sailing around New Britain and New Guinea, he went back to Manila, took on freight for Spain, and finally dropped anchor in New York on 27 August 1831.

Morrell and his wife both wrote accounts of their experiences. Benjamin Morrell's extensive *A Narrative of Four Voyages to the South Sea, North and South Pacific Ocean, Chinese Sea, Ethiopic and Southern Atlantic Ocean, Indian and Antarctic Ocean . . . 1822 to 1831*, was published in New York in 1832. Abby Jane Morrell's *Narrative of a Voyage to the Ethiopic and South Atlantic Ocean, Chinese Sea, North and South Pacific Ocean in the Years 1829, 1830, 1831* appeared in 1833. Both works, but especially the husband's, abound in exaggerations and errors and need to be treated with caution. They were popular works nevertheless, Benjamin's being reprinted in 1841 and serving as source material for James

Fenimore Cooper. But his reputation among serious explorers was not high, and Dumont d'Urville *(q.v.)* turned down his offer to sail with him to the Pacific in 1837.

While on a trading voyage to Africa in 1839, Benjamin Morrell died of fever in Mozambique.

## Mortimer

LT. GEORGE MORTIMER was asked by the British merchant John Henry Cox *(q.v.)* to take charge of his newly built ship the *Mercury* for a voyage to the Pacific. Cox as owner was officially in command.

The *Mercury* sailed from Gravesend on 26 February 1789, for Tenerife, the Cape of Good Hope, Amsterdam Island, and Australia. On 5 July the *Mercury* sailed into Oyster Bay, Tasmania, where Mortimer established contact with the aborigines, of whom he wrote a lively and valuable account. The *Mercury* then sailed to the central Pacific, past Tubuai to Tahiti, arriving on 12 August 1789 for a stay of three weeks. After this, Mortimer took the *Mercury* to the Hawaiian Islands and north to Unalaska in the expectation of buying furs from the Aleuts. Trade, however, was not satisfactory, and the *Mercury* sailed on 6 November for Canton by way of Tinian and Macao.

Mortimer brought the ship to Canton on 1 January 1790. The fur trade was facing difficulties after its heyday of 1785–1789, and Mortimer returned to England. He wrote a short but interesting record of his voyage, published in 1791 after his return to England, with a title that is almost a narrative in itself: *Observations and Remarks made during a Voyage to the islands of Tenerife, Amsterdam, Maria's Islands near Van Diemen's Land, Otaheite, the Sandwich Islands, Owyhee, the Fox Islands, the North-West Coast of America, Tinian, thence to Canton in the brig "Mercury" commanded by John Henry Cox, Esq.*

## Mortlock

A BRITISH MERCHANT CAPTAIN about whom little is known except that he was trading in New South Wales and China in the mid-1790s, Captain Mortlock was sailing through the Caroline Islands in 1795 in command of the *Young William* when he discovered a group of small islands that in 1798 appeared on Arrowsmith's chart under the name of Mortlock Islands. They are now known as the Namoi (or Nomoi) Islands—Etal, Lukunor, and Satawan. The date of this discovery is sometimes given as 1793, and these atolls may in fact have been sighted in 1790 by another China-bound English trader, Wilkinson, captain of the *Indispensable.*

## Mouat

ALEXANDER MOUAT, son of Patrick Mouat *(q.v.)*, was born in England in 1761. At the age of 15 he sailed as a midshipman with James Cook *(q.v.)* on his third voyage to the Pacific. On 23 November at Raiatea, Mouat deserted with the gunner's mate, Thomas Shaw, and fled to Borabora, intending to make for Huahine, the home of an island girl with whom Alexander had fallen in love.

Cook, however, knew the island chiefs and was able to obtain their cooperation, with a little hostage seizing to jog them along, in recapturing the deserters. Shaw was flogged, Mouat was sent before the mast, and both men were kept in irons until the ship sailed.

Mouat redeemed himself both during the voyage and in later service in the Royal Navy. He died a lieutenant in Antigua, in 1786, aged 25.

## Mouat

PATRICK MOUAT, of Scottish extraction, was born in 1712. As a young man he was apprenticed to a shipbuilder. He later joined the navy and was promoted to lieutenant on 20 January 1746 and to commander on 22 May 1758, when he took over the fireship *Cormorant*, a command he retained until 1762.

He had become a friend of Commodore John Byron *(q.v.)*, and when the latter was appointed to lead an expedition to the South Seas in the *Dolphin*, Mouat was chosen to accompany him in the sloop *Tamar*. The two vessels sailed from the Downs on 21 June 1764, put in at Port Desire in Patagonia, and eventually, on 9 April 1765, emerged from the Strait of Magellan into the Pacific. Some minor discoveries were made in the Tuamotus in early June, and later in the same month Atafu was discovered in the northern Tokelaus. On 2 July an island was sighted and named Byron: it was one of the Gilbert archipelago. The *Dolphin* and the *Tamar* had given up their western course, Byron having lost hope of coming upon the Solomons. The ships then passed east and north of the Marshalls, and on 31 July Byron and Mouat dropped anchor off Tinian, in the Ladrones (Marianas). After obtaining fresh food for their scurvy-ridden crews, the two captains continued westward, rounding the north of the Philippines, making for Batavia. They left the East Indies in early December 1765, toward the Cape of Good Hope and on to home. Near the equator, however, Mouat's *Tamar* suffered some rudder damage and had to first make for Antigua for repairs.

Back in England in 1766, Patrick Mouat was appointed post-captain. Although his career in the navy continued for some years, he did not have an opportunity to return to the Pacific. This good fortune—a mixed blessing, as it turned out—fell to his son Alexander (*q.v.*). Patrick Mouat died on 5 May 1790, aged 78, at Westminster, London.

## Musgrave

CAPTAIN MUSGRAVE sailed from Britain to New South Wales in 1792 in the *Sugar Cane*. On his return home by way of Canton in 1793 he reported coming across uncharted islands in the Carolines.

The first island discovered was Pingelap, an atoll consisting of two islets; the others consisted of a cluster of seven islets forming the atoll of Ngatik, which, however, had already been reported in 1773 by Felipe Tompson (*q.v.*). Musgrave, according to details found on some charts, may also have been the first navigator to sight Kusaie (Kosrae). He gave no names to his discoveries, which remain known today by their native names.

## Najera

JORGE MANRIQUE DE NAJERA was captain of the caravel *Santa Maria del Parral*, one of the seven ships that sailed from Coruna, Spain, on 24 July 1525 under the overall command of Loaysia (*q.v.*). They sailed out of the Strait of Magellan into the Pacific on 26 May 1526, but on 1 June a wild gale blew up and scattered the fleet.

Najera decided to cross the Pacific to the Philippines in accordance with the general plan of the voyage. No details of his crossing are available, although it can be assumed that some hitherto unknown islands were encountered on the way, and it is known that at least one mutiny occurred. What is clear is that the crew suffered great hardships and that numbers were severely depleted when the *Santa Maria del Parral* finally reached Mindanao, where the ship was wrecked, possibly because the survivors were too weak to maneuver it inshore. The remaining Spaniards were held captive by the islanders. Three were eventually rescued by Saavedra *(q.v.)* in 1528; one later deserted, one was hanged for mutiny, and only one remained with Saavedra. Knowledge of the caravel's route across the Pacific is therefore very slight, and Najera's precise date of death is not known.

## Nares

GEORGE STRONG NARES was born on 24 April 1831 at Aberdeen, the son of Commander William Henry Nares. He entered the Royal Naval College at New Cross in 1845. He acquired early experience in the Australian station and in 1852 was mate of the *Resolute*, which sailed to the Arctic under Capt. Kellett and Sir Edward Belcher *(qq.v.)* in 1852 in a fruitless attempt to find traces of the lost expedition of Sir John Franklin. Back in 1854, Nares was promoted to lieutenant and served in the Mediterranean and the Black Sea.

Nares next worked for several years in naval cadet training ships, including the *Illustrious*, the *Britannia*, and the *Boscawen*. He was raised to the rank of commander in 1862; 1864–1866 was spent on surveys off the Australian coast in the *Salamander*, and in 1867 he began hydrographic work in the Mediterranean in the *Newport* and later the *Shearwater*, carrying out oceanographic research in the Gulf of Suez and around Gibraltar.

This research formed part of a growing interest in the sea floor and deep sea exploration. Several expeditions were organized for work in European waters, but by 1870–1871 a major cruise was being planned. Nares was given command of the *Challenger*, a steam corvette of 2,300 tons with a complement that included an impressive array of scientists. The *Challenger* sailed from Portsmouth on 21 December 1872 and spent almost a year in the Atlantic before making for the Crozet Islands and Kerguelen in the southern Indian Ocean, going down to the Antarctic ice barrier and on to Melbourne, where it arrived on 17 March 1874.

*Challenger* went on to New South Wales, left for New Zealand on

12 June, and dropped anchor in Wellington on the twenty-eighth. It next proceeded to Tonga and Fiji. An observatory was set up on the island of Matuku. Nares left Fiji for the New Hebrides (Vanuatu) on 10 August and went on to Cape York, passing through Torres Strait and reaching Amboina on 4 October. The expedition called at Ternate and Manila in November and ended the first stage of the Pacific survey at Hong Kong. There Nares found instructions awaiting him to return to England to take charge of an Arctic expedition. Accordingly, he handed over command of the *Challenger* to Capt. Frank Thomson *(q.v.)* at the beginning of January 1875 and made his way back to Europe.

In the spring of 1875, Nares set off with the *Alert* and the *Discovery* toward Greenland and the heavy Arctic ice barrier—which Nares named the palaeocrystic sea. The expedition returned to England in October 1876, the *Alert* having reached a higher latitude and wintered farther north than any ship had ever done. On his return Nares was knighted. He received the Royal Geographic Society's Founder's Medal in 1877 and the Gold Medal of the Paris Société de Géographie in 1879. In 1878 he was sent with the *Alert* to carry out survey work in the Strait of Magellan.

Sir George Nares was raised to rear admiral in 1877. He retired from active service and in 1892 became a vice-admiral. His role in the *Challenger* expedition is described in the *Narrative* of the multivolume official account of the expedition the *Reports on the Scientific Results of the Voyage of HMS "Challenger"*; his own *Narrative of a Voyage to the Polar Sea* appeared in two volumes in 1878. He died at Surbiton, Surrey, on 15 January 1915. His wife, Mary Grant, whom he had married in 1858, had died in 1905.

## Narvaez

JOSÉ MARIA NARVAEZ was born at Cadiz in 1765, joined the Spanish navy in 1780, and served in South America. In 1788 he was at San Blas on the Mexican coast with the grade of second pilot when he was selected for the expedition of Martinez *(q.v.)* to the northwest coast. In 1789 he was at Nootka Sound when Martinez seized vessels under the command of John Meares *(q.v.)*; the seizure led to the famous Nootka Incident, which almost caused a war between Britain and Spain.

One of the seized ships was the *Princess Royal*, which Narvaez took south to Monterey. The Nootka dispute took some time to settle, but in 1791 Narvaez was given command of the *Santa Saturnina* for a further voyage of exploration to the northwest coast, with Francisco Eliza in command of the *San Carlos*. In July, Narvaez sailed past the San Juan Islands from Juan de Fuca Strait into the Strait of Georgia and probably discovered the Fraser River.

In later years, Narvaez sailed across the Pacific to the Philippines and China, and when Mexico became independent of Spain served in the fledging Mexican navy. He died at Guadalajara in 1840.

## Oliver

NOT A GREAT DEAL is known of Oliver, master's mate of the *Pandora*, commanded by Captain Edwards *(q.v.)*, who sailed from Portsmouth on 7 November 1790 on a voyage in search of the *Bounty* mutineers. Oliver appears to have been a reliable, resourceful man, an experienced seaman, and a good leader of men when the occasion demanded it.

Edwards was sufficiently impressed by him to place him in command of the *Resolution*, a small schooner he had built in Tahiti to assist in seeking out the missing mutineers by sailing close inshore among the islands of the Pacific.

With him went the midshipman Renouard, the quartermaster James Dodd, and six seamen. On 22 June 1791, in gloom and a violent rain squall, the *Resolution* lost sight of the *Pandora*. The two vessels were then among the Samoas. Oliver made for Anamuka, the prearranged rendezvous in case of separation, but got to Tofua in the Tongan group by mistake and after looking in vain for the *Pandora* decided to sail west toward the Dutch East Indies. The area he traversed was still very imperfectly known, and Oliver displayed considerable navigational skill. The small band of men, however, suffered severe hardship through lack of supplies and water.

Oliver had some difficulty persuading the authorities in the Dutch settlements that he was not a mutineer. Edwards found him there, and the two returned to England in June 1792.

It is likely that Oliver discovered one or more of the many islands that constitute the Fiji group, but his log has not been found, and precise information is not easy to obtain. The schooner's journey was nevertheless an epic struggle by a handful of men.

## Ortega

PEDRO DE ORTEGA was born in Guadalcanal, province of Valencia, Spain, probably in the 1520s. He made his way to Peru, serving in the armed forces, and in 1567 was appointed *maestro de campo*, in charge of seventy soldiers, on the expedition of Alvaro de Mendaña *(q.v.)*, undertaken to discover a southern continent in the South Seas. In this capacity he was involved in negotiations with the natives of Santa Ysabel in the Solomon Islands; in spite of a number of difficult incidents, he appears to have been a humane man, anxious to control his men while at the same time protecting the Spanish encampment and obtaining much-needed supplies.

He was put in command of the brigantine *Santiago*, in which from 7 April to early May he carried out a detailed exploration of part of this large island group. As Ortega lacked navigational experience, the maneuvers were controlled by Hernán Gallego *(q.v.)*. However, as commander of this operation, Ortega can be recognized at least as the nominal discoverer of Malaita, the Florida group, Guadalcanal, Savo, part of the New Georgia group, and Choiseul.

The Mendaña expedition sailed from San Cristobal on 11 August and lost sight of the last of the Solomons on the seventeenth. Ortega favored going to New Guinea, but the majority preferred to return to South America. They finally reached Callao on 11 September 1569.

Ortega had been at the point of death during the return crossing, but he apparently recovered. There are, however, no details of his subsequent activities.

## Padilla

FRANCISCO PADILLA was captain of the *Santissima Trinidad*, chartered by Jesuits from Manila to explore the ocean east of the Philippines. In December 1710 the *Trinidad* reached Sonsorol, on the western fringe of the Marianas group, where Padilla learned that additional islands lay to the north-northeast. Leaving Sonsorol on 9 December, he came upon an island the natives called Panloq; more islands were then seen, but as the islanders proved unwelcoming, no attempt was made to go ashore to begin the work of evangelization.

Padilla spent from 11 to 13 December among what is now known as the Palau Islands, the largest of which is Babelthuap. He then returned to Manila, but beyond adding any information he brought back with him to their charts, the Spanish did little to develop or control the isolated island group. An account of the *Trinidad*'s voyage was written by Josefe Somera, the expedition's pilot.

## Peard

GEORGE PEARD was born on 18 February 1783, the son of Vice-Admiral Shuldham Peard. He entered the Royal Naval College in 1807 and served in various ships from 1809, being taken prisoner in 1811. He was appointed lieutenant in the gunboat service in 1815 in Canada.

Between 1818 and 1821 he served in the frigate *Hyperion*, which gave him the opportunity to sail to South America, including the Pacific coast. In March 1825 Peard was appointed first lieutenant of HMS *Blossom* and sailed on it to the Pacific and Bering Strait under Frederick William Beechey *(q.v.)*. He was promoted to commander in May 1827.

Peard completed his service in the *Blossom* when the ship was paid off in England in October 1828 but was unable, possibly on the grounds of ill health, to obtain another appointment. He died in London on 17 February 1837.

The journal he kept on board the *Blossom* in the years 1825–1828 is a valuable record of the voyage. It remained unpublished until 1973, when it was edited by B. M. Gough.

## Pendleton

ISAAC PENDLETON, captain of the brigantine *Union*, sailed from New York in late 1803 on a sealing expedition. He had planned to work among the Crozet group in the southern Indian Ocean but was unsuccessful in his attempt to find the islands. He sailed on to southwest Australia but found few seals. He was more fortunate along the south coast, where he discovered an island he named Borders and constructed a small schooner, the first European vessel to be built in Australia outside New South Wales. With the *Union* and the schooner, which he named *Independence*, he sailed through

Bass Strait and southeast toward the south of New Zealand, putting in at the lonely Antipodes Islands.

He found large numbers of seals on the islands and left a party of eleven men in charge of an officer to collect furs for a season while he sailed to Port Jackson, arriving in September 1804 with the first stocks.

The *Union* was then chartered by the merchant Simeon Lord to sail to the Fijis for sandalwood. When the ship put in at Tongatabu, in the Tonga group, to engage an interpreter, Isaac Pendleton was massacred together with a boat's crew. The mate, Wright, took the ship back to Port Jackson to secure replacements for the crew and sailed to the Fiji Islands, where the *Union* was wrecked with the loss of all hands.

The party Pendleton had left behind on the Antipodes suffered great hardships before their eventual rescue, but they brought some 60,000 skins back to Sydney, starting a sealskin rush that led to the near-extermination of the seal population.

## Perez

JUAN JOSEF PEREZ HERNÁNDEZ was born in Majorca around 1725, entered the Spanish naval service, graduated as a pilot, and served on the Manila galleon route. In 1767 he was at San Blas, Mexico, and was named in 1768 as a member of a commission established to study problems caused by Russian penetration into northern Alaska. Part of the response was the colonization of California, and in 1769 Perez was sent in command of the *Principe* with a shipload of colonists to San Diego and Monterey. In subsequent years he commanded vessels that supplied food and equipment to the nascent settlements.

In 1774 the viceroy, Antonio Bucareli, decided to obtain a better knowledge of the northern American coast and ascertain the extent of Russian activity. Juan Perez sailed in the *Santiago* on 25 January 1774 from San Blas to San Diego and Monterey, leaving in June for the north. On 15 July he reached the present Alaska-Canada border, traded with Indians at the north of Queen Charlotte Islands, and went on as far as 55°30′ north, off Prince of Wales Island, where, in fog and faced with unfavorable winds and currents, he turned back. It was 30 July.

Sailing down the coast of Vancouver Island, Perez discovered on 8 August Nootka Sound, which he named San Lorenzo, but he was prevented by contrary winds from sailing into it. Fog hampered his further exploration of the coast, although he probably sighted the entrance to Juan de Fuca Strait. His only discovery of significance after this was Mt. Olympus in present-day Washington state, which he named Sierra Nevada de Santa Rosalia. The *Santiago*, its crew badly afflicted with scurvy, sailed south to San Blas, where another expedition was planned to consolidate Perez's pioneering reconnaissance.

Perez sailed again in 1775 in the *Santiago*, but as second-in-command, the expedition being led by Bruno de Hezeta. Perez's health had been undermined by the hardships endured on the first voyage, and scurvy developed again in 1775. He died on board the *Santiago* on 2 November 1775 on his way from Monterey to San Blas and was buried at sea with full naval honors.

## Perry

MATTHEW CALBRAITH PERRY was born in Rhode Island on 10 April 1794 and entered the navy in 1809, first serving aboard the *Revenge*, commanded by his brother, then transferring to the *President* under Commodore John Rogers in 1810 and later to the *United States*.

After the war he served for a time in merchant ships, sailing to Europe. In 1820 he returned to the naval service as executive officer of the *Cyane*, sailing to Africa. In 1822 he went to the West Indies on operations against pirates and in 1825–1826 to the Mediterranean in the *North Carolina*. In 1830 he sailed to Russia in the *Concord*, then returned to service in the Mediterranean. He had been promoted to master commandant in 1826; in 1833 he was second officer in the New York naval yard; in February 1837 he was promoted to captain. He returned to sea for a time on the *Fulton*, the first naval steamship, but in 1841 was appointed commandant of the New York naval yard. In 1843 he led the African squadron sent to supervise the elimination of the slave trade, then took over command of the *Mississippi* in the Mexican War.

The years 1848 to 1851 were spent on special duties in New York. In January 1852 he was selected to head an American mission to Japan. Perry sailed from Norfolk, Virginia, in the *Mississippi* and proceeded to Hong Kong. Other ships placed under his command for the expedition included the frigate *Susquehanna* and the sloops *Plymouth* and *Saratoga*. He sailed from Shanghai on 17 May 1853 for Naha on Okinawa Island in the Ryukyus, organizing scientific surveys ashore as well as a survey of the Bonin Islands. On 2 July he sailed in the *Susquehanna* with the two sloops, reaching Yedo Bay on the eighth. He handed over the official letter the president had entrusted to him and on the seventeenth sailed back to Naha while the Japanese considered their response.

During the autumn Commodore Perry had a detailed survey of the coast of Okinawa carried out and sent Commander Kelly of the *Plymouth* to the Bonin Islands to complete the earlier survey and to lay a formal claim to the southern islands of the group on the basis of an earlier visit by an American whaler. Perry then took his squadron back to Tokyo Bay in February 1854 and went to Yokohama, where he signed the treaty opening up Japan to western trade on 31 March 1854. He sailed back to Naha and on to China, but despatched one of his ships to Formosa (Taiwan) to carry out hydrographic work.

Ill health forced Perry to sail home from Hong Kong by an English steamer. He reached New York on 12 January 1855 and died there on 4 March 1858. On his return he had compiled his useful *Narrative of the Expedition of an American Squadron to the China Seas and Japan*, which was edited by Francis L. Hawks.

## Peyster

ARENDT SCHUYLER DE PEYSTER was a merchant trader born in the American colonies but with strong links to England. In 1819 he was given command of the armed English brigantine *Rebecca*, in which he sailed to Valparaiso and crossed the Pacific to India. In late 1819 he discovered a cluster of some fourteen low-lying islands, which he named Ellice's Group in honor of his friend and benefactor, Ellice, who was Member of Parliament for Coventry, England, and soon after another group of seventeen islands, which he called De Peyster's Islands.

From the positions given by Peyster, they can be identified as Fanufuti and Nukufetau, both part of the Ellice Islands (present-day Tuvalu).

## Pigafetta

ANTONIO PIGAFETTA was born, probably in 1486, into a patrician family of Vicenza, northern Italy. He probably fought against the Turks in the eastern Mediterranean; by 1519 he had become a Knight of Rhodes. He was taken on the staff of Francesco Chiericati, the Papal Nuncio to the Court of Spain, and traveled to Saragossa, Valladolid, and Barcelona, where he learned of the voyage to the Pacific proposed by Magellan *(q.v.)*. He traveled to Seville, where in June 1519 he was accepted by Magellan as *criado del capitán* (aide to the admiral).

The expedition sailed from Sanlúcar on 20 September 1519, entered what is now known as the Strait of Magellan on 21 October 1520, emerged into the Pacific on 28 November, and reached the Marianas on 6 March 1521. Magellan was killed in the Philippines on 27 April. Antonio Pigafetta survived this and later affrays, landing back at Seville on 8 September 1522.

Pigafetta's importance lies in his detailed narrative of the voyage, which gained him well-deserved fame. It is full of important observations and helped to counteract many of the claims and accusations made by other participants. The main manuscript account was dedicated to the Grand Master of the Knights of Malta, as Pigafetta's order was now known. It has been reprinted and translated in many editions. Nothing is known, however, of the later life of this invaluable chronicler of Magellan's voyage except that he died in Malta in 1534.

## Porter

DAVID PORTER was born on 1 February 1780 in Boston, Massachusetts, the son of a seagoing family. He accompanied his father on a voyage to the West Indies and in 1798 joined the American navy as a midshipman; he was promoted lieutenant in 1799, but was captured and held prisoner from 1803 to 1805. He was commissioned master commandant in 1806 and, following a series of successful engagements, was raised to captain in 1812.

Porter was given command of the frigate *Essex* and in February 1813 took it round the Horn, raided English whalers in the south Pacific, and took formal possession of Nuku Hiva in the Marquesas in October. Early in 1814, while raiding along the coast of Chile, he was pursued by British warships and took refuge in Valparaiso harbor where, on 28 March, he was attacked by the frigate *Phoebe* and the sloop *Cherub*. Forced to surrender, Porter was later paroled and returned to New York.

From 1815 to 1823 he was a member of the Navy Board in Washington, but then with the rank of commodore took an active part in the suppression of piracy along the Mosquito Coast and the islands of the Caribbean. He overstepped his powers, however, and was recalled and court-martialed in 1825. He resigned in the following year, became for a time commander-in-chief of the Mexican navy, and in 1831 was appointed American representative in Turkey. He died in Constantinople on 3 March 1843.

His *Journal of a Cruise made to the Pacific Ocean in the United States frigate "Essex"*, published in two volumes in 1815, contains much very valuable ethnographic information on the Marquesan islanders.

## Portlock

NATHANIEL PORTLOCK was born in the American colonies around the year 1748 and entered the navy as an able-seaman on board the *St. Albans* in 1772, his seagoing experience presumably having been gained in the merchant service. After serving in the *Ardent* and the *Ramillies*, he joined the *Discovery* in 1776 and sailed as mate under James Cook *(q.v.)* during his third voyage, which ended in London on 4 October 1780.

Portlock, promoted to lieutenant, then served in the *Firebrand*, which was part of the Channel Fleet. In 1785 he was offered the command of an expedition to the northwest coast organized by Richard Cadman Etches and other London traders calling themselves the King George's Sound Company. Portlock sailed from Spithead on 16 September 1785 in the *King George*, accompanied by the smaller *Queen Charlotte*, commanded by George Dixon *(q.v.)*. The expedition sailed to the Falklands, rounded Cape Horn, and put in at Kealakekua Bay, Hawaii, in late May 1786, the first ships to arrive there after Cook's murder. Leaving the islands on 13 June, Portlock reached Cook Inlet on the northwest coast on 19 July.

Trade was slow, Portlock was beset by ill health and storms, and the expedition sailed back to Hawaii in October with a sense of relief.

The second trading season began with Portlock's departure from the islands in March 1787, making for Prince William Sound, where the Englishmen found Capt. John Meares *(q.v.)*, who had been wintering there in his snow *Nootka* and was in great need of assistance. Portlock and Dixon went their separate ways on 14 May to trade along the coast. Portlock left on 24 August for Hawaii, arriving on 28 September; after laying in supplies, he set off for China to dispose of his cargo of furs. He anchored in Macao Roads on 21 November and joined Dixon shortly after.

Selling the furs and buying a cargo of tea kept Portlock and Dixon in China until 9 February 1788. The ships separated on 1 April and met up again as arranged in St. Helena. Portlock ended his voyage in Margate Roads on 24 August 1788, Dixon dropping anchor at Dover three weeks later. They brought with them not only tea, but valuable natural history specimens. Portlock's *A Voyage round the World, but more particularly to the North-West Coast of America* was published in London in 1789.

Two years later (on 3 August 1791) Portlock sailed with William Bligh *(q.v.)* as captain of the *Assistant* to fetch breadfruit plants from Tahiti and deliver them to the West Indies. They set off by way of the Cape of Tasmania. They anchored in Matavai Bay, Tahiti, on 9 April 1792 and sailed again, their mission completed, on 19 July. The return voyage took them to Aitutaki, Tonga, Fiji, and Torres Strait, with a call at Koepang in October. The breadfruit plants were delivered in January 1793 and, sailing with caution as war had broken out with France, Portlock reached Dungeness on 2 August.

Portlock was promoted to commander on 9 September and served in the war. He was captain of the *Arrow* when in September it captured the Dutch ship *Draak*. He was raised to the rank of captain shortly after but gave up active service as peace approached. He died at Greenwich Hospital on 12 September 1817.

## Prado

DIEGO DE PRADO Y TOVAR was a resident of Lima, well connected and well educated, who sailed with Quiros *(q.v.)* in 1605. He was an engineer of some ability, a cartographer, and by the time he sailed for Peru, an experienced navigator with the rank of captain. He was appointed *capitán-entretenido*, but whether he had valid claims to be Quiros' second-in-command or the captain of one of the ships is open to argument.

He was granted five hundred pesos for the voyage and may have had some official status as the king's or the viceroy's agent on the expedition. He sailed in the *San Pedro y Pablo* on 21 December 1605 but transferred to the *almiranta San Pedrico* when the expedition reached Taumako in the Duff Islands on 6 April 1606. When Quiros made his landfall at Espiritu Santo and set up the colony of New Jerusalem, he was appointed public trustee, one of the many titles bestowed by Quiros on members of the expedition. It should not be regarded as evidence of Prado's particular worthiness, for he seems to have been ambitious and something of an intriguer. When Quiros' ship became separated from the *San Pedrico*, Prado laid claim to becoming its commander. All the evidence, however, points to Torres *(q.v.)* being in charge of the difficult navigation that now faced them.

Failing to meet up with Quiros' *San Pedro*, the *San Pedrico* worked its way west between New Guinea and Australia through the strait that now bears Torres' name and in time reached Ternate in the Moluccas. There, according to a letter written by the commander, "Don Diego de Tovar, a good engineer and moreover very expert in foundry work" drew up plans for fortifying the town. In May 1607 Prado was in Manila, where again his services were called upon to design fortifications and supervise their building.

In 1608 he wrote a "Relación" of the voyage, which was forwarded to the king of Spain together with a number of charts. A later version was made around 1615, by which time he had returned to Spain; his role in the expedition became magnified in the later version and his criticisms of Quiros became increasingly severe and unfair. Prado appears to have left the Philippines in 1613 and sailed to Goa, from where he wrote another letter to the king in December. He is believed to have reached Spain sometime in 1614. The last record of him is dated 1618, when he joined the Order of St. Basil in Madrid.

## Pribilov

LITTLE IS KNOWN of the Russian Gavriil (Gerasim) Loginovich Pribilov, a captain of the Russian American Company. He was in command of the ship *Sv. Georgii* from 1781 to 1788, sailing mostly from the Sea of Okhotsk and Kamchatka along the Aleutian chain, engaging in the fur trade, as far as the northwest coast of America. In 1786 and 1787 he passed through the Aleutians into the Bering Sea and began exploring the little-known northern waters, where reportedly there were numerous islands rich in fur seal rookeries. He came upon the only islands of any significance north of the Aleutians and certainly rich in seals, which he named St. Paul and St. George. The group was named Pribilof Islands in his honor in 1789 by the navigator G. I. Shelikov. Pribilov died in 1796.

## Puget

PETER JOHN PUGET was born in London in 1765, the son of a merchant. He joined the Royal Navy in 1778 as a midshipman and in 1783 was appointed to the *Europa*, serving in the West Indies. He then met George Vancouver *(q.v.)*, who had also been appointed to the *Europa*, as a lieutenant.

The two became close associates over a three-year period, and Vancouver welcomed Puget's assistance for his voyage to the Pacific in 1791. Puget sailed as second of the *Discovery* on 1 April 1791, making for Tenerife, the Cape, New Zealand, and Tahiti. After a call at the Hawaiian Islands, the expedition sailed to the northwest coast of America, reaching Juan de Fuca Strait on 30 April 1792. During the careful exploration that followed, Puget's name was given to the complex southern extension of the strait, Puget Sound, on which present-day Seattle has been built. Puget's name is also commemorated in Puget Island in the Columbia River and in Cape Puget in the Gulf of Alaska.

The lengthy exploration of the coastline was complicated by disputes with the Spanish, who claimed prior rights to much of the coast. Puget, already promoted to first lieutenant of the *Discovery*, took over command of the *Chatham* from William Broughton *(q.v.)*, whom Vancouver sent back to Europe. Puget assumed a role of growing importance, setting off for the Hawaiian Islands with Vancouver in January 1793. He returned to the northwest coast in April ahead of his commander. But Vancouver soon followed, and for four months the two ships carried out survey work as far as 56° north; toward the end of the year they went down to California, Puget surveying Bodega Bay while Vancouver remained embroiled with the Spanish authorities in Monterey.

The following year was almost a repetition of 1793 until 2 December 1794, when the *Discovery* and the *Chatham* left Monterey for Valparaiso, Cape Horn, and St. Helena, the *Chatham* reaching Plymouth on 16 October 1795, just a day after the *Discovery*'s arrival.

Peter Puget had a period of leave after the exertions of the previous five years, but war was raging and his services were soon called upon. In 1807 he led a successful attack during the second battle of Copenhagen; later he was appointed commissioner of the navy at Madras. His health began to deteriorate, and he retired to Bath; there he died, a rear admiral in 1822.

## Quiros

PEDRO FERNANDEZ DE QUIROS was born in Evora, Portugal, in 1565. It is likely that he went to sea quite young as a ship's boy and apprentice pilot, serving in ships trading out of Libson and eventually with vessels bound for the Indies. By his late twenties he was recognized as a skilled and knowledgable pilot. He married Ana Chacon de Miranda in 1589 and sailed to Peru with her and their son in 1591 or 1592. We find him in Peru in 1594, questioning an English geographer taken prisoner with Richard Hawkins, who had been raiding along the coast.

It is not surprising, therefore, that he should have been selected in March 1595 as captain of the *San Jerónimo* and chief pilot of the expedition of Mendaña *(q.v.)*. This expedition sailed from Paita, Peru, on 16 June 1595 and on 8 September reached Santa Cruz, where it was decided to form a settlement in Graciosa Bay. The undertaking proved to be a disaster: Mendaña and many others lost their lives, and the ships sailed away on 18 November. Mendaña's widow became the nominal commander, but the expedition's sur-

vival depended on Quiros' navigational ability and innate leadership.

He knew next to nothing about the seas through which he would
have to sail to reach Manila, where help could be expected. The voyage, in rotting vessels with a starving and dying company, was one
of the greatest feats in Pacific navigation, made all the more difficult
by Dona Ysabel Mendaña's selfish and haughty behavior. The island
of Ponape was sighted just before Christmas and Guam on 1 January,
but the *San Jerónimo*, now the only vessel left, had no equipment
and not enough fit men to attempt a landing.

Finally, on 12 January 1596 the coast of the Philippines hove into
sight; natives came with food and provided some directions. The
*San Jerónimo* slowly made its way to Manila, where it anchored on
11 February. The survivors needed time to recover, and the ship had
to be extensively refitted. On 10 August it sailed for Mexico, arriving in Acapulco on 11 December 1596, whence Quiros set off for
Peru.

He had become convinced that the Solomon Islands could be
found and that the southern continent was not far from where the
Mendaña expedition had been forced to turn away. He was also
moved by a great desire to bring Christianity to the peoples of the
Pacific. Unable to persuade the viceroy of Peru to finance a voyage
back to the Pacific, Quiros went to Spain and to Rome, where he
met the pope. In 1603 the Spanish monarch agreed to support him;
after a series of delays and setbacks Quiros returned to Peru, where
he was given three ships—*San Pedro y Pablo*, *San Pedrico*, and *Los
Tres Reyes Magos*. The expedition included six Franciscan friars and
assumed under Quiros a more religious character than other participants were ready to accept.

The ships sailed from Callao on 21 December 1605. Various small
islands were discovered in the Tuamotus, as Quiros adopted a route
that was at first more southerly than Mendaña's. Then he rejoined
that route, past the Tokelaus, on to Taumako (not far from Santa
Cruz), and on 1 May 1606 anchored in the Bay of St. Philip and St.
James, in Espiritu Santo, in present-day Vanuatu, which he identified with the southern continent and named Austrialia del Espiritu
Santo.

There Quiros established a settlement he called New Jerusalem;

but establishing a Christian Spanish beachhead proved too daunting a task, and within a few weeks he sailed away to explore the area further, whereupon the ships became separated. The *San Pedrico*, commanded by Torres *(q.v.)*, sailed southwest and made a number of further discoveries, while Quiros aboard the *San Pedro* decided to return to America. To reach the appropriate westerly winds, he sailed north through the Gilbert Islands, discovering Makin Meang on 8 July, which he named, perhaps a little ruefully, Buen Viaje; he sighted the coast of North America on 23 September and reached Acapulco on 23 November 1606.

He had made a number of discoveries, although apart from Espiritu Santo, most were small islands and deserted atolls. The viceroy of Mexico was not unkind, but recriminations about the failure of the colonization attempt and his own leadership began to accumulate. Quiros traveled to Spain to report to the king and seek support for yet another expedition. In time, partly to rid himself of a man who had become an importunate visionary, the king agreed, and Quiros sailed for America in April 1615.

His increasing preoccupation with converting and saving the people of the Pacific, and particularly with the imaginary southern continent, has at times given rise to conflicting verdicts on his personality, which needs to be set against the background of contemporary Spanish cupidity for gold and disregard for native people. In the end, it did impair his judgment and result in decisions that remain hard to explain, but his ability as a navigator and his contribution to Pacific exploration cannot be challenged. His death, which occurred in Panama on his way back to Peru, sometime in mid-1615, saved him from the final disappointment that awaited him—since the Spanish authorities had no intention of allowing him to sail once more into the Pacific—but his place in Pacific history could only gain in stature as the years passed.

## Raven

WILLIAM RAVEN was born in England in October 1756 and joined the merchant service at an early age. He entered the navy in March 1779, when he became master of the sloop *Tobago*. In the following year, while master of the *Albion*, he suffered severe wounds; nevertheless, he later took over the *Grampus* until 1786. Little is known about him until 1791, when he is recorded as master of the *Duke*.

In 1792 he sailed to New South Wales as captain and part owner of the *Britannia*. In October of the same year he was sent from Sydney to fetch provisions for the settlement from the Cape; but he first went to Dusky Sound, New Zealand, where he left a sealing party on Anchor Island. Back in Sydney in June 1793, he returned to New Zealand in September to collect his sealers and the furs, went on to Norfolk Island, and thence to Batavia for supplies. On the way he discovered a group of islands between New Caledonia and the New Hebrides (Vanuatu), which he named the Loyalty Islands.

He was back in Sydney in June 1794 and the following year went to the Cape and to Bengal. He was back in New South Wales in mid-1796, and in 1797 sailed home to England, arriving in June. He then took over the *Buffalo*, in which he returned to New South Wales. The authorities provided him with a passage home in the *Supply*, which left Sydney at the end of 1799; but the ship was captured near the Isle of Wight, and Raven spent several months as a prisoner in France. His health was beginning to fail. He was put on half-pay and served for a while with the Trinity House Volunteers. He was soon forced to retire; he died in London on 14 August 1814.

## Receveur

CLAUDE-FRANÇOIS JOSEPH RECEVEUR was born on 25 April 1757 at Noel-Cerneux, a small French village close to the Swiss frontier. Although his father was but a laborer, several members of his pious family, including a brother, entered the priesthood. He himself became associated with the Franciscan order, later joining the Grey Friars in Paris, where he took the name of Brother Laurent. However, his real interest was natural history, and he presented a number of papers to the French Academy of Science and acquired a reputation as a sound researcher.

Between 1776 and 1780 he was sent on a number of research expeditions. Then in 1785, aged only 28, he was selected as naturalist for the voyage of La Pérouse *(q.v.)*, acting also as chaplain. He sailed in the *Astrolabe* from Brest on 1 August 1785, for Cape Horn, Easter Island—where he charitably forgave the islanders for stealing some of his belongings—the Hawaiian Islands, the northwest coast of America, California, and China. After sailing north to Kamchatka the expedition veered south for the Samoan group.

On 11 December 1787 a party of Frenchmen was attacked on shore, several, including the *Astrolabe*'s captain, Fleuriot de Langle *(q.v.)*, being killed. Father Receveur was wounded in the head and almost lost an eye. He later wrote to his brother saying that his wounds were not as serious as had been thought. However, he was known for his mildness and self-effacing nature, and he may have been minimizing his condition so as not to worry his friends.

The ships sailed from Tutuila, Samoa, on 14 December, going west along the other islands of the group. On 27 December they reached the northern Tongas, then went on to Norfolk Island and Botany Bay, New South Wales, where La Pérouse dropped anchor on 26 January 1788.

Although Receveur's letter stating that his wounds were not serious and had healed is dated 7 February 1787, Joseph Receveur died on the seventeenth, ten days later, and was buried ashore at Botany Bay, the first European to earn the dubious honor of a formal burial on Australian soil. There is a strong possibility that he had indeed recovered from his wounds and was killed while on a botanizing trip inland.

A Père Receveur Commemoration Committee keeps his memory alive in Australia. His collections, unhappily, were all lost in the wreck of the expedition at Vanikoro.

## Retes

YNIGO ORTIZ DE RETES was a Spanish captain sent out on 16 May 1545 in the *San Juan de Letran* from Tidore to Spanish America, an earlier attempt by de la Torre *(q.v.)* having failed. Retes sailed south to New Guinea, coasting along there until 12 August, reaching a point close to the mouth of the Sepik River, but constant contrary winds forced him to turn back; he arrived at Tidore in September.

The interest of this voyage lies in the islands Retes encountered during July and August. Few could be claimed as discoveries, most having been sighted by Saavedra *(q.v.)*. They include the Hermit Islands, Lio and Ninigo group. It was on this voyage that, on 20 June

1545, the main island was given the name of Nueva Guinea and formally if ephemerally claimed as a Spanish possession.

## Ringgold

CADWALADER RINGGOLD was born in Washington County, Maryland, on 20 August 1802 and entered the navy in 1819 as a midshipman. He served with Commodore Porter's fleet suppressing piracy in the West Indies. A lieutenant in 1828, he took part in the Pacific cruise of the *Vandalia* in 1828–1832, then went to the Mediterranean in the *Adams* in 1834–1835.

In 1838 Ringgold was given the command of the *Porpoise* and the rank of third officer of the Wilkes *(q.v.)* expedition. The fleet sailed from Hampton Roads, Norfolk, Virginia, on 18 August 1838, bound for Madeira, Porto Praya in the Cape Verde Islands, and Rio, where it spent November to early January, sailing next for Tierra del Fuego and the Antarctic. After exploration work in difficult conditions, the expedition went to Valparaiso and Callao. Since the expedition comprised a number of vessels, Wilkes was able to despatch several of them on separate surveying missions.

Thus in 1839 Ringgold went ahead of Wilkes to Tahiti and was sent to survey the western Tuamotus with instructions to rendezvous with Wilkes at Rose Island, where they met on 7 October. Then they sailed to Samoa, where the *Porpoise* was detached to carry out a survey of Savaii.

The squadron then assembled at Apia in November before sailing to Sydney, where Ringgold arrived on the twenty-seventh. A return to Antarctic exploration in January 1840 brought about further separations, the *Porpoise* sailing to the Bay of Islands, New Zealand, where Wilkes found it on 30 March. A week later, they left for Tonga and the Fijis, Ringgold then being sent off to survey the eastern Fiji islands and to search for the crew of a wrecked ship. Wilkes made his way back to Honolulu; Ringgold completed some hydrographic work in Tonga and Samoa before joining him on 8 October 1840.

The *Porpoise* was sent to the Tuamotus in November, returning on 24 March 1841. Ringgold's work had been particularly thorough and demanding. The *Porpoise* needed to be recoppered at Honolulu before it could leave with Wilkes' *Vincennes* on 5 April for the northwest coast. They arrived off the mouth of the Columbia River on 28 April and went on to Puget Sound. Both hydrographic work and exploration work ashore were carried out during the months following. In mid-July the *Peacock* arrived off the Columbia River but was wrecked on the bar. In the subsequent reorganization, Cadwalader Ringgold was given command of the *Vincennes* with orders to survey San Francisco Bay; he went as well to the San Joaquin River and up the Sacramento River.

In November, the expedition returned to Honolulu, where the *Porpoise* was detached with the *Flying Fish* for a survey of the reefs and shoals northwest of the Hawaiian group. The fleet reassembled at Singapore, where the *Flying Fish* was sold. Only the *Vincennes* and the *Porpoise* completed the circumnavigation, returning home by way of the Cape and St. Helena, Ringgold arriving at New York at the end of June 1842.

Ringgold was promoted to commander in 1849. U.S. interest in California was growing rapidly, and Ringgold became known as a specialist in its coastal geography. Following his surveys and further work in 1849 and 1850, he published in 1851 *A Series of Charts with sailing directions* on California. Then in 1853 he was appointed to the *Vincennes* to lead a five-ship North Pacific Exploring Expedition; he sailed from Norfolk on 11 June 1853 and began the work of exploration, going to Australia and the western Pacific, but his health broke down. Matthew C. Perry *(q.v.)* considered Ringgold unfit to continue with the expedition and sent him home from Hong Kong in the *Susquehanna* in September 1854, a decision Ringgold resented.

He was promoted to captain in 1856, having sufficiently recovered to return to active service. He commanded the frigate *Sabine* during the Civil War and was raised to the rank of commodore in July 1862 and to rear admiral in 1866, the year in which he retired. He died in New York on 29 April 1867.

## Rocha

DIOGO DE ROCHA was a Portuguese captain sent by Jorge de Meneses, governor of the Moluccas—himself the reputed discoverer of New Guinea—on a voyage from Ternate to the Celebes. Rocha is believed to have sailed in June 1525, been blown off course by a violent gale in August or September, and driven east into the Pacific. Struggling to make his way back from those uncharted waters, Rocha came upon some islands through which he took his ship safely and where he was able to land and refresh his crew. The islands, in latitude 9° or 10° north, were named Ilhas de Gomez de Sequeira, after the ship's pilot. Rocha arrived back in Ternate in January 1526.

From the description given, it is evident that he had reached the Yap Islands, and it is possible that he also sighted some other islands on the western fringe of the Carolines.

## Rodgers

JOHN RODGERS, born on 8 August 1812 near Havre de Grace, Maryland, served as a midshipman from April 1828 in the *Constellation* and the *Concord* in the Mediterranean. He later entered the naval school at Norfolk, Virginia, graduating in 1834. After further studies, he sailed to Brazil and later worked on surveys of the Florida coast.

He was promoted to lieutenant in January 1840. In 1842–1844 he commanded the *Boxer*, was then sent to Africa and the Mediterranean, and returned in 1849 to join the Coast Survey. On 12 October 1852 he was appointed to the North Pacific Exploring Expedition, commanding the bark-rigged steamer *John Hancock*. The expedition sailed from Hampton Roads on 11 June 1853, making for Australia and in the case of Rodgers proceeding to Batavia. The *Hancock* spent January through to May 1854 surveying Karimata Strait and the islands between Batavia and Singapore. The expedition came together again in Hong Kong, but in September the expedition's commander, Cadwalader Ringgold (*q.v.*), fell ill and had to be sent home, his place being taken by John Rodgers.

Rodgers spent the rest of the year surveying the Bonin and the Ryukyu islands. In the following year, exploration work was carried out around Formosa (Taiwan) and Japan, Rodgers surveying in detail the coast of Japan, ignoring the objections of the Japanese. The expedition then sailed north, toward Sakhalin and Kamchatka, Rodgers himself continuing through Bering Strait into Arctic waters; he then sailed for San Francisco along the Aleutian chain. He went home by way of the Hawaiian and Society islands, where he carried out more hydrographic work and added to the very considerable collections of zoological specimens the expedition brought back.

Rodgers had been appointed commander during this voyage, in September 1855. After his return to the United States in 1856 he was placed in charge of an office in Washington to oversee the preparation of a narrative and other publications on the voyage. This work, however, was never completed, owing to the outbreak of the Civil War, in which he served from May 1861 to early 1865. He was promoted to commodore following his capture of the Confederate ironclad *Atlanta.*

His further activities in the Pacific were largely associated with American efforts to open up Asia to Western trade. In September 1865 he sailed to the Pacific with the *Vanderbilt* and several smaller vessels to protect American interests, and in 1870, promoted to rear admiral, he was appointed to command the Asiatic Squadron. In 1871 he sailed to Korea in the *Colorado*, anchored his fleet of five ships in the Han River, and sent a party ashore. The party was fired upon, and any possibility of a treaty was one of the casualties. After a bloody engagement, Rodgers sailed out of Korean waters.

John Rodgers left the Asiatic Squadron in 1872 and took up various posts ashore, eventually becoming president of the Naval Institute. He died in Washington on 5 May 1882.

## Rodriguez

JUAN RODRIGUEZ was a Spanish pilot sailing south of Guam in 1696 when he came upon an uncharted island. He reported this discovery to Spanish missionaries, adding that close by were two smaller islands. The native name (Farroilep) and Rodriguez's detailed description of his landfall enabled the island to be identified as Faraulep and the smaller islands as Pigue and Eate, part of the western Carolines.

## Rogers

WOODES ROGERS was born in 1678, possibly in Poole, Dorset. He was apprenticed to a merchant captain in 1697 but had probably worked with coastal vessels previously. He took part in several trading ventures, including some wartime privateering.

In 1708 he sailed with the *Duke* and the *Duchess* on an expedition financed by a group of Bristol merchants who had become his partners. One of his officers was William Dampier *(q.v.)*, making his third voyage to the Pacific. The ships left Bristol on 1 August, making for Cork in Ireland and the Canaries. They rounded the Horn in early January and on the thirty-first sighted Juan Fernandez Islands, where they took on board Alexander Selkirk *(q.v.)*, the man on whom the character of Robinson Crusoe was modeled. The next months were spent working their way up the coast of South America, raiding and plundering with fair success. A stay in the Galapagos in May 1709 provided an opportunity to refresh the weary crew and careen the ships in preparation for further raids. A Spanish frigate from Manila with a crew exhausted and sick after the long voyage yielded a rich cargo, but the great Manila galleon, the *Nuestra Señora de la Encarnación*, which Rogers finally encountered at the end of the year, was too strong for his two ships. After two days of fighting, the outgunned and outmatched *Duke* and *Duchess* called off the fight and sailed away.

On 10 January 1710 Woodes Rogers left from Puerto Seguro in Lower California, taking along with him the *Marquis*, a renamed prize captured off Guayaquil earlier on the voyage, and the Spanish frigate, renamed the *Batchelor*. They traveled almost due west along the thirteenth parallel, passing well to the south of the Hawaiian Islands through seas empty as far as the eye could see, until on 11 March they came upon Guam. Rogers took on supplies for the next stage of the voyage, to the Celebes and the Moluccas, reaching Batavia in June. The *Marquis* was sold and the other three ships repaired. On 12 October they left the Dutch East Indies for the Cape. It was safer to make for Europe as part of a convoy, which meant some delay. Rogers left on 6 April 1711 and arrived in Holland on 23 July, but he was forced to await clearance before sailing to Bristol, as the East India Company was claiming that the *Duke* and *Duchess* had breached their monopoly. The voyage finally ended on 2 October after the incensed company had been pacified with a share of the voyage's quite considerable profits.

Woodes Rogers' account of his expedition, *A Cruising Voyage round the World* (London, 1712), helped to establish his reputation and widen his contacts. In 1713 he sailed in the *Delicia* for Sumatra and Madagascar on a slave-trading expedition and endeavored to arouse interest in a colonizing venture on Madagascar. More practical was the development of the Bahamas, which he leased in 1717 for twenty-one years. It proved a difficult enterprise, pitting him against the pirates who infested the area and the ever-vigilant Spanish. It also proved a heavy drain on his financial resources. He returned to England in 1721 and went through a period of severe financial stress.

Finally, on 25 August 1729 he returned to the Bahamas with a formal appointment as governor. He died in Nassau on 15 July 1732.

## Roggeveen

JACOB ROGGEVEEN was born at Middelburg, Holland, on 1 February 1659. His father, Arend, planned a voyage to the Pacific in 1675, but the proposal did not eventuate and Arend died in 1679. Jacob was well educated, attending the Protestant University at Saumur, France. In 1693 he became a notary in Middelburg and in 1706 was appointed to the Council of Justice in Batavia, where in 1708 he married Anna Clement. She died before his return to Holland in 1715; they had no children.

He became involved in religious controversies and found himself persona non grata in his home town. In 1721, he revived his father's project centering his plan on the discovery of a southern land in order not to infringe upon the wider monopoly of the Dutch East India Company. He obtained sufficient support for an expedition of three ships—the *Arend*, under Capt. Jan Koster; the *Thienhoven*, under Capt. Cornelis Bouman; and the *Afrikaansche Galey*, under Capt. Roeloef Rosendaal *(qq.v.)*.

They sailed from Texel on 1 August 1521. Roggeveen first sailed down to the Falkland Islands (which he renamed Belgia Australis), passed through the Strait of Le Maire, and continued south to beyond 60° south latitude to enter the Pacific. He made a landfall near Valdivia, Chile, and went for refreshment to Juan Fernandez, where he spent 24 February 1522 to 17 March. He had hopes of finding the land believed to have been discovered by Edward Davis *(q.v.)* but instead came upon an island which, it being Easter Day (5 April 1522), he named Easter Island.

Roggeveen spent a week at Easter Island before setting out once more in search of Davis Land. Nothing was seen but empty seas until mid-May, when he found himself among the Tuamotus. There were enough small islands in this vast archipelago for the Dutch to claim a number of discoveries, although the names they bestowed on them have not lasted. On 18 May they discovered Tikei, then Manihi, Apataki, Aratua, and Makatea. One island was named Schadelijke (Disastrous; it is Takapoto) because the *Afrikaansche Galey* was lost on it with a vast store of provisions. The entire group was given the not inappropriate name of the Labyrinth. On 4 June Roggeveen came upon two high islands. These were Bora Bora and Maupiti; he had reached the present-day Society Islands. Strong swells pushed the two ships northward; Roggeveen then veered to a westerly course, which took him to the Samoa group. Small islands were sighted at first—Rose Island, which he called Bird Island; then the Manua group on 13 June; and two days later a large island he called Thienhoven and another he named Groeningen; these were Tutuila and Upolu, all being discoveries.

Roggeveen wisely chose to cease his search for the southern continent and instead to make for New Guinea and the Dutch East Indies, where he hoped to get help for his scurvy-ridden crew. He passed, without seeing them, between the Gilbert and Ellice Islands (Kiribati and Tuvalu) and reached New Ireland on 17 July 1722. He made a brief landing on New Hanover. Scurvy and other diseases were now making frightful inroads, and although he could not be certain that he would be made welcome by his commercial rivals in the Dutch settlements, he had to press on. In September he sighted Java and anchored in Batavia on 4 October. Although food and other assistance were supplied, his vessels were seized.

Roggeveen made his way back to Holland, leaving with the regular merchant fleet on 3 December 1722 and arriving at Texel on 11 July 1723. Protracted negotiations over the seizure of his ships, eventually deemed illegal, resulted in compensation being paid. Jacob Roggeveen returned to Middelburg, where he died in 1729.

## Roquefeuil

CAMILLE DE ROQUEFEUIL was born in France around the year 1780 and served in the French navy, rising to the rank of lieutenant. At the end of the Napoleonic wars he found himself, like many other mid-career officers, with few immediate prospects. He was offered the command of the *Bordelais*, a merchant ship of 200 tons being readied by a couple of Bordeaux merchants for a voyage to the north-west coast of America and China.

He sailed from Bordeaux on 11 October 1816, making for the Canaries and South America. He turned Cape Horn in January 1817 and dropped anchor at Valparaiso on 5 February. The political situation there led him to move to Callao, where he laid in goods for barter along the coast and copper for China. On 29 May he sailed for San Francisco, arriving on 6 August, then left a week later for the north.

On 1 September he began trading near Nootka, but the season was too far advanced to find more than a few furs. He eventually made his way back to California, anchoring at San Francisco on 19 October. There was some illness and even more disaffection among the crew, Roquefeuil even suspecting a mutiny. The *Bordelais* sailed on 19 November and reached the Marquesas on 22 December. Roquefeuil spent two months in the archipelago, where he bought eighty tons of sandalwood as well as food supplies. On 28 February 1818 he returned to America, in due course making his way to the Russian settlement in Sitka Sound, where he renewed his acquaintance with the Russian Hagemeister *(q.v.)*, with whom he went otter hunting.

Roquefeuil next sailed to Kodiak Island, which he reached on 12 May, and back to Prince of Wales Island, where his expedition was attacked by Indians. His further travels along the coast produced only meager results, and the ship nearly grounded on Queen Charlotte Island. Roquefeuil decided to return to San Francisco, where he stayed a month, leaving on 18 October with corn for the Russian outpost at Sitka.

On 13 December 1818 the *Bordelais* sailed for the Hawaiian Islands, first anchoring off Kailua on 9 January 1819, then going on to Oahu, buying food and more sandalwood. Leaving on 26 January, Roquefeuil made westward, sighting Asuncion and Agrihan in the Marianas on 24 February and pressing on to the Philippines Sea and Macao, where he dropped anchor on 11 March. His hope for profitable trading in China was only partly realized, and he sailed for home on 27 April, making for Mauritius and the Cape of Good Hope. The *Bordelais* ended its three-year circumnavigation in the estuary of the Gironde on 21 November 1819.

The expedition had not shown a profit, but for the French it was a valuable reconnaissance of a region from which they had been excluded for many years. Roquefeuil wrote an account that contains useful reports on the northwest coast and on the natives of the Marquesas and Hawaii; it was published in an English edition in 1823, the same year as it appeared in France, as *A Voyage round the World between the Years 1816–1819*.

After surpervising this work, Roquefeuil concluded that his prospects of employment had not improved, and he resigned from the navy. His later years are obscure.

## Rosendaal

NOTHING IS KNOWN of the date and place of birth of Roelof Rosendaal, who was captain of the *Afrikaansche Galey*, the smallest of the three ships that sailed from Texel on 1 August 1721 under Jacob Roggeveen *(q.v.)*. In spite of its name, it was a sailing vessel, not a galley with oars.

Rosendaal kept up with Roggeveen's *Arend*, although the third vessel, the *Thienhoven*, became separated from the others in December and did not meet up with them again until February 1722 at Juan Fernandez. All three sailed to Easter Island, which Rosendaal, scouting ahead in his *Afrikaansche Galey*, sighted on the afternoon of 5 April 1723; technically, therefore, he can be credited with the discovery of Easter Island.

After a brief stay, the Dutch sailed on east and northeast toward the Tuamotus where, on 19 May, the *Afrikaansche Galey* ran aground on Takapoto, which they named Schadelijke (Disastrous) Island. Only one man lost his life, but the vessel had to be abandoned, its complement—a mere thirty-one men—being allocated to the other two ships.

Rosendaal, who was ill at the time, was transferred to the *Thienhoven*, in which he continued as far as Batavia. His health deteriorated further, especially since the later part of the voyage was marked by the spread of scurvy and dysentery. The Dutch reached Batavia on 4 October 1722. Roelof Rosendaal died there on 27 November.

## Ross

JAMES CLARK ROSS was born in London on 15 April 1800 to a family with strong naval affiliations: his uncle was rear admiral Sir John

Ross. James entered the Royal Navy in 1812, serving in the *Briseis* and subsequently the *Isabella*. He accompanied his uncle on his 1818 expedition to the Arctic, and in 1819 sailed in the *Hecla* with William Edward Parry, who was endeavoring, like Capt. John Ross, to discover a northwest passage. Parry advanced westward for a considerable distance until stopped by pack ice. He returned on three further occasions, making important contributions to geographical knowledge of the Arctic regions. In 1829 James Clark Ross transferred back to his uncle's ship *Victory* for yet another voyage to the Arctic, during which he discovered the position of the north magnetic pole.

The expedition returned to England in 1833, and the following year Ross was promoted to captain. The years 1835 to 1838 were spent in more congenial surroundings, carrying out a magnetic survey of the British Isles, but in 1839 he obtained command of his own expedition to polar regions, this time to the Antarctic. He was given two ships, the *Erebus*, which he commanded, and the *Terror*, commanded by Francis Crozier *(q.v.)*, who had also sailed under Ross and Parry in the Arctic.

The two ships weighed anchor from Margate Roads on 30 September 1839, making for Hobart, where they arrived in August 1840. On 12 November Ross set out toward the southernmost waters of the Pacific, crossing the Antarctic Circle on 1 January. On the ninth he reached what is now known as the Ross Sea and took possession of the land beyond, which he named Queen Victoria Land. Further discoveries made in January and February include Ross Island (which he called High Island), the active volcano of Mt. Erebus, and the vast Ross Ice Shelf. Unable to proceed farther south in his search for the south magnetic pole, Ross returned to Hobart in March.

In November 1841 the *Erebus* and the *Terror* sailed back into Antarctic waters, steering southeast from New Zealand to approach the ice barrier from the east. Ross sighted the ice shelf on 22 February 1842 but was unable to find a break and turned back to clearer waters, sailing across the southern Pacific to Cape Horn and wintering in the Falkland Islands.

His third voyage—in February–March 1843—took him to the Weddell Sea, where he again crossed the Antarctic Circle. He then returned to England, where he was hailed for his great achievements. He received the gold medals of the geographical societies of

London and Paris and was knighted, given an honorary doctorate by Oxford University, and elected to the Royal Society. The account of his voyages was published in 1847.

*Erebus* and *Terror* were to sail in 1845 on yet another attempt to discover a northwest passage, but they left under the command of Sir John Franklin. It is reported that Ross, who married Anne Coulman in 1843, was prevented from accepting the command by an agreement with his wife's family not to sail on dangerous voyages for a period of years. Franklin's expedition was lost, and with him died also Francis Crozier. Several attempts were made to ascertain the expedition's fate and to rescue any survivors: Ross led one of these, with *Enterprise*, in 1848.

Sir James Ross died at Aylesbury on 3 April 1862.

## Rossel

ELISABETH-PAUL-EDOUARD DE ROSSEL was born on 11 September 1765 at Sens, south of Paris, of a noble family. He joined the navy in 1780 and was almost immediately appointed to ships involved in the bloody engagements of the American War of Independence. Between 1784 and 1789 he served on the *Résolution*, commanded by d'Entrecasteaux *(q.v.)*, in which he sailed to the Dutch East Indies and Canton. He was promoted lieutenant on 15 February 1789.

D'Entrecasteaux selected Rossel for his own *Espérance*, which sailed with the *Recherche* from Brest on 29 September 1791 in search of the lost expedition of La Pérouse. It was an arduous and long voyage to Australia, New Zealand, and many Pacific islands. Kermadec *(q.v.)*, who commanded the *Recherche*, died on 6 May 1793, d'Entrecasteaux died on 20 July, and the second-in-command of the *Espérance*, d'Auribeau *(q.v.)*, was dangerously ill. As a result, Rossell was in effective command of the expedition from August 1793, when it called briefly at Waigeo Island in the Dutch East Indies, until the end of September, when Rossel, with the concurrence of the still ailing d'Auribeau, was steering the expedition to the major Dutch settlements to get assistance and bring the voyage to an end.

Rossel sided with d'Auribeau and other royalists when political dissension led to a final break with supporters of the republican cause among the French, especially scientists and crew members.

He sailed back to Europe in 1794; but the Dutch ship he was in was captured in the Atlantic, and Rossel eventually taken to London, where his main concern was to save the documents and natural history specimens of the expedition. Still unreconciled with the republican government of France, Rossel did not return to Paris until after the Peace of Amiens in 1802. He then devoted himself to writing the official account of the expedition (others, favoring the republican viewpoints, had already appeared), the *Voyage de Dentrecasteaux Envoyé à la "Recherche" de La Pérouse*, which appeared in two volumes in 1808.

Rossel was appointed a member of the Académie des Sciences in 1811, given the Legion of Honor in 1820, and the rank of honorary rear admiral in 1822. He took a leading part in planning the expeditions of Duperrey *(q.v.)* and Dumont d'Urville *(q.v.)*. Appointed director-general of the Dépôt de la Marine in 1826, he died on 20 November 1829.

His name was given to the westernmost island of the Louisiade Archipelago, west of New Guinea, and to the northernmost cape of Uvea in the Loyalty group.

## Rule

GEORGE RULE was a trading and whaling captain who was born in Scotland in 1781 but settled at Nantucket, where he became associated with the Gardner and Starbuck families *(qq.v.)*.

He retained his links with Great Britain, sailing on two occasions from London for the South Pacific in command of whaling ships—the *Spring Grove*, leaving on 29 October 1818 and returning on 5 May 1821, and the *Fanny*, leaving on 7 July 1822 and returning on 29 June 1824. According to reports, Rule discovered an island in latitude 11°48′ south and longitude 164°47′ west; this approximates fairly closely with the island of Nassau in the Cook Islands, also known as Mitchell and Newport Island, and in that case Rule was the discoverer of this atoll, to which he gave the name of Lydra Island. George Rule died in 1859.

## Saavedra

ALVARO DE SAAVEDRA CERON was a relative of Hernán Cortes, the conquistador, whom he joined in the New World around the year

1520. In 1526 when Saavedra was in his thirties Cortés received orders from Spain to despatch an expedition to the Moluccas to ascertain the fate of the Loaysia *(q.v.)* expedition. Cortés entrusted the command to Saavedra, who sailed with three locally built ships from the port of Zihuatanejo, Mexico, on 31 October 1527. Two of the ships vanished in a storm on 15 December, only the flagship *Florida* continuing on its way.

On the twenty-ninth Saavedra came upon the islands of Utirik and Taka in the Marshalls, and on 1 January 1528 he discovered Rongelap and Ailinginae in the same group. A week was spent in this area, contact being established with local people. Unfortunately, the Spanish believed they had arrived among the Mariana Islands, a confusion that confounded geographers and cartographers. On 1 February the *Florida* came in view of Mindanao; the ship was careened on an islet, and at this time several survivors from the *Santa Maria del Parral* of Najera *(q.v.)* were rescued. Sailing by way of the Sarangani Islands, Saavedra reached Tidore in the Moluccas on 30 March 1528, thus completing the first east-to-west crossing of the Pacific north of the equator, a remarkable feat in such a small vessel: the *Florida* had a crew of only twelve, with thirty-eight landsmen aboard.

The problem now was how to return to America with his report on the Loaysia expedition. Saavedra set out on 3 June 1528 from the Moluccas, rounding Halmahera and sailing east toward the coast of New Guinea. He discovered the Kepulauan Schouten (Islas de Oro to the Spaniards, although the name also applied to the New Guinea mainland) and the Admiralty Islands, as well as Manus and some smaller islands of the Bismarck Archipelago that cannot be identified with any certainty. He then proceeded north toward the Carolines, where more discoveries were made, probably Namoluk or the Nomoi Islands, but again it is not possible to identify these landfalls with any degree of precision as the manuscript of this part of the voyage is defective.

Unable to find favorable winds for the Americas, Saavedra was forced to skirt the Marianas and return to Mindanao and the Moluccas. He made a second attempt to take the *Florida* back to Mexico or Peru in 1529, leaving on 3 May and following a similar course to the one he took the previous year, down to New Guinea and Manus Island, which was reached on 15 August. His efforts to go east were foiled until the end of the month, when he struck northeast for

America. On 14 September he discovered the islands of Ponape and Ant in the eastern Carolines. Still going northeast, Saavedra discovered a number of islands in the western Marshall group: Ujelang on 21 September and Eniwetok on 1 October. A landing was effected on the latter island, which the Spaniards called Islas de los Jardines. After about a week, the *Florida* continued on its northeasterly course, but Saavedra died a few days later and was buried at sea. The expedition began to lose its impetus, but nevertheless continued on its route as far as 31° north, well past Wake Island; not finding the hoped-for easterly winds, it turned back toward the Moluccas.

The diary Saavedra had kept of his voyages formed the basis for subsequent published reports. Depositions made by Vicente de Napoles, one of the few survivors of the expedition, in 1534 in Spain are also valuable in reconstructing the itineraries and achievements of this important expedition, which was led by a man of great determination and courage.

## Salazar

TORIBIO ALONSO DE SALAZAR was the *contador* (accountant) of the fleet of Garcia Jofre de Loaysia *(q.v.)*. He sailed in the flagship *Santa Maria de la Victoria*, leaving Coruna, Spain, on 24 July 1525. Loaysia died on 30 July 1526, to be succeeded by Elcano *(q.v.)*, who did not survive him by more than five days. The command then fell upon Salazar, who decided to make for Japan. However, on 9 August this course was abandoned in favor of the Moluccas and then of Guam.

On 21 August 1526 land was sighted to the north; it was an island to which the Spanish gave the name of San Bartolomeo. The current was too strong to permit a landing, so on the twenty-third Salazar sailed on, reaching Guam twelve days later.

Salazar died at Guam on 4 September. The island he had discovered was Taongi in the Marshall Islands; it was the only tangible result of the voyage of the *Santa Maria de la Victoria*.

## Salcedo

FELIPE DE SALCEDO was the captain of the *San Pedro* which sailed from Cebu, in the Philippines, on 1 June 1565. The flagship of the fleet under Legazpi *(q.v.)*, it had on board as pilot Rodrigo de la Isla Espinosa as well as the monk Andrés de Urdaneta *(q.v.)*. The *San Pedro* sailed north through the Bonin Islands and in a wide arc to the coast of California, sighting land on 18 September, then continuing on to Acapulco where Salcedo dropped anchor on 8 October 1565.

On 21 June the Spanish had sighted an atoll consisting of a ring of rock and a small lagoon. It was named Parece Vela (Like a Sail) by Urdaneta for its appearance. It is Orino-Torishima, a lonely island west of the Marianas.

## Sarmiento

PEDRO SARMIENTO Y GAMBA (de Gamboa) was born at Alcala de Henares, near Madrid, in 1532, joined the army at eighteen, and left for South America after taking part in various military campaigns from 1551 to 1555 and devoting himself to studies. He had a tendency to dabble in magic, although it was rather the result of a driving curiosity than a challenge to religious conformism. Nevertheless, it aroused the suspicions of the powerful Inquisition and placed him in real danger, especially in faraway Peru.

Sarmiento, however, was well regarded by the Spanish authorities and well connected. He wrote the important *Historia de los Incas* (1572) and urged the exploration of the Pacific Ocean as a means of extending the Spanish empire and bringing enlightenment to as yet undiscovered lands. He was instrumental in organizing the expedition of Alvaro de Mendaña *(q.v.)* of 1567–1568, which at first he had hoped to lead, and went with it to the Solomon Islands as chief pilot. On his return to Peru, he assisted the viceroy on his campaigns against the Indians as well as in the defense of the Spanish-held coast against the raids of Francis Drake *(q.v.)*.

On 11 October 1579 he sailed from Callao with the *Nuestra Señora de Esperanza* and the *San Francisco* to survey the various bays and islands along the south Chilean coast where raiders might hide. In the *Esperanza* he continued into the Strait of Magellan, emerged into the Atlantic on 24 February 1580, and reached Spain in August. Having reported to the king, he set off in September 1581 with orders to take steps to curb further English incursions. He eventually (in 1584) reached the Strait of Magellan, where he hoped to erect defensive forts, but in 1586 he was captured and taken to England.

Sarmiento was at first treated as a prisoner but was soon liberated and consulted by prominent English cartographers and geographers. On his way back to Spain he was captured by Huguenots and held prisoner in France for three years. Crippled by debts, he died in Spain in 1592.

## Sarychev

GAVRIIL ANDREEVICH SARYCHEV was born at St. Petersburg in 1763 and joined the navy in 1775. In 1785 he became associated with the expedition of Joseph Billings (q.v), which occupied him until 1794. Sarychev's travels, independently and with Billings, took him into the Sea of Okhotsk—whose shores he surveyed—and to the Bering Sea, the Kuril Islands, and the Aleutian chain. He carried out detailed survey work among the Pribilof Islands and the Diomede group and mapped in particular Unalaska, St. Lawrence Island, and King Island.

From 1802 to 1806 he headed the Baltic Hydrographic Expedition and in 1808 supervised the Russian Hydrographic Survey. Elected an honorary member of the St. Petersburg Academy of Sciences in 1809, he was raised to the rank of admiral in 1829. He wrote an account of his voyages with Billings, *Travels of Naval Captain Sarychev in the northeastern part of Siberia, the Arctic Ocean and the Eastern Ocean*, published in two volumes in St. Petersburg in 1802, as well as a valuable *Atlas of the Northern Part of the Eastern Ocean* (1826). Sarychev Volcano on Matua, one of the Kurils, is named after him.

Gavriil Sarychev died at St. Petersburg on 30 July 1831.

## Saumarez

PHILIP SAUMAREZ was born at St. Peter Port, Guernsey, on 17 November 1710 of a distinguished naval family. He entered the Royal Navy and served in various ships until 1739, when he was appointed third lieutenant to the *Centurion*, the flagship of Commodore Anson (q.v.) on his voyage around the world. Also on board was Saumarez's younger brother Thomas, serving as midshipman.

Anson's squadron of six ships and two small supply vessels sailed from St. Helens, Isle of Wight, on 18 September 1740, making for Madeira, Cape Horn, and the Pacific coast of Spanish South America, where a number of raids were carried out. On 28 April 1742 the *Centurion* sailed from Chequetan, Mexico, to begin a crossing of the Pacific. On 28 August the English dropped anchor at the island of Tinian in the Ladrones (Marianas) and then went on to Macao, where the ship was refitted. Warping out of Canton River on 11 April 1743, the *Centurion* made for the Philippines, capturing the rich Spanish galleon *Nuestra Señora de Cobagonda* on 20 June and bringing it back to Canton. The voyage home was completed by way of the Cape of Good Hope.

Saumarez reached England on 15 June 1744, greatly weakened by the hardships endured on the voyage, during which he had risen to first lieutenant and become Anson's confident. He spent some time recuperating at Bath, then in 1746 was given his own command, the *Nottingham*, in which he captured the French warship *Mars*. He was killed in action in 1747. He wrote a valuable *Journal* of the voyage.

## Schantz

IVAN IVANOVICH VON SCHANTZ (Fonchants) was born on 1 November 1802 of an old Finnish family and originally sailed in Finnish merchant ships. He joined the Russian navy as a midshipman in 1821, serving in the Baltic Sea. In 1828 he was sent to the Dardanelles during the Russo-Turkish War. Then in 1834 he was given command of the *Amerika*, a transport ship in which he sailed to the Pacific, concentrating in particular on the Marshall Islands. During this survey, in 1835, he discovered some thirteen islands, mostly uninhabited, in the Ralik group. These received the name of Schantz Islands. However, it is likely that they had been seen by Villalobos and Legazpi (*qq.v.*) in 1543 and 1565. Schantz, nevertheless, can be credited with giving the first precise position and description of these islands.

The *Amerika* returned to Russia in 1836, and Schantz resumed his naval career. He was raised to the rank of rear admiral in 1847 and to full admiral on his retirement in 1866. He died on 22 December 1879.

## Schapenham

GEEN HUYGEN SCHAPENHAM was born at Rotterdam during the last quarter of the sixteenth century, the son of a sea captain. In 1615 he sailed for the first time to the East Indies in command of a Dutch East India Company vessel, and we find him in 1621 in the Mediterranean, sailing to the Middle East. It is clear that he was well regarded in Dutch trading circles and an experienced navigator, perhaps no great leader, but "of a sweet disposition."

In 1623 he was appointed vice-admiral to Jacques L'Hermite (q.v.), who sailed on 29 April with eleven ships and sixteen hundred men—the so-called Nassau Fleet—sent by the Dutch to challenge Spanish supremacy in the eastern Pacific and set up a base in South America. It took until February 1624 for the ships to sail through Le Maire's Strait. The ships sailed close to Tierra del Fuego into Nassau Bay, discovering an island, which received the name of Hermite, and a bay, which was named after Schapenham. This led to the realization that Cape Horn was actually part of an island group.

The fleet was scattered during a gale when it entered the Pacific but was reunited at Juan Fernandez in April. It then made for the coast of Peru. Jacques L'Hermite, who had been in ill health since leaving the coast of West Africa, died on 2 June off Callao, and Schapenham took over command. The next few weeks were spent in inconclusive raids and foiled attempts to effect landings. The only attack that could be termed successful was one against Guayaquil, but a second raid failed. Suffering from scurvy and the inability to use their troops in a major engagement, the Dutch left the coast of South America in mid-September and headed toward Mexico, hoping to intercept the Manila galleon. On 27 October Schapenham arrived at Acapulco, which was defended by a small but determined garrison. On 1 November Schapenham gave up, sailed uncertainly in the hope of sighting the galleon, then set course for Guam, where he arrived on 25 January 1625. He left for the Moluccas on 11 February and on the fifteenth made the only discovery for which the expedition can be credited in the Pacific, the island of Yap in the eastern Carolines. On 2 March Schapenham in his flagship the *Eendracht* established contact with the Dutch authorities in the Moluccas and in due course made his way to Batavia, where the fleet was split up.

On 28 October 1625 Schapenham sailed for Holland from Batavia with the *Eendracht* and the *Wapen van Hoorn*, but he died a week later in Sunda Strait and was buried on one of the Bantam Islands, his remains being transferred to Batavia a year later for a formal reinterment in Batavia church on 13 November 1626.

## Schouten

WILLEM CORNELISZOON SCHOUTEN was born at Hoorn, northern Holland, probably in 1567. He went to sea at an early age, gaining wide experience in merchant ships and making at least three voyages to the Dutch East Indies. He provided the seafaring experience needed by the Amsterdam merchant Isaac Le Maire and his partners to send an expedition to the South Seas by what they believed would be a new access through open sea to the south of the Strait of Magellan. Schouten shared the Amsterdamers' belief. The benefit in such a route was that, in theory at least, it would circumvent the monopoly rights of the Dutch East India Company. A charter was obtained from the Dutch states for a rival "Austral Company."

Schouten brought in financial support from several merchants of Hoorn and the experience of his younger brother, Jan Schouten, who took command of the smaller ship *Hoorn* while Willem captained the *Eendracht* (Unity, or Concord). Isaac Le Maire's son Jacob *(q.v.)* came as supercargo and general supervisor of the expedition. The two ships sailed from Texel on 14 June 1615, made first for Sierra Leone in Africa, where 25,000 lemons—invaluable against scurvy—were obtained, and on 6 December dropped anchor at Port Desire, in Patagonia. There the *Eendracht* and the *Hoorn* were cleaned, but the latter was so covered with weeds that it was decided to burn off the growth. Unfortunately, the ship caught fire, and the *Eendracht*, with the *Hoorn*'s crew, together with what could be saved from the disaster, sailed on alone on 13 January 1616. On the twenty-fifth the Dutch discovered a wide channel, which they named Le Maire's Strait, and on the evening of the twenty-ninth a high, barren headland, which they named after the *Eendracht*'s lost consort: it was Cape Horn. The next day they found themselves undeniably in the open Pacific. Their theory about a passage in the far south had been proved right.

Schouten first sailed north toward Juan Fernandez, which he reached in early March, but he could not land. A call here might have saved his sick brother Jan, who died on 9 March. Veering west, the Dutch came upon the Tuamotus, then the northern Tonga group; edging north, they discovered on 19 May Futuna and Alofi, which they named the Hoorn Islands and where they were able to trade. Schouten's experience became of increasing importance as they began to approach the East Indies, discovering new islands north of the Solomons, then New Ireland, where they landed.

On 3 July they came upon the Admiralty Islands, sailed along the coast of New Guinea, and named Schouten Islands, a large island group in Geelvinck Bay, northwest New Guinea. This part of the voyage took up all of July and August. As Schouten advanced toward the Dutch possessions, he reached islands where the inhabitants understood him and were able to help the exhausted crew. On 17 September 1616 the *Eendracht* dropped anchor at Ternate in the Moluccas.

The authorities were helpful, providing food and a welcome respite from the hardships of navigation. Fifteen men agreed to transfer to East India Company ships, and after a week at Ternate the *Eendracht* sailed on to Jacatra where, on 28 October, the voyage was declared to be at an end. The company founded by Isaac Le Maire and his associates was now faced by its larger and intransigent rival, which challenged the validity of its charter and refused to admit that any new passage into the Pacific Ocean had been found. The *Eendracht* was impounded and Le Maire and Schouten sent back to Holland in December, Jacob dying on the twenty-second, a few days after sailing. Willem Schouten reached Hoorn safely and assisted Isaac Le Maire in his determined and eventually successful lawsuit against the East India Company. Schouten died in 1625.

The expedition had made a number of important discoveries, not the least being the Cape Horn route, but also islands in the Tuamotu archipelago, several in the Tonga group, the Hoorn Islands, the Green and Feni islands in the Bismarck Archipelago, New Ireland and a number of offshore islands, New Hanover, and a number of islands north of New Guinea. Whether these should be credited to Schouten as the man in charge of navigation or to Le Maire as the official head of the expedition remains a matter of opinion. An account of the voyage first published in 1618 gave pride of place to Schouten; another, published in 1622, gave greater prominence to Jacob Le Maire. The modern practice, and probably the fairer, is to refer to "the expedition of Schouten and Le Maire"—a subtle bracketing that takes into account the major sponsoring role of Isaac Le Maire as well as his son's part in the voyage.

## Selkirk

ALEXANDER SELKIRK (or Selcraig) was born at Largo, Fifeshire, in 1676. Accused of improper behavior in church, he ran away to sea in August 1695. In May 1703 he joined William Dampier *(q.v.)* on a privateering voyage to the Pacific.

Selkirk went as sailing master of the *Cinque Ports*, being promoted to quartermaster some months later when the captain died and Thomas Stradling, the senior lieutenant, succeeded him. *Cinque Ports* called at Juan Fernandez Islands in February 1704, the crew already rebellious toward Stradling. Matters did not improve, the privateering expedition met with little success, and on a second call at Juan Fernandez in September, Selkirk asked to be put ashore with his belongings and enough supplies to sustain him for a few weeks. He had a change of heart before *Cinque Ports* sailed on its way back to England, but the fiery Stradling refused to take him back.

Selkirk remained alone on the island until 31 January 1709, when Woodes Rogers *(q.v.)* put in at Juan Fernandez. On 12 February Selkirk left his makeshift home as mate of Rogers' *Duke*. Later he was given command of a captured Spanish coaster, renamed *The Increase*. When Rogers decided to sail for home across the Pacific, Selkirk was appointed master of another prize, a Spanish frigate renamed *Batchelor*. In it he sailed from Lower California on 10 January 1710. Rogers reached Guam in March and went on to the Dutch East Indies, where Selkirk transferred as master to the *Duke*.

Selkirk returned to England on 14 October 1711 after an absence of more than eight years. He went back to visit his relatives in Largo in 1712 and returned to sea in 1717, but by then he had become famous, first through Rogers' narrative of his voyage, then through an account of his adventures published in *The Englishman* of 2 December 1713, followed by *Providence Displayed*, a pamphlet largely based on Woodes Rogers' account. All this, however, was but a prelude to the success of *The Life and Surprizing Adventures of Robinson Crusoe*, Daniel Defoe's fictionalized account of Selkirk's solitary life on his island, which appeared in 1719.

Alexander Selkirk died on 12 December 1721 while serving as master's mate in HMS *Weymouth*. He is commemorated by the modern name of the westernmost island of the Juan Fernandez group, now Isla Alejandro Selkirk, while the easternmost has become Isla Robinson Crusoe, a rare instance of naming an island after a work of fiction.

## Sever

WILLIAM CROPTON SEVER was a merchant navy captain employed by the East India Company and private shipowners who was given command of the *Lady Penrhyn*, 330 tons, a transport ship chartered for the First Fleet destined for Botany Bay, New South Wales. The *Lady Penrhyn* was a new ship, built in 1786, but a slow sailer with a troublesome crew and an even more troublesome collection of convicts, mostly women. It left England with the fleet on 13 May 1787, enduring a difficult voyage and reaching Botany Bay and eventually Port Jackson in January 1788.

Sever's health had been poor during much of the voyage out, but he recovered in New South Wales and sailed from Port Jackson on 5 May 1788, intending to take the *Lady Penrhyn* back to England by way of China, where he could pick up a cargo for the journey home.

On 31 May he discovered and named Curtis and Macauley islands in the Kermadec group (Alderman Curtis being one of the *Lady Penrhyn*'s owners). He landed on the latter island, which he found to be uninhabited and barren. He had been able to take little in the way of supplies from New South Wales and was concerned about scurvy on the long voyage to Canton. This is probably why he decided to make a wide arc into the central Pacific and head for the Society Islands.

On 10 July the *Lady Penrhyn* dropped anchor in Matavai Bay, Tahiti, and began to lay in supplies of hogs, poultry, greens, and fruit. Leaving Tahiti on 23 July, Sever went on to Huahine, and on 8 August sighted a low, flat island to which he gave the name Penrhyn's Island. This was a discovery, but it has reverted to its native name of Tongareva; it forms part of the northern Cook Islands.

William Sever saw no further islands until he reached the Ladrones (Marianas), anchoring at Tinian on 19 September and then going on to Macao, where he arrived on 19 October. He took on a cargo of tea and other goods and made his way back to England.

The *Lady Penrhyn* was sold to new owners some time after her return to England and put to service on the London-Jamaica run. The ship was captured in 1811 in the West Indies during the Napoleonic wars. Nothing more is known of William Sever's life story.

## Shelvocke

GEORGE SHELVOCKE was born in England in the late 1670s and joined the Royal Navy sometime before 1690. He is believed to have served under Admiral Benbow on Benbow's expedition of 1698 to the West Indies. Shelvocke was apparently master on the *Scarborough* in 1703 and purser of the *Monck* in 1707–1713.

He seems to have left the navy after this. In 1718 he was put in charge of a privateering expedition to the South Seas, but an abortive attempt to sail under a foreign flag with a largely Flemish crew caused a financial loss to his backers, and he was replaced by his second-in-command, Clipperton *(q.v.)*. Shelvocke, in the *Speedwell*, and Clipperton, in the *Success*, sailed from Plymouth on 12 February 1719; but Shelvocke soon went his own way, and the two did not meet again—and briefly at that—until 25 January 1721.

His route took him by way of Cape Horn to the Juan Fernandez Islands. He carried out a few raids on Spanish shipping with limited success until 25 May 1720, when *Speedwell* was wrecked. Shelvocke succeeded in capturing a Spanish vessel, which he hopefully renamed *The Happy Return*, later exchanging it for another prize, *Sacra Familia*. Further raids on the coast produced only moderate gains and, peace having been declared between Spain and England, the Spanish governor asked for the return of *Sacra Familia*. Shelvocke declined, alleging he could not understand Spanish, and by his action turned himself and his crew from privateers into pirates.

Already some of his men had suggested they should return home by way of China. Shelvocke delayed by a few more months, laying in supplies and capturing one rich prize. On 17 August 1721 the *Sacra Familia* sailed from San Lucar in Baja California for China. Shelvocke's well-stocked vessel made it possible to avoid a call at the dangerous Spanish-held Marianas. A Shelvocke Island he claimed to have discovered on the way was probably Roca Partida, one of the Revilla Gigedo group discovered by Ruy de Villalobos *(q.v.)* in 1542.

Shelvocke reached Macao on 11 November 1721, sold *Sacra Familia*, and sailed home on an English Indiaman, the *Cadogan*. He arrived at Dover in June 1722, was arrested on grounds of piracy at the request of the Spanish and Portuguese ambassadors, was acquitted and then rearrested for fraud at the instance of the *Speedwell*'s owners, but he escaped from jail and fled to France. He remained abroad for at least another five years and at some time returned to London where he died, possibly in late 1728 or early 1729.

Shelvocke's highly unreliable *A Voyage round the World by Way of the Great South Sea* was published in 1726. Its redeeming feature is a reference to the shooting of "a disconsolate black albatross," the only living creature to follow *Speedwell* as it battled toward Cape Horn, an incident later transmuted and immortalized by the poet Samuel Taylor Coleridge in *The Rime of the Ancient Mariner*.

## Shimaya

ICHIZAEMON SHIMAYA was a seaman from Nagasaki, born probably in the 1640s, who had some experience of Western navigation, obtained presumably through contacts with the European sailors who were allowed to travel to Japan for trade through Nagasaki. In April 1675 Shimaya was sent in a specially built "foreign style" ship with a crew of thirty-two to the Bonin Islands. The islands were not unknown to the Japanese: they were referred to as the Ogasawara Archipelago from their alleged discoverer, one Sadayori Ogasawara, a nobleman said to have sailed there in 1593.

The islands were believed to have been uninhabited, or at least not settled, hence their other name *bunin* (islands with no people on them). In February 1670 the crew of a wrecked ship led by one Kanemon struggled ashore on the Bonins, built a small craft, and made its way back to Japan. This aroused the shogunate's interest in the lonely island group, leading to the Shimaya expedition. It spent a month surveying the entire island group, drew maps, and brought natural history specimens back to Japan in June 1675. Further attempts to explore and annex the Bonins ended in failure, however, and the Japanese showed no further interest in exploration until the second half of the nineteenth century.

## Shishmarev

GLEB SEMENOVICH SHISHMAREV was born at St. Petersburg in 1781. He entered the Naval Cadet Corps in 1796, graduating in 1801. Unlike his fellow cadets, he did not join the British Royal Navy at this stage, but served in Russian ships until in 1815 he was appointed second-in-command to Kotzebue *(q.v.)* aboard the *Riurik*. He sailed from Kronstadt in July 1815, rounded Cape Horn, and called at Chile before going on to Kamchatka and Alaska. The *Riurik* put in at Honolulu in November 1816 and in December sailed for the Carolines. A second call was made in the Hawaiian Islands in October 1817. The Russians began their homeward voyage by way of Manila, Sunda Strait, and Capetown.

Not long after the *Riurik*'s return to Kronstadt in August 1818, Shishmarev was given his own command, the transport *Blagonamerennyi*, with which he completed a three-year voyage, reversing the route followed by the *Riurik*: leaving Kronstadt in July 1819, he sailed down the Atlantic to the Cape of Good Hope, to Kamchatka and Alaska, with a call at the Hawaiian Islands, and home by Cape Horn. A number of geographical features commemorate his work: Shishmaref Inlet and the town of Shishmaref at the western end of the Seward Peninsula of Alaska, a group of small islands in the Kara Sea, a pass in the Marshall Islands, and a peak in the Antarctic.

He was promoted to captain, second class, after his return to Russia in 1823, commanded the 67th and 11th naval equipages from 1824 to 1827, when he was raised to captain, first class, and took over command of the frigate *Imperatriska Ekaterina*. A rear admiral in 1829, he held commands in the Gulf of Finland. He died at St. Petersburg on 22 October 1835.

## Shortland

JOHN SHORTLAND was born near Plymouth in 1739. He entered the Royal Navy in 1755 as a midshipman, serving under Admirals Boscawen off Newfoundland, Byng at Minorca, and Rodney in the West Indies. In 1763 he was a lieutenant aboard a transport service between England and the American colonies. This experience culminated in his being appointed in 1782 to command the transports taking reinforcements to Gibraltar and in 1786 to organize the First Fleet's transports to Botany Bay with the title of agent.

He arrived on 17 January 1788 ahead of the main fleet. As soon as practicable, the new governor sent him back to England with despatches and news of the successful establishment of the colony and penal settlement. Shortland sailed from Port Jackson on 14 July 1788 in command at first of the *Alexander*, the *Borrowdale*, the *Prince of Wales*, and the *Friendship*. He discovered lonely Middleton Reef north of Norfolk Island and at the end of July sighted a large island. This was San Cristobal in the Solomon Islands, although Shortland did not identify the island or the archipelago. By now the *Prince of Wales* had become separated from the convoy with the *Borrowdale*, both making for Batavia. Shortland skirted San Cristobal and Guadalcanal; on 2 August he discovered the Russell Islands. He sailed on toward the northwest and over the next few days discovered more islands: Gatukai, Vangunu, and Simbo, part of a group he named New Georgia. Defective maps and an incorrect interpretation of his whereabouts led to bitter argument between French and English geographers, but Shortland can be credited with some useful contributions to the exploration of the large Solomon Islands group. His name is commemorated by the Shortland Islands in the western area of the archipelago.

Shortland fell in with the Palau Islands on 10 September and reached Mindanao on the twenty-seventh. By then he was so shorthanded—his crews were ridden with scurvy—that he was forced to sink the *Friendship* and carry on with the *Alexander*. He arrived at Batavia on 18 November, was assisted by the Dutch authorities, and reached England on 29 May 1789.

Shortland was promoted to commander in 1790. He later retired to spend his last years at Lille, northern France, where he died in 1803.

## Solander

DANIEL CARL SOLANDER was born in 1733 at Pitea, northern Sweden. He studied medicine, but his real interest was botany. A disciple of Linnaeus, he was sent to England in 1760 to promote the ideas of Linnaean classification. Soon popular with English natural historians, he was appointed assistant at the British Museum and elected a Fellow of the Royal Society in 1764. Acquainted with Sir Joseph Banks *(q.v.)*, he offered his services as naturalist on the first voyage of James Cook *(q.v.)* and was accepted.

The *Endeavour* left from Plymouth on 26 August 1768 and returned to England on 13 July 1771, having sailed to Madeira and Rio, round Cape Horn to Tahiti, New Zealand, the east coast of Australia, Batavia, and the Cape of Good Hope. At each stop Dr. Solander (the title is largely honorary) botanized energetically and was of great assistance to Sir Joseph Banks. James Cook named Botany Bay, in New South Wales, to mark the great quantity of plants collected there by the two men and further gave the names of Point Banks and Point Solander to the two headlands at its entrance. The notes taken by Solander on this voyage were voluminous, but they were not separately published.

James Cook was appointed to leave on a second voyage soon after his return from the first, and both Banks and Solander were to go with him. Difficulties raised by Banks' claims for accommodation and additional passengers on board ship led to the cancellation of this proposal. Instead, Banks took Solander on an expedition to Iceland; from this Solander produced his *Flora Islandica*. By now, Solander was Banks' main collaborator and secretary, and putting their work in order took up most of his time. In 1773 Solander and Banks were appointed to the Royal Academy of Sciences at Ulrichstadt. Although Banks was better known, Solander was a respected and popular member of London's scientific community with a growing reputation in Europe. Elected a member of the Council of the Royal Society in 1774, he became increasingly influential. His death on 16 May 1782, aged 49, put an end to Banks' hopes of completing his major book on natural history—for which much of the work was being undertaken by Solander. Apart from the headland in New South Wales, the naturalist's name is commemorated in Solander Island, a lonely, uninhabited island to the south of New Zealand.

## Spanberg

Morten (or Martin) Petrovich Spanberg was a Dane born early in the eighteenth century who entered the Russian service and was serving at St. Petersburg with the rank of lieutenant in 1726. He was appointed to the expedition of Vitus Bering *(q.v.)*, whom he joined at Okhotsk in January 1727. A year later the expedition sailed from Kamchatka, going north and northeast. By 13 August the Russians were out of sight of land, at around 65°30' north. Asked for his advice, Spanberg urged Bering to sail north for only a few days more and then go back to Kamchatka for the winter. His views prevailed, although Bering's *St. Gabriel* reached as far north as 67°18'n. On 2 September they were back at Nizhnekamsk.

Spanberg returned to St. Petersburg but was appointed, again with Bering, to take a major part in the projected Great Northern Expedition. He started on his way back to Siberia in 1733, facing a difficult logistical operation to take the necessary supplies across vast roadless distances. He arrived at Okhotsk in 1735 to find that a great deal still needed to be done. Finally, on 29 June 1738 he sailed from Okhotsk with three ships—the reconditioned *St. Gabriel*, the *Arkhangel Mikhail*, and the *Nadezhda*. His task was to go south, exploring the islands north of Japan.

His 1738 attempt was foiled by ice and fog. He had to sail to Bolsheretsk in Kamchatka, leaving on 26 July and getting no farther than Urup in the Kurils, having lost sight of the *Nadezhda* commanded by Walton *(q.v.)*. Spanberg sailed again from Bolsheretsk on 21 May 1739, and although he once again lost contact with Walton he went south as far as Japan, trading with the people of Honshu, turning back toward Hokkaido, and following the line of the Kurils to Kamchatka and on to Okhotsk, where he dropped anchor in early September. The charts that resulted from this voyage were of considerable assistance to geographers. Spanberg set off for a third voyage in 1742. But although the island of Sakhalin was sighted, the voyage resulted in no tangible results.

Spanberg had been promoted to captain, first class, in 1736. He returned to St. Petersburg to assist in the compilation of atlases incorporating the results of the Great Northern Expedition, but there was considerable dissension among the surviving participants. He died in 1761.

# Spilbergen

JORIS VAN SPILBERGEN (found also under the names Spielbergen and Speilbergen) was born at Antwerp on 2 November 1568. He gained fighting and navigational experience on the expedition of Balthasar de Moucheron to Africa in 1596 and in various raids to Africa and Brazil in 1598 and 1600. Then followed further voyages, to Ceylon (Sri Lanka) and Africa.

He was appointed in 1614 to head an expedition to the East Indies by way of the Strait of Magellan to reassert Dutch claims to access into the Pacific from the east. Sponsored by the States-General, the expedition consisted of six vessels, including two 600-ton fighting ships, the *Groote Sonne* and the *Groote Manne*. Spilbergen sailed from Texel on 8 August 1614, entered the strait on 28 March 1615, and enjoyed a remarkably speedy passage, emerging into the Pacific on 6 May. The first attack on the Spanish was made on the small town of Santa Maria in Chile, part of Spilbergen's instructions being to challenge Spanish claims to exclusivity along the American coastline. He sailed north to Valdivia, Valparaiso, and Arica in order to meet the Spanish defense fleet head-on. On 17 July they engaged in an indecisive battle off Canete, south of Callao: the Spanish were defeated and Spilbergen then blockaded Callao, but he was forced to give up within a few days. He went on to Acapulco, meeting only token resistance, then sailed further along the Mexican coast to Cape Corrientes where, on 20 November, the Dutch decided to await the expected Manila galleon. But after a fruitless ten days of cruising, they gave up and set off on a westerly course, sighting the Revilla Gigedo group on 3 December and lonely Roca Partida the following day. On 23 January 1616 Spilbergen reached Guam and continued his route toward Manila, where he arrived at the end of February.

After ten days in Manila Bay spent provisioning the ships, Spilbergen sailed to Ternate, where he arrived on 29 March, and thence to Java. He left in December 1616, having on board as passenger Jacob Le Maire *(q.v.)*, and reached Flushing on the Schelde on 2 July 1617. As the fleet had been split up in the Moluccas, there is some uncertainty as to which ships Spilbergen took home with him.

An account of his voyage appeared at Leyden in 1619 under the title *Oost en West Indische Spiegel der nieuwe navigatie, waarin*

*vertoond wordt de eerste zeize gedaan door Joris van Spilbergen.* He
died at Bergen-op-Zoom in January 1620.

## Staines

THOMAS STAINES was born near Margate, Kent, in 1776 and
entered the Royal Navy at the end of 1789, when he was appointed
to the *Solebay*, in which he served in the West Indies until 1792,
transferring to the *Speedy* for a cruise to the Mediterranean. He was
later moved to the *Victory* and in 1796 was promoted lieutenant and
given the sloop *Petrel*, which was captured by Spanish frigates in
1798. The sloop was retaken, but Staines spent a period as a prisoner
before he could return to active service under Nelson and Lord
Keith. In 1802 he took over command of the brig *Cameleon*, taking
part in a number of engagements in the Mediterranean and the
Adriatic.

The *Cameleon* returned to England in September 1805. Staines
was advanced to post rank and appointed to the frigate *Cyane*, in
which he sailed to the Mediterranean in 1808. Wounded and sent
back to England in October 1809, he was later appointed to convoy
work to Newfoundland and South America. On 30 December 1813
he took the frigate *Briton* from Spithead to Rio, where he received
orders to proceed to Valparaiso to intercept the U.S. frigate *Essex*,
commanded by David Porter *(q.v.)*. Staines reached Valparaiso on 21
May 1814 to find that the *Essex* had already been captured by two
other British ships. Staines sailed up the coast to Callao and out to
the Galapagos, accompanied by the *Tagus*, which he had found at
Valparaiso.

On 4 August the two ships sailed for the Marquesas, arriving at
Nuku Hiva a fortnight later. On 2 September, having removed traces
of Porter's earlier visit, they left for Valparaiso, but on the way came
upon Pitcairn Island; Staines was able to confirm reports that
descendants of the *Bounty* muntineers were living there. He also
called at Juan Fernandez. He headquartered at Valparaiso, cruising
along the South American coast until April 1815, when he sailed for
Rio and England. He arrived back at Plymouth on 7 July 1815.

Thomas Staines was knighted at the beginning of 1815. The wars
now being over, he was able to enjoy some time ashore and, in 1819,
get married. He commanded the *Superbe* from 1823 to 1825 in the

West Indies and the Atlantic and the *Isis* in the Mediterranean from 1827 to 1830. He died at Margate, England, on 13 July 1830.

## Staniukovich

KONSTANTIN MIKHAILOVICH STANIUKOVICH (the name is also found as Stankovich) was born on 18 March 1843 at Sebastopol. The son of Admiral M. N. Staniukovich *(q.v.)*, he followed in the family naval tradition and entered the Naval Cadet School at St. Petersburg in 1857. Completing his studies, he went to sea in 1860. In 1864 he retired with the rank of lieutenant, spending two years in a remote village of Vladimir province, teaching at the local school, but in reality devoting himself to writing.

In 1867 he published his first book of sketches, (the English equivalent of the title is *From a Voyage around the World*). Writing and political activities then took up most of his time; in 1872 he began contributing to the journal *Delo*; in 1884 he was arrested for associating with Populist émigrés, spent a year in jail, and was exiled for three years in Tomsk. He continued to write, mostly novels criticizing the Russian bourgeoisie. In 1901 he won the Pushkin Prize for a collection of sea stories. Staniukovich died in Naples on 7 May 1903.

## Staniukovich

MIKHAIL NIKOLAEVICH STANIUKOVICH (also commonly found as Stankovich) was born in 1785, joined the Naval Cadet Corps, and, like many of his contemporaries, was sent to gain experience with the British Royal Navy. He spent the years 1803 to 1809 as a volunteer with the British fleet in the Atlantic and the Mediterranean. He returned to Russia and served with the Baltic Fleet from 1814 to 1826.

In 1826 he was given command of the sloop *Moller* and set out for a three-year surveying campaign in the Pacific. He carried out extensive hydrographic work around the Hawaiian Islands and surveyed and described part of the Aleutians and the Alaska Peninsula from Isanotski Strait to Bristol Bay. During his surveys of the Hawaiian Islands in 1827 he made two discoveries: Laysan Island, an atoll at $25°46'$ north, sighted but only vaguely reported by an American whaler, and Kure Island in the northwest of the group.

After his return to Russia, Staniukovich served in the Black Sea, spending part of the 1840s in the Odessa and Sebastopol area. He was raised to the rank of admiral in 1855 and died on 29 December 1869.

## Stanley

OWEN STANLEY was born on 13 June 1811, the son of Edward Stanley, who became bishop of Norwich; one of his brothers, Arthur, became dean of Westminster. He entered the Royal Navy in 1826, serving in the *Druid* and the *Ganges*, and gained experience as a surveyor and hydrographer in the Strait of Magellan area while with the sloop *Adventure*, commanded by Philip Parker King, in 1830. In 1831 he served as a lieutenant aboard the *Belvidera* in the Mediterranean and in 1836 sailed with Sir George Back in the *Terror* on his expedition to the Arctic.

In 1838 Stanley joined the *Britomart*, in which he went to the East Indies and Australia, going in particular to Port Essington, where he served as a magistrate and was promoted to commander. He was sent in the *Britomart* to New Zealand during the first months of British rule in 1840 and was at the Bay of Islands when the French frigate the *Aube* arrived from Bordeaux a few weeks ahead of the *Comte de Paris*, which was to land a substantial party of French colonists at Akaroa in the South Island. Stanley was despatched to Akaroa to ensure British sovereignty over the South Island. He handled a potentially difficult situation with tact, spending from 10 to 27 August 1840 at Akaroa, returning to the Bay of Islands in mid-September and thereafter to Sydney.

Stanley sailed to Singapore, Burma, and England in 1841. He was raised to full captain in 1844, commanded the *Blazer* on a voyage to the North Sea, and transferred to the *Rattlesnake*, leaving Portsmouth in late 1846 with two naturalists to assist him. One was Thomas Henry Huxley, serving as assistant surgeon, who later acquired fame as a professor of natural history in London and whose work on the voyage earned him the Fellowship of the Royal Society and the Royal Medal.

The *Rattlesnake* sailed to southern Africa, Mauritius, and Hobart, where it arrived on 24 June 1847. After a brief stay in Sydney, Stanley began a careful and detailed survey of the northwest coast of Australia, the Cape York and Torres Strait area, and the Gulf of Papua, completing and perfecting the work of Blackwood *(q.v.)* in the *Fly*. The ethnographic information gathered on the voyage was in many respects as valuable as the hydrographic work. The work, including periods for rest and refits, took almost three years. The strain, complicated by a growing tendency toward depression, worsened by news of the death of his father and one of his brothers, proved too much for Stanley, and he killed himself in Sydney on 13 March 1850. The *Rattlesnake* was brought back to England by Lt. C. B. Yule and paid off at Chatham on 9 November 1850.

## Starbuck

OBED STARBUCK was born on 5 May 1797 at Nantucket, Massachusetts. He went to sea from an early age and was linked through marriage with other seafaring New England families.

He sailed to the Pacific as captain of the whaling ship *Hero* on 4 January 1822, returning on 9 February 1824 with 2,173 barrels of sperm oil. On 5 September 1823 he discovered an isolated island at 5°32' south and 155°55' west, part of the Line Islands, which has become known as Starbuck Island. It has been referred to by a variety of names over the years, including Hero Island.

Obed Starbuck next sailed on a whaling voyage to the Pacific on 7 December 1824 in the *Loper*, returning on 19 October 1826. On this occasion he made another discovery, an island in the Phoenix group, which he named New Nantucket Island. Reported in 1835 by Michael Baker, another American seafarer, it is now known as Baker Island. Later on the same voyage Obed Starbuck came upon two more islands, which he called Loper and Tracy respectively. These were Niutao and Vaitupu in the Ellice group. The latter was a discovery, but Niutao may have been seen by Mendaña *(q.v.)* in the sixteenth century and named by him Isla de Jesus. Other islands reported as first sighted by Starbuck lack the accurate details that would enable them to be identified with certainty.

On 21 June 1829 Starbuck sailed for a second voyage to the Pacific in the *Loper*, returning on 7 September 1830 with 2,280 barrels of sperm oil. However, his next venture, in the *Rose* in 1831, failed when the ship grounded. Obed Starbuck's last whaling expedition to the Pacific was in the *Zone*, starting on 13 October 1843 and ending on 10 November 1846. He died in 1882.

Obed Starbuck is sometimes confused with Valentine Starbuck *(q.v.)*, the captain of the British whaler *Aigle* chartered in 1823 by King Liholiho of Hawaii to take him and his suite on a visit to England. In 1823 Valentine Starbuck had sighted an island in the Line Islands group, which he had named Volunteer Island; George Anson Byron *(q.v.)*, sailing in the area in August 1825, renamed it Starbuck Island after Valentine, although it now seems clear that it had been discovered earlier by Obed.

### Starbuck

VALENTINE STARBUCK was born in the 1790s, a member of the Nantucket seafaring family. In 1823 he was sailing in the Pacific in command of the British whaler *Aigle* when, having put in at Honolulu, his ship was chartered by Liholiho, the Hawaiian ruler, who was eager to visit England. On 27 November 1823, Starbuck sailed with Liholiho and a large party of Hawaiian dignitaries. At the king's request, the *Aigle* avoided calling at Boston, which American missionaries in Hawaii suggested, and made for Portsmouth, where Starbuck dropped anchor in May 1824.

The visit, unexpected as far as the British government was concerned, was successful enough to begin with, but on 8 July Queen Kamamalu died of measles; Liholiho died on the fourteenth. Starbuck meanwhile was dismissed by his British employers for disregarding his instructions and forsaking the rich Pacific whaling ground; they followed their action with a lawsuit over the financial loss his actions had caused. Starbuck fought back and left England.

George Anson Byron *(q.v.)*, who took the royal remains back to Hawaii in the *Blonde*, came upon an island in the Pacific known as Volunteer Island, which he knew Valentine had sighted in 1823. Accordingly, he named it Starbuck in his honor. It had, however, been visited previously by another Starbuck, Obed *(q.v.)*.

### Stewart

WILLIAM STEWART was born in Scotland around the year 1776, served in the navy from 1793 to 1797, sailed to India, and arrived at

Port Jackson, New South Wales, in June 1801. He bought a share in a sealing undertaking, operating mostly around Bass Strait. In 1805 he joined the Sydney firm of Campbell and Company and led several sealing expeditions to the Antipodes Islands.

In 1809 Stewart sailed as first officer of the *Pegasus* to New Zealand and worked on a survey of the southernmost coast, proving first that Stewart Island (named after him) was an island and not a projection of the mainland and second that what James Cook *(q.v.)* had described as Banks's Island was really a peninsula. He then went on to the Chatham Islands to complete their charting. He returned to England, reaching Gravesend in August 1810. His next years are shrouded in mystery, apart from the publication in 1816 of his chart of Port Pegasus, New Zealand, in the *Oriental Navigator.* In 1824 he became involved in plans to establish a trading settlement at Stewart Island. He sailed there on the first of three occasions in early 1826 and for many years traded both in New Zealand and in various Pacific islands. In 1834 he is recorded as being in the Hawaiian Islands, where, as captain of the *Bee*, he played an honorable role in a kidnapping incident. He died in New Zealand on 10 September 1851.

## Stokes

JOHN LORT STOKES was born in 1811 near Haverfordwest, Pembrokeshire, and entered the Royal Navy in 1824 as a first-class volunteer aboard the *Prince Regent*. He was then transferred to the *Beagle*, which was about to sail for a major voyage of exploration under the overall command of Capt. Philip Parker King. The *Beagle*, in which Stokes first sailed as midshipman, was commanded by Pringle Stokes, who committed suicide in August 1828, being replaced by Lt. W. G. Skyring. With the *Beagle* sailed the *Adventure* under Captain King.

The two ships left Plymouth on 22 May 1826, making first for Rio and then for Patagonia, Tierra del Fuego, and the Strait of Magellan. Survey work lasted until late 1828, when command was taken over by Capt. Robert Fitzroy *(q.v.)*. The first part of the voyage ended at Plymouth on 14 October 1830. The *Beagle* was refitted at Devonport and sailed again on 27 December 1831, this time with Charles Darwin *(q.v.)* on board. Hydrographic work continued in the

Falkland Islands and Tierra del Fuego area until early 1835, when the expedition began to survey off the Pacific coast of America, the Tuamotus, and Tahiti. At the end of 1835 the *Beagle* reached New Zealand, went on to Australia in 1836, then began its journey home by way of Mauritius and the Cape, dropping anchor at Falmouth on 2 October 1836.

During all this time, Stokes had risen steadily in rank, eventually becoming commander. In due course he took over the *Beagle*, whose captain he became for a period of six years. His long association with the ship could even be said to have extended into his private life, for he married Philip Parker King's younger sister. He received promotion to full captain in July 1846 and in October 1847 was appointed to command the *Acheron* for a detailed survey of the coast of New Zealand. He took his wife with him, as well as his daughter, but Mrs. Stokes died on board not long after leaving the Cape. Stokes left his daughter in Sydney in the care of relatives while he carried out some hydrographic work in Australian waters. He then sailed, on 3 November 1848, for Auckland and began one of the most detailed and comprehensive explorations of New Zealand's lengthy and indented coastline. The *Acheron* spent four years on this work, sailing back to Sydney, where its crew was paid off.

John Stokes returned to England and carried out survey work on the English coast; he was promoted to rear admiral in 1864 and to vice-admiral in 1871. He retired from active service in 1877 and died, a full admiral, on 11 June 1885.

## Strange

JAMES CHARLES STUART STRANGE was born in Scotland in 1753 of a well-connected Jacobite family (he was a godson of Bonnie Prince Charlie). He went to India for the East India Company and became one of its senior merchants in Madras. He was invited to join in a syndicate of other traders, with the leave of the India Company, for a voyage of discovery and commerce to the northwest coast of America, including survey work in the Kamchatka and Bering Strait areas.

Two ships were placed at his disposal—the *Captain Cook*, commanded by Henry Laurie, and the smaller *Experiment*, under Henry Guise. They sailed from Bombay on 8 December 1785, making for

Batavia, Borneo, and the Celebes instead of, as had been planned, Goa and Macao. The change in plans resulted from his inability to obtain a cargo for China, and it severely affected the financial viability of the project.

On 25 June 1786 the two ships reached Vancouver Island, but they did not anchor in Friendly Cove, Nootka, as intended, until 7 July. Strange purchased a native house as a shore establishment for sick crew members, the first purchase of property in the area by the British. The place, however, was unsuitable, and Strange gained a poor impression of Nootka and its natives. As a consequence, he spent most of his time on board, leaving it to Alexander Walker, a young army ensign, to visit ashore and collect some highly valuable ethnologic data. Strange was able to purchase only a limited number of furs and, on 28 July, sailed north, discovering Queen Charlotte Sound, after rounding and naming Cape Scott after one of his partners.

Proceeding toward Cook Inlet in northern Alaska, Strange bought a few more furs, but he was constantly frustrated by poor weather and further discomfitted by the presence of a competitor in William Tipping (*q.v.*). In September he decided to sail for China to dispose of his cargo and return for a second voyage. The *Captain Cook* reached Macao on 15 November 1786, the *Experiment*, which had made for the Aleutians in the hope of finding copper, arriving a month later.

The voyage had been a financial disaster, and Strange did not get a second chance. He reentered the East India Company's service in Madras until 1795, when he went back to England. He was elected a member of Parliament, returned to Madras as postmaster general in 1804, and died in 1840, having retired to Scotland. His *Journal and Narrative of the Commercial Expedition from Bombay to the Northwest Coast of America* was published in Madras in 1928.

## Surville

JEAN-FRANÇOIS-MARIE DE SURVILLE was born on 18 January 1717 at Port-Louis, Brittany, the son of a government official. He went to sea at the age of 10 for the French India Company and served mostly in the Indian Ocean and the China seas. During the War of the Austrian Succession and the Seven Years War he served in the French navy. He was twice taken prisoner, in 1745 and again in 1746, and was wounded and received the Cross of St. Louis in 1759.

Together with the French administrators of the Indian cities of Chandernagore and Pondicherry, he began a series of trading voyages in Indian waters from 1766. In late 1768, on the basis of confused reports about the expedition of Wallis *(q.v.)*, the partners backed him for a voyage of combined exploration and trade to the central Pacific. He sailed from India in the *Saint Jean-Baptiste* on 2 June 1769, making for the Strait of Malacca, Trengganu, and the northern Philippines, and entered the Pacific on 24 August. His course took him through western Micronesia, but he failed to sight any islands, and veered east before reaching New Guinea. Finally, on 7 October, his crew already seriously affected with scurvy, he made his first landfall at Choiseul Island in the Solomons. He anchored for a week in Santa Ysabel, where his crew were attacked by a party of islanders. Between twenty and thirty islanders were killed in the affray, and as a consequence Surville continued eastward, surveying the coastline of the Solomons, a task that greatly contributed to European knowledge of this complex island group. But the condition of his crew compelled him to postpone any further exploration and go in search of supplies in New Zealand.

He arrived off Hokianga on 12 December 1769 and rounded North Cape on the seventeenth in a storm that had blown James Cook *(q.v.)*, at that time sailing north up the east coast, out of sight of land. The two navigators probably passed within only twenty-five miles of each other. The French spent from 18 to 31 December 1769 at anchor in Doubtless Bay. Plants found along the shore helped in restoring the health of the crew, although seven men died of scurvy.

For much of the time relations between Maori and French were friendly; the local people brought in supplies of greens in exchange for hogs, a cock and a hen, wheat, rice, peas, and cloth. It is likely that Father de Villefeix, the ship's chaplain, celebrated the first Christian service held in New Zealand, on Christmas Day 1769.

Their stay was cut short by a violent storm, which revealed Doubtless Bay to be a poor anchorage. Surville sailed east in the southern Pacific, but made no new discoveries. Since they encountered no land, and as his crew became increasingly debilitated, he decided to seek help at the port of Chilca, Peru. On 7 April 1770 Surville attempted to go ashore in heavy seas to get assistance; he was drowned in the heavy surf. His journal and that of his first officer, Guillaume Labé, who eventually brought the ship back to France, were published in English in 1981 under the title *The Expedition of the St. Jean-Baptiste to the Pacific 1769–1770*. They contain valuable ethnographic details on the people of the Solomon Islands and on the Maori of northern New Zealand.

## Swan

CHARLES SWAN was one of the notorious buccaneers who roamed the Pacific in the 1680s. He is first reported as sailing in 1670 with Henry Morgan to the Caribbean, was present at the sacking of Panama in 1671 when Morgan captained the *Endeavour*, and remained associated with him for some years.

In 1683 he sailed to the Pacific by way of Cape Horn in charge of the aptly named *Cygnet*. His intentions at this stage were to trade among the Spanish settlements along the South American coast, but in attempting to put in at Valdivia, in Chile, he alerted the authorities to the presence of English interlopers and had little option but to revert to his old trade of piracy. He fell in with a group of English buccaneers who were soon joined by a band of Frenchmen. In May 1685 they intercepted a Spanish fleet in the Gulf of Panama, but the well-armed Spaniards fought them off and escaped. After several raids ashore that proved only moderately successful, Dampier *(q.v.)* joined Swan in the *Cygnet* and convinced him that, rather than struggle on trying to control an undisciplined fleet of buccaneers, he should sail across the Pacific.

The *Cygnet*, accompanied by a smaller vessel, sailed from Cape Corrientes on the northern coast of South America on 31 March 1686, reaching Guam fifty-one days later. Their hopes of finding the rich Manila galleon were dashed, so they sailed on to Mindanao, where Swan settled ashore to trade and to enjoy what fruits he had remaining of his three years of piracy. Dampier and a number of the crew sailed away in the *Cygnet* on 13 January 1687.

Later that year Swan fell out with the local Malay authorities and wisely decided to sail home in a Dutch vessel, but he was drowned in a boat accident. His journal, which he had sent on earlier, has not been discovered.

## Tasman

ABEL JANSZOON TASMAN was born in 1603 in Lutjegast, Holland. He began his working life as an ordinary seaman based in Amsterdam. By the age of 31 he was serving as first mate on Dutch East India Company ships. In May 1634 the governor of Ambon appointed him skipper of the *Mocha;* he spent the next two years cruising around Ambon and to Ceram. He went back to Holland in the *Banda* at the end of 1636, returning with his wife in 1638 as skipper of the *Engel* to settle in Batavia.

In the following year, the governor-general and his council sent the *Engel*, commanded by Mathijs Quast, and the *Gracht*, commanded by Tasman, to search for rich islands believed to lie east of Japan and to explore the coast of Korea and north China. They sailed on 2 June 1639, going to Luzon, sighting various small islands near Japan, and ending up at the Dutch post of Zeelandia on Formosa (Taiwan). Tasman brought the *Gracht* back to Batavia, which he reached on 19 February 1640, and soon after was despatched on a further voyage to Formosa and Japan, this time in charge of a flotilla of four ships. He returned by way of Cambodia, to which he was sent back in May 1641, going on to Formosa; he was again in Batavia on 20 December 1641.

Tasman was therefore one of the company's most experienced and trusted captains. His selection for a long voyage of exploration in unknown waters came as no surprise. The *Heemskerck* and *Zeehaen* left Batavia on 14 August 1642, making first for Mauritius, then south of the Australian continent. In late November Tasman came in sight of a new land, which he named Anthoni van Diemens Landt after the governor-general; it is now Tasmania. Proceeding east—across what is now the Tasman Sea—he discovered another unknown land on 13 December 1642. It was the west coast of the South Island of New Zealand. A few days later, proceeding north, four of his men were attacked and killed by Maoris. He continued north, endeavoring to keep close to the unknown coast, as far as the furthest tip of the North Island, which he named Cape Maria van Diemen, and a nearby group of small islands, which he named the Three Kings.

On 6 January 1643 the Dutch sailed north to Tonga, where further discoveries were made, to Fiji, and home to Java by way of New

Guinea, thereby proving that the Australian continent was separate from the discoveries they had made in the southwest Pacific. After his return to Batavia on 15 June 1643 Tasman was sent on another voyage of exploration to New Guinea and northern Australia. On his return he was appointed to the Batavia Council of Justice, chiefly as a naval specialist. He sailed on a number of missions—to Ceylon, to eastern Sumatra, to Thailand, and to the Philippines in an unsuccessful attempt to intercept Spanish ships coming from Mexico.

Tasman retired from active service in 1652 or 1653 and died in 1659. His achievements were considerable, although the East India Company's overriding interest being trade, none of his discoveries led to any Dutch attempt at colonization and their true extent was not known outside Holland for some years.

## Tipping

WILLIAM TIPPING joined the newly formed Bengal Fur Company as a captain in 1785. He was given command of the *Sea Otter* and sailed from Bengal in March 1786 accompanied by the *Nootka*, commanded by John Meares *(q.v.)*. However, the two ships soon separated, Tipping calling at Malacca and then making for northern Alaska.

On 5 September Tipping entered Prince William Sound, where he found James Strange *(q.v.)*. He elicited enough information from his competitor to realize that there would be little profit in sailing south along the coast, where Strange had found it hard to purchase adequate supplies of furs, so Tipping decided to sail west to Cook Inlet, forestalling Strange. In February he was back in Macao, where he disposed of his cargo of furs at a handsome profit before returning to India. He made no further voyage to the Pacific.

## Thomson

FRANK TURLE THOMSON (the middle name appears in his service record as Tourle) was born on 14 October 1829. He joined the *Indefatigable* in October 1850, rising to mate in the following year; in 1852 he transferred as mate to the *Sidon*, part of the Western Squadron, and was commissioned lieutenant on 23 May 1854. Until January 1863, when he was made commander, he served in various ships in the Mediterranean and the Channel: the *Rodney*, the *Illustrious*, the *Defence*.

In January 1864 he took over command of the *Hector*, attached to the Channel Squadron, until 6 January 1866, when he became captain of the royal yacht *Victoria and Albert*, a post he held for three years. He was raised to the rank of captain at the end of 1868 and spent three years away from active service. On 6 January 1873 he was appointed to the Royal Naval College, Greenwich, until the following year, when he took command of the *Modeste*, which he sailed to China. He relinquished the command at the beginning of January 1875 to take over the *Challenger* from George Nares *(q.v.)*, who was being recalled to England.

The *Challenger* sailed from Hong Kong on 6 January 1875, making for Manila, passed through the Philippine Islands toward New Guinea, and reached Humboldt Bay on the north coast on 23 February. The expedition went on to the Admiralty Islands, where the scientists carried out important ethnographic work and named a coral reef after the French navigator d'Entrecasteaux. On 10 March *Challenger* sailed for Japan, putting in at Yokohama in mid-April for an overhaul. This done, the ship sailed for the Hawaiian Islands, whence, after a three-week stay, it made for Tahiti. On 3 October the expedition left Papeete on the final leg of the Pacific voyage, reaching Valparaiso, after a call at Juan Fernandez, on 11 December 1875. The journey home was made via the Strait of Magellan and the Atlantic. The *Challenger* dropped anchor at Spithead on 24 May 1876 after a voyage of almost 70,000 nautical miles.

Thomson spent a short time in the *Royal Adelaide* in August 1876, then took command of the *Bellerophon* on 9 September for a cruise to North America and the West Indies that lasted until 21 March 1877, at which point he went back to command the *Victoria and Albert* until his retirement on 14 October 1884. He had a consultative role in the preparation of the expedition's *Narrative*, but the fifty large volumes entitled *Report on the Scientific Results of the Voyage of HMS "Challenger"*, published between 1880 and 1885, were prepared under the supervision of the scientist Charles Wyville Thomson, and John Murray, both of whom had sailed in the *Challenger*.

Frank Turle Thomson died in London shortly after his retirement.

## Tompson

FELIPE TOMPSON was an officer *(primer piloto)* in the Spanish navy who commanded a privately owned ship, the *Nuestra Señora de la Consolación*, bound from Manila to San Blas in Mexico by way of New Guinea in 1773.

He first came upon a reef east-northeast of Morotai in the western Carolines, which he named Bajo de San Feliz. It was the first recorded discovery of Helen Reef in the Palau group. Then, on his way north from New Guinea, on 5 April 1773, he discovered an island group to which he gave the name Islas de la Pasión; on the seventh and eighth he sailed along a reef and an island that he named San Agustin. These were the atolls of Ngatik and Oroluk in the eastern Carolines.

## Torre

BERNARDO DE LA TORRE was sent by Ruy López de Villalobos *(q.v.)* in the *San Juan de Letran* from the Sarangani Islands, south of Mindanao in the Philippines, to America. He sailed in August 1543 via Leyte and Samar, north and east through the central Marianas as far as latitude 30° north. In September Torre discovered three islands in the Mariana archipelago, probably Farallon de Medinilla, Anatahan, and Sariguan. He also sighted the Volcano Islands, which included Iwo Jima in the Bonin Islands, and Marcus Island (Minami-Torishima). On 18 October wild seas assailed the *San Juan*, forcing it to turn back. On his way home, Torre passed through San Bernardino Strait, the first European to do so; he completed his voyage by circumnavigating Mindanao, which was also a European first.

Torre's return to the Sarangani Islands was not a happy one: Portuguese intrigues had forced Villalobos to leave the area, and he had sought refuge on Gilolo. Torre therefore took the *San Juan* to safer waters, where eventually, at Tidore, it was refitted for another attempt to sail to Spanish America, this time under Ortiz de Retes *(q.v.)*.

## Torres

NOTHING IS KNOWN of Luis Vaez (or Baez) de Torres' early life, except that he was born in Spain, traditionally of a Breton or Celtic family, which could argue for a birthplace in northwest Spain, more especially Galicia, in the late 1560s or early 1570s. He became an experienced seaman—and, if Galician, probably lived and worked at Coruna. He was in Lima at the beginning of the seventeenth century, had acquired a reputation as a navigator and leader, and possessed enough personal property to warrant granting a power of attorney to a local businessman to look after it for him.

He was appointed at the request of Quiros *(q.v.)* and of his sailors as captain and pilot of the *San Pedrico,* in which he sailed from Callao on 21 December 1605, part of Quiros' fleet of two ships and a tender or launch. In January a number of Tuamotu atolls were sighted, then the Duff group and the Banks group. On 9 April Torres went ashore on the island of Taumako, not far from Santa Cruz, which was Quiros' destination. On 3 May the ships anchored in a wide bay at the island of Espiritu Santo, one of the New Hebrides (Vanuatu).

It was here that Quiros hoped to set up a Christian colony to begin converting the peoples of the Pacific, but after three weeks he decided to leave and seek a more suitable site. Illness forced him back, but the fleet sailed again on 8 June. However, the ships became separated. Torres sailed along the coast accompanied by the launch *Los Tres Reyes,* hoping to meet up with his commander. He then went down to 21° south, in accordance with sealed orders he had opened, and reached a point in the Coral Sea that was less than two hundred miles from Australia and dangerously close to the Great Barrier Reef.

There was no sign of the fabled southern continent. In early July Torres veered north, hoping to make his way to Manila, but on 14 July 1606 he sighted the high island of Tagula, part of the Louisiade Archipelago. He was unable to veer east to turn what he believed would be the eastern extremity of New Guinea. He consequently sailed west along the dangerous line of reefs and islands that forms the entrance to what is now known as Torres Strait. He tried on several occasions to find a passage to the north, so for much of this perilous passage he hugged the southern coast of New Guinea. His precise course has been the subject of much argument over the centuries, but it seems now established that he passed through Endeavour Strait, forced toward the south by reefs and shallows, sailing along the tip of Cape York Peninsula, working his way north whenever he could. He did not sail down the west coast of the peninsula, but veered back to New Guinea.

On 27 October Torres reached the western extremity of New Guinea and made his way north of Ceram and Misool toward the Halmahera Sea. At the beginning of January 1607 he reached Ternate, where he left the *Los Tres Reyes*. He sailed on 1 May for Manila, arriving on 22 May. Nothing is known of Torres after this point. The voyage was over and the *San Pedrico* was needed in the Philippines for operations against the Dutch. Torres sent a letter to Quiros from Manila in June reporting on his voyage, but the original has been lost; a letter written by Torres to the king of Spain a few weeks later was received at court in June 1608; but the main account of the voyage is a somewhat biased narrative by Diego de Prado y Tovar *(q.v.)*, a senior officer who endeavored to claim much of the credit for himself. Torres' skill and achievements, however, cannot be challenged.

## Trobriand

JEAN-FRANÇOIS-SILVESTRE-DENIS DE TROBRIAND was born at Ploujean, Brittany, on 7 June 1765. He joined the navy at the age of 15, being first appointed to the *Languedoc*, commanded by Louis de Bougainville *(q.v.)*. He saw service during the American War of Independence and had opportunities to serve in a number of ships after the peace and following the outbreak of the French Revolution, at which time he was completing a three-year spell in the *Astrée*.

He was promoted to lieutenant in March 1788 and received the Cross of St. Louis in June 1791. He was serving in the *Fine* when he was appointed first officer to Kermadec *(q.v.)* on the *Espérance*, to take part in the expedition of d'Entrecasteaux *(q.v.)*. His health stood up well during this long and difficult voyage, which began from Brest on 29 September 1791 and ended in the Dutch East Indies on 27 October 1793. By then both d'Entrecasteaux and Kermadec had died, and Trobriand was in effective command of the *Espérance* for several weeks. In Surabaya the expedition broke up, dissensions developing between royalists and republicans.

Trobriand threw in his lot with the former and eventually sailed for Europe in the *Houghly*, which was captured by the English and wrecked. He succeeded in making his way back to France, where he was given command of the *Vestale* in 1797 and promoted to the rank of captain. He died in Santo Domingo in the West Indies on 16 March 1799.

The Trobriand Islands, off western New Guinea, still bear his name today. They lie, appropriately, to the north of the d'Entrecasteaux group.

## Tromelin

Louis-François-Marie-Nicolas Le Goarant de Tromelin was born at Girnin in Brittany in 1786; he joined the navy in 1800. He served in various ships during the Napoleonic wars. On 21 December 1826 he sailed from Toulon in command of the corvette *Bayonnaise* for South America. He was given instructions to report on the political situation in the Hawaiian Islands, where the French had been unable to establish a lasting settlement and where French missionaries were facing an equally difficult task.

He was in Callao in Febrary 1828 and sailed for Honolulu, where he spent 21 March to 17 April. He called on members of the Hawaiian ruling family and on the British and American consuls and felt confident, quite wrongly, that he had strengthened the French missionaries' hand. He then sailed for Fanning Island and Rotuma. He gave an accurate position for Phoenix Island, which until then was imperfectly known. Tromelin next sailed to Tikopia and Vanikoro in the Santa Cruz group, arriving on 17 June. His voyage home took him to Guam, Timor, Mauritius, St. Helena, and Ascension. He was back in Toulon on 19 March 1829.

He was to return to the Pacific in 1846 with the rank of rear admiral as commander of the French naval forces in the Pacific. In August 1849 he clashed with the Hawaiian authorities and occupied for a time the fort of Honolulu and the customs office; he left on 5 September, having done little to improve relations between France and the rulers of Hawaii.

Tromelin died in 1867. His main contribution to Pacific hydrography was his report on Phoenix Island; he is often credited with the discovery of Fais, in the Carolines, but it was probably first sighted by Francisco de Castro *(q.v.)*.

## Tupac

TUPAC INCA YUPANQUI, presuming he is not a mythical character, was born around the middle of the fifteenth century in Peru. He conquered much of present-day Ecuador and, having heard of the existence of islands in the mid-Pacific, sailed out with a fleet of warriors on balsa rafts. He returned with black prisoners, gold, and various artefacts. This event may have taken place in the 1480s.

The story, narrated by his grandchildren to Spanish conquerors, may contain the embellishment of gold in order to please and attract the Spanish listeners, whose main interest was in finding treasure—the possibility is that the Incas were trying to persuade the Spanish to sail away in search of the islands and leave them in peace—but it is not implausible. If Tupac's voyage in fact took place, then the islands visited may have been the Galapagos or Mangareva in the Gambier archipelago: traditions of a chief named Tupa arriving at Mangareva have been recorded, and a pass on the eastern side of the island was known as Tupa's Passage.

## Turnbull

JOHN TURNBULL sailed to China in 1799 as second lieutenant of the merchant ship *Barwell.* He became a close friend of the first officer, John Buyers *(q.v.),* and with him on their return to England persuaded various investors to back a trading voyage to the northwest coast. They left in the *Margaret* on 2 July 1800, Turnbull being the supercargo and Buyers the captain. They reached New South Wales in January 1801, Buyers then taking the *Margaret* to North America while Turnbull remained in Australia trading and eventually joining a whaling ship that took him to Norfolk Island, where Buyers, returning after an unprofitable voyage, joined him. On 9 August 1802 they left in the *Margaret* for Tahiti and the Hawaiian Islands, arriving on 2 December.

The *Margaret* set off for Tahiti on 21 January 1803, arriving in March. Turnbull went ashore to buy hogs and salt pork, intending to sail for China and England; Buyers meanwhile sailed in the *Margaret* in search of further supplies and pearls. The ship was wrecked on a reef in the Tuamotus. Buyers managed eventually to make his way back to Matavai Bay, and the two partners obtained passage on a ship bound for Port Jackson, where they landed in December 1803. They sailed for England in the *Calcutta* on 16 March 1804, completing their voyage in June.

On his return, John Turnbull wrote an account of their travels, *A Voyage round the World* (1805), which was very popular and soon translated into French. It is short on navigational details and dates but is a valuable source of information on life in Tahiti, Hawaii, and New South Wales in the early 1800s.

## Ulloa

FRANCISCO DE ULLOA was born in Merida, Estramadura, Spain, toward the end of the fifteenth century. He sailed from Seville in June 1527 together with his brother Nicolas and reached Yucatan, subsequently becoming a trusted associate of Hernán Cortés, the conqueror of Mexico.

In 1536 Cortés discovered the peninsula of Baja California, although he was unable to ascertain with certainty whether it was an island or a part of the American continent. He sent Ulloa to investigate further in the *Santa Agueda*. Ulloa sailed from Acapulco on 8 July 1539, exploring the Mar Vermejo (the Gulf of California) and satisfying himself that it was not a strait; he then explored the Pacific coast of Baja California, discovering Cedros Island and a number of features along the coast as far as modern-day San Diego.

Although some hold the view that Ulloa died on the return voyage, a Francisco de Ulloa sailed from Valparaiso in October 1553 to carry out a detailed survey of the southern Chilean coast in company with Cortés Ojea, penetrating deep into the Strait of Magellan, as part of the Spanish hydrographic exploration of this complex and storm-battered part of South America.

## Urdaneta

ANDRÉS DE URDANETA was born at Villafranca de Guipúzcoa, Northern Spain, in 1508. As a young man, he sailed with the 1525–1529 expedition of Loaysia *(q.v.)*, as an officer aboard the *Santa Maria de la Victoria*, reached the Moluccas, where he remained until early 1535, and made his way back to Spain by way of Cape of

Good Hope. At Valladolid, he reported on his travels to the Spanish king, then went to New Spain (Mexico), where he became an adviser to the viceroy Antonio de Mendoza.

He took part in planning the expedition of Villalobos *(q.v.)* of 1542–1543, but further attempts to send Spanish ships across the Pacific were prevented by the king in order to appease Portugal, with whom Spain was allied. On 20 March 1553, Urdaneta took vows as an Augustinian friar at a religious house in Mexico.

As Spanish policies toward Pacific exploration changed, expeditions began to be planned. Upon the recommendation of the viceroy, Luis de Velasco, Philip II approved a voyage of discovery to the "Islas del Poniente". This change of policy eventually led to the expedition of Miguel de Legazpi *(q.v.)*, which sailed from Mexico on 20 November 1564. Urdaneta sailed in the flagship, *San Pedro*. On 5 January 1565, the island of Meijit, in the Marshall group, was discovered, then two more islands during the days following, but Legazpi next entered seas where few islands could be encountered and, on 22 January, reached Guam. On 14 February the Spanish reached Samar in the Philippines and began to establish and consolidate the Spanish dominion over the Philippines.

Urdaneta's importance lay in helping to establish the idea that the best return route to Mexico was along the northern latitudes. On 1 June 1565 the *San Pedro*, with him on board, set out to seek a route back to America. On the twenty-first the Spanish sighted a small rocky island, having the appearance of a ship in full sail; they named it Parece Vela. It is Orino-Torishima and lies to the west of the Marianas. No more land was seen until 18 September, when they reached the American coast. The practicality of return voyages between America and the Philippines was thus established.

Friar Urdaneta reached Acapulco on 8 October 1565 and made his way back to Mexico City, where he died in 1568.

## Vaillant

AUGUSTE-NICOLAS VAILLANT was born in France in 1793; he joined the French navy and saw service in the Napoleonic wars, rising to the rank of post-captain by the time he was given command of the corvette *Bonite*, which sailed from Toulon on 6 February 1836, making for the Canary Islands, Rio de Janeiro, and Cape Horn, which he turned on 16 May in cold, stormy weather; this prevented him from reaching Valparaiso before 10 June.

The aim of the voyage was to report on trade prospects in the Pacific and to protect French interests in the islands. Help to the many French whalers then operating in the Pacific was an early priority: Vaillant found that the entire crew of the *Geneviève* had deserted in Chile. Vaillant next sailed up the coast to Callao and Guayaquil before setting off west to the Galapagos, where, however, he was unable to stop. Instead, he went up to Hawaii, dropping anchor in Kealakekua Bay on 1 October. Time was spent in negotiations over the rights of French citizens on the islands and especially those of missionaries. Vaillant sailed on 24 October, proceeding mostly along the eighteenth parallel toward the Philippines. He met with no islands until he reached the Marianas on 17 November, went on toward the Babuyan Islands north of Luzon, and sailed down the west coast of that island until he put in at Manila on 7 December.

Vaillant left a fortnight later for Macao, then proceeded to Indochina for negotiations, which proved fruitless, with the Vietnamese authorities. He went on to Singapore, arriving on 17 February 1837, thence to Penang, Bengal, Pondicherry, and the island of Bourbon (Réunion), where he arrived on 11 July. The final stage of the voyage included a brief call at St. Helena. The *Bonite* finally dropped anchor at Brest on November 1837.

Although scientific research was a secondary aim of the expedition, the *Bonite* brought back several thousand natural history specimens. A three-volume account of the voyage, including its scientific achievements, was published in 1845–1852 as *Voyage autour du Monde exécuté pendant les Années 1836 et 1837 sur la corvette "La Bonite"*.

Vaillant became a rear admiral in 1849 and minister of marine in 1851.

## Vancouver

GEORGE VANCOUVER was born at King's Lynn, Norfolk, on 22 June 1757, the son of a local customs officer. He entered the navy in 1772, when he was accepted by James Cook *(q.v.)* for the *Resolu-*

*tion*, which sailed from Plymouth on 13 July 1772 for the Antarctic and the Pacific. Vancouver claimed that by standing on the bowsprit in the Antarctic just before the ship turned back north he had been farther south than anyone else.

The *Resolution* was back in England in July 1775 but was soon made ready to leave, with the *Discovery*, for yet another voyage. Vancouver sailed in the *Discovery* this time, as a midshipman. The ship left at the beginning of August, rejoining the *Resolution* at the Cape in November and reaching New Zealand in February. The voyage was devoted mostly to the exploration of the northern Pacific, including the northwest coast of America. In Hawaii, where Cook was killed, Vancouver was himself attacked and slightly injured. The ships were back in England on 4 October 1780 and on the nineteenth Vancouver received his promotion to the rank of lieutenant.

At the end of 1780 he joined the sloop *Martin*, doing escort duty in the North Sea and later in the Caribbean. Service then followed in the *Fame* and the *Europa*, enabling him to gain experience in West Indian waters. He returned to England in August 1789. His next assignment was to the *Discovery* (a different vessel from Cook's ship of 1775) for a surveying voyage to the northwest coast. Vancouver reported for duty in early 1790, but the possibility of war breaking out with Spain caused delays during which Vancouver served in the *Courageux*. Once the danger of war was over, Vancouver lost no time in preparing to sail, as commander of an expedition of two ships, the *Discovery* and the *Chatham* commanded by William Broughton (*q.v.*).

They got under way from Falmouth on 1 April 1791. The voyage to the Pacific was relatively slow, by way of Tenerife, the Cape, the south of Australia, and New Zealand, where Vancouver anchored—in Cook's Dusky Sound—on 2 November 1791. Leaving three weeks later, the ships became separated in a gale. Vancouver discovered the lonely Snares islets (which in fact Broughton had just named the Knights) and sailed on to Tahiti, where he arrived at the end of December. A few days earlier, on the twenty-second, he had discovered Rapa in the Austral Islands. Meanwhile, Broughton had discovered and named the Chatham Islands. The two ships were reunited in Matavai Bay, Tahiti. They carried out repairs and left on 24 January 1792 for Hawaii. After brief calls at Oahu and Kauai, the vessels went on to the northwest coast, dropping anchor in Juan de Fuca Strait on 30 April.

Survey work began, including the discovery of Puget Sound; it was complicated by negotiations with the Spanish. Broughton was sent to England from San Francisco in November with despatches, Puget *(q.v.)* taking over command of the *Chatham*. On 14 January 1793 Vancouver set off for Hawaii. Surveys were carried out around the islands; on 16 March the *Chatham* under Puget was sent to Nootka Sound, and at the end of the month Vancouver followed him to the northwest coast. The summer was spent on survey work, and in December the expedition set off from California for a third wintering in Hawaii. On this occasion, Vancouver formally took possession of the islands in the name of King George III, an action that had no consequences.

April to August 1794 was spent on more exploration of the Alaskan coast from the Aleutians to Nootka Sound. The ships then prepared for the homeward journey, which took them to Monterey in California and round Cape Horn. The two ships once more became separated, but they met again at St. Helena in early July 1795. Puget went with the *Chatham* to Brazil, while Vancouver made for home, arriving at Deal on 15 October 1795.

Vancouver's painstaking and accurate surveys of the northwest coastline are a major accomplishment. His name is commemorated in Vancouver Island and in that of the largest city of British Columbia. His health, however, had suffered during his voyages, and he did not live to see the publication of his *A Voyage of Discovery to the North Pacific Ocean and round the world*, published in three volumes in late 1798 in London and completed by his brother John, aided by Puget. George Vancouver died at Petersham, Surrey, on 12 May 1798.

## Van Noort

OLIVIER VAN NOORT was born in Utrecht in 1558 or 1559. Little is known of his earlier years, beyond the suspicion that he joined in privateering expeditions to the West Indies. He became a merchant in a small way in Rotterdam but by 1590 was mostly known as a tavern keeper. He had enough influence, however, and displayed enough knowledge of the geography of the Pacific seaboard of South America and of the exploits of Drake and Cavendish *(qq.v.)* to gain support for a two-ship voyage to the Pacific.

He sailed on 4 July 1598 in command of the *Mauritius* and was joined in September by two ships from Amsterdam. Progress down the Atlantic, with calls in Africa and South America, was slow and beset by outbreaks of scurvy. One ship of the three was abandoned as unseaworthy. Reaching the entrance to the Strait of Magellan on 4 November 1599, Van Noort emerged into the Pacific on 29 February 1600. The *Hendrick Frederick* became separated from the other two ships; its captain raided Spanish shipping as far north as Nicaragua but, finding no sign of Van Noort, sailed to Ternate in the Moluccas, where his ship ran aground and had to be sold off to the local sultan.

Van Noort raided Valparaiso but found that the Spanish were forewarned and in fact faster than his cumbersome vessel, the *Mauritius*, or the smaller *Eendracht*. In May he decided to give up and sail across the Pacific to Guam, which he reached on 15 September. He went on to the Philippines, capturing a few small vessels on the way, which produced little more than supplies for the onward voyage. By November the Dutch were off Manila, hoping to capture Chinese merchant ships. Instead, they aroused the fears of the Spanish authorities, who organized a fleet of two vessels of 300 tons each, supported by a number of smaller craft.

The Spanish sailed out of Manila on 13 December 1600 to engage the two Dutch ships off Marivoles Island. Considerably outnumbered, the outsiders were soon in danger, the *Mauritius* being boarded and almost captured. Desperation and a fire on board that seemed about to cause the ship to explode saved the Dutch: the Spanish turned back and the *Mauritius* seized the opportunity to flee. The *Eendracht*, however, was captured, and most of its small crew were executed as pirates.

Van Noort sailed to Brunei, where he traded until the end of the year, then south to the Bali Strait, the Indian Ocean, the Cape, and home. He reached Rotterdam on 27 August 1601 with a mere 45 out of the 248 men who had originally set out, but the *Mauritius* could claim the first Dutch circumnavigation of the globe. Van Noort's reputation did not suffer from the poor financial results of the voy-

age: he played a role in the continuing Dutch wars and was associated with several mercantile undertakings until his death on 22
February 1627 at Schoonhoven.

## Vasilev

MIKHAIL NIKOLAEVICH VASILEV (found also as Vassiliev) was born
in 1770, graduated from the Cadet Naval School, and served in the
Russian navy during the Napoleonic wars. In 1819, as a lieutenant
captain, he was given command of a two-ship expedition to the
Pacific, with his own corvette *Otkrytie* (Discovery) and the sloop
*Blagonamerennyi* (Well-Intentioned), under G. S. Shishmarev *(q.v.)*

Vasilev sailed from Kronstadt in July 1819 with instructions to
seek a northern passage into the Atlantic along the northern coasts
of America or Eurasia. He rounded the Cape of Good Hope, called at
Sydney, and made his way north to Kamchatka. The next two years
were devoted to surveys of the northern coasts of Asia and America.
Vasilev sailed along the Aleutian chain from Unalaska into Bristol
Bay, following the coast of eastern Alaska, identifying Nunivak as
an island (on which the name Otkrytie Island was bestowed), and
around to Norton Sound and into Norton Bay. He passed through
Bering Strait to Point Hope and Cape Lisburne and westward into
the Chukchi Sea. The positions of the various headlands were determined with precision, but the Russians found nothing to suggest
that a northern passage into European seas could be discovered. The
expedition made a valuable contribution to the knowledge of the
northern coasts and brought back useful information about the people encountered in the Pacific, including a more scientific appraisal
of the Aleuts than had been available to anthropologists until then.

The return voyage began in mid-October 1821 from Petropavlovsk in Kamchatka and took the two vessels across the Pacific
to Honolulu, arriving in late November, then south to Cape Horn.
Vasilev was back at Kronstadt in August 1822. He ended his career
as a vice-admiral and died on 23 June 1847.

## Villalobos

JUAN DE VILLALOBOS was captain of the *San Francisco*, which
accompanied Pedro Sarmiento *(q.v.)* on a voyage of exploration to

the Strait of Magellan. Having sailed from Callao on 11 October 1579, they reached Golfo Trinidad in southern Chile on 17 November and began a detailed survey of the coast down to the entrance of the strait. On 30 January 1580 Sarmiento entered the strait, but the *San Francisco* had been driven south in a gale, possibly as far as latitude 56° south, where an open sea passage to the Atlantic could be found. However, being unable to join up with Sarmiento and possibly in no mood for further hardships, Villalobos turned back north to Valparaiso.

## Villalobos

RUY LÓPEZ DE VILLALOBOS, a relative by marriage of the viceroy of Mexico, Antonio de Mendoza, was sent in 1542 with six ships—*Santiago, San Anton, San Jorge, San Juan,* and two smaller vessels—to lay a Spanish claim to the Moluccas and other territories that might be held under arguable claims by the Portuguese. He sailed from Navidad, Mexico, on 1 November 1542, passed through the Revilla Gigedo Islands, and continued on a westerly course to the Marshalls, where he discovered, from 25 December, a number of low, tree-covered islands, on one of which he landed on the twenty-sixth and to which he gave the name of Santo Esteban. On 6 January 1543 ten islands were sighted, named Los Jardines; on the twenty-third another island was found where the inhabitants seemed to have some knowledge of Christianity and called out what the sailors understood to be "Buenos dias, matelotes."

The precise identification of each one of these discoveries is not easy. They were probably Wotko, Erikub, Maloelap, Likiep, Kwajalein, Lao, Ujae, and Wotho, while Los Matelotes is certainly Fais in the Carolines. On 26 January Villalobos sailed past more of the Carolines, probably Yap, less probably Ulithi, but he was by now sailing in waters already known to the Portuguese and could not claim any more discoveries. After the expedition left Fais, a storm led to the separation of the small ship *San Antonio;* it struggled alone on a northwesterly course toward the Philippines, eventually meeting up with Villalobos but, having sailed through relatively empty or known waters, is unlikely to have come upon islands.

On 2 February 1543 Villalobos reached northeastern Mindanao, where he remained for a month, resting his crew and repairing his vessels; he then sailed south to the Sarangani Islands from where he sent Bernardo de la Torre *(q.v.)* in the *San Juan* in an attempt to send a report to the viceroy. In 1544 Villalobos was forced by Portuguese pressure and shortage of supplies to move to Tidore, where a new attempt was made to send a ship back to Mexico. Eventually, he was forced to accept repatriation to Spain, setting out in January 1546; but he died on the journey, at Amboina, on Good Friday, being attended in his last hours by the great missionary Francis Xavier.

## Vizcaino

SEBASTIÁN VIZCAINO was born in Spain around the year 1550 and joined the army in Portugal in 1567. He took part in a number of engagements during the period, which saw Spain take over Portugal. He went to Mexico in 1585 and made at least one Pacific crossing in the Manila galleon between 1586 and 1589; he certainly was on board the *Santa Ana* in 1587 when Cavendish *(q.v.)* captured it off Lower California.

In 1593 Vizcaino set about organizing a company for the exploration of the Gulf of California, which was little known and reputed to be a rich source of pearls. A first attempt in 1594 was a failure, but Vizcaino led a fleet of three ships from Acapulco in June 1596 and claimed to have reached 29°30′ north.

On 5 May 1602 Vizcaino again led an expedition of three ships from Acapulco; this time he sailed along the Pacific coast of Lower California to San Diego; continuing northward on 15 December he discovered Monterey Bay. The expedition was suffering great hardships, with frequent storms, fog, and scurvy. Nevertheless, Vizcaino drove on north, charting the coast as far as Cape Mendocino, which he reached on 12 January 1603, and possibly to Cape Blanco in present-day Oregon. However, he had the misfortune to miss the great bay of San Francisco. He returned to Mexico, dropping anchor in Mazatlán on 18 February.

Monterey offered the possibility of a good harbor for galleons on their way to and from Manila. Vizcaino traveled to Spain for permission to establish a garrison there; he was granted his wish in 1607, but the new viceroy was not enthusiastic about the proposal. As a consolation, Vizcaino was sent on 22 March 1611 in the *San Francisco* on a voyage of exploration across the Pacific to seek the fabled islands of Rica de Oro and Rica de Plata somewhere to the east of Japan and to endeavor to open up trade relations with the Japanese. Unsuccessful in both enterprises, he sailed back to Mexico in January 1614. He is recorded as being in Avalos and other places in Mexico, engaged in military duties, in 1615, but most of his life after this period is obscure. He is believed to have died in 1628.

## Vries

MAARTEN GERRITSZOON VRIES (also de Vries or Fries) was a captain of the Dutch East India Company who was sent in 1643 to explore the Pacific east of Japan to check on the possible existence of islands rich in precious metals supposedly discovered by the Portuguese in 1582, Rica de Oro and Rica de Plata. The latitude was very vague—somewhere between 37° and 40° north—and the longitude even more uncertain. At the same time, Vries was told to investigate the possibility of a northern passage from the Pacific to the Atlantic or the North Sea. Vries sailed from Batavia in February 1643 with two ships, his own *Castricum* and the *Breskens*, making first for Ternate.

He soon lost contact with the *Breskens* and failed to find it at the agreed rendezvous point of northern Hokkaido; the *Breskens* was in fact detained by the Japanese in Honshu until the end of the year.

On 14 June Vries sighted Kunashir, just north of Hokkaido; because of the fog he took it to be a projection of the Japanese island, but it was the beginning of the long Kuril chain, which he was the first European to see. The next day he discovered the island of Iturup, which he named Staten Eylandt, and on 18 June the island of Urup on which he landed, naming it Compagnies Landt. The difference in name was due to his belief that, whereas Iturup was clearly an island, Urup was a projection of North America. The strait between the two, through which he had sailed and which still bears his name, thus appeared to him as dividing Asia from America and opening the way to northern waters. He did not, however, continue north, but veered west toward the Sea of Okhotsk and to Sakhalin, where he landed, and to Aniwa Bay, at the south of the island, where he anchored on 1 August. He returned to the Pacific by Vries Strait, sailed fairly cautiously eastward in the hope of sighting the Gold and Silver islands, but wisely returned to the coast of Japan, caught up with the *Breskens* (now released by the Japanese), and returned to Batavia in mid-December.

Vries brought back nothing of interest to the Dutch trading company, but some useful data about the previously unknown waters north of Japan. His contribution was marred, however, by his mistaken view of Urup, which confused cartographers for many years. Accounts of the voyage, published in Dutch in 1858 and in English in 1975 shed light on his achievements and his doggedness in the face of considerable hardships.

## Wallis

SAMUEL WALLIS was born at Fentonwoon, Cornwall, in early 1728 (the date of his christening is 23 April). He joined the Royal Navy and was promoted to lieutenant on 19 October 1748. In 1753 he was appointed to the *Anson* and in April 1755 to the *Torbay*, the flagship of Vice-Admiral Boscawen. In the following year he was transferred to the *Invincible* and on 30 May 1756 was given command of the sloop *Swan*. The Seven Years War was beginning, and until it ended Wallis obtained a number of appointments, serving mostly in the North American theater of war.

He was now a highly regarded and experienced commander, one of a small group from which the Admiralty could draw on when expeditions were being planned to the South Seas. He was given command of the *Dolphin*, which had just returned from a circumnavigation under John Byron *(q.v.)* and was due to return on a second voyage. Along with the *Dolphin* was to go the *Swallow*, placed under the command of Philip Carteret *(q.v.)*. Wallis sailed from Plymouth on 22 August 1766, making for Madeira, the Cape Verde Islands, and the Strait of Magellan, which he reached on 17 December. A third vessel, the storeship *Prince Frederick*, was unloaded and sent back to England by way of the Falklands. The *Dolphin* and the *Swallow* then began a long and painful navigation through the strait, emerging into the Pacific on 11 April 1767. The two ships lost sight of each other in fog and each completed its circumnavigation separately.

Wallis sailed on a northwest and northerly course, his crew soon becoming affected by scurvy. It was with great relief that an island was sighted on 6 June, Whitsun Island (Pinaki), followed by a second one, which the English named Queen Charlotte Island (Nuku-tavake). These were part of the Tuamotus, of which several more were seen during the next few days. The archipelago was not unknown, but Wallis discovered in all five new islands. On 17 June he discovered Mehetia in the Society Islands, and the next day made his major discovery, the island of Tahiti, where he stayed for five weeks. He sailed on 27 July, going westward and meeting a number of new islands on the way, although only three—Tubai Manu, Mopi-haa, and Motu One—can be claimed as discoveries: others were sub-sequently identified as having been reported by previous navigators.

In mid-August, realizing how badly his ship was leaking and doubtful of obtaining adequate supplies from the succession of quite small islands he was encountering, Wallis began to steer north and northwest toward the Ladrones (Marianas). This new course led him to a hitherto unknown island, which his officers called Wallis Island; it was Uvea, seen on 16 August. On 3 September he discov-ered Rongerik in the Marshall Islands. Then, on the nineteenth, the *Dolphin* dropped anchor at Tinian, where it stayed until 15 October. Batavia was reached at the end of November; the route home included a call at the Cape on 4 February 1768 for a refit; on 20 May 1768, Wallis dropped anchor in the Downs.

The discovery of Tahiti and the accounts of the island's people and customs given by Wallis and by the *Dolphin*'s master, George Robertson, aroused considerable interest. The accounts found their way into many collections of voyages, notably John Hawkesworth's in 1773. Wallis was given a substantial gratuity on his return as well as two years' leave. He then resumed his career, being appointed to the *Torbay* in November 1770, to the *Queen* in 1780, and becoming a Commissioner of the Navy in 1782–1783 and again, when the office was reinstituted, from 1787 until his death, which occurred at London on 21 January 1795.

## Walton

WILLIAM WALTON (or Vilim Valton) was a captain in the Russian navy of English origin who was appointed to command the *Nadezhda* (Hope), one of the three ships that made up the expedition of Martin Spanberg *(q.v.)* of 1738–1739. The aim was to ascertain the extent of the Japanese archipelago and its relationship to the Kurils. The first attempt, in 1738, was foiled by ice, and the ships were unable at first to get out of the Sea of Okhotsk, making instead for Bolsheresk in Kamchatka, which they managed to leave on 26 July, sailing south, only to encounter almost impenetrable fog in which they became separated. Walton succeeded in reaching the neighborhood of eastern Hokkaido but brought back no precise information.

Walton tried again in 1739, this time in the *St. Gabriel (Sv. Gavriil)*. He became separated from Spanberg, probably intentionally, and sailed beyond Hokkaido to the island of Honshu. He anchored just off the Beso Peninsula east of Tokyo Bay and was well received by the Japanese. The *Sv. Gavriil* continued south along the coast of Wakayama in southern Honshu, then veered back to Kamchatka, where it arrived in early September, the crew badly afflicted by sickness.

In 1741 and 1742 William Walton carried out survey work to the northwest and west of the Sea of Okhotsk as far as eastern Sakhalin, but he was bedeviled by fog and hopelessly inaccurate charts. He died in 1743; and his achievements, which included landing in Japan and charting, however roughly, twenty-six of the Kurils, were not recognized until some years after his death.

## Waterhouse

HENRY WATERHOUSE was born in London on 13 December 1770 and joined the navy at an early age. Beginning with the *Portland* he served on various ships until 1786, when he was appointed midshipman on the *Sirius* and sailed to New South Wales. In December 1789, as acting lieutenant, he took the *Sirius* to Norfolk Island, where it was wrecked. In February 1791 he transferred to the *Supply* and later in the year returned to England.

In May 1792, promoted to lieutenant, he served on the *Swallow* and in March 1793 transferred to the *Bellerophon*. In July 1794 he was appointed to the *Reliance*, in which he sailed for New South Wales, arriving in Port Jackson in September 1795. He was sent to the Cape in 1796, returning in June 1797 with the first merino sheep to be landed in Australia. Waterhouse then received a grant of land and bought further tracts in 1798–1799.

He made several further voyages to Norfolk Island and in March 1800 was authorized to sail back to England in the *Reliance*. It was on this return journey that he discovered an island he named Penantipode. It is present-day Antipodes Island to the south of New Zealand. A commander since 1794, he was promoted to captain on his return to England in October 1800. Shortly after, he took over command of the *Raison*. He died in London on 27 July 1812.

## Weatherhead

MATTHEW WEATHERHEAD was captain of the *Matilda*, an English whaler operating in the southern Pacific in 1790–1792. His was the second ship to enter Jervis Bay, Australia, which had been visited and named in August 1791 by Lieutenant Bowen of the transport *Atlantic*. Weatherhead put in at Jervis Bay in November and drew a detailed chart of it that was published in March 1794 by Alexander Dalrymple.

Weatherhead then sailed to the central Pacific, but the *Matilda* was wrecked on 25 February 1792 on a long atoll that became known as the Matilda Rocks. The survivors struggled back to Tahiti, where they met Bligh *(q.v.)* and reported both the disaster and their discovery. Matilda Rocks were included on Arrowsmith's chart of 1798, but in 1826 Beechey *(q.v.)* called at Mururoa in the Tuamotus, where he found clear evidence of the 1792 wreck. Weatherhead can therefore be acknowledged as the discoverer of Mururoa, which has gained modern notoriety as a center for nuclear tests.

## Wilkes

CHARLES WILKES was born in New York on 3 April 1798 and entered the United States Navy as a midshipman in 1818. By 1826 he was a lieutenant and making a name for himself in survey and hydrographic work. Pressure had been mounting for some years for an American voyage of exploration into the Pacific, which so far had been the preserve of European nations. Edmund Fanning *(q.v.)* in particular had been urging the United States government to act. War and apathy meant that nothing was done until 1825, when President John Quincy Adams put forward a proposal. Even then, Congress did not act until 1828.

Wilkes, recently appointed superintendent of the Depot of Charts and Instruments, was sent to England and the Continent to buy scientific instruments, but money was not forthcoming and the project was postponed. Pressure continued to mount, with captains reporting that charts of the Pacific coast were inadequate and the area around the Columbia River dangerously ill-delineated. In 1836 funds finally became available for what was to be called the United States Exploring Expedition, but delays occurred as officials wrangled over supplies and who was to command the expedition. On 10 March 1838 the appointment was given to Wilkes.

The expedition was a major undertaking, with two sloops, the *Vincennes* and the *Peacock*, commanded by William L. Hudson *(q.v.)*, a brig, the *Porpoise*; and a storeship, the *Relief*. Two schooners were added for shallow coastal work, the *Sea Gull* and the *Flying Fish*. Nine scientists and artists were included in the complement. Wilkes sailed on 18 August 1838 from Hampton Roads, Virginia, for Madeira, Rio, and Tierra del Fuego. At this point, the ships separated, some going southwest in an attempt to reach beyond the farthest point south that Cook *(q.v.)* had reached. They met again in Callao in May, except for the *Sea Gull*, which was never seen again.

Wilkes began a survey of the Tuamotus in August, painstakingly correcting charts, before putting in at Tahiti on 14 September 1839. The ships separated again, the *Vincennes* and the *Porpoise* going to Samoa while the *Peacock* and the *Flying Fish* stayed in Tahiti until October for repairs (the *Relief* had been sent home). The squadron assembled in Apia on 10 November, having completed a detailed survey of the entire Samoan group, and made for Sydney, where they arrived on 26 November. A month was spent there, after which Wilkes sailed for the Antarctic. More than two months of determined work along the ice barrier produced valuable information and a lasting tribute to the explorer—the naming of the vast stretch of the continent south of the Indian Ocean, Wilkes Land. The *Peacock* was forced to return to Sydney for repairs, where Wilkes joined it on 11 March 1840, while the other two ships sailed to the Bay of Islands, New Zealand.

Leaving the *Peacock* in New South Wales, Wilkes crossed to New Zealand and, on 6 April 1840, left for a lengthy survey of the Fiji group. In September he went to Honolulu, where *Peacock* joined him on the thirtieth. *Peacock* and *Flying Fish* were sent to Samoa for more hydrographic work, and *Porpoise* to the Tuamotus, while Wilkes carried out scientific work in Hawaii. On 5 April 1841 *Vincennes* and *Porpoise* set off for the northwest coast. *Peacock* and *Flying Fish* arrived there in July, but *Peacock* was wrecked at the mouth of the Columbia River. Wilkes purchased the *Oregon* as replacement and continued his survey work until November, when he returned to Honolulu. Soon after, he sailed for Manila. *Flying Fish*, which was in a poor condition, was sold in Singapore. Wilkes then sailed home with the remaining vessels by way of the Cape; he finally dropped anchor off Sandy Hook, New Jersey, on 10 June 1842.

Charles Wilkes had been an efficient commander, but a harsh and unpopular one. His behavior led to a court-martial on his return; he was officially censured, but his achievements were too impressive to be overlooked. His five-volume *Narrative of the United States Exploring Expedition*, published in 1844, was widely read; the twenty-two volumes of scientific reports that followed had a lesser readership. Wilkes, who was promoted to commander after the troubles associated with the aftermath of his return died down, spent much of his time on these publications and on coastal survey advisory work until the outbreak of the Civil War, when he was given command of the *San Jacinto* and later put in charge of a squadron bound for the Indies. His character, however, led to various incidents, and in 1864 he was again court-martialed. He was then forced to retire. He had been raised to commodore in 1862 and was promoted to rear admiral in 1866. He died in Washington on 8 February 1877.

## Williams

JOHN WILLIAMS was born at Tottenham, England, in 1796. He was attracted to the work of the London Missionary Society (L.M.S.), volunteered to serve in the Pacific Islands, and on 17 November 1816 sailed for New South Wales in the *Harriet* with his young bride, Mary. From Sydney he went in the *Active* to the Bay of Islands, New Zealand, and on to Tahiti, where he arrived on 16 November 1817.

Williams eventually settled in Raiatea. Realizing the need for interisland communications, he went to Sydney in 1822 and prevailed on the local L.M.S. representatives to purchase a small vessel, the *Endeavour*, in which he sailed back to Raiatea, again by way of the Bay of Islands.

In July 1823 he took the *Endeavour*, captained by John Dibbs, to the Cook Islands, having on board the Reverend Bourne and six Raiatean teachers, intending to set up a mission on Aitutaki. During this voyage, he discovered the two small islands of Mitiaro and Mauke, east of Atiu. He was back in Raiatea in August. The London directors of the L.M.S., however, did not approve of his shipping venture, and the *Endeavour* had to be disposed of. Williams later had another small vessel built, the *Messenger of Peace*, in which he traveled to Rarotonga and Samoa.

He sailed home to London in the whaler *Sir Andrew Hammond* in 1834, spending the next four years in England where, in 1837, he published his popular *A Narrative of Missionary Enterprises in the South-Sea Islands*.

On his return to the Pacific, John Williams made Samoa his headquarters. He was killed by islanders at Erromango, New Hebrides, during a visit there, on 20 November 1839.

## Wilson

HENRY WILSON was a captain in the employ of the British East India Company who in June 1783 was in command of the *Antelope* in Macao when he received orders to sail to the western Pacific. He left Macao on 21 July, sailing east and southeast. On 9 August the *Antelope*, a 300-ton packet boat, struck a reef off Oroolong in the Palau Islands. Thanks to a crew member who spoke Malay and a Malayan who had himself been wrecked on the islands, Wilson was able to establish contact with the islanders and their chief, Abba Thule.

From the wreckage of the *Antelope* Wilson built a small schooner, which he named *Oroolong*, in which the British, with the exception of one man who elected to stay behind, sailed for China on 12

November. With him Wilson took the chief's son, Lee-Boo, whom Abba Thule wanted to see England and become educated in the ways of Europeans. The *Oroolong* reached Macao on 30 August, and Wilson sailed home with Lee-Boo as passenger in the ship *Morse*.

They reached Portsmouth on 14 July 1784. Wilson kept his promise to Abba Thule and began educating the youth, but in spite of all his care Lee-Boo died of smallpox on 27 December. The East India Company had a monument erected to his memory in Rotherhithe cemetery. Henry Wilson returned to sea, in the service of the company, later retiring to Colyton, Devon, where he died in August 1810 "at an advanced age."

An account of the wreck *The History of Prince Lee Boo, a Native of the Pelew Islands brought to England by Captain Wilson* (London, 1788; Philadelphia, 1802), written by George Keate, was widely read and contains useful information about the little-known Palau group.

## Wilson

JAMES WILSON was born in England in 1769 and went to India at an early age, working for the East India Company. He gained experience as a seaman and a navigator. He was taken prisoner by the French, escaped, but was recaptured by soldiers of the maharajah of Mysore, who was then a bitter enemy of England, and suffered great hardships. Eventually released, he went into trade, acquired considerable wealth, and retired in 1792.

Back in England, Wilson settled near Portsea in Hampshire and in 1795 was converted to active Christianity. The London Missionary Society, which had been founded in that year, came to Wilson's attention; and when he learned that it had bought a ship, the *Duff*, in April 1796, to take missionaries to the South Seas, he wrote offering his services as captain and was accepted.

The *Duff* sailed from the Thames on 10 August 1796 making for Portsmouth, where it joined the East India convoy, leaving on the twenty-fifth. Aboard were four clergymen, a number of artisans, and their wives and children. Wilson made for Port Praya and Rio, where the travelers were well received but expressed their disapproval of this "popish place" where the people seemed "sunk in idolatry." His intention was to enter the Pacific by way of Cape Horn, but the weather was so bad and the passengers so affected by the wild seas that on 3 December he decided to make for Australia. The southern Indian Ocean was no gentler than the South Atlantic, but progress was better. In late January 1797 the *Duff* was far to the south of Tasmania, going toward southern New Zealand, then sailing past the lonely Bounty Islands in early February, and north toward the Society Islands.

Tupai was sighted on 22 February, fourteen weeks since they had last seen land, at Rio. The aim being to set up the first missionary settlement at Tahiti, they went on their way, in storms and heavy rain, and anchored in Matavai Bay, Tahiti, on 6 March. On the twenty-sixth the *Duff* sailed for Tongatabu, where another missionary outpost was planned, and thence to the Marquesas. On 19 May, Wilson came upon two uncharted islands on the southeastern fringe of the Tuamotus. He named them Gambier's Islands; they are Timoe and Mangareva. On the twenty-eighth another discovery was made, which Wilson named Serle's Island; it was Pukarua.

On 5 June 1797 the *Duff* arrived at Resolution Bay, Tahuata, in the Marquesas. After leaving one missionary ashore, Wilson sailed to the neighboring islands of Huapu and Nuku Hiva and then left for Tahiti, where he again dropped anchor on 6 July. Satisfied that the missionaries were settling in adequately, he left finally on 4 August for Tonga, where he found the small missionary outpost coping well in the new environment.

On 7 September 1797 the *Duff* sailed for home. A sighting was made the next day of various small islands in the Lau group of the Fiji archipelago that can be claimed as discoveries. On the twenty-fifth, a group of islands hove into sight; these were named the Duff Islands (Santa Cruz Islands group), a name they retain. Situated to the northeast of Santa Cruz, they had been seen by Spanish navigators, but Wilson was the first to give their precise bearing. He continued on a northwesterly course and on 25 October discovered a number of small islands belonging to the Palau group.

James Wilson sailed on to China, passing north of the Philippines to Macao, where he dropped anchor on 21 November 1797. He took in a cargo of tea for England and had the *Duff* repaired. The strict moral code enforced on board Wilson's ship led sailors from other vessels to nickname it "The Ten Commandments."

The *Duff* sailed from China on 5 January 1798 with a convoy of merchantmen for Malacca and the Indian Ocean, reaching Cork in Ireland on 24 June, and finally dropping anchor in the Thames on 11 July 1798. James Wilson did not return to sea. He settled in London, married in 1799, and died in 1814, leaving a son and four daughters. The narrative of his voyage, published in 1799 as *A Missionary Voyage to the Southern Pacific Ocean*, contains much valuable ethnologic and geographic information.

## Wrangel

FERDINAND PETROVICH (VON) WRANGEL (Vrangel) was born of a noble family at Pskov, northwest Russia, on 29 December 1796. He graduated from the Cadet Naval School in 1815 and two years later sailed with Golovin *(q.v.)* in the *Kamchatka* by way of Cape Horn and South America to Kamchatka, and from there across the central Pacific, calling at the Hawaiian Islands and Manila. The circumnavigation was completed by the Cape of Good Hope and the Atlantic.

Wrangel was back in Russia in 1819 to prepare for the Kolyma expedition, which he led from 1820 to 1824. His work in the frozen wastes of northern Siberia established that an open sea lay to the north—the great East Siberian Sea—and helped to delineate the continent. As soon as he was back in Russia he began to prepare for the circumnavigation of the *Krotkii*, which sailed under his command in 1825. The voyage, which lasted three years, made no discoveries but carried out important scientific experiments in the Pacific Ocean and called at the Russian settlements in North America. When the *Krotkii* expedition came to an end in 1827, Wrangel enjoyed only a brief respite before returning to the Pacific: he was appointed chief administrator of the Russian settlements in America, a post he held from 1829 to 1835. He had already supervised the post at Sitka, and his interest in defending Russian interests in North America deepened when he was appointed director of the Russian American Company in 1840, a position he kept for ten years. He later became naval minister, using all his influence to stall plans to sell Russian Alaska to the United States.

Wrangel retired with the rank of admiral in 1864 and lived long enough to witness the sale of Alaska in 1867. He died at Tartu on 25 May 1870. A number of geographical features are named after him, including Wrangel Island in the East Siberian Sea (this was not discovered by him but by an American who gave it the name because Wrangel had reported its rumored existence), Cape Wrangell *(sic)* on Attu Island, the Wrangel Mountains, and Wrangell-Saint Elias National Park in Alaska.

His *Voyage along the Northern Coast of Siberia and the Arctic* was published in 1841.

# Selected Bibliography

Among the works cited here, some deserve special note. Certain general studies of Pacific voyages are especially useful in providing concise descriptions of the various navigators' travels, trials, and accomplishments. J. C. Beaglehole's *The Exploration of the Pacific* is excellent for the first period up to 1789; Ernest S. Dodge's *Beyond the Capes* takes up the story at 1766 and carries it on to 1877. Herman R. Friis edited a useful nation-by-nation survey, *The Pacific Basin: A History of Its Geographical Exploration*. Andrew Sharp's *The Discovery of the Pacific Islands* analyzes the achievements of each discoverer on a chronological basis. John Dunmore's *French Explorers in the Pacific* deals with the French from the earliest years to 1840. Colin Jack-Hinton's *The Search for the Islands of Solomon 1567–1838* is useful for the Spanish and the southwest Pacific, although skimpy on biographical information. Glynn Barratt's three-volume work, *Russia and the South Pacific 1696–1840*, is most useful for Russian navigators, as is his *Russia in Pacific Waters 1715–1825*. The voyages of American whalers are surveyed in E. A. Stackpole's *The Sea Hunters*, although here again biographical details are skimpy. O. H. K. Spate's history of the Pacific since Magellan most successfully brings these many strands together. Marginal to the present work but useful in the analysis they provide of the meeting of European and Polynesian-Melanesian cultures are such works as Bernard Smith's *European Vision and the South Pacific 1768–1850* (Oxford, 1969), Kerry R. Howe's *Where the Waves Fall*, and Dorothy Shineberg's *They Came for Sandalwood*.

Biographies have been written of a number of major figures in Pacific exploration, namely Cook, Magellan, Drake, Bougainville, La Pérouse, Dampier, Bligh, Vancouver. Many are featured in the various national dictionaries of biography. The British multivolume *Dictionary of National Biography* lays stress on the senior figures of the Royal Navy, consolidating earlier specialized collected biographies such as J. Charnock's *Biographia Navalis*, J. Campbell's *Lives of the British Admirals*, J. Marshall's *Royal Naval Biography or Memoirs of the Services*, and W. R. O'Byrne's *A Naval*

273

*Biographical Dictionary.* The Frenchman Hoefer edited a useful *Nouvelle Biographie Générale* (Paris, 1853–1866), now superseded by the great *Dictionnaire de Biographie Française.* The *Australian Dictionary of Biography* appeared in Melbourne between 1966 and 1982, the *Dictionary of Canadian Biography* began publication in Toronto in 1966, and the large *Dictionary of American Biography*, started in New York in 1928 and reprinted in 1946, was still adding new volumes in the 1980s. All these have been drawn upon for the present work, as were the *Great Soviet Encyclopedia*, the Spanish *Galería Biográfica de los Generales de Marina*, the *Biblioteca Maritima Española* (ed. M. F. de Navarrete, 1851), and the *Diccionario de Geografía, Historia y Biografía Méxicanas.*

Apart from general works of references, titles are grouped according to the country with which the voyage or voyages were associated. An edited text is usually listed under the name of the editor; a translated text appears under the name of the author.

## General Works

*Allgemeine Deutsche Biographie.* Leipzig, 1885–1891.

*Australian Dictionary of Biography.* Melbourne, 1966–1982.

Bancroft, H. H. *History of Alaska from 1730 to 1883.* San Francisco, 1886.

———. *History of California.* San Francisco, 1884.

———. *History of the Northwest Coast.* 2 vols. San Francisco, 1884.

Beaglehole, J. C. *The Discovery of New Zealand.* 2d ed. London, 1961.

———. *The Exploration of the Pacific.* London, 1934. (New editions 1947 and 1966.)

Bellwood, P. *Man's Conquest of the Pacific.* Auckland, 1978.

Bériot, A. *Grands Voiliers autour du Monde: les Voyages Scientifiques 1760–1850.* Paris, 1962.

Besson, M. *The Scourge of the Indies: Buccaneers, Corsairs and Filibusters.* New York, 1929.

*Biographie Universelle Ancienne et Moderne.* Paris, 1843–1865.

Bradley, H. W. "The Hawaiian Islands and the Pacific Fur Trade 1785–1813." *Pacific Northwest Quarterly* 30 (1934): 275–299.

Brosses, C. de. *Histoire des Navigations aux Terres Australes.* 2 vols. Paris, 1756.

Brosses, J. *Great Voyages of Exploration: the Golden Age of Discovery in the Pacific.* Translated by S. Hochman. Lane Cove (Australia), 1983.

Burney, J. *A Chronological History of the Discoveries in the South Sea or Pacific Ocean.* 5 vols. London, 1803–1807.

———. *A Chronological History of North-Eastern Voyages of Discovery.* London, 1819.

Callander, J. *Terra Australis Cognita, or Voyages to the Terra Australis or*

*Southern Hemisphere during the sixteenth, seventeenth and eighteenth centuries.* 5 vols. London, 1766–1768.

Campbell, J., and Stevenson, W. *Lives of the British Admirals.* 8 vols. London, 1816–1817.

Charnock, J. *Biographia Navalis.* 6 vols. London, 1794–1798.

Charton, E. *Voyageurs Anciens et Modernes.* 4 vols. Paris, 1854–1857.

Cortesaõ, A. "A Expansaõ Portuguesa atraves do Pacifico." In *Historia da Expansaõ Porguesa no Mundo,* edited by Baiao et al. Lisbon, 1939.

Dalrymple, A. *An Account of the Discoveries made in the South Pacifick Ocean previous to 1764.* London, 1767.

——. *An Historical Collection of the Several Voyages and Discoveries in the South Pacific Ocean,* 2 vols. London, 1770–1771.

*Dansk Biografisk Leksikon.* Copenhagen, 1933–1944.

*Deutsch-Baltisches Biographisches Lexicon 1710–1960.* Cologne, 1970.

*Diccionario Biográfico Colonial de Chile.* Santiago, 1906.

*Diccionario de Geografía, Historia y Biografía Méxicanas.* Mexico, 1910.

*Diccionario Histórico-Biográfico del Peru.* Lima, 1931–1934 (with Appendices, Lima, 1935–1938).

*Diccionario Marítimo Español.* Madrid, 1864.

*Dictionary of American Biography.* New York, 1946 rept., 11 vols. and supplements.

*Dictionary of Canadian Biography.* Toronto, 1966–1982.

*Dictionary of National Biography.* London, 1885–1927.

*Dictionary of New Zealand Biography.* Wellington, 1940; 1990–.

*Dictionnaire de Biographie Française.* Vols. i–. Paris, 1933–.

Dodge, E. S. *Beyond the Capes: Pacific Exploration from Captain Cook to the "Challenger" 1776–1877.* London, 1971.

——. *Islands and Empire: Western Impact on the Pacific and East Asia.* Minneapolis, 1976.

Friis, H. R., ed. *The Pacific Basin: A History of its Geographical Exploration.* New York, 1967.

*Galería Biográfica de los Generales de Marina, Jefes y Personages Notables . . . desde 1700 à 1868.* Madrid, 1873.

Gosse, P. *The Pirate's Who's Who.* London, 1924.

*Great Soviet Encyclopedia.* Moscow and New York, 1973–1980.

Heawood, E. *A History of Geographical Discovery in the Seventeenth and Eighteenth Centuries.* London, 1912.

Heyerdahl, T. *American Indians in the Pacific: The Theory behind the Kon-Tiki Expedition.* London, 1952.

——. *Sea Routes to Polynesia.* London, 1968.

Howard A. "Polynesian Origins and Migrations: A Review of Two Centuries of Speculation and Theory." In *Polynesian Culture History,* edited by G. A. Highland, pp. 45–101. Honolulu, 1967.

Howe, K. R. *Where the Waves Fall: A New South Sea Islands History from First Settlement to Colonial Rule.* Sydney, 1984.

Jack-Hinton, C. *The Search for the Islands of Solomon 1567-1838.* Oxford, 1969.

Jenkins, J. S. *Recent Exploring Expeditions to the Pacific and the South Seas, under the American, English and French Governments.* London, 1853.

Judd, B. *Voyages to Hawaii before 1860.* Honolulu, 1929.

Laird-Clowes, W. *A History of the Royal Navy.* 7 vols. London, 1899-1904.

Langdon, R. "The Maritime Explorers." In *Friendly Islands: A History of Tonga,* edited by N. Rutherford, pp. 40-62. Melbourne, 1977.

Lewis, D. *We, the Navigators: The Ancient Art of Landfinding in the Pacific.* Canberra, 1973.

Lloyd, C. *Pacific Horizons: The Exploration of the Pacific before Captain Cook.* London, 1946.

Major, R. *Early Voyages to Terra Australis.* London, 1859.

Marshall, J. *Royal Naval Biography: or Memoirs of the Services.* 12 vols. London, 1823-1835.

National Maritime Museum. *The Commissioned Sea Officers of the Royal Navy 1660-1815.* 3 vols. London, 1954.

Navarette, M. F. de. *Biblioteca Maritima Española.* 2 vols. New York, 1968 (reprint of 1851 ed.).

*Neue Deutsche Biographie.* Berlin, 1952-1987.

*Nouvelle Biographie Générale.* Paris, 1853-1866.

O'Byrne, W. R. *A Naval Biographical Dictionary.* London, 1849.

Ogden, A. *The California Sea Otter Trade 1784-1848.* Berkeley, 1941.

O'Reilly, P. *Calédoniens: Répertoire Bio-bibliographique de la Nouvelle-Calédonie.* Paris, 1953.

———. *Hébridais: Répertoire bio-bibliographique des Nouvelles-Hébrides.* Paris, 1957.

———, and Teissier, R. *Tahitiens, répertoire bio-bibliographique de la Polynésie française.* Paris, 1962.

Pearson, W. H. "The Reception of European Voyagers on Polynesian Islands 1568-1797." *Journal de la Société des Océanistes* 26 (1970): 121-154.

Pierce, R. A., ed. *F. W. Howay: A List of Trading Vessels in the Maritime Fur Trade 1785-1825.* Kingston (Ontario), 1973.

Ralfe, J. *Naval Biography.* 5 vols. London, 1828.

Rainaud, A. *Le Continent Austral: Hypothèses et Découvertes.* Paris, 1893.

Randier, J. *Hommes et Navires au Cap Horn 1616-1939.* Paris, 1966.

Sharp, C. A. *Ancient Voyagers in the Pacific.* Wellington, 1956.

———. *The Discovery of Australia.* Oxford, 1963.

———. *The Discovery of the Pacific Islands.* Oxford, 1960.

Skelton, R. A. *Explorers' Maps.* London, 1958.

Slevin, J. R. *The Galapagos Islands: A History of their Discovery.* San Francisco, 1959.

Smith, B. *European Vision and the South Pacific 1768–1850.* Oxford, 1969.

Snow, P., and Waine, S. *The People from the Horizon: An Illustrated History of the Europeans among the South Sea Islanders.* London, 1986.

Spate, O. H. K. *The Pacific since Magellan:* I. *The Spanish Lake;* II. *Monopolists and Freebooters;* III. *Paradise Lost and Found,* 1987. London and Canberra, 1979–1987.

Stephan, J. J. *Sakhalin: A History,* Oxford, 1971.

———. *The Kuril Islands.* Oxford, 1974.

Thévenot, M. *Relations de Divers Voyages Curieux.* 4 vols. Paris, 1663–1672.

Wagner, H. R. "Apocryphal Voyages to the Northwest Coast of America." *Proceedings of the American Antiquarian Society* 61 (1931): 179–234.

———. *The Cartography of the Northwest Coast of America to the year 1800.* 2 vols. Berkeley, 1937.

Wright, H. *New Zealand 1769–1840: Early Years of Western Contact.* Cambridge (Mass.), 1959.

Wroth, L. C. *The Early Cartography of the Pacific.* New York, 1944.

Wycherley, G. *Buccaneers of the Pacific.* London, n.d.

### France

*An Account of the Visit of the French frigate "L'Artémise" to the Sandwich Islands.* Honolulu, 1839.

Allen, E. W. "Jean François Galaup de Lapérouse, a checklist." *California Historical Society Quarterly* 20 (1941): 47–64.

Amalric, P., et al., eds. *Bicentenaire du Voyage de Lapérouse 1785–1788.* Albi, 1988.

Arago, J. E. V. *Promenade autour du monde . . . sur les corvettes du Roi "L'Uranie" et "la Physicienne".* 2 vols. Paris, 1822.

Audouard, J. *Une Famille Provençale au XVIIIe Siècle: les Bruny d'Entrecasteaux.* Paris, 1910.

Bassett, F. M. *Realms and Islands: The World Voyage of Rose de Freycinet in the corvette "Uranie" 1817–1820.* London, 1962.

Baudin, N. T. *The Journal of Post-Captain Nicolas Baudin.* Translated by C. Cornell. Adelaide, 1974.

Bellec, F. *La Généreuse et Tragique Expédition Lapérouse.* 2 vols. Paris, 1985.

———. "Le Naufrage de l'Expédition Lapérouse." *Neptunia* 149 (1983): 1–11, and 150 (1983): 1–14.

Bellesort, A. *La Pérouse.* Paris, 1926.

Berthelot, P. "Antoine-Raymond-Joseph Bruny, Chevalier d'Entrecasteaux, contre-amiral (1737–1793)." *Bulletin de la Société d'Études Scientifiques et Archéologiques de Draguignan* 12 (1968): 75–107.

Blosseville, E. P. de. *Jules de Blosseville.* Evreux, 1854.

Blosseville, J. A. R. P. de. "Mémoire géographique sur la Nouvelle-Zélande." *Nouvelles Annales des Voyages* 29 (1826): 5–35.

Bougainville, H. Y. P. de. *Journal de la Navigation Autour du Globe de "La Thétis" et "L'Espérance" pendant les années 1824, 1825, et 1826.* 2 vols. Paris, 1837.

Bougainville, L. A. de. *Voyage autour du monde par la frégate du Roi "La Boudeuse" et la flute "L'Etoile" en 1766–1769.* Paris, 1771.

Bouvier, R., and Maynial, E. *Une Aventure dans les Mers Australes: l'Expédition du commandant Baudin (1800–1803).* Paris, 1947.

Brossard, M. de. *Lapérouse: des Combats à la Découverte.* Paris, 1978.

———. *Rendez-vous avec Lapérouse à Vanikoro.* Paris, 1964.

Buffet, H. F. "L'Explorateur Malouin Marion de Fresne." *Mémoires de la Société d'Histoire et d'Archéologie de Bretagne.* Rennes, 1959.

———. "L'Explorateur port-louisien Julien Crozet, Eponyme des îles Crozet dans la Mer des Indes." *Mémoires de la Société d'Histoire et d'Archeologie de Bretagne.* Rennes, 1943.

———. "Voyage à la Découverte du port-louisien Surville." *Mémoires de la Société d'Histoire et d'Archéologie de Bretagne.* Rennes, 1950.

Buick, T. L. *The French at Akaroa.* Wellington, 1929.

Burney, J. *A Memoir of the Voyage of d'Entrecasteaux in search of La Pérouse.* London, 1820.

Busson, J. P., ed. "Des Gambiers à Upolu avec Dumont d'Urville. Souvenirs d'un quartier-maître de l'*Astrolabe* 1838." *Revue Historique de l'Armée* 21, 3 (1965): 49–61.

Cabrié, M. *Éloge de l'Amiral Dumont d'Urville.* Versailles, 1843.

Cap, P. A. *Philibert Commerson, naturaliste, voyageur.* Paris, 1861.

Chevalier, A. "Un Grand Voyageur Naturaliste Normand J. J. La Billardière (1755–1834)." *Revue Internationale de Botanique Appliquée,* March–June 1953.

Chevrier, R. *Bougainville: Voyage en Océanie.* Paris, 1846.

Chinard, G. *Le Voyage de Lapérouse sur les Côtes de l'Alaska et de la Californie.* Baltimore, 1937.

Cooper, H. M. *French Exploration in South Australia.* Adelaide, 1952.

Cordier, H. "La Mission de M. le Chevalier d'Entrecasteaux à Canton en 1787." *Bulletin de Géographie Historique et Descriptive* 3 (1911): 407–446.

Cornell, C. *Questions Relating to Nicolas Baudin's Australian Expedition 1800–1804.* Adelaide, 1965.

Crozet, J. *Crozet's Voyage to Tasmania, New Zealand, the Ladrones Islands and the Philippines 1771–1772.* Translated by H. L. Roth. London, 1891.

Dahlgren, E. W. *Les Relations Commerciales et Maritimes entre la France et les côtes de l'Océan Pacifique (Commencement du XVIIIe Siècle).* Paris, 1909.

———. "L'Expédition Martinez et la fin du commerce français dans la Mer du Sud." *Revue d'Histoire des Colonies Françaises* (1913): 257–332.

———. "Voyages Français à Destination de la Mer du Sud avant Bougainville (1695-1749)." *Nouvelles Archives des Missions Scientifiques* 14 (1907): 423–568.

Day, G. *Dumont d'Urville.* Paris, 1947.

Demeulenaere, O. "Quand la Nouvelle-Zelande était Française." *Cahiers d'Histoire du Pacifique* 8 (Jan. 1978): 39–68.

Dezos de la Roquette, J. B. "Notice sur la Vie, les Travaux et les Services de M. le Chavalier de Rossel." *Annales Maritimes* 32 (1847): 49–57.

Dixon W. "Dumont d'Urville and Lapérouse." *Journal of the Royal Australian Historical Society* 21 (1936).

Dondo, M. M. *La Pérouse in Maui.* Hawaii, 1959.

Dorsenne, J. *La Vie de Bougainville.* Paris, 1930.

Duhaut-Cilly, A. *Voyage autour du Monde principalement à la Californie et aux îles Sandwich.* 2 vols. Paris, 1834–1835.

Dumont d'Urville, J. S. C. *Mémoires sur les îles Loyalty.* Paris, 1829.

———. *Voyage au Pôle Sud et dans l'Océanie sur les corvettes "L'Astrolabe" et "La Zélée".* 10 vols. Paris, 1841–1846.

———. *Voyage de Découvertes autour du Monde . . . sur la corvette "L'Astrolabe" pendant les Années 1826-1829.* 5 vols. Paris, 1832–1848.

———. *Voyage pittoresque autour du Monde.* 2 vols. Paris, 1835.

Dunmore, J. *French Explorers in the Pacific.* 2 vols. Oxford, 1965–1969.

———. *Pacific Explorer: The Life of Jean-François de La Pérouse.* Annapolis, 1985.

Dunmore, J., ed. *The Expedition of the "St. Jean-Baptiste" to the Pacific 1769-1770.* London, 1981.

———, and Brossard, M. de. *Le Voyage de Lapérouse 1785-1788.* 2 vols. Paris, 1985.

Duperrey, L. I. *Mémoire sur les opérations géographiques faites dans la campagne de la corvette de S.M. "La Coquille".* Paris, n.d. [1827].

———. *Voyage autour du Monde exécuté par ordre du Roi sur la corvette "La Coquille" pendant les Années 1822-1825.* Paris, 1826.

Dupetit-Thouars, A. A. *Voyage autour du Monde sur la Frégate "La Vénus" pendant les Années 1836-1839.* 4 vols. Paris, 1840–1843.

Duplomb, C. *Campagne de "L'Uranie": Journal de Madame Rose de Saulces de Freycinet.* Paris, 1937.

———. *D'Entrecasteaux: Rien que la Mer, un Peu de Gloire.* Paris, 1983.

———. "Le Contre-Amiral Rossel." *La Géographie* 59 (1933): 151–153.

———. See also under Freycinet, Rose de.

Emmanuel, M. *La France et l'Exploration Polaire de Verrazano à La Pérouse 1523–1788*. Paris, 1959.

Emmons, G. T. "Native Account of the Meeting between La Pérouse and the Tlingit." *American Anthropologist*. April–June 1911, pp. 294–298.

Faivre, J. P. "La France découvre l'Australie: L'Expédition du *Geógraphe* et du *Naturaliste* 1801–1803." *Australian Journal of French Studies* 2, 1 (1963): 45–58.

———. *Le Contre-amiral Hamelin et la Marine Française*. Paris, 1962.

———. "Les Idéologues de l'An VII et le Voyage de Nicolas Baudin en Australie 1800–1894." *Australian Journal of French Studies* 3, 1 (1966): 3–15.

———. *L'Expansion Française dans le Pacifique de 1800 à 1842*. Paris, 1953.

Fleurieu, C. P. C. de. *Découvertes des François en 1768 et 1769 dans le Sud-Est de la Nouvelle-Guinée*. Paris, 1790.

———. *Voyage autour du Monde pendant les Années 1790, 1791 et 1792 par Etienne Marchand*. 6 vols. Paris, 1789–1809.

Fleuriot de Langle, I. *Le Voyage Extraordinaire de Lapérouse*. 3 vols. Nice, 1971–1972.

Fleuriot de Langle, P. *La Tragique Expédition de Lapérouse et Langle*. Paris, 1954.

Freycinet, L. C. D. de. *Voyage de Découvertes aux terres australes exécuté sur les Corvettes "Le Géographe", "Le Naturaliste" et la Goélette "La Casuarina" . . . 1800–1804*. 2 vols. Paris, 1815.

———. *Voyage autour du Monde entrepris par ordre du Roi . . . sur les corvettes de S.M. "L'Uranie" et "La Physicienne"*. 5 vols. Paris, 1827–1839.

Freycinet, Rose de. *Journal du Voyage autour du Monde à bord de "L'Uranie"*. Edited by C. Duplomb. Paris, 1927.

Froger, F. *Relation d'un Voyage fait en 1695, 1696 et 1697 aux côtes d'Afrique et au Détroit de Magellan par une Escadre du Roi*. Paris, 1698.

Froment-Guiyesse, G. *La Pérouse*. Paris, 1947.

Gautier, A. "Le Père Receveur, Aumonier de l'Expédition La Pérouse." *Courrier des Messageries Maritimes*, no. 140 (1974): 24–34.

Gazel, A. *French Navigators and the Early History of New Zealand*. Wellington, 1946.

Gaziello, C. *L'Expédition de Lapérouse (1785–1788): Réplique Française aux Voyages de Cook*. Paris, 1984.

Girault de Coursac, P. and P. *Le Voyage de Louis XVI autour du Monde: l'Expédition de Lapérouse*. Paris, 1985.

Grille, F. *Louis de Freycinet: sa Vie de Savant et de Marin*. Paris, 1853.

Hapdé, J. B. A. *Expédition et Naufrage de Lapérouse: Recueil Historique*. Paris, 1829.

Hogg, G. H. *D'Entrecasteaux: An Account of his Life, his Expedition and his Officers*. Hobart, 1937.

Horner, F. *The French Reconnaissance: Baudin in Australia 1801–1803.* Melbourne, 1987.

Hulot, G. T. *D'Entrecasteaux 1737–1793.* Paris, 1894.

Inglis, R. *The Lost Voyage of Lapérouse.* Vancouver, 1986.

Jacquier, H. "Jeanne Baret, la première femme autour du monde." *Bulletin de la Société des Études Océaniennes* 12, 141 (1962): 150–156.

Joubert, F. *Dumont d'Urville 1790–1842.* Tours, 1873.

Jurien de la Gravière, J. P. E. *L'Amiral Baudin.* Paris, 1888.

Juteau, R. "Journal de Bord du Capitaine Etienne Marchand, commandant le *Solide.*" *Bulletin de la Société des Études Océaniennes.* 11, 135 (1961): 247–260.

Kelly, L. G. *Marion Dufresne at the Bay of Islands.* Wellington, 1951.

Kerallain, R. de. *La Jeunesse de Bougainville.* Paris, 1896.

Kerneis, A. A. "Le Chevalier de Langle, ses Compagnons de l'*Astrolabe* et de la *Boussole.*" *Bulletin de la Société Académique de Brest,* 1889–1900, pp. 221–288.

La Billardière, J. J. H. de. *Relation du Voyage à la Recherche de La Pérouse.* 2 vols. Paris, 1799.

Lacroix, L. *Les Derniers Baleimiers Français.* Nantes, 1947.

Laplace, C. P. T. de. *Campagne de Circumnavigation de la Frégate "L'Artémise" pendant les Années 1837–1840.* 6 vols. Paris, 1841–1854.

Laplace, C. P. T. *Voyage autour du Monde par les mers de l'Inde et de la Chine exécuté sur la Corvette de l'Etat "La Favorite".* 5 vols. Paris, 1833–1839.

La Roncière, C. G. M. de. *Bougainville.* Paris, 1942.

———. *Histoire de la Marine Française.* 5 vols. Paris, 1899.

———. "Le Premier Voyage Français autour du Monde." *Revue Hebdomadaire.* Sept. 1907, pp. 22–36.

———. "Routier Inédit d'un Compagnon de Bougainville." *La Géographie* 69 (1939): 112–114.

Lefranc, G. *Bougainville et ses Compagnons.* Paris, 1929.

Lesson, R. P. *Journal d'un Voyage Pittoresque autour du Monde exécuté sur la Corvette "La Coquille" commandée par M. L. I. Duperrey.* Paris, 1830.

———. *Voyage autour du Monde entrepris par ordre du Governement sur la Corvette "La Coquille".* 2 vols. Paris, 1838–1839.

———. *Voyage Médical autour du Monde.* Paris, 1829.

———. *Notice Historique sur l'Amiral Dumont d'Urville.* Rocheford, 1846.

Lussan, R. de. *Journal du Voyage fait à la Mer du Sud avec les Flibustiers de l'Amérique en 1684 et Années Suivantes.* Paris, 1689.

Maine, R. *La Pérouse.* Paris, 1946.

Mancy, J. de. *Jules de Blosseville.* Paris, 1835.

Marcel, G. *La Pérouse.* Paris, 1881.

———. *Les Corsaires Français.* Paris, 1902.

Marchand, E. *Découvertes des îles de la Révolution.* Marseilles, 1792.

Marchant, L. R. *France Australe.* Perth, 1982.

————. "The French Discovery and Settlement of New Zealand 1769–1840: A Bibliographical Essay on Naval Records in Paris." *Historical Studies* (Melbourne) 10 (1963): 511–518.

Martin, J. E. "Essai sur Bougainville Circumnavigateur: la Genèse de sa Carrière Maritime." *La Géographie,* 1929, pp. 321–345.

Martin-Allanic, J. E. *Bougainville Navigateur et les Découvertes de son Temps.* Paris, 1964.

Milet-Mureau, N. L. A., ed. *Voyage autour du monde . . . de La Pérouse.* 4 vols. Paris, 1797.

Moerenhout, J. A. *Voyages aux îles du Grand Océan.* 2 vols. Paris, 1837.

Montemont, A. *Relation du Voyage autour du Monde de 1785 à 1788 par La Pérouse, Relation du Voyage de Marion en 1771–1772.* Paris, 1855.

Montessus, F. B. de. *Martyrologe et Biographie de Commerson.* Chalons-sur-Saône, 1889.

Oexmelin, A. *Histoire des Aventuriers qui se sont Signalés dans les Indes.* 2 vols. Paris, 1688.

Oliver, J. J. *Life of Ph. Commerson.* London, 1909.

Péron, F. *Voyage de Découvertes aux Terres Australes . . . sur le "Géographe", le "Naturaliste" et la "Casuarina" pendant les Années 1800–1804.* Paris, 1807.

Pisier, G. *D'Entrecasteaux en Nouvelle-Calédonie.* Noumea, 1976.

Plomley, N. J. B. *The Baudin Expedition and the Tasmanian Aborigines.* Hobart, 1982.

Pomeau, R. "Lapérouse Philosophe." In his *Approches des Lumières,* pp. 357–370. Paris, 1974.

Raulin, G. de. *Dupetit-Thouars.* Paris, 1943.

————. *Rose de Freycinet, Exploratrice Maritime.* Paris, 1944.

Richard, H. *Le Voyage de D'Entrecasteaux à la Recherche de Lapérouse.* Paris, 1986.

————. "L'Expédition de d'Entrecasteaux (1791–1794) et les origines de l'implantation anglaise en Tasmanie." *Revue Française d'Histoire d'Outre-mer* 69 (1982); 289–306.

Rochon, A. M., ed. *Nouveau Voyage à la Mer du Sud commencé sous les ordres de M. Marion du Fresne. On a joint à ce voyage un extrait de celui de M. de Surville.* Paris, 1783.

Roquefeuil, C. de. *Voyage autour du Monde pendant les Années 1816–1819.* Paris, 1823.

Rosenman, H. ed. *Two Voyages to the South Seas, by Captain (later Rear-Admiral) Jules S. C. Dumont d'Urville.* 2 vols. Melbourne, 1987.

Rossel, E. P. E. de, ed. *Voyage de Dentrecasteaux Envoyé à la "Recherche" de La Pérouse.* 2 vols, Paris, 1808.

Roy, B. *Dans le sillage de La Pérouse.* Paris, 1946.

Rudkin, C. N. *The First French Expedition to California*. Los Angeles, 1959.

Saint-Yves, G. *Le Voyage autour du Monde du Capitaine Etienne Marchand*. Paris, 1897.

Scott, E. "Baudin's Voyage of Exploration to Australia." *English Historical Review*, 1913, pp. 341–346.

Scott, E. *Lapérouse*. Sydney, 1912.

————. *Terre Napoleon: A History of French Explorations and Projects in Australia*. London, 1910.

Sharp, C. A. *Duperrey's Visit to New Zealand in 1824*. Wellington, 1971.

Sinclair, K. V. "Laplace at Hobart Town and Sydney Town in 1831: The Humanism of a French Naval Captain." *First Louis Triebel Memorial Lecture*. Hobart, 1986.

Spencer, R. H. "The Visit of the *St. Jean-Baptiste* to Doubtless Bay, New Zealand, 17–31 December 1769." *Cartography*, 14 Sept. 1985, pp. 124–143.

Taillemite, E. *Bougainville et ses Compagnons autour du Monde*. 2 vols. Paris, 1977.

————. "Charles-François Lavaud, de la Nouvelle-Zélande à Tahiti." *Journal de la Société des Océanistes* 38 (1982): 93–97.

————. "Le Lieutenant Caro et sa relation inédite du séjour de Bougainville à Tahiti". *Journal de la Société des Océanistes* 18 (1962): 11–19.

Taylor, N. M. "French Navigators in the Pacific." In *The Pacific: Ocean of Islands*, edited by C. L. Barrett. Melbourne, 1950.

Thiery, M. *Bougainville, Soldier and Sailor*. London, 1932.

Tremewan, P. J. *French Akaroa*. Christchurch (New Zealand), 1990.

Vaillant, A. N. *Voyage autour du Monde exécuté pendant les Années 1836 et 1837 sur la corvette "La Bonite"*. Narrative by A. de La Salle. 3 vols. Paris, 1845–1852.

Vergniol, C. *Dumont d'Urville*. Paris, 1931.

Vieules, P. M. *Centenaire de La Pérouse: Notice sur la Famille et la Vie Privée du Célèbre Marin*. Albi, 1888. Supplement, 1892.

Wilbur, M. E., ed. *Raveneau de Lussan, Buccaneer of the Spanish Main and Early Filibuster of the Pacific*. Cleveland, 1930.

Wright, O., trans. *New Zealand 1826–1827*. Wellington, 1950.

————. *The Voyage of the "Astrolabe", 1840*. Wellington, 1955.

## Great Britain

Alekseev, A. I. "Joseph Billings." *The Geographic Journal* 132, 2 (1966): 233–238.

Anderson, B. *Surveyor of the Sea: The Life and Voyages of George Vancouver*. Seattle, 1960.

Andrews, K. R. *Drake's Voyages*. London, 1967.

Anson, G. *A Voyage round the World, compiled from papers and other materials of the Right Honourable George Lord Anson.* London, 1748.

Austin, K. A. *The Voyage of the "Investigator" 1801–1803: Commander Matthew Flinders R.N.* Adelaide, 1964.

Bach, J. *William Bligh.* Melbourne, 1967.

————, ed. *The Bligh Notebook.* Canberra, 1987.

Barlow, N., ed. *Charles Darwin and the Voyage of the "Beagle".* London, 1945.

————. *Diary of the Voyage of HMS "Beagle".* Cambridge, 1933.

Barrow, J. *Eventful History of the Mutiny and Piratical Seizure of HMS "Bounty".* London, 1831.

————. *The Life of George, Lord Anson.* London, 1839.

Bassett, F. M. *Behind the Picture: HMS "Rattlesnake".* Melbourne, 1968.

Beaglehole, J. C. *The Life of Captain James Cook.* London, 1974.

————, ed. *The "Endeavour" Journals of Joseph Banks 1768–1771.* 2 vols. Sydney, 1962.

————. *The Journals of Captain James Cook on his Voyages of Discovery.* 4 vols. Cambridge, 1955–1974.

Beddie, M. K. *Bibliography of Captain James Cook.* Sydney, 1970.

Beechey, F. W. *Narrative of a Voyage to the Pacific and Beering's Strait . . . in the ship "Blossom".* 2 vols. London, 1831.

Belcher, Edward. *Narrative of a Voyage round the World performed in HMS ship "Sulphur" during the years 1836–1842.* 2 vols. London, 1843.

————. *Narrative of the Voyage of HMS "Samarang" during 1843–1846.* 2 vols. London, 1848.

————. *The Last of the Arctic Voyages.* London, 1855.

Bell, E., ed. "The Log of the *Chatham* (by Peter Puget)," *Honolulu Mercury* 1, 4 (1929).

Bennett, F. D. *Narrative of a Whaling Voyage round the Globe from the year 1833 to 1836.* London, 1842.

Bladen, F. M. "Notes on the Life of John Hunter." *Journal of the Royal Australian Historical Society* 1 (1901), 21.

Bligh, F. S. *Captain Tobias Furneaux R.N.* Plymouth, 1952.

Bligh W. *A Narrative of the Mutiny on board His Majesty's Ship the "Bounty".* London, 1790. Australiana Facsimile. Canberra, 1952.

————. *A Voyage to the South Sea undertaken by command of His Majesty . . . in HM's ship the "Bounty".* 2 vols. London, 1792.

————. *The Log of the Bounty.* 2 vols. London, 1937.

Bodi, L. "Georg Forster: The Pacific Expert of Eighteenth Century Germany." *Historical Studies of Australia and New Zealand* 8, 8 (1954): 345–363.

Bonner, W. H. *Captain William Dampier: Buccaneer-Author.* Palo Alto (Calif.), 1934.

Bowden, K. W. *George Bass, 1771–1803.* Melbourne, 1952.

Brent, P. *Charles Darwin.* London, 1981.

Broughton, W. R. *A Voyage of Discovery to the North Pacific Ocean*. London, 1804.

Bulkeley, J., and Cummins, J. *A Voyage to the South-Seas by His Majesty's Ship "Wager"*. London, 1743.

Byron, G. A. *The Voyage of HMS "Blonde" to the Sandwich Islands 1824–1825*. London, 1826.

Byron, J. *A Journal of a Voyage round the World in HM's Ship the "Dolphin"*. London, 1767.

Cameron, H. C. *Sir Joseph Banks K.B., P.R.S.: The Autocrat of the Philosophers*. London, 1952.

Campbell, A. *A Voyage round the World from 1806 to 1812*. Edinburgh, 1816.

Campbell, G. G. *Log-Letters from the "Challenger"*. London, 1877.

Carrington H. ed. *The Discovery of Tahiti: A Journal of the Second Voyage of HMS "Dolphin" under the command of Captain Wallis RN*. London, 1948.

Cheyne, A. *A Description of Islands in the Western Pacific Ocean north and south of the Equator*. London, 1852.

———. *Sailing Directions from New South Wales to China and Japan; including the whole islands and dangers in the Western Pacific Ocean*. London, 1855.

Chisholm, J. *Brind of the Bay of Islands*. Wellington, 1979.

Cobley, J. *Sydney Cove 1788*. London, 1962.

Collins, D. *An Account of the English Colony in New South Wales*. 2 vols. London, 1798.

Colnett, J. *A Voyage to the South Atlantic and round Cape Horn into the Pacific Ocean*. London, 1798.

Cook, J. *A Voyage to the Pacific Ocean in the years 1776 . . . 1780*. 3 vols. (Vol. 3 by Capt. J. King.) London, 1784.

———. *A Voyage towards the South Pole and round the World . . . in the years 1772 . . . 1775*. 2 vols. London, 1777.

Cooke, E. *A Voyage to the South Sea and round the World*. London, 1712.

Cooper, H. M. *The Unknown Coast: Flinders on the South Australian Coast, 1802*. Adelaide, 1953. *Supplement*, 1955.

Corbett, J. *Drake and the Tudor Navy*. 2 vols. London, 1898.

Corney, P. *Voyages in the North Pacific: the narrative of several trading voyages from 1813 to 1818 between the Northwest Coast, the Hawaiian Islands and China*. Honolulu, 1896.

Dampier, W. *A New Voyage round the World*. London, 1697.

———. *A Voyage to New Holland in 1699*. London, 1703.

———. *Vindication of his Voyage to the South Seas*. London, 1707.

Danielsson, B. *What Happened on the "Bounty"*. London, 1963.

Darwin, C. *Journal of Researches during the Voyage of the "Beagle"*. London, 1840.

———. *The Voyage of the "Beagle"*. London, 1845.

Darwin, F. *Charles Darwin*. London, 1908.

Davidson, J. W. "Peter Dillon and the South Seas." *History Today* 6 (1956): 307–317.

———. *Peter Dillon of Vanikoro: Chevalier of the South Seas*. Melbourne, 1975.

Dawson, W. R., ed. *The Banks Letters*. London, 1958.

Dillon, P. *Narrative and Successful Result of a Voyage in the South Seas . . . to ascertain the fate of La Pérouse's expedition*. 2 vols. London, 1829.

Dixon, G. *A Voyage round the World*. London, 1789.

———. *Further Remarks on the Voyages of John Meares, Esq*. London, 1791.

———. *The Navigator's Assistant*. London, 1791.

———. *Remarks on the Voyages of John Meares, Esq*. London, 1790.

Drake, F. *The World Encompassed*. With an appreciation by R. C. Temple. London, 1926.

Duncan, A. *A Short Account of the Life of the Rt Hon. Sir Joseph Banks*. Edinburgh, 1821.

Edwards, E., and Hamilton, G. *Voyages of HMS "Pandora"*. London, 1917.

Elliott-Joyce, L. E., ed. *A New Voyage and Description of the Isthmus of America*. Oxford, 1934.

Ellis, J. *John William*. London, n.d.

Enderby, C. *The Auckland Islands: A Short Account*. London, 1849.

Engel, L., ed. *The Voyage of the "Beagle"*. New York, 1962.

Erskine, J. E. *Journal of a Cruise among the Islands of the Western Pacific*. London, 1853.

Esquemeling, J., and Ringrose, B. *The Buccaneers of America*. London, 1678.

Fanning, E. *Voyages and Discoveries in the South Seas, 1792–1832*. Salem (Mass.), 1924.

———. *Voyages round the World*. New York, 1833.

———. *Voyages to the South Seas, Indian and Pacific Oceans, China Sea, North-west Coast, Feejee Islands, South Shetlands, etc*. New York, 1838.

Fisher, R., and Johnston, H., eds. *Captain James Cook and his Times*. Vancouver, 1979.

Fitzhardinge, L. F., ed. *Watkin Tench: Sydney's First Four Years*. Sydney, 1979.

Fitzroy, R. *Narrative of the Surveying Voyages of His Majesty's Ships "Adventure" and "Beagle"*. 3 vols. (vol. 3 by Charles Darwin). London, 1839.

Flinders, M. *A Voyage to Terra Australis . . . in the ship "The Investigator"*. 2 vols. London, 1814.

Forster, G. *A Voyage round the World in His Britannic Majesty's sloop "Resolution" . . . during the years 1772,3,4 and 5*. 2 vols. London, 1777.

Forster, J. R. *Observations made during a Voyage round the World*. London, 1778.

Fry, H. T. *Alexander Dalrymple (1737-1808) and the Expansion of British Trade*. Toronto, 1970.

Fryer, J. *The Voyage of the "Bounty" Launch*. Adelaide, 1979.

Funnell, W. *A Voyage round the World, containing an Account of Captain Dampier's Expedition into the South Seas in the Years 1703 and 1704*. London, 1707.

Furneaux, R. *Tobias Furneaux, Circumnavigator*. London, 1960.

Gallagher, R. E., ed. *Byron's Journal of his Circumnavigation 1764-1766*. Cambridge, 1964.

Gerhard, P. *Pirates on the West Coast of New Spain 1575-1742*. Glendale (Calif.), 1960.

Gilbert, T. *Voyage from New South Wales to Canton in the Year 1788*. London, 1789.

Godwin, G. *Vancouver: A Life 1757-1798*. London, 1930.

Gough, B. M. *The Royal Navy and the Northwest Coast of North America 1810-1914: A Study of British maritime ascendancy*. Vancouver, 1971.

————, ed. *To the Pacific and Arctic with Beechey: The Journal of Lieutenant George Peard of HMS "Blossom" 1825-1828*. Hakluyt Society, Cambridge, 1973.

Graham, M. *Voyage of HMS "Blonde" to the Sandwich Islands 1824-1825*. London, 1826.

Gutch, J. *Beyond the Reefs: The Life of John Williams*. London, 1974.

Hampden, J., ed. *Francis Drake, Privateer*. London, 1972.

Hawkesworth, J. *An Account of the Voyages . . . by Commodore Byron, Captain Wallis, Captain Carteret and Captain Cook*. 3 vols. London, 1773.

Hawkins, R. *Observations in his Voyage into the South Sea*. London, 1622.

Heaps, L., ed. *Log of the "Centurion", based on the original papers of Captain Philip Saumarez on board HMS "Centurion", Lord Anson's flagship during his circumnavigation 1740-1744*. London, 1973.

Henry, D. *An Historical Account of all the Voyages round the World performed by English Navigators*. London, 1774.

Hoare, M. E. "Johann Reinhold Forster: The Neglected Philosopher of Cook's Second Voyage (1772-1775)." *Journal of Pacific History* 2 (1967): 215-224.

————. "The Legacy of J. R. Forster to European Science and Letters before Cook's Second Voyage." In *James Cook: Image and Impact*, edited by W. Veit, vol. 2, pp. 64-75. Melbourne, 1982.

————. *The Tactless Philosopher: Johann Reinhold Forster*. Melbourne, 1976.

————, ed. *The "Resolution" Journal of Johann Reinhold Forster 1772-1775*. 4 vols. Cambridge, 1982.

Hooker, J. D. *The Journal of the Rt Hon. Sir Joseph Banks during Captain Cook's First Voyage.* London, 1896.

Hooper, B. *With Captain Cook in the Antarctic and Pacific: The Private Journal of James Burney.* Canberra, 1975.

Hough, R. *Captain Bligh and Mr. Christian.* London, 1972.

Howay, F. W. "James Colnett and the *Princess Royal.*" *Oregon Historical Quarterly* 25 (1924): 36–52.

———, ed. *The Dixon-Meares Controversy.* Toronto, 1929.

———. *The Journal of Captain James Colnett aboard the "Argonaut" from April 26, 1789 to November 3, 1791.* Toronto, 1940.

Hunter, J. *An Historical Journal of the Transactions at Port Jackson and Norfolk Island.* London, 1793.

Huxley, T. H. *Diary of the Voyage of HMS "Rattlesnake", July 1847 to October 1850.* London, 1935.

Joerger, P. K., ed. *To the Sandwich Islands on HMS "Blonde".* Honolulu, 1971.

Jore, L. "Le Capitaine irlandais Thomas Ebrill, sauveteur de la frégate *L'Artémise.*" *Bulletin de la Société des Études Océaniennes* 11 (1961): 261–280.

Jukes, J. B. *Narrative of the Surveying Voyage of HMS "Fly" commanded by Captain F. P. Blackwood . . . during the years 1842–1846.* 2 vols. London, 1847.

Keate, G. *An Account of the Pelew Islands composed from the Journals and Communications of Captain Henry Wilson and some of his Officers.* London, 1789.

———. *The History of Prince Lee Boo, a Native of the Pelew Islands brought to England by Captain Wilson.* London, 1788.

Kemp, P. K., and Lloyd, C. *The Brethren of the Coast.* London, 1960.

Kersten, K. *Der Weltumsegler: Johann Georg Adam Forster 1754–1794.* Bern, 1957.

Keynes, R. D., ed. *The "Beagle" Record.* London, 1979.

King, J. *The First Fleet: The Convict Voyage that founded Australia 1787–1788.* Melbourne, 1982.

Laird Clowes, G. S., ed. *Anson's Voyage round the World.* London, 1928.

Lamb, W. Kaye, ed. *The Voyage of George Vancouver 1791–1795.* 4 vols. London, 1984.

Lee, I., ed. *Captain Bligh's Second Voyage to the South Sea.* London, 1920.

Linklater, E. *The Voyage of the "Challenger".* London, 1972.

Little, B. *Crusoe's Captain: Woodes Rogers.* London, 1960.

Lloyd, C. *William Dampier.* London, 1966.

Lubbock, A. *Owen Stanley R.N. (1811–1850), Captain of the "Rattlesnake".* Melbourne, 1968.

MacGillivray, J. *Narrative of the Voyage of HMS "Rattlesnake" Commanded by the late Captain Owen Stanley R.N. during the years 1846–1850.* 2 vols. London, 1852.

Mack, J. D. *Matthew Flinders 1774–1814.* Nelson, 1966.

Mackaness, G. *Sir Joseph Banks, Bart.* Sydney, 1962.

——. *The Life of Vice-Admiral William Bligh.* Sydney, 1931.

Macrae, C. *With Lord Byron at the Sandwich Islands in 1825.* Honolulu, 1922.

Maiden, J. H. *Sir Joseph Banks.* Sydney, 1909.

Mainwaring, G. E. *My Friend the Admiral* [James Burney]. London, 1931.

——. *Woodes Rogers, Privateer and Governor.* London, 1957.

Masefield, J., ed. *Voyages* [by W. Dampier]. 2 vols. London, 1906.

Maynarde, T. *Sir Francis Drake and his Voyage.* London, 1949.

Meares, J. *An Answer to Mr George Dixon, late commander of the "Queen Charlotte".* London, 1791.

——. *Voyages made in the years 1788 and 1789 from China to the North-West Coast of America.* London, 1790.

Mellersh, H. E. L. *Fitzroy of the "Beagle".* London, 1968.

——. *The Missionary Voyages to the South Sea Islands performed in the years 1796 . . . 1798 in the ship "Duff", commanded by Captain James Wilson.* London, 1841.

Moresby, J. *Discoveries and Surveys in New Guinea and D'Entrecasteaux Islands; a Cruise in Polynesia and Visits to the Pearl-Shelling Stations in Torres Strait of HMS "Basilisk".* London, 1876.

Mortimer, G. *Observations and Remarks made during a Voyage . . . in the brig "Mercury" commanded by John Henry Cox, Esq.* London, 1791.

Moseley, H. N. *Notes by a Naturalist on the "Challenger".* London, 1879.

Narborough, J. *An Account of Several Late Voyages & Discoveries to the South and North, towards the Streights of Magellan, the South Seas, etc.* London, 1694.

——. *Voyage to the South Sea.* 2 vols. London, 1711.

Nares, G. S. *Narrative of a Voyage to the Polar Sea.* 2 vols. London, 1878.

——, et al. *Report on the Scientific Results of the Voyage of HMS "Challenger".* 40 vols. London, 1880–1895.

Nuttall, Z. *New Light on Drake.* London, 1914.

Pack, S. W. C. *Admiral Lord Anson.* London, 1960.

Penzer, N. M., ed. *A New Voyage round the World by William Dampier.* London, 1927.

Phillip, A. *The Voyage of Governor Phillip to Botany Bay.* London, 1789.

Pisier, G. *Les Aventures du Capitaine Cheyne dans l'Archipel Calédonien.* Noumea, 1975.

Portlock, N. *A Voyage round the World, but more particularly to the North-West Coast of America, performed in 1785–1788 by Captains Portlock and Dixon.* London, 1789.

Prout, E. *Memoirs of the Life of the Rev. John Williams.* London, 1843.

Purdy, J. *The Oriental Navigator.* London, 1816.

Quinn, D. B., ed. *The Last Voyage of Thomas Cavendish.* Chicago, 1975.

Rawson, G. *"Pandora's" Last Voyage.* London, 1963.

————. *Matthew Flinders' Narrative of his Voyage in the Schooner "Francis" in 1798*. London, 1946.

Ritchie, G. S. *"Challenger": The Life of a Survey Ship*. London, 1957.

Robertson, G. *The Discovery of Tahiti: A Journal of the Second Voyage of HMS "Dolphin"*. Edited by H. Carrington. London, 1948.

Roe, M., ed. *The Journal and Letters of Captain Charles Bishop on the Northwest Coast of America, in the Pacific and in New South Wales 1794–1799*. Cambridge, 1967.

Rogers, P. G. *The First Englishman in Japan*. London, 1956.

Rogers, W. *A Cruising Voyage round the World*. London, 1712.

Ross, J. C. *A Voyage of Discovery and Research in the Southern and Antarctic Regions*. 2 vols. London, 1847.

Ross, M. J. *Ross in the Antarctic*. Whitby, Yorkshire, 1982.

Russell, W. C. *William Dampier*. London, 1889.

Rutter, O. *The Journal of James Morrison, Boatswain's Mate of the "Bounty"*. London, 1935.

Sauer, M. *An Account of a Geographical and Astronomical Expedition to the Northern Parts of Russia performed by Commodore Joseph Billings in the years 1785–1794*. London, 1802.

Scott, E. *The Life of Captain Matthew Flinders RN*. Sydney, 1914.

Shelvocke, G. *A Voyage round the World by Way of the Great South Sea*. London, 1726. (Reprinted 1928 with notes by W. G. Perrin).

Shillibeer, J. *A Narrative of the "Briton"'s Voyage to Pitcairn Island*. London, 1817.

Shineberg, D. *They Came for Sandalwood: A Study of Sandalwood Trade in the South-West Pacific 1830–1865*. Melbourne, 1967.

————, ed. *The Trading Voyages of Andrew Cheyne 1841–1844*. Canberra, 1971.

Shipman, J. C. *William Dampier: Seaman-Scientist*. Lawrence (Kansas), 1962.

Smith, E. *The Life of Sir Joseph Banks*. London, 1911.

Somerville, B. T. *Commodore Anson's Voyage in the South Sea and around the World*. London, 1934.

Spry, W. J. J. *The Cruise of Her Majesty's Ship "Challenger"*. New York, 1877.

Stead, E. H. *Captain James Wilson*. London, n.d.

Stanbuzy, D., ed. *A Narrative of the Voyage of HMS "Beagle"*. London, 1977.

Stockdale, J., ed. *The Voyage of Governor Phillip to Botany Bay . . . to which are added the journals of Lieutenant Shortland*. London, 1790.

Strange, J. C. S. *Journal and Narrative of the Commercial Expedition from Bombay to the Northwest Coast of America*. Madras, 1928.

Swire, H. *The Voyage of the "Challenger": A Personal Narrative of the His-*

*toric Circumnavigation of the Globe in the Years 1872–1876.* 2 vols. London, 1938.

Tench, W. *A Narrative of the Expedition to Botany Bay.* London, 1789.

Thomson, B., ed. *The Voyage of HMS "Pandora".* London, 1915.

Thomson, C. W., and Murray, J. *Reports on the Scientific Results of the Voyage of HMS "Challenger" during the Years 1873–76 under the command of Captain George S. Nares R.N., F.R.S. and the late Captain Frank Tourle Thomson R.N.* 50 vols. London, 1880–1885.

Thomson, C. W. *The Voyage of the "Challenger": The Atlantic.* 2 vols. London, 1877.

Thomson, G. M. *Sir Francis Drake.* London, 1988.

Turnbull, J. *A Voyage round the World in the Years 1800, 1801, 1802, 1803 and 1804.* 2 vols. London, 1805.

Uhlig, L. *Georg Forster.* Tübingen, 1965.

Vancouver, G. *A Voyage of Discovery to the North Pacific Ocean and round the World.* 3 vols. London, 1798. Reprinted New York, 1967.

Wafer, L. *A New Voyage and Description of the Isthmus of Panama.* London, 1699.

Wagner, H. R. *Sir Francis Drake's Voyage around the World.* San Francisco, 1926. Reprinted. Amsterdam, 1969.

Wallis, H., ed. *Carteret's Voyage round the World 1766–1769.* 2 vols. Cambridge, 1965.

Walter, R., comp. *A Voyage round the World . . . by George Anson.* London, 1748.

Wilcox, L. A. *Anson's Voyage.* New York, 1970.

Wild, J. J. *At Anchor: A Narrative of Experience Afloat and Ashore during the Voyage of HMS "Challenger" from 1872 to 1876.* London, 1878.

Wilkinson, C. *William Dampier.* London, 1929.

Williams, G. *The British Search for the Northwest Passage in the Eighteenth Century.* London, 1962.

Williams, G., ed. *Documents relating to Anson's Voyage round the World 1740–1744.* London, 1967.

Williams, J. *A Narrative of Missionary Enterprises in the South-Sea Islands.* London, 1837.

Williamson, J. A. *Cook and the Opening of the Pacific.* London, 1946.

———. *Hawkins of Plymouth.* London, 1949.

———. *Sir John Hawkins: The Times and the Man.* Oxford, 1927.

———, ed. *The Observations of Sir Richard Hawkins.* London, 1933.

Wilson, J. *A Missionary Voyage to the Southern Pacific Ocean.* London, 1799.

Woodward, R. L. *Robinson Crusoe's Island: A History of the Juan Fernandez Islands.* Chapel Hill (N. Carolina), 1969.

Young, J. M., ed. *Australia's Pacific Frontier: Economic and Cultural Expansion into the Pacific 1795–1885.* Melbourne, 1967.

## Holland

Behrens, C. F. *Histoire de l'Expédition de trois Vaisseaux envoyés par la Compagnie des Indes Occidentales.* 2 vols. The Hague, 1739.

Bouman, C. *Scheespjournaal gehouden op het Schip "Tienhoven".* Middelburg (Holland), 1911.

Boxer, C. R. *The Dutch Seaborne Empire 1600–1800.* New York, 1965.

Cannenburg, W. V. *De Reis om de Wereld van de Nassausche Vloot 1623–1626.* The Hague, 1964.

Decker, A. de. "L'Amiral Georges van Spilbergen et son temps." *Revue Générale* (Brussels) 45 (1887).

Engelbrecht, W. A., and Van Herwerden, P. J. *De Ontdekkingsreis van Jacob Le Maire en Willem Cornelisz Schouten in de jaren 1615–1617.* 2 vols. The Hague, 1945.

Heeres, J. E., ed. *Abel Janszoon Tasman: Journal.* Amsterdam, 1898.

Ijzerman, J. W. *De Reis om de Wereld door Olivier van Noort.* The Hague, 1926.

Laroche, M. C. "Circonstances et Vicissitudes du Voyage de Découvertes dans le Pacifique Sud de l'Explorateur Roggeveen 1721–1722." *Journal de la Société des Océanistes.* 38 (1982): 19–23.

Le Maire, J. *Spieghel der Australische Navigatie.* Amsterdam, 1622.

Leupe, P. A., ed. *Reize van Maarten Gerritsz. Vries in 1643 naar Japan.* Amsterdam, 1858.

Meyjes, R. P., ed. *De Reizen van Abel Janszoon Tasman en Franchoys Jacobszoon Visscher in 1642–3 en 1644.* Amsterdam, 1919.

Mulert,F. E. *De Reis van Mr Jacob Roggeveen.* The Hague, 1919.

Noort, O. van. *Beschryvinghe van de Voyagie.* Rotterdam, 1602.

Robert, W. C. H., ed. *Voyage to Cathay, Tartary and the Gold- and Silver-rich Islands East of Japan 1643.* Amsterdam, 1975.

Roggeveen, J. *Daagverhall der Ontdekkings Reis van Myn. Jacob Roggeveen.* Middelburg (Holland), 1838.

———. *Extracts from the Official Log of Mynheer J. Roggeveen 1721–1722.* London, 1908.

———. *Tweejaarige Reyze rondom de Wereld.* Dordrecht, 1728.

Schouten, W. C. *Journal ou Description du Merveilleux Voyage de Guillaume Schouten.* Amsterdam, 1618.

Sharp, C. A., ed. *The Journal of Jacob Roggeveen.* Oxford, 1970.

———. *The Voyages of Abel Janszoon Tasman.* Oxford, 1968.

Sluiter, E., etal., eds. *New Light from Spanish Archives on the Voyage of Oliver van Noort.* The Hague, 1937.

Spilbergen, J. van. *Oost en West Indische Spieghel der nieuwe navigatie, waarin vertoond wordt de eerste reize gedaan voor Joris van Spilbergen, admiraal van deze vloot.* Leyden, 1619.

Walker, J. B. *Abel Janszoon Tasman: His Life and Voyages.* Hobart, 1896.

Warnsinck, J. C. M., ed. *De Reis om de Wereld van Joris van Spilbergen 1614–1617.* The Hague, 1943.

Wieder, F. C., ed. *De Reis van Mahu en de Cordes door de Straat van Magalhaes naar Zuid-Amerika en Japan 1598–1600.* The Hague, 1923.

### Russia

Andreev, A. I., ed. *Russian Discoveries in the Pacific and in North America in the Eighteenth and Nineteenth Centuries: A Collection of Materials.* Translated by C. Ginsburg. Ann Arbor (Mich.), 1952.

Armstrong, T. *Russian Settlement in the North.* Cambridge, 1965.

Barratt, G. R. *Bellingshausen: A Visit to New Zealand 1820.* Palmerston North (New Zealand), 1979.

————. "Russia and New Zealand: the Beginnings." *New Zealand Slavonic Journal* 2 (1972): 25–49.

————. *Russia and the South Pacific. I. The Russians and Australia; II. Southern and Eastern Polynesia.* Vancouver, 1988.

————. *Russia in Pacific Waters 1715–1825: A Survey of Russia's Naval Presence in the North and South Pacific.* Vancouver, 1981.

————. *Russian Exploration in the Mariana Islands 1816–1828.* Saipan. 1985.

————. *The Russian Discovery of Hawaii 1804: The Journals of Eight Russian Explorers.* Honolulu, 1988.

————. *The Russian View of Honolulu 1809–1826.* Ottawa, 1988.

Brun, X. *Adelbert de Chamisso de Boncourt.* Lyons, 1896.

Chamisso, A von. *Reise um die Welt . . . in den Jahren 1815–1818 auf der Brigg "Riurik".* In *Chamissos Werke,* edited by J. E. Hitzig. Vol. 1 of 6. Leipzig, 1836–1842.

Chevigny, H. *Russian America.* New York, 1965.

Choris, L. *Voyage Pittoresque autour du Monde.* Paris, 1822.

Coxe, W. *An Account of the Russian Discoveries between Asia and America.* London, 1780.

Cross, A. G. *By the Banks of the Thames: Russians in Eighteenth Century Britain.* Newtonville (Mass.), 1980.

Debenham, F., ed. *The Voyage of Captain Bellingshausen to the Antarctic Seas 1819–1821.* 2 vols. Cambridge, 1945.

Doring, H. *August von Kotzebues Leben.* Weimar, 1830.

Dufour, C. J., et al. "The Russians in California." *California Historical Quarterly* 12 (1933): 210–216.

Feudel, W. *Adelbert von Chamisso: Leben und Werk.* Leipzig, 1971.

Fisher, R. H. *Bering's Voyages: Whither and Why.* London, 1977.

————. *The Russian Fur Trade 1550–1700.* Berkeley, 1943.

Golder, F. A. *Bering's Voyages.* 2 vols. New York, 1922–1925.

———. *Russian Expansion on the Pacific 1641–1850: An Account of the Earliest and Later Expeditions.* Cleveland, 1914.

Golovnin, V. M. *Around the World on the "Kamchatka" 1817–1819.* Translated by Ella L. Wiswell. Honolulu, 1979.

———. *Recollections of Japan.* London, 1819.

Hitzig, J. E. "Leben und Briefen von Adelbert von Chamisso." In *Chamissos Werke,* edited by J. Hitzig. Vols. 5, 6. Leipzig, 1842.

Ivanshintsev, N. A. *Russian Round-the-World Voyages from 1803 to 1849.* Translated by G. R. Barratt. Kingston (Ontario), 1980.

Kotzebue, O. von. *A New Voyage round the World during the Years 1823–1826.* 2 vols. London, 1830.

———. *A Voyage of Discovery into the South Sea and Beering's Straits in the Years 1815–1818.* Translated by H. E. Lloyd. 3 vols. London, 1821.

Kruzenshtern, I. F. *A Voyage round the World in the Years 1803–1806.* Translated by R. B. Hoppner. 2 vols. London, 1814.

Langsdorff, G. H. von. *Voyages and Travels in Various Parts of the World during the Years 1803–1807.* London, 1813.

Lauridsen, P. *Vitus Bering: The Discoverer of Bering Strait.* Translated by J. O. Olson. Chicago, 1889.

Lisyansky, U. F. *A Voyage round the World in the Years 1803–1806.* London, 1814.

Lütke, F. P. *Voyage autour du Monde.* 3 vols. Paris, 1835–1836.

Mahr, A. C. *The Visit of the "Riurik" to San Francisco in 1816.* Stanford (Calif.), 1932.

Makarova, R. V. *Russians on the Pacific 1743–1799.* Translated by R. A. Pierce and A. S. Donnelly. Kingston (Ontario), 1975.

McCartan, E. F. "The Long Voyages: Early Russian Circumnavigations." *Russian Review* 1 (1963): 30–37.

Mehnert, K. *The Russians in Hawaii 1804–1819.* Honolulu, 1939.

Nozikov, N. *Russian Voyages round the World.* Translated by E. and M. Lesser. London, 1944.

Pierce, R. A. *Russia's Hawaiian Adventure 1815–1817.* Berkeley, 1965.

———. "Two Russian Governors: Hagemeister and Yanovskii." *Alaska Journal* 1,2 (1971): 49–51.

Rabanie, C. G. *Kotzebue: sa Vie et son Temps.* Paris, 1893.

Riegel, R. *Adelbert de Chamisso: sa Vie et son Oeuvre.* 2 vols. Paris, 1834.

Ross, J., ed. *The Memoirs of the Celebrated Admiral Adam John de Krusenstern, the First Russian Circumnavigator.* London, 1856.

Schweizer, N. R. *A Poet among Explorers: Chamisso in the South Seas.* Bern, 1973.

Simonov, I. M. "Précis du Voyage de Découvertes fait par ordre du Gouvernement Russe en 1819–1821 par le Capitaine Bellingshausen." *Journal des Voyages* 23 (1824): 12–15.

Sokol. A. E. "Russian Expansion and Exploration in the Pacific." *Slavonic and East European Review* 11 (1952): 85–105.

Solovev, A. I., ed. *Zapiski o Plavanii Voennogo shliupoi "Blagonamerennyi".* (By A. P. Lazarev). Moscow, 1950.

Staehlin, J. von. *An Account of the New Northern Archipelago lately Discovered by the Russians in the Seas of Kamchatka and Anadir.* London, 1774.

Veselago, F. F. *Admiral Ivan Fedorovich Kruzenshtern.* St. Petersburg, 1869.

Waxell, S. *The Russian Expedition to America.* New York, 1962.

Wrangel, F. von. *Voyage along the Northern Coast of Siberia and the Arctic.* London, 1841.

### Spain

Alcala-Galiano, D. *Relación del Viaje hecho por las Goletas "Sutil" y "Mexicana" en el año 1792 para Reconecher el Estracho de Fuca.* Madrid, 1802.

Amherst, W. A. T., and Thomson, B., eds. *The Discovery of the Solomon Islands by Alvaro de Mendaña in 1568.* 2 vols. London, 1901.

Anderson, C. L. *The Life and Letters of Vasco Nuñez de Balboa.* New York, 1941.

Arciniega, R. *Pedro Sarmiento de Gamboa: el Ulissa de América.* Buenos Aires, 1956.

Bayldon, F. J. "The Voyage of Luis Vaez de Torres from the New Hebrides to the Moluccas." *Journal and Proceedings of the Royal Australian Historical Society.* 11 (1925); 158–194.

Beltrun y Rozpide, R. *Descubrimiento de la Oceania par los Españoles.* Madrid, 1895.

Blanco, L. C., et al. *Colección de Diarios y Relaciónes para la Historia de los Viajes y Descrubrimientos.* Madrid, 1943.

Bona, E. *Alessandro Malaspina: sue Navigazioni ed Esplorazioni.* Rome, 1935.

Caamano, J. "The Journal of Jacinto Caamano, edited by H. R. Wagner and W. A. Newcombe." *British Columbia Historical Quarterly* 2 (1938): 189–222, 265–301.

Cameron, I. *Magellan and the First Circumnavigation of the World.* London, 1974.

Careri, G. F. B. *A Voyage to the Philippines.* Translated by A. Churchill. Manila, 1963.

Caster, J. G. "The Last Days of Don Juan Perez, the Mallorcan Mariner." *Journal of the West* (Los Angeles) 2 (1963): 15–21.

Chapman, C. E. *The Founding of Spanish California.* New York, 1916.

Clissold, S. *Conquistador: The Life of Don Pedro Sarmiento de Gamboa.* London, 1954.

Cook, W. *Flood Tide of Empire: Spain and the Pacific Northwest 1543–1819*. New Haven (Conn.), 1973.

Cordejuela, A. R. de. *Magellanes-Elcano: la Primera Vuelta al Mundo*. Saragossa, 1940.

Corney, B. G., ed. *The Quest and Occupation of Tahiti by the Emissaries of Spain during the Years 1772–1776*. 3 vols. London, 1913–1919.

———. *The Voyage of Don Felipe González . . . to Easter Island in 1770–1771*. Cambridge, 1908.

Cutter, D. C. "California, Training Ground for Spanish Naval Heroes." *California Historical Society Quarterly* 40 (1961): 109–122.

———. *Malaspina in California*. San Francisco, 1960.

Day, A. G., et al. *The Spanish at Port Jackson: The Visit of the Corvettes "Descubierto" and "Atrevida" 1793*. Sydney, 1967.

Duncan, W. A. *An Account of a Memorial presented to His Majesty by Captain Pedro Fernandez de Quir*. Sydney, 1874.

Galvano, A. *Tratado dos Descubrimientos*. London, 1862.

Guillemart, F. H. H. *The Life of Ferdinand Magellan and the First Circumnavigation of the Globe*. London, 1890.

Hamy, E. "Luis Vaez de Torres et Diego de Prado y Tovar, Explorateurs de la Nouvelle-Guinée." *Bulletin de Géographie Historique et Descriptive* 22 (1907): 47–72.

Hesse, E. W., ed. *Balboa*. New York, 1944.

Hezel, F. X., and Del Valle, M. T. "Early European Contact with the Western Carolines." *Journal of Pacific History* 5 (1972): 26–44.

Hilder, B. *The Voyage of Torres*. Brisbane, 1980.

Kelly, C. *Austrialia Franciscana*. 2 vols. Madrid, 1963–1965.

———. *La Austrialia del Espíritu Santo*. 2 vols. Cambridge, 1966.

———. "The Narrative of Pedro Fernández de Quirós." *Historical Studies of Australia and New Zealand* 9 (1960): 181–193.

Kubler-Sutterlin, O. *Kolumbus Australiens: das Wagnis des Pedro Fernández de Quiros*. Munich, 1956.

Lagoa, V. de. *Fernao de Magalhais: a sua Vida e a sua Viagem*. Lisbon, 1938.

Landin Carrasco, A. *Vida y Viajes de Pedro Sarmiento de Gamboa*. Madrid, 1945.

Langdon, R. *The Lost Caravel*. Sydney, 1975.

Lapa, A. *Pedro Fernandes de Queiros o Ultimo Navegador Portugues*. Lisbon, 1951.

Markham, C. R., ed. *Early Spanish Voyages to the Strait of Magellan*. London, 1911.

———. *The Voyages of Pedro Fernández de Quirós 1595–1606*. 2 vols. London, 1904.

Medina, J. T. *El Piloto Juan Fernández*. Santiago, 1918.

———. *El Descubrimiento del Océano Pacífico*. 2 vols. Santiago, 1913–1914.

Merriman, R. B. *The Rise of the Spanish Empire*. New York, 1918.

Mitchell, M. *Elcano; The First Circumnavigator*. London, 1958.

———. *Friar Andrés de Urdaneta O.S.A.* London, 1964.

Navarette, E. F. de. *Historia de Juan Sebastián del Cano*. Vittoria, 1872.

Navarrete, M. F. de. *Colección de los Viajes y Descubrimientos que hicerón por Mar los Españoles*. 5 vols. Madrid, 1825–1837.

Novo y Colson, P. de, ed. *Viaje Político-científico alrededor del Mundo por las Corbetas "Descubierta" y "Atrevida" al mando de los Capitánes de navío D. Alejandro Malaspina y Don Jose de Bustamente. . . .* Madrid, 1885.

Nowell, C. E., ed. *Magellan's Voyage round the World by Antonio Pigafetta: Three Contemporary Accounts*. Evanston (Ill.), 1962.

Pacheco, J. F., Cardenas, F. de., Mendoza, L. T., eds. *Collección de Documenos Inéditos relativos al Descubrimiento*. Madrid, 1866.

Paige, P. S. *The Voyage of Magellan*. Englewood Cliffs (N.J.), 1969.

Parr, C. M. *So Noble a Captain: The Life and Times of Ferdinand Magellan*. New York, 1953.

Parry, J. H. *The Spanish Seaborne Empire*. Harmondworth, 1973.

Pigafetta, A. *Magellan's Voyage around the World*. Translated and edited by J. A. Robertson. 2 vols. Cleveland, 1906.

———. *Magellan's Voyage: A Narrative Account of the First Circumnavigation*. Translated by R. A. Skelton. 2 vols. New Haven (Conn.), 1969.

Prieto, C. *El Océano Pacífico: Navegantes Españoles del Siglo XVI*. Madrid, 1972.

Ramusio, G. B. *Delle Navigatione e Viaggi*. 3 vols. Venice, 1550–1559.

Roditi, E. *Magellan of the Pacific*. London, 1972.

Romoli, K. *Balboa of Darien, Discoverer of the Pacific*. New York, 1953.

Rosenblat, A., ed. *Pedro Sarmiento de Gamboa: Viajes al Estrecho de Magallanes 1579–1584*. 2 vols. Buenos Aires, 1950.

Sanderlin, G., ed. *Pigafetta: A Journal of Magellan's Journey*. London, 1960.

Samiento de Gamboa, P. *The Narrative of the Voyage of Pedro Sarmiento de Gamboa*. Translated by C. R. Markham. London, 1895.

Schurz, W. L. *The Manila Galleon*. New York, 1939.

Sharp, C. A. *Adventurous Armada: The Story of Legazpi's Expedition*. Christchurch (New Zealand), 1961.

Stanley, H. E. J. *The Philippine Islands . . . and a Letter from Luis Vaez de Torres, describing his Voyage through Torres Straits*. London, 1868.

Stanley of Alderley, ed. *The First Voyage round the World by Magellan translated from the accounts of Pigafetta and other contemporary writers*. London, 1874.

Stevens, H. N., and Barwick G. F., eds. *New Light on the Discovery of Aus-*

*tralia as Revealed by the Journals of Captain Don Diego de Prado y Tovar*. London, 1930.

Thurman, M. E. "Juan Bodega y Quadra and the Spanish Retreat from Nootka 1790–1794." In *Reflections of Western Historians*, edited by J. A. Caroll and J. R. Kluger. Tucson (Ariz.), 1969.

Viana, F. X. de. *Journal [de la Descubierta]*. Montevideo, 1849.

Wagner, H. R. *Spanish Explorations in the Strait of Juan de Fuca*. Santa Ana (Calif.), 1933.

————. *Spanish Voyages to the Northwest Coast of America in the Sixteenth Century*. San Francisco, 1929.

Wright, I. S. "Early Spanish Voyages from America to the Far East." *Greater America*, 1945, pp. 59–78.

————. "The First American Voyage across the Pacific 1527–1528: The Voyage of Alvaro de Saavedra Ceron." *Geographical Review* 29 (1939): 472–482.

Ybarra y Berge, J. de. *De California à Alaska: Historia de un Descubrimiento*. Madrid, 1945.

Zaragoza, J. *Historia del Descubrimiento de los Regiones Austriales hecho por le General Pedro Fernández de Quirós*. 3 vols. Madrid, 1876–1882.

Zweig, S. *Magellan: Pioneer of the Pacific*. London, 1938.

## United States

Amarat, P. *They Ploughed the Sea*. St. Petersburg (Florida), 1978.

Brooke, G. M., Jr. *John M. Brooke, Naval Scientist and Educator*. Charlottesvillle (Va.), 1980.

————, ed. *John M. Brooke's Pacific Cruise and Japanese Adventure 1858–1860*. Honolulu, 1986.

Clune, F. *Captain Bully Hayes*. Sydney, 1970.

Delano, A. *Narrative of Voyages and Travels in the Northern and Southern Hemispheres*. Boston, 1817.

Dodge, E. S. *New England and the South Seas*. Cambridge (Mass.), 1965.

D'Wolf, J. *A Voyage to the North Pacific and a Journey through Siberia*. Cambridge (Mass.), 1861.

Griffis, W. E. *Matthew Calbraith Perry, a typical American Naval Officer*. Boston, 1887.

Hale, H. *The United States Exploring Expedition . . . under Charles Wilkes*. Philadelphia, 1846.

Haskell, D. C. *The United States Exploring Expedition 1838–1842 and Its Publications 1844–1874*. New York, 1942.

Hawks, F. L., ed. *Narrative of the Expedition of an American Squadron to the China Seas and Japan . . . under command of Commodore M. C. Perry*. 2 vols. New York, 1856.

Henderson, D. M. *The Hidden Coasts: A Biography of Admiral Charles Wilkes.* New York, 1953.

Howay, F. W., ed. *Voyages of the "Columbia" to the Northwest Coast 1787–1790 and 1790–1793.* Boston, 1941.

Ingraham, J. "An Account of a recent discovery of seven islands . . . by Joseph Ingraham, citizen of Boston and commander of the brigantine *Hope* of 70 tons." *Collections of the Massachusetts Historical Society for the Year 1794.* Pp. 20–24.

———. *Joseph Ingraham's Journal of the Brigantine "Hope" on a voyage to the Northwest Coast of America.* Edited by M. D. Kaplanoff. Barre (Mass.), 1971.

Jacobs, T. S. *Scenes, Incidents and Adventures in the Pacific Ocean or the Islands of the Australasian Seas during the Cruise of the Clipper "Margaret Oakley" under Captain Benjamin Morrell.* New York, 1844.

Kirker, J. *Adventures to China: Americans in the Southern Oceans 1792–1812.* New York, 1970.

Langdon, R. *American Whalers and Traders in the Pacific: A Guide to Records on Microfilm.* Canberra, 1978.

Lubbock, B. *Bully Hayes: South Seas Pirate.* London, 1931.

Morgan, W. J., et al., eds. *Autobiography of Rear Admiral Charles Wilkes U.S. Navy 1798–1877.* Washington, D.C., 1978.

Morison, S. E. "Boston Traders in the Hawaiian Islands 1789–1823." *Washington Historical Quarterly* 12 (1921): 166–201.

———. *Old Bruin: Commodore Matthew Calbraith Perry.* Boston, 1967.

Morrell, A. J. *Narrative of a Voyage.* New York, 1833.

Morrell, B. *A Narrative of Four Voyages to the South Sea . . . from the year 1822 to 1831.* New York, 1832.

Porter, D. *Journal of a Cruise made to the Pacific Ocean in the United States frigate "Essex" in 1812 . . . 1814.* 2 vols. New York, 1815.

Porter, D. D. *Life of Commodore David Porter.* New York, 1875.

Reynolds, J. N. *Voyage of the United States Frigate "Potomac" during the Circumnavigation of the Globe.* New York, 1835.

Sherman, S. C., et al. *Whaling Logbooks and Journals 1613–1927: An Inventory of Manuscript Records.* New York, 1986.

Stackpole, E. A. *The Sea-Hunters: The New England Whalemen during Two Centuries 1635–1835.* Philadelphia, 1953.

Stanton, W. *The Great United States Exploring Expedition.* Berkeley, 1975.

Starbuck. A. *History of the Whale Fishery from its Earliest Inception to the year 1876.* Waltham (Mass.), 1876.

Stevens, J. K. *American Expansion in Hawaii.* Harrisburg, 1955.

Tyler, D. B. *The Wilkes Expedition: The First United States Exploring Expedition (1838–1842).* Philadelphia, 1968.

Walach, S., ed. *Narrative of the Expedition of an American Squadron . . .*

*under command of Commodore M. C. Perry.* New York, 1952. [Abridged version.]

Ward, R. G. *American Activities in the Central Pacific 1790–1870.* 8 vols. Ridgewood (N.J.), 1966–1970.

Whipple, A. *Yankee Whalers in the South Seas.* New York, 1954.

Wilkes, C. *Narrative of the United States Exploring Expedition during the Years 1838, 1839, 1840, 1841 and 1842.* 5 vols. Philadelphia, 1844–1845.

# Index

## Names of People

## Names of Ships

*Only ships associated with Pacific voyages are included.*